MW00848740

GERT DUMBAR

GENTLEMAN MAVERICK OF DUTCH DESIGN

MAX BRUINSMA, AUTHOR/EDITOR
LEONIE TEN DUIS, AUTHOR

RENATE BOERE, VISUAL EDITOR/BOOK DESIGN

VALIZ, AMSTERDAM

CONTENTS

CHILDHOOD AND FORMATIVE YEARS
Leonie ten Duis   09

TEL DESIGN 1966–1976
Leonie ten Duis & Max Bruinsma   41

FOREWORD
Leonie ten Duis & Max Bruinsma

*L'ORDRE EST LE
PLAISIR DE LA RAISON,
MAIS LE DÉSORDRE
EST LE DÉLICE DE
L'IMAGINATION.
(ORDER IS THE
PLEASURE OF REASON,
BUT DISORDER IS
THE DELIGHT OF
IMAGINATION)*
Paul Claudel

How can things be done differently? Where's the unexpected outcome that proves to be a useful alternative that breaks through boring routines? Such questions, and the unstoppable curiosity that triggers them, define Gert Dumbar's work attitude — and his philosophy of life. As a graphic designer, he takes ingrained traditions to task, always seeking to expand the designer's playing field and, if he finds it necessary, crossing the lines. He likes to provoke and cast new light on things, put them into a new, sometimes absurd perspective. In all of this, he delights in being an agent of creative insubordination. You may call him a joker — as long as you don't forget he's a pretty serious designer as well.

Dualism runs through the man's entire life and oeuvre, starting with his dual roots in sub-tropical Indonesia and moderate Holland, and in the seeming opposites of modernism's rationality and the quirky associativeness of the visual arts that inspire him — Mondrian versus Pop Art. Or, to paraphrase the philosopher Bataille, he constantly explores the boundaries between the homogeneous — the raked lawn of functionalist graphic design — and the heterogeneous — the explorative playground of the arts. Without the first, there will be chaos, but discarding the second leads to dictatorship. So one needs to find connections, hybrids, amalgams of the two, with humour and wit as binding essence.

In the course of his life, Gert — together with many collaborators — has built an impressive body of work, spearheaded by a number of prominent house styles for public companies such as the Dutch Railways, the PTT, KPN, the Rijksmuseum, the Dutch police, and several ministries. His studio also designed many remarkable identities and posters for cultural institutions, such as the Holland Festival and the Mickery Theater in Amsterdam and Theater Zeebelt in The Hague. For this highly influential oeuvre, he was awarded the prestigious Piet Zwart Prize in 2009, named after one of the founding fathers of Dutch graphic design. The jury report characterized the awardee as an 'icon' in his field and an example and source of inspiration for young designers. The eulogy also mentioned the fact that Gert has always worked in close collaboration with others, first at the Tel Design agency and then at his own Studio Dumbar. There he surrounded himself with mostly young designers from all over the world, who were attracted by the playful, experimental design environment and the opportunity for personal development.

The many honours he received for his work did not silence the many voices of critique — another dualism, characteristic of Gert's life and work. His studio's designs would be 'too baroque', his posters sometimes 'unreadable'. Critic Lambert Tegenbosch once called Gert 'artistically in heat' because of what he saw as a plethora of frivolous elements in Studio Dumbar's posters for the Holland Festival. This and similar criticism eventually even produced another, albeit derogative, accolade: to his critics his name became synonymous with a certain style of designing. 'To dumbar' meant the designer guilty of this act was working in a shamelessly decorative manner. It's a rare honour for a designer to become a verb, and it shows how influential his studio's output was at the time, the 1980s and 1990s.

In this monograph, we follow a predominantly chronological path, sometimes anticipating future developments. Art historian Leonie ten Duis describes Gert's childhood in Indonesia, his period at the Royal Academy of Art in The Hague where he studied painting and graphic design — and where he and Leonie met — his studies at the Royal College of Art in London and his first decade as professional designer at design firm Tel Design. Max Bruinsma adds his voice to the description of the Tel Design period and follows up with an analysis of the work in Studio Dumbar. In between we look at overarching themes, connecting Gert's work and life with contemporary phenomena and cultural tendencies.

Despite his undisputed success and significance, Gert has never championed an overarching design theory or philosophy. And perhaps this is one of the reasons why he became so influential. His openness to experimentation and to a broad range of individual approaches in Studio Dumbar produced a 'let a hundred flowers bloom' environment, which was not founded on an ideology, but on a vision and a mentality. The origins and development of this vision, and the ways it was put into practice, are the subject of this book. Underlying questions are: how does Gert connect or merge a modernist rationalism with the more irrational aspects of the visual arts? How does he find a balance between order and chaos, between freedom and constraints? During his formative years and his early career, he was not the only one to pick holes in the stern rationality of modernism and the International Style. Pop Art, Punk and Postmodernism, Antidesign, Flower Power, Fluxus and Vernacular were all 'digging like moles through the carefully cultivated meadow of graphic design', as Anthon Beeke once put it. But Gert never identified with one of these groups and instead forged his own brand of 'post-ideological' design. His main concern was not to found a new school but to reintroduce the joy of experimentation —joy itself— in design, which at the time was a rather irreverent stand vis-à-vis the almost religious zeal with which various sides of the trade were arguing their positions.

This research was inspired by Gert's work and how it is reflected in archives, publications, and correspondence. Besides the archival research, Max has talked extensively with Gert and many others who have worked at or with Studio Dumbar. So did Leonie, who can of course also draw on the many conversations she has had with him in the by now sixty years they are together. Gert's voice resonates clearly in her text below, as his spirit inspires this entire publication.

CHILDHOOD AND FORMATIVE YEARS

INTRODUCTION

Gert and I met in 1962 at the Royal Academy of Art in The Hague, where we both studied graphic design, and we got married in 1965. I became intrigued by his attitude, his enthusiasm and his work, strongly attracted by his humour and light-heartedness, and his self-assurance when it came to design solutions. His wonderment and sensitivity for the absurdity of reality, and the relativization that ensues, have always fascinated me; a sensitivity for the absurd that stimulated him and that he, when convenient, utilized in his designs, without impeding applicability. Since our first meeting at the academy, we have exchanged views on the profession with great regularity and I have been able to follow day by day how Gert's work came about — often against the prevailing views.

Speaking about the background of his work, Gert tells the following anecdote: 'In 1976, Stephen Pile, author of *The Book of Heroic Failures*, founded a gaffe club, the Not Terribly Good Club of Great Britain. The club has since collapsed under its success: too many people wanted to become members. To qualify for membership, you had to be not particularly good at something. Evenings were organized where people demonstrated their inability. For the

THE MIND IN ITS FREEWHEELING STATE, THAT IS WHAT BRINGS YOU NEW IDEAS
Gert Dumbar

artists, there was a Salon des Incompétents. To mark the founding of the blunder club, a meal was held in an exquisitely bad restaurant. When the waitress dropped a soup bowl, it was caught by the chairman. Because he thus succeeded in preventing a disaster, he was immediately disqualified.'

Gert adds: 'This is what I mean. Sometimes you have to purposefully short-circuit things in life. Blunders are normally out of the question. You have to keep things on

Gert Dumbar, drawing, 1959

track. And that can be boring. At times you have to break through all that and react in a non-obvious way. It's like your mind goes on vacation for a while then. The mind in its freewheeling state, that is what brings you new ideas.'

11

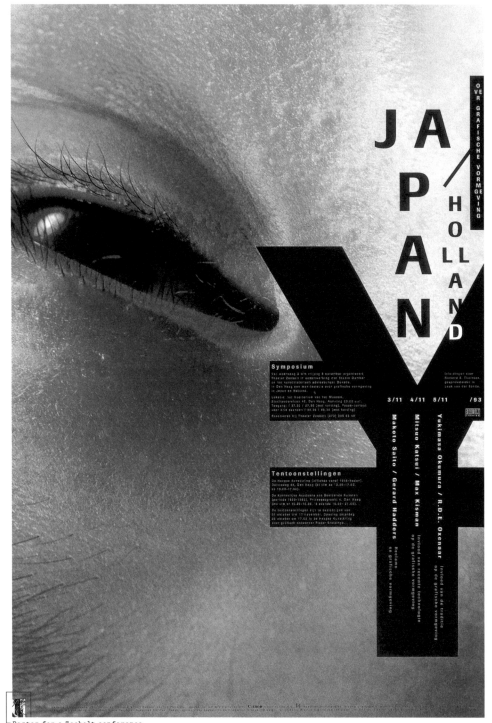

Poster for a Zeebelt conference
on Japanese graphic design, 1993
(design: Bob van Dijk)

DUTCH INDIES

'A SMALL MOBILE WAR MEMORIAL'

In 1993, together with Bob van Dijk in the Studio, Gert designed a poster for a conference on Japanese graphic design to which several renowned Japanese designers were invited as speakers. On the right-hand side of the poster a large Yen symbol is printed with the text Japan / Holland above it, in a typography consisting of separate, vertically arranged letters which, because of their position, are somewhat reminiscent of scripts on a Japanese sign. In the centre of the poster, the eye of a Japanese girl is depicted. Something strange is going on with that eye. A closer look reveals that it is upside down, which somehow intensifies its oriental character. The colour of the poster, blue, with orange lighting around the eye, evokes associations with classical Japanese opera. But there is more to it. Hardly noticeable in the lower left corner of the large poster there's a small black and white photograph, printed like a postage stamp. The picture shows a little boy behind barbed wire, curiously looking at what is going on outside. It is a reference to Gert's first years in life, which he spent

Detail of the poster for a conference on Japanese graphic design, 1993. In the left bottom corner, a little boy behind barbed wire

in a 'Jappenkamp' (the derogative Dutch term for a Japanese prison camp during the Second World War) on Java, Indonesia, and to which he wanted to draw attention in the poster.

Gert grew up in extreme circumstances, marked by danger, imprisonment, and the struggle for survival. It would instil in him a strong desire for freedom and an aversion to authorities and uniforms. Camp life was his first encounter with the world. Fifty years later, he made a reference to his childhood by leaving a personal mark on the poster. 'A small mobile war memorial,' says Gert, 'to remind us of that period.' It was a modest token; he did not want either side to lose face so many years later. Few people will have noticed that it is nevertheless an indictment of the Japanese occupation: 'I just wanted to show that because of the Japanese, part of my life has been rather confusing. My father died working on the Burma Railway, I was locked up for two years under harsh conditions. Taking advantage of the fact that there would be a number of Japanese present at the conference, I took the opportunity for a silent protest, a protest that does not immediately reveal its message, but that the Japanese guests, on closer inspection — they were given the poster to take back to Japan — would probably notice. As long as it isn't seen, the light stays on orange. It was a strategic, personal intervention, but it does involve a historical event. You indicate that there is something else going on with the poster other than what it was intended for. I can do that as a designer.'

'THERE IS NO IMMEDIATE DANGER HERE'

Gert was born in Batavia (now Jakarta) on 16 May 1940, six days after the German invasion of the Netherlands. 'These are evil times in which the new Dumbar will see the light of day,' his father Derk said in a letter to his parents about two weeks before Gert's birth. In the Dutch East Indies one still hoped to stay out of the war: 'It is at present Sunday evening and the radios have just been echoing the latest war news through the sultry evening air. An invigorating message that makes me realize once again how privileged we are, at least for the moment, sitting quietly together in our comfortable pavilion.'[1]

Descendants of the Scottish Dumbar clan settled in the Dutch town of Deventer in the mid-seventeenth century, where they would subsequently live for more than 200 years; Overijssel gentry, who held important positions in public administration. Independent thinkers, sometimes with progressive ideas and great oratory talent. They have spoken out at various times in history. They had the gift of the word, which Gert inherited. His father Derk, after studying law in Leiden, left for the Dutch East Indies in 1938, where he became deputy legal clerk at the Dutch Court of Audits. In contrast to his forebears, who were reasonably progressive within the limits of

Gert, 1941

their environment, Derk turned out to be a conservative Dumbar, very attached to tradition and wary of 'divisive new ideas'.[2] He emerges as moderate and sensible, with a sense of humour. Someone who loved parties, was good at drawing and accepted life as it came. In 1939 Derk married, by proxy, Anna Helena Toe Laer, from an Amsterdam family of vicars and notaries.

1   Derk Dumbar in a letter to his parents, 14 April 1940.
2   Derk Dumbar in a letter to his parents, 1932.

An was a flamboyant woman with a keen sense of humour — 'slightly posh' in

Left: Derk Dumbar, Gert's father
Right: Derk Dumbar and Gert's mother
An in Hilversum, NL

Gert's words. A strong personality, who did not mince words and commented on everything. Gert's mother had a taste for the dashing. 'Compared to Derk, she was rather exuberant,' said an old college friend.

'JAP' CAMP

After the bombing of Pearl Harbor on 7 December 1941, the Dutch East Indies were also sucked into the war. Just three months later, March 1942, the immense archipelago was conquered by the Japanese. Gert ended up with his mother and sister Petra (born 14 April 1941) in camp Tjihapit, a closed European city district of Bandung, after which they were transported to Banjoebiroe in central Java. While in Tjihapit one was still somewhat free — there was no barbed wire, one could enter and leave the neighbourhood — in Banjoebiroe they were prisoners. The camp was closed off by barbed wire and gedek (bamboo fencing). The detainees slept in barracks divided into small rooms, with bars in front of the windows. Packed tightly together, they had to survive under great hardship, fear and uncertainty, on the brink of starvation and with continuous bouts of disease.

Despite his tender age at the time, Gert has strong memories of the

Banjoebiroe camp. Part of his youth and his first emotions were formed there. But he did not, in his own words, experience any trauma from it. 'I experienced the camp, despite the hardships, as an exciting boys' book. As a child in such a situation of being trapped, you don't know what danger is and how miserable you are. You had no material for comparison. This was the world.'

He was only two-and-a-half when he entered the camp and five when he came out. His memories of the camp are fragmentary, but sharp, and the boys' book's narrative was tainted by an omnipresent mood of fear, insecurity and humiliation. For example, an image emerges of the torture of women who, tied to bamboo poles, were laid out for hours in the burning sun. They were given nothing to drink. 'The mothers tried to keep the children away from that, but you slipped away and peeked... You were curious. You did feel that it was bad and that you really shouldn't be looking at it. That's what those women conveyed to you.' Gert also remembers bowing to 'the Japs'. 'Every morning the whole camp had to line up, on the morning roll call, and stand in long rows to be counted, with the children in front. You had to stand perfectly still in the glowing sun while the Jap shouted orders. After everyone had bowed deeply to the Japanese emperor, you had to shout the number of the row you were in, in Japanese: ichi, ni, san, shi... That's how I learned to count to ten in Japanese. When

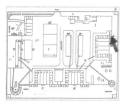

Left: plan of the prison complex in Banjoebiroe, central Java, where Gert was detained during the war
Right: aerial photo of the prison facility

15

everyone was counted, another deep bow was made and they had to get to work. For the children that meant weeding and looking for snails for dinner.'

Gert endured the miserable aspects of camp life more or less resignedly; he learned to shut himself off and take refuge in his own fantasy world. And he was curious and explorative. He loved tinkering. With sticks and pieces of wire he built houses and made furniture, chairs and tables. Sometimes in the afternoon two Indonesian girls would appear as if in a dream, 'flappers', on silver shoes, tap-dancing by the washroom to the rhythmic crackling of a wind-up gramophone. 'They practiced there. I went to watch them every afternoon.' A magical image in the drab reality of camp life.

Gert's mother An was not easily intimidated. For months she and a friend listened at night to a clandestine radio, which 'Tante Lenie', a friend of An, had

Daily morning ritual: bowing to the 'Jap'

somehow smuggled in, which allowed them to follow the course of the war. They then spread the news through a limited number of confidants among the camp's residents. In doing so they ran a great

risk; radios were strictly forbidden. Gert: 'Every night before the broadcast we had a 'singing quarter' so they could turn up the radio and tune in to the Australian BBC. Then they turned the sound very low. I remember there was electricity, there was a lamp in our room and —I remember that image— my mother would unscrew the bulb and wriggle the wire from the radio into the socket and then they would listen to radio Australia. One night they heard Churchill's voice saying that the war in Europe was over. That's when things got really dangerous. The 'Japs' knew that there was a radio in the camp, because messages were circulating that could not possibly be known in the camp. Fortunately, they were able to quickly destroy the radio and make it disappear into the sewer.'

An was a courageous woman. She did not let 'the Jap' or the circumstances get her down. Her self-assurance and courage ensured that her children generally felt safe and it was from that feeling of relative safety that Gert faced the world around him. He went his own way, was enterprising, enjoyed a certain freedom of movement. 'The freedom of a farm dog,' he says, 'who can run around the farm all day, barking at everything, sniffing at everything, but who cannot leave the premises.'

Father Derk, meanwhile, had been put to work on the Burma Railway. From letters and stories that circulated about him Derk emerges as a strong personality, someone with a cheerful character and concern for others: 'After the heavy day's work for the Jap, he brought us food, washed our soiled clothes and all while we were too sick to do so,' wrote a fellow prisoner.[3] Early in February 1943, Derk was sent by freight train to Siam (now Thailand). After arriving at the 'base camp' he and a number of fellow-sufferers were

3   Letter J. Barendrecht to Mr. and Mrs. Hämisch ten Kate-van de Wall Bake, Bangkok 19 January 1946.

4   Puncak or Puncak Pass (Indonesian for 'top' or 'peak') is a mountain pass in West Java, Indonesia.

sent on foot into the jungle to work on a section of the railroad. Eventually, because he was reasonably healthy considering the circumstances, he was sent even further into the jungle and finally, after several months, succumbed to exhaustion and dysentery. Gert hardly knew his father. When he looks at an old photograph, vague memories come up: 'I remember going with my parents to the Poentjak[4] in the mountains. He would be standing there in a white tropical suit with his knee socks pulled up high.'

Derk and Gert Dumbar, 1942

GERT ENDURED THE MISERABLE ASPECTS OF CAMP LIFE MORE OR LESS WILLINGLY; HE LEARNED TO SHUT HIMSELF OFF AND TAKE REFUGE IN HIS OWN FANTASY WORLD

After the atomic bombs on Hiroshima and Nagasaki, Japan capitulated, a fact the prisoners were only informed of some time later. In the meantime, the Indonesian revolution ignited. This development came as a complete surprise to most prisoners, who had heard little from the outside world for three years. On 17 August 1945, Sukarno and Hatta had proclaimed Indonesia's independence. The consequences were felt everywhere on Java. In a short time, the 'spirit of the revolution' had penetrated broad layers of the Indonesian population. Expressions of strong anti-Dutch sentiment led to many forms of violence. In the week after the capitulation the prisoners could still go outside the camp, but after a few weeks that became too dangerous. Rampok parties (looting),

murders and general chaos made life outside the camp fence increasingly unsafe. Now 'the Japs' had to protect the Dutch from the Indonesians. The inhabitants of Banjoebiroe were taken to Fort Willem I, in Ambarawa, where they were somewhat less vulnerable. In the days that followed, most were evacuated, in long convoys protected by Gurkhas, (soldiers of Indian heritage in service of the British army) to Semarang and from there to Batavia (now Jakarta). The first convoys were attacked by murderous permudas (Indonesian freedom fighters). Gert, who was in one of the last trucks, remembers 'On the way we saw 'rampassed' (captured and set on fire by the permudas) villages and towns. Merchandise everywhere, broken warongs and houses, garbage on the streets, a stopper bottle of katjang idjoe, the green peas scattered everywhere. But everything was completely deserted. I couldn't stop watching.'

After the war, Gert, his sister Petra and his mother ended up in Kandy in the interior of Ceylon (now Sri Lanka) where they were housed in a former British army camp for six months to

17

regain strength. From Ceylon they went by cargo boat to the Netherlands. On the way they stopped in Attaka, another former army camp not far from the Suez Canal, where warm clothes — underwear, winter coats, shoes — were distributed in a large hangar in the desert because of the harsh winter in Europe. The hangar was manned by German prisoners of war. 'Off the boat you were loaded into freight trains and then you drove a long way into the scorching hot desert. The wagons stopped in the middle of nowhere. There were no platforms. You jumped out of the wagon right into the sand and then you walked to a big hangar. There was a battery of swings there. That's where you raced as a kid. Behind each swing was a German prisoner of war, in German uniform, from Rommel's army. They had to stand in a long line and if a child wanted to be rocked, they pushed. In the distance you could hear fragments of a music band playing.' Such images seem like the stuff of surrealist theatre or movies, and they must have instilled in Gert a basic awareness of the normality of the absurd.

The images and anecdotes evoked here tell something about Gert's early childhood, his earliest life experiences and how he reacted to them. He never felt like a 'victim'. 'There were hardships, we were locked up, we were hungry. There was a lot of complaining about the camps, but complaining has no grandeur,' says Gert, echoing Dutch writer Rudi Kousbroek. 'It was a way of survival. You were confronted early on with risky situations and learned how to respond to them. You learned to improvise and to adapt quickly to new circumstances. There was fear but at the same time curiosity about the unknown.' The striking imperturbability with which he underwent everything was not lost on his mother. 'Gert will glide through life easily,' An wrote from Kandy.[5]

Drawing by Gert Dumbar, 8 years old

UNDER THE IMMENSE GREY SKY

Gert arrived in the Netherlands in early 1946, almost six years old and dressed in ill-fitting winter clothes. With traces of the recent occupation still visible everywhere, the new, cold, flat land under an 'immense, grey sky' made an unattractive impression. The postwar reconstruction had only just begun and everything was in short supply. The family moved in with grandmother Dumbar in Hilversum, a painter of considerable skill, and Gert went to school for the first time. Drawing was his favourite pastime and when he came home from school in the afternoon, he often found his grandmother painting in her studio, a cozy chaos of paint tubes and brushes lying around, wonderfully smelling of turpentine. One of his oldest surviving drawings dates from this period. A human body surrounded, like in a comic strip, by the names of its body parts. Not averse to creating myths, Gert considers the way he combined text and image in this drawing as one of his first steps towards graphic design.

In 1947, Gert's mother remarried, to the lawyer Karel Raue whose wife had died shortly before. Gert was joined by a stepbrother and sister: Bart and Fiet. Later followed by a half-sister, Heleen. In 1948

5 Letter to Gladys, 29 March 1946.
6 Hella Haasse, *Zelfportret als legkaart*, Amsterdam, 1954.

the new family went back to Indonesia where Karel became a high-ranking official with the Indonesian pension funds in Bandung. There was unrest in the country as a result of the 'policing action' (as the Dutch government called its colonial war at the time) with which the Netherlands tried to counter the Indonesian independence struggle with often excessive military force. It was a confusing time. On the one hand the remains of the comfortable

THE OVERWHELMING NATURE, THE VAST GREEN SPACE, THE SCORCHING SUN, THE BRIGHT COLOURS OF THE BIRDS, THE SNATCHES OF GAMELAN MUSIC SHAPED HIS SENSES, NURTURING A SENSITIVITY FOR THE MAGIC OF VISUAL EXPRESSION

colonial life, on the other hand chaos and the ever-present feeling of danger. Yet Gert led a fairly carefree life. He went to the Zeelandiaschool, an elementary school in Bandung and on Saturday afternoons he took drawing lessons at the people's university. He often set out into nature, making day trips, on foot or by bike, equipped with a sketchbook and pencils. He enjoyed the silence, with no one around except an occasional tani (farmer) working in the rice fields. He was impressed by the overwhelming nature, the vast green space, the scorching sun, the bright colours of the birds, the snatches of gamelan music from the kampong, (native village). It all made a deep impression of a surreal world, full of visual variety, rich in imagination, colourful, sensual. Life in the tropics cultivated in

him a sensitivity for the (visual) magic of things.

After a five year's stay, the family returned to the Netherlands and Gert had to finally get used to the style of life in his new homeland, which was considerably less loose, and less sensual, than in Indonesia. 'Following Dutch writer Hella Haasse, I can say: "I was born and raised in the Dutch Indies. My first emotions are connected with that country and it has shaped my senses. The atmosphere you grow up in, the influence of nature, the air you breathe, the sunlight, the rains... something of that atmosphere settles in you." [6] Hella Haasse put that very well. You could say that what I experienced in the Dutch East Indies —particularly in the camp— nourished my later attitude, also in my work, and I don't just mean a craving for freedom and an aversion to uniforms, but also that you know how to keep your balance in all kinds of difficult situations, like a tightrope walker, that you dare to take risks and that you can put things in perspective.' The child, as they say, is the father of the man.

19

20

Dick Stapel, *Portrait Gert Dumbar*, 1957
'They read Sartre, wore black turtlenecks,
and loved jazz', as did Gert

BREAKING OUT
OF THE CODE

THE 1950S AND 1960S

Back in the Netherlands, Gert sees a Piet Mondrian retrospective at the Gemeentemuseum in The Hague.[7] He is 15 years old and deeply impressed. 'A revelation', is how he remembers

Piet Mondriaan, *Victory Boogie Woogie* (1942-1944), Kunstmuseum Den Haag

the confrontation with Mondrian: 'The bright colours, the open compositions, the order, the logical development of the work towards an ever greater abstraction,

the search for the essential, suddenly I understood. And then those beautiful Boogie-Woogies in which the rigid grid is broken open again, the vibrancy of jazz in those paintings, so much more cheerful and lighter than the preceding work. It was of a great optimism.' For the first time, Gert was consciously seized by the meaning of modern art — its surprising power.

He had returned from Indonesia two years earlier and became a pupil at the Maerlant Lyceum in The Hague where his passion for drawing and painting revealed itself. 'A great talent,' said the drawing teacher, 'a second Picasso!' Gert felt somewhat of an outsider. He had fallen behind in learning and was two years older than most of the pupils in his class — partly because of that he had a certain preponderance. Because of his Indonesian background he had a looser way of life. Gert was very much his own man, a bit distinguished too — 'someone who stood a bit above everything,' says fellow student Dick Stapel.[8]

7 Gemeentemuseum Den Haag, 'Mondriaan', exhibition 10 February–12 April 1955.

8 Interview Dick Stapel, November 2002.

Gert Dumbar, second row, third from left, Maerlant Lyceum, 1954

He was enterprising, had original ideas, wild ideas and, more importantly, the drive to put them into action. He was a passionate organizer of (beach) parties and loved jazz. 'I loved parties where you had to put things on stage. For example, we sometimes ended a party with a breakfast on the streetcar rails. On the track of the famous blue streetcar that ran from The Hague to Leiden, we would place a tablecloth with soft-boiled eggs on it, plates, knives forks, a jar of jam, a teapot, and then we would have breakfast. Halfway through our breakfast, we could already hear the whistle of the streetcar in the distance, approaching at great speed. Then we would quickly run and stand ten meters away to see how our breakfast was being crushed, the highlight being an opened can of applesauce clattering against the window of the streetcar. With a small hand-operated window wiper, the driver wiped the applesauce off the windowpane while shaking his fist at us in rage out the window. At five in the morning we went home satisfied.' Dick Stapel, who has experienced many such parties remembers: 'Gert was always good at shaping the fun of life.'[9]

Gert had trouble getting used to the 'stuffy and bourgeois' Dutch society, which, so soon after the war, longed for peace and order and where decency and conformism were important virtues. 'The voice of G.B.J. Hilterman[10] on the radio, an authoritarian stepfather who smoked cigars, a plate of mashed potatoes with a dent for gravy and a side of overcooked cauliflower', is how Gert remembers the stuffy 1950s. 'The confrontation with Mondrian at that time was a liberation. I was not only impressed by the visual power, but also by the attitude that spoke from the work: Just as Mondrian investigated art, you could also investigate life, break out of the code and escape the rigid norms of bourgeois existence. Thank God there are people who can think differently. Only much later did I start to realize how archetypally Dutch Mondrian's oeuvre and spirit were — the clarity, the order, the geometry, as it can be found in the Dutch landscape.'

JAZZ

There were also rays of hope in the stuffy fifties, which anticipated developments of the turbulent sixties, counter-movements of young people,

Gert Dumbar's cartoons for *Forum Academiale* student magazine, 1959

students, artists who rebelled against what they called the 'prissying of society'. They wore black sweaters, read Sartre

9   Interview Dick Stapel, November 2002.
10 Mr. G.B.J. Hilterman (1914–2000). An influential journalist, jurist, Indologist and political commentator, whose weekly radio (and later TV) column 'The Situation in the World' was somewhat of the official conservative opinion for decades between the 1950s and 1980s.

and loved jazz, as did Gert. He first came into contact with jazz in the 1950s. At this time The Hague was jazz capital of the Netherlands, with big concerts in Scheveningen where Duke Ellington, Lionel Hampton, Gerry Mulligan, and many others performed. Gert could be found regularly in the Vliegende Hollander ('The Flying Dutchman'), a 'slightly bohemian' jazz cellar close to the Kurhaus in Scheveningen. He indulged his enthusiasm for jazz in a number of cartoons he made for a student magazine during this period, drawings in which the 'flutteriness' of bebop emerges, in which guys in tight pants blow their clarinets, or in which a horn player whooshes abstract shapes. Another one plays to the rhythm of a cubist painting. Jazz stood for 'modern'.

Gert was, at a young age, well aware of what was going on internationally in the art field. There was, so soon after the war, a great desire for freedom in the arts. Prominent innovators, such as Willem Sandberg, director of the Stedelijk Museum in Amsterdam, where CoBrA set the tone, enthusiastically embraced new developments. This was echoed in The Hague, where abstract and experimental painters such as Hussem, Nanninga and Ouborg produced important work, where artists' groups had been thriving since the 1920s and an active exhibition policy was pursued, with the Haags Gemeentemuseum — home to the largest Mondrian collection in the world — as its epicentre. But The Hague was less fierce than Amsterdam, more demure. Where CoBrA was deliberately primitive, The Hague's abstracts were more aesthetic and civilized. Gert was drawn to The Hague art scene like a moth to a flame. He visited the most important galleries and could regularly be found in the Posthoorn, 'the most distinguished café in the

Netherlands', where The Hague's painters, writers and actors met regularly and where art was often discussed until midnight at the artists' table, headed by Jaap Nanninga

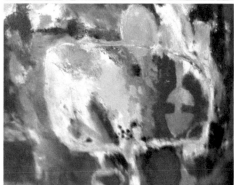

Gert Dumbar, top: gouache, 1957;
Bottom: Oil painting on canvas, 1957

and Willem Hussem. Painters were given the opportunity to hang their work on the café walls and in 1956 the Posthoorn's manager Jan Knijnenberg rented a room next door as an art room.

In 1957 Gert went to Paris for six weeks, at that time still Europe's cultural Mecca. He took drawing lessons at the Académie de la Grande-Chaumière, a mythical place in Paris, where an Atelier d'Art Abstrait had been established in 1950, which caused a great deal of controversy because, according to critics, abstract art did not belong in an academy. Gert became

Gert Dumbar, *Jazz*, 1959
(illustration)

11   Jan van Keulen (1913–1994) was a painter, photographer
and graphic designer who reshaped the graphic design
course at the Royal Academy in The Hague in 1957.
In 1968 he became professor at the Rijksakademie in
Amsterdam, where he started the department of Visual
Communication, which he headed till 1983.

fascinated by the Abstraction Lyrique (Lyrical Abstraction) a group of artists from various countries who worked independently and who, in the years immediately after the war, exhibited together in Paris. Like the painters of CoBrA, they wanted the greatest possible freedom in their work, an absolute independence from all kinds of prevailing stylistic notions and a liberation from political, aesthetic, and moral values. They did not have a common style, but they did share an urge for self-expression in which spontaneity, improvisation and coincidence played an important role. Gert recalls: 'No mapped-out roads, a terra incognita in which you could participate and help map it out. The challenge of making your own rules, making them visible. There was an incredibly creative energy in it.'

ROYAL ACADEMY OF ART IN THE HAGUE

In 1958 he was admitted to the Royal Academy of Art in The Hague, in the department of painting. The attitude of independence and the emphasis on autonomy that were fostered there were decisive for his development as a graphic designer. 'You were given the time and the opportunity to think about things and to be critical. Visual art forces you to think about your own form and attitude.' The few works that have survived from that period, made outside the academy's programme, show once again that he was strongly led by the international developments in art at that time, which were dominated by abstraction and expressionism. The direct expression of personal feelings came first. But even more important for his further development were the conversations he had with Jan van Keulen,[11] who taught composition in the painting department. Van Keulen became

head of a renewed graphic and typographic design department in 1957, and while still teaching in the painting department he looked for talented students who showed an interest in the subject. He convinced Gert of graphic design's importance for

Gert Dumbar, 1959 (illustration)

the society of the future and Gert decided to change direction. 'A part of this,' says Gert, 'was that in the end the solitary life of the artist didn't appeal to me that much. I needed an outside perspective, a client, with a clear and concrete problem. I was more interested in a direct communication with society. In the visual arts you are so terribly left to your own devices. I would rather play in an orchestra than as a soloist.' Later he adds: 'Within the compelling framework of the client, the challenge is greater. You're more aware of your sense of freedom when you're trying to escape from prison than when you're already outside.' Before he changed direction, however, he had to serve in the army for 21 months. But even there, he did not abstain from drawing and other artistic activities. When he was caught one evening in the attic of the barracks making collages and cartoons, accompanied on the violin by his friend Thomas Tichelman, he was expelled from the officer training programme 'for artistic nonchalance.'

25

In September 1961, after his military service, Gert returned to the academy in the department of graphic and typographic design headed by Jan van Keulen, who had rigorously transformed the old 'Reclame'[12] (Advertising) department into a new graphic design department. 'It was a kind of coup d'état, the old guard out and the new one in, the whole programme was transformed,' says former student Hans van Westen.[13] Founded

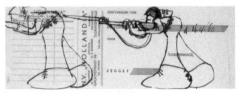

Gert Dumbar, Cartoon made during military service, 16 April 1960

in 1930 by Paul Schuitema[14] and Gerrit Kiljan[15], the 'Reclame' department in The Hague had a glorious history — it was the first specialized training school for graphic designers in the Netherlands, set up according to principles related to the Bauhaus. Schuitema and Kiljan were called 'the maniacs' because of the fanaticism with which they tried to implement the principles of New Objectivity in their classes. Together they laid the foundation for a functionalist way of designing that would be followed by many generations of design students. They placed a strong emphasis on the social relevance of the profession as Schuitema, a communist, believed in the social engineering of a better world. Responsible design could contribute to that. Van Keulen and his director J.J. Beljon took a different course. Pre-war functionalism had lost its momentum and had to disappear, they felt. 'A pathetic little club,' says Beljon, speaking of Schuitema and Kiljan. 'One has the feeling that one has bowed too

deeply to the machine and that the complete human being with his caprices, his feeling for the irrational, for play, etc. is no longer in demand.'[16] Nonetheless, also Van Keulen's course was dominated by a form of modernism associated with the Swiss School, which asserted itself as the rightful heir to functionalism in the 1950s, advocating a minimalist use of imagery, abstracted forms and sans serif fonts. Like in the earlier avant-gardes, the idea remained that graphic design could play an important role in society by providing clarity and order in communication through a well-ordered, objective formal language. But Van Keulen had his own interpretation of modernism, which did not always include functionalism. Strictly speaking, Van Keulen felt designers should determine the starting points for a good design by themselves, rather than mechanically following the client's briefing or fulfilling some 'objective' function. He remained the designer with the attitude of a free artist. And in this Gert would follow him. 'The grey theory broken; life proves stronger than doctrine' is a famous Van Keulen statement. And: 'Suddenly a certain design captivates even without an emphatic argument and is then simply visually interesting.'[17]

YOU ARE MORE AWARE OF YOUR SENSE OF FREEDOM WHEN YOU'RE TRYING TO ESCAPE FROM PRISON THAN WHEN YOU'RE ALREADY OUTSIDE

Van Keulen was inspired more by form than by function, and good results had more to do with the pleasure a designer took in his work than with a design philosophy. He was wary, he said,

12   'Reclame' at the time stood for a broader concept of public communication than today's term 'advertising' suggests. In a manifesto-like article in the avant-garde magazine *iiro*, Schuitema contrasted 'Yesterday — Art' with 'Today — Reality.' In it, the term 'Reclame' summarized the new characteristics: 'real, direct, photographic, ... practical, technical.' Ref. Paul Schuitema: 'Reclame', *iiro*, Vol.I, #16 p. 76, Amsterdam, November 1928.

13   Interview Hans van Westen, October 2002.

14   Paul Schuitema (1897–1973) was a Dutch graphic designer, photographer and artist, who together with Piet Zwart shaped a new direction in using photos in design. His designs for advertising Van Berkel scales pioneered the expressive use of photography in advertising. A member of the 'Union of worker photographers' in the 1930s, he spearheaded a new generation of photographers.

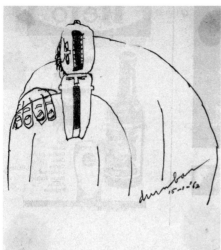
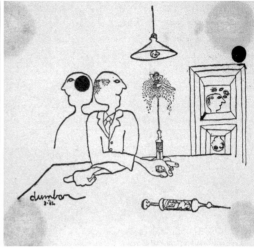

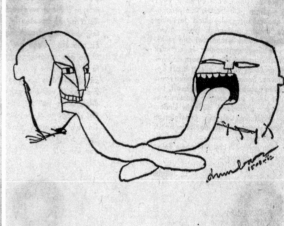

Gert Dumbar's illustrations at the
Royal Academy of Art, The Hague,
1961-1962

15   Gerrit Kiljan (1891–1968) was a Dutch graphic designer and, with Piet Zwart and Paul Schuitema, one of the pioneers of the 'new photography' of the 1930s. He was among the first to use photos in designs for postage stamps, but is most known for his work in education, most notably as initiator of the 'Reclame' department at the Royal Academy in The Hague, in 1930.

16   Jan Middendorp, *Ha, daar gaat er een van mij*, Rotterdam, 2002, p. 90.

17   NAGO News, 2–1997.

of the overly strict dogma of functionalist designers. An enormous expansion of the 'publicity world' was anticipated and, according to Van Keulen, designers had not yet been involved enough at that time. This had to change: 'It's not about why it is designed well, but that it is designed well, that's the most important thing'.[18] But despite his freer, more 'humanistic' attitude, Van Keulen maintained strict rules when it came to aesthetics and formal requirements (based on the rules of the Swiss School), with minor freedom for the student's personal interpretation. Gert, by the way, would care little about this. He was initially impressed by Van Keulen, with whom he had also kept in touch during his period of military service. But gradually this changed into an attitude of scepticism. According to Gert, Van Keulen was authoritarian and dogmatic and had too little eye for the student's personal development. 'The whole class produced little Van Keulens. He was above all an aesthete who, despite

Posters, 1962

his background as an autonomous artist and a liberal attitude, used authoritarian formal rules: lots of white, sans serif fonts, primary colours and the Gill font. You were inexorably forced into a straitjacket.'

Posters, 1962

Gert allowed all this to sink in. He frequently rebelled against the strict formal rules, though, sometimes in unexpected ways. For example, when for an exhibition for the Gemeentemuseum in

I HAD STAGED IT ALL WITH A FEELING OF EUPHORIA LIKE THE DADAISTS MUST HAVE KNOWN, A BUNCH OF MADMEN WHO, IN AN INVENTIVE WAY, TURNED EVERYTHING UPSIDE DOWN IN ORDER TO ARRIVE AT SOMETHING NEW

The Hague, instead of producing a single poster designed according to Van Keulen's purist principles, he produced no fewer than eight two- and three-dimensional posters, including one with flashing lights, one with a little motor that set water in motion in a glass tube, aquarium-like, and several typographical experiments in which different fonts — serif and sans serif — were used indiscriminately. One poster (for a Kandinsky exhibition) folded out like a sandwich board, with a photograph

18   Ibid.

of Kandinsky and on the tray a piece of cake with a stack of napkins on which the word 'Kandinsky' was printed in gold. 'I just couldn't stop,' Gert explains. 'I was so fascinated by that profession! How you could combine shapes, images, and letters and how you had to communicate with the client and the public. Earlier I had sent a telegram to Van Keulen: 'Tomorrow poster exhibition.' I had staged it all with a feeling of euphoria like the Dadaists must have known, a bunch of madmen who, in an inventive way, turned everything upside down in order to arrive at something new. I tried to bring back something of that enthusiasm, that euphoria. To see how

Record sleeve, 1962

things could be done differently. It was not common practice at the time and was not understood by other teachers either.' Van Keulen, who initially had great expectations of Gert, did not know what to think of it. 'Well, one could do it that way…' he cautiously remarked, adding: 'brilliant nonsense.'

During the two years in Van Keulen's department, Gert nevertheless became familiar with the functionalism prescribed there. At the same time he continued to experiment. 'I had to come up with a solution, but not by following the appropriate route.' Gradually he became more and more critical of Van Keulen: 'He

Book illustration, 1962

was not society-minded enough and paid too little attention to the potential of the students themselves.' A criticism that Gert expressed during a dinner at the latter's home, which was not appreciated. His design deviated too much from the then prevailing standard. He would pass his final exam with a meagre 6-. Unfortunately, little of Gert's work from that period has survived.

In June 1963 Gert left the Royal Academy to continue his studies at the Royal College of Art in London, at that time one of only two academies in Europe where advanced study was possible (the other was the Hochschule für Gestaltung in Ulm, a strict functionalist course elaborating on the ideals of the Bauhaus). Although he had experienced the training at The Hague's Royal Academy as too limited, it did lay the basis for his further career. He had learned the basic principles of graphic design, typography, type design and visual communication and had mastered the instruments with which he could now develop the profession in his own way.

Poster for *Bluebeard's Castle* by the
RCA Music Society, 1964.
Model: Peter Blake

THE SWINGING SIXTIES

ROYAL COLLEGE OF ART IN LONDON, 1963–1965

'I believe there is no city in the world where so many illogical things are brought together,' Gert wrote, October 1963, a month after his arrival in London. 'In this vast chaos of insane things, one is making an active contribution to the art development of Europe.'[19]

In September he had started his studies at the Royal College of Art (RCA) in London — then the world Capital of 'the swinging sixties'. 'The city is alive with birds and beatles, buzzing with minibars and tellystars, pulsing with half a dozen separate veins of excitement,' wrote the American weekly *Time* magazine.[20]

It was the age of the Beatles, the Rolling Stones, the Who, Mary Quant's miniskirts and Carnaby Street, the new fashion Mecca where young people bought their new gear to the beat of pop music, in stores crafted by designers from the RCA. The vitality of the city, the new lifestyle — eccentric, bohemian — was infectious. There was a sense of lightness, optimism, and excitement about everything that suddenly seemed possible. For many young people in England and also in the rest of the world, London at that time was a symbol of liberation and renewal, of great expectations for the future. Gert fell into a state of euphoria. 'It fizzes and buzzes inside me,' he wrote, 'There is so much to see and do that it sometimes makes me feel disheartened.'[21] Life in London seemed like one big party, a burst of merriment after a period of great gloom and poverty in the years during and just after the war. The spectacle of city life as expressed in advertising images, film, fashion, slogans, and other expressions of a burgeoning mass culture was celebrated by Pop Art painters and transformed into colourful images of great vitality, ushering in a new phase in the development of art. 'Pop' also had a big influence on Gert during his studies at the RCA.

19   Letter Gert to Hans van Westen, former classmate at the KABK, 23 October 1963.
20   'London "the swinging city"', in *Time*, 15 April 1966.
21   Letter Gert to Leonie ten Duis, 21 October 1963.

Gert Dumbar's work station at RCA

A SMALL NON-CONFORMIST SCHOOL

The RCA was a small non-conformist school of international stature, a dense community of young, sometimes eccentric artists and designers, coming from all parts of the world, who provided a unique cross-pollination of influences and ideas — a focal point of the new developments.

Head of the RCA since 1948 had been Robin Darwin (Charles's great-grandson), an Eton-educated club man who wanted artists and designers to have 'the amused and well-tempered mind of a gentleman'. The faculty room designed under his direction had as its model a senior common room in Cambridge. There was a good cuisine, excellent wines were served, ties were mandatory for men. Darwin regularly invited speakers of international standing, such as Isaiah Berlin, George Steiner, Kenneth Clark, John Betjeman.

Although Darwin's patrician attitude seemed rather absurd at first glance, there was a strong logic behind his gentrification programme. Darwin wanted to attract prominent people to make the RCA the number one Art & Design school in the world. And he was quite successful.[22] He befriended important industrialists and brought them to the College, thus raising

the status of 'designing for industry' and breaking down the snobbish divide between the 'useless' fine arts and the 'useful' applied arts. Thanks to Darwin, the RCA would become one of the most progressive academies in Europe at that time. The defining factor was a relaxed attitude in education, aimed at innovation and experimentation. But even more than the education, it was the creative climate and the vibrant activity generated by the painters, filmmakers, industrial and graphic designers, which played such an important role in the years of pop culture, that so impressed Gert.

The contrast between Darwin's somewhat curious upper-class attitude and the rebellious eccentricity of the students at the RCA also surprised Gert at first. Students regularly mocked Darwin, who did not take offense. An annual event, for example, was convocation day, the day on which the students, dressed in toga and beret, received their degrees. Darwin gave

Robin Darwin, drawing by Arthur Lismer

his usual speech, and as he started, all the students present put on a silk-screened mask — a portrait of Darwin with his

22 Peter Conradi, *Iris Murdoch: A Life*, London, 2001, p. 470.
23 Richard Guyatt, 'Design at the Royal College of Art', in *Graphics RCA*, catalog 1963.

24 Ibid.

heavy glasses and striking moustache. No one laughed and Darwin continued his speech unruffled. For Gert, this was proof that the spirit of Dada in England lay just below the surface. The sense of the absurd that he found at the college held an irresistible attraction for him.

THE SCHOOL OF GRAPHIC DESIGN

IT IS THROUGH THE VISUAL ARTS, THE 'USELESS' ARTS, THAT THE 'USEFUL' ARTS OF DESIGN ACQUIRE THEIR POWER
Professor Richard Guyatt

Despite the relaxed attitude at the college, graphic design students had to meet high standards. 'Self-awareness, ambition, social responsibility, a sense of ethics, logical but also emotional intelligence and — crucially — intellectual curiosity' were required. Students were further expected to have 'a broad mind and be able to work well together, debate and respond to criticism.'[23] Much importance was given to the theoretical context of the work, supported by a well-focused humanoria programme of lectures, seminars, and work groups, covering a broad range of subjects from philosophy, architecture, and art history. In addition, a central premise was that the visual arts were the source of inspiration for the applied arts. Hence the importance given to the painting class in graphic design. 'It is through the visual arts, the "useless" arts, that the "useful" arts of design, acquire their power,' wrote Professor Richard Guyatt, then head of the graphic design department.[24] There was a lively exchange

between the two departments and, although initially the visual arts had been the inspiration for graphic design, since the early 1960s there had been more of a two-way exchange between the 'useful' and 'useless' arts. From a reservoir of images and motifs — mostly drawn from the idiom of mass culture — painters drew freely for their paintings as did designers for their posters, increasingly blurring the traditional divisions between art and design.

Poster for RCA dance party, 1964

POP ART
Gert began his studies in London at a time when the RCA was the centre of Pop Art. Peter Blake taught in the painting department, David Hockney had graduated the year before but was

Gert with a papier-mâché model used
in the RCA dance party poster, 1964

still a regular at the college, the American painter R. B. Kitaj studied there and stayed on. Embracing popular culture — comic strips, advertisements, movies, pin-up girls and the like — rather than honouring the sacrosanct models from tradition, Pop Artists opened up a treasure trove of new motifs while at the same time unhinging both traditional and modernist artistic dogma. Pop Art was anarchic, humorous with ample room for contradiction and ambiguity and an aversion to everything that was too serious, pompous and pedantic.[25] Unsurprisingly, Gert felt at home with Pop Art, which in England was 'more gentle' then the much rawer American version. This tendency of the English not to go to extremes and keep a somewhat ironic distance fitted in seamlessly with Gert's attitude to life. He was fascinated by the freedom and visual inventiveness of Pop Art: 'You had to look at mundane things in a new way. You had to somehow transfer them into a high-quality visual image. How can you take a vulgar cliché to a higher level? That's a visual exercise. That fascinated me.' Pop Art gave him greater visual latitude and the opportunity to use a more personal artistic expression. He rediscovered a form of open-mindedness, for which there had been (too) little room in the education provided at the art academy in The Hague, with its unequivocal, formalistic starting point.

Darwin put a strong emphasis on professionalism, and in line with this much attention was paid to the practical aspects of the profession. For the student, there was the opportunity to work for the RCA's Design Department, which was responsible for designing all the printed materials for the college. In addition to these printing jobs, students were given the opportunity to design posters for the various clubs within the College, including the drama club, the film club, the jazz club and the 'school dance', which took place once a week in the College. Gert would design several posters for these events, which were also printed at the College.

Poster for Tarkovsky's film *Ivan's Childhood* at the RCA film club. The film is about a Russian boy who fights the Germans as youngest partisan (design: Gert Dumbar, 1964)

ARK

A sensitive indicator of what was happening in London in the 1950s and 1960s in the field of graphic design was the RCA's magazine *ARK*, which reflected the growing influence of Pop Art. Edited and designed by graphic design students, *ARK*'s content and form were experimental, closely following current developments in art and culture and providing a platform to discuss them. For its time, it was a revolutionary magazine — idiosyncratic, surprising, often sporting rather absurd designs, which inspired many up-and-coming designers and artists. For Gert, who had bought a few issues on his first visit to London in 1963, it provided another shock of recognition:

35

25   See Barnice Martin, *A Sociology of Contemporary Cultural Change*, Oxford, 1981.

Various *ARK* magazines, 1962-1964

'The use of accidentally encountered typographical elements, the fragmented, illogical structure, the deliberately primitive lettering — the design, the imagery, the incitements to Pop Art, it all made me think about graphic design in a different way, putting it into perspective, humorously. The magazine's use of images and colour was extraordinarily innovative for the time. I was confronted with a different way of seeing that could be built upon. And it was different every time. It created an enormous expectation pattern: this is where it happened. The new *ARK* was always eagerly anticipated.'

The content and form of the magazine were inspired by Dada. There is an interest in collage and breaking down the conventional narrative structure, with an important role for coincidence. Notwithstanding the often quite ideological tenets of their sources of inspiration, *ARK*'s issues from the 1960s were not overtly political. 'The significance of the magazine lay rather in the attempt to understand and appreciate the cultural changes that were taking place at the time and especially in an appreciation of metropolitan culture,' says Denis Postle, *ARK*'s art director at the time: 'We were looking for images that weren't the accustomed ones… trying to give legitimacy to things which up until that time had been illegitimate.'[26] The magazine gradually became more and more experimental, occasionally printing pages in invisible ink on brown packing paper, or in luminous colours on cellophane. Articles by Jack Kerouac and William Burroughs appeared, fragmented chunks of poetry, and Dada icon Kurt Schwitters wrote an article. In the fragmentedness, the breaking down of narrative structure, the use of collage, the magazine was ahead of later developments, in particular postmodernism, foredating 1980s magazines like Neville Brody's *The Face* by almost two decades. Gert. 'I saw parallels with how I myself thought about design. It put me on the track of a design that suited a new era. I also realized then that you shouldn't see design as a separate discipline but that it was part of a greater whole. It was about an attitude.'

FUNCTIONALISM
The visual arts may inspire the applied arts, but a designer's work remains based on function, stated Professor Guyatt. A stark contrast to the euphoria of Pop

26   Alex Seago, *Burning the Box of Beautiful Things*, Oxford, 1995, p. 173.

every
dog
has
his
day......,
it
could
be
friday
at
the
r. c. a.

*bar
party*

royal college of art, friday march 25 1966, 8-12 pm, 3 bands 2 bars

Poster for RCA bar party, 1966
(design: Gert Dumbar)

Art were the classes of Anthony Froshaug, head of the first year of graphic design. Here Gert was again confronted with a form of functionalism. 'They have about the same work mentality here as the old Kilian and Schuitema group, everything is about "problem solving". Every step has to be rationalized. Every dot, every stripe that even slightly hints at copying is condemned in our work.'[27]

Froshaug had taught at the Bauhaus-inspired Hochschule für Gestaltung in Ulm, Germany, from 1957 to 1961, a school that was dominated by a 'sachlich' functionalism, as neutral as a machine. A logical, methodical thinker, Froshaug brought his Ulm background to his London teaching programme. He saw design as an analytical, mathematical thinking process. Through Froshaug, Gert gained access to areas of graphic

design unfamiliar to him at the time — information design, semantics, designing structures. He learned how to efficiently organize and graphically represent complicated matter, a thorough preparation for designing the corporate identities for government and large companies that would later become a central part of his studio's work. But as functionalist as it was at root, Froshaug's thinking about design wasn't dogmatic. Analysis and organization of the programme of requirements were key, but should not automatically lead to a fixed and unambiguous graphic solution. He rather argued for flexible systems, open to new developments: 'It is precisely the development of "open-ended" problems and systems, that we should be concerned with,' Froshaug said.[28] This 'open-endedness' would become one of the pillars of Gert's future practice.

RCA, first year graphic design, 1962/'63. Anthony Froshaug (centre), Gert Dumbar second from left

27   Letter Gert to Leonie ten Duis, 23 October 1963.
28   Robin Kinross, *Anthony Froshaug, Documents of a life*, London, 2000, p. 131.
29   Ibid.
30   Ibid., p. 197.

31   Ibid., p. 142. Here, Gert touches on the bedrock conviction of one of the most prominent of his future colleagues in the Netherlands, Wim Crouwel, a hardened functionalist who famously stated that 'Relevant and necessary information is purely original in itself, the designer has

In Froshaug's classes, a number of Gert's other essential design convictions were addressed as well. For instance, Froshaug pointed out the role and importance of intuition as often decisive for solving a design problem, even within a functionalist approach.[29] And he advocated a form of 'controlled self-expression'. Students should be encouraged in the first year to learn techniques of 'random creativeness' as well as the techniques of control.[30] Froshaug also raised a question that would continue to fascinate Gert: 'The problem of whether a design that gives only the necessary information and exercises the greatest restraint conveys its message better than a design that has a degree of noise, of redundant information.'[31] Gert had great admiration for Froshaug. 'You have to analyse but also bring in something of yourself.' 'There is room for emotion. There is room for humour,' he wrote enthusiastically about Froshaug's functionalism to his friend and former fellow student at the The Hague Academy Hans van Westen.[32]

Froshaug was a charismatic teacher who deeply influenced many students. Someone with an 'underground reputation', who, when asked by students 'What do you teach?' replied 'Technics and ethics'. 'Froshaug wanted to emphasize that design is always much more than just an end product,' writes Robin Kinross. 'The projects and the material products may have been the immediate reason for students and teachers coming together, but his greater interest lay in the people.'[33] Unlike many other teachers, Froshaug had an informal way of teaching, as Gert recalls: 'For example, he allowed himself to be called Anthony and not Mr. Froshaug at a time when that was not customary at all. He also regularly joined students for a beer in the pub at the corner, The Hoop and Toy, to talk about the subject in a more informal setting.' The stories that circulated around him — about his turbulent life, with lots of drinking and women — also made a big impression. It would become the ground for his dismissal. 'A functionalist with human traits,' Gert said, admiringly.

POP ART OR FUNCTIONALISM?

Gert experienced a period of strict functionalism at the RCA, while at the same time designing posters inspired by Pop Art. He liked 'designs where nothing is superfluous', a stainless-steel ruler with a hole in it to hang on the wall, the design of a car such as the Citroen 2CV, or 'the purity of the thumbtack'. Still, he rejected the omission of capitals, as prescribed by Schuitema and the Bauhaus functionalists. 'It has been scientifically proven that the omission of capitals is utterly foolish. Indeed, it tires the reader much more than when capitals are used,' he wrote to Hans van Westen. Hans had written a manifesto in the spirit of Paul Schuitema, entirely set in lower case. 'It is not virtuous, it is false,' Gert writes about the use of only lower case. After which Gert attacks Hans for using elements in his design that he could not justify: 'What are all those dashes doing at the top of your manifesto. What is their function? They are superfluous; indeed, they are confusing. Madness, madness,'[34] stated Gert in a letter to his friend, unsuspecting of the fact that his own name would one day become a verb for exactly this 'madness'.

To Hans' great surprise, Gert seemed to be quite serious about functionalism — surely Gert was more of an artist, wasn't he? Failing to understand what Pop Art had to do with functionalism, he asked

nothing to add to it.' See Max Bruinsma: 'Points of View on Design Education', in *Rietveld Project* nr.23, Gerrit Rietveld Academie / AGI, 1984.
32 Letter Gert to Hans van Westen, 21 October 1963.
33 Robin Kinross in *Octavio*, 1986/1, p. 4.
34 Letter Gert to Hans van Westen, 23 February 1964.

somewhat desperately, 'What are you going to do now? Pop Art or think about every stroke you put on paper?'[35]

Pop Art continued to captivate, but Gert gradually began to have his doubts about its content: 'It's a kind of super-comedy, graphically extremely interesting, but it doesn't carry a message.'[36] And: 'They play with their props on the canvas, very cleverly. No doubt about that. But I believe that in a few years this style will be over, because it is more fashion than art.'[37]

Gert tried to find a balance between the freedom of art and the discipline of functionalism. But instinctively, he ultimately stayed closer to a subjective, expressionist design. Froshaug's functionalism was nevertheless crucial. 'Here I learned to think in systems of order, with panache and not dogmatically.'

Another important teacher at the RCA was Jock Kinneir, whose classes Gert took for two years. Between 1957 and 1967, Kinneir designed the signage system for Britain's roads, one of the most ambitious and effective 'information design' projects ever undertaken in the United Kingdom. Together with his partner Margaret Calvert, Kinneir designed a coherent and easy to read signage system with carefully coordinated lettering — in a bespoke typeface, later named Transport — colours, shapes, and symbols. This was unique for the time and the system became widely imitated. For a long time it served as an example for road signage all over the world. Jock Kinneir taught Gert to design signage systems based on examples and experiences from everyday life. 'Clear, unadorned, and functional. I learned to think in systems and to use grids, in which features such as colour, size and font were brought together. But also, how a design was tested for readability in practice and even how things were manufactured. I got a lot out of that later.'

A connection to the lessons of Froshaug and Kinneir were F.H.K. Henrion's classes. Henrion was a pioneer in the field of house styles and had designed a new corporate identity for KLM in the early 1960s, the first corporate identity in the public sector in the Netherlands. He familiarized students with examples from practice. Gert: 'It wasn't until Henrion came on board that it became clear to us what designing a corporate identity entailed. Henrion taught us how to approach designing a corporate identity in a coherent way and pointed out the importance of a concept that would last for years.' Henrion's corporate identity for KLM proved to be the start of a totally new development of designing for government in the Netherlands. For the first time a Dutch state-owned company presented itself as a unity in such an outspoken way. NS, the Dutch Railways, followed not long after. Responsible for that project were Siep Wijsenbeek, industrial designer and design manager at NS, and Gert Dumbar, freshly returned to the Netherlands from the Royal Academy.

In the 1980s and 1990s Gert would return to the Royal College of Art two more times. First as professor from 1985 till 1987, and from 1999 till 2001 as visiting professor. In a commemorative book published by the RCA in 2014, Adrian Shaughnessy writes: 'Perhaps the most radical appointment of the post-1960s era was the introduction of Gert Dumbar. A former RCA student, he was appointed Visiting Professor in 1985. ... A true radical, Dumbar brought with him a whiff of anarchy and transformation. ... his philosophy of uncompromising self-expression found willing disciples among his students.'[38]

35   Letter Hans van Westen to Gert, 27 February 1964.
36   Letter Gert to Leonie ten Duis, 9 November 1964.
37   Interview in *de Volkskrant*, June 1964.

38   Teal Triggs e.a, *GraphicsRCA: Fifty Years and Beyond*, London: Royal College of Art, 2014.

Cover of an undated brochure
with Tel Design logo and 'pin-up'
wallpaper

BUILDING A CURIOSITY-BASED STRUCTURE

In the summer of 1966, Gert returned to the Netherlands, 26 years old, with bolstered self-confidence and a focused view of the profession. The many encounters with inspiring personalities and ideas at the RCA 'taught me to think about design with that typically British combination of analysis and witticism'. Added to this were his numerous visits to the Institute of Contemporary Arts (ICA), a famous meeting place in London for artists, writers and critics where the latest developments in art were shown and discussed. British Pop art had been launched there in the 1950s.

The atmosphere of freedom and experimentation he had experienced at the RCA contrasted sharply with the unambiguous modernism that still set the tone as an ideology and as a style in Dutch design in 1966. The purified, functionalist design of Wim Crouwel's Total Design was the benchmark for good design at the time. But 1966 also marked the beginning of a new era in the Netherlands, the era of Provo with its playfully anarchistic political activism, its plea for an open and versatile attitude and its emphasis on individual freedom, rebellion against conventions, provocation of established authorities. It was inspiring not just politically, but also aesthetically, says Gert, evoking 'the euphoria that this was also possible in a limited field like graphic design'.

Not long after his return to the Netherlands, Gert was approached by Tel Design in The Hague, a young, thriving, business-oriented industrial design agency. They were looking for a designer to set up Tel Design's new graphic design department in connection with a possible assignment for a corporate identity for the Dutch National Railways, the NS. Tel Design's founders, Emile Truijen and Jan Lucassen, both industrial designers, had started it in 1962 with the ambition to become the first large design agency in the Netherlands, predating Total

Tel Design, 1967

Design by a year. Both were inspired by large multidisciplinary British design agencies such as Design Research Unit (led by Mischa Black) and Fletcher, Forbes and Gill. Such agencies were a new phenomenon in the early 1960s in the Netherlands, where graphic design had always been considered a predominantly aesthetic affair, done by individual designers or small studios — not the kind of organizational, constructive activity more associated with architecture and urbanism. Tel and Total Design introduced a more businesslike approach, mirroring to a certain extent the managerial and organizational DNA of their targeted clientele. Mindful of F.H.K. Henrion's famous quote 'institutions like to talk to institutions', the two design agencies wanted to become institutions themselves. In the Netherlands, Henrion had

introduced the idea of 'house style' with his design for KLM in 1963. Other key examples in Dutch business were oil company PAM (1965, by Total Design) and Albert Heijn (1966, by Allied Industrial Designers, UK). In the course of the 1960s, the concept of corporate identity would gradually grow on both designers and clients in the Netherlands.[1]

NS — THE DUTCH RAILWAYS

On the advice of Siep Wijsenbeek, an industrial designer at the NS who, like Gert, had studied at the RCA and knew his work well, Truijen and Lucassen contacted Gert. 'We liked his work and we liked each other,' wrote Truijen.[2] Gert was the first graphic designer to be permanently employed by the firm, which

1   In 1968 an ICOGRADA (international association of national graphic design organizations) congress took place in Eindhoven, where much attention was paid to the subject of house style. There F.H.K. Henrion presented, with co-author Alan Parkin, their book *Design coordination and corporate image* (London, 1967), which would soon

become the bible for everyone involved with house styles.
2   Emile Truijen, *Brieven van een ontwerper*, Faculteit Industrieel Ontwerpen, Delft, 1993, p. 104.

previously had only worked with freelance graphic designers. His job was to establish and lead a new graphic design department and he managed to form a good team. His department's internal structure, however, was not very conventional: 'I didn't like to have too much authority and power structures; my war camp experiences probably played a role in this. My credo in setting up a design team was actually quite simple: to build a structure based on curiosity and entrepreneurial spirit with a large degree of responsibility for the designers and as much freedom as possible, while directing this in the background

> *MY CREDO IN SETTING UP A DESIGN TEAM WAS ACTUALLY QUITE SIMPLE, TO BUILD A STRUCTURE BASED ON CURIOSITY AND ENTREPRENEURIAL SPIRIT WITH A LARGE DEGREE OF RESPONSIBILITY FOR THE DESIGNERS*
>
> Gert Dumbar

and reacting alertly to the possibilities it offered. That was more or less what I had in mind.' Of course, Gert did retain final responsibility, setting the tone and determining the mindset regarding the profession and the clients. He was committed to innovative design and not afraid to stand up for his convictions, even against the grain, also convincing traditional clients of the importance of unconventional solutions. At Tel Design, the foundations were laid for a working method and a mentality that would later, at Studio Dumbar, be fully developed.

The commissions the agency received were diverse, from commercial clients such as Simon de Wit supermarket and construction company HBG to government clients such as the National Railways (NS) and the national Mail, Telegraphy, and Telephony (PTT). The — in contemporary terms — extensive and comparatively unconventional corporate identity for the NS brought Tel Design national and international fame. It was a major commission requiring a complex, well-ordered, functional design system but at the same time — to quote Gert — 'it contained a music box here and there'. Equally important and striking were the designs for the cultural sector on which Gert could leave a more personal imprint, exploring a freedom that bordered on that of the visual arts, with a central role for staged photography. That was his experimental playground, and later that of his studio, exploring what design critic Hugues Boekraad would characterize as 'diagonal modernism', as if Gert were a Van Doesburg among designers.

Train colours in 1966
In: Wibo Bakker, *Droom van Helderheid*, 2009

With the design commission of the NS corporate identity, and the task to set up a new graphic design department, Gert was immediately thrown in at the deep end, although Truijen and Lucassen remained responsible for the business side. 'It was an adventurous beginning.

It was my first big assignment and I felt an enormous responsibility. I was aware that the NS corporate identity would have a national impact and would add a striking element to the environment. But I felt supported by my education at the RCA. There I had come into contact with a number of inspiring personalities, including Anthony Froshaug, who taught us to think in structures and systems, and Henrion who taught us to think in fields, where it wasn't just about the function of a logo, a typography, a colour but about their place in the whole, and how to bring unity to that.'

EXPLORING WHAT DESIGN CRITIC HUGUES BOEKRAAD WOULD CHARACTERISE AS 'DIAGONAL MODERNISM' AS IF GERT WERE A VAN DOESBURG AMONG DESIGNERS

The NS commission was given to Tel Design after a pitch against Total Design on the merit of Tel's 'more focused and concrete plan of action'.[3] Siep Wijsenbeek may have played a role too in advocating Tel — and advising Lucassen to hire Gert specifically for this job. Wijsenbeek became an important member of the NS steering group that would oversee the entire process. The NS had two faces: an internal study showed a well-organized company with high technical standards, but a survey conducted among the Dutch public revealed that it was seen as old-fashioned, dull, complacent and conservative. That had to change. At the same time, the Railways — long a linchpin in the Dutch infrastructure — felt increasing competition from cars. New roads were

built, and people used the train less. As a result, the NS was struggling with losses from 1963 onwards; one of the reasons why a new corporate identity was being considered. The brief was to give the NS a more 'contemporary' and 'modern' look.

1 Oud NS-embleem, tot 1946   2 NS-embleem 1946-1968

Old NS vignettes, 1946-1968

Beyond improving the company's public image (a word that was emerging in the Dutch design field at the time), designing the NS identity centred on informing a large and diverse public in a clear and accessible way in a distinctive visual language that could serve over a longer period of time without losing vigour. The actual design task was preceded by a thorough analysis and research of the NS's organization of infrastructure and transport. Converting the results into a solid house style was a complex and extensive operation, to which end a strict functionalist starting point was applied in order to unify all the different components. But with room for a contrarian note.

The research revealed a motley array of visual forms, including three colours of trains, more than thirteen emblems or logos, a variety of typefaces, all of which now had to be brought under one visual umbrella: one colour for the trains, one new vignette, one typeface, a new corporate typography, signage for the stations, a new layout for the railway timetables. After first developing the basic principles and elements of the identity — the logo, the colours, the typeface — Gert gradually recruited more designers, including Gertjan Leuvelink and René van Raalte.

3   In part because, as Wibo Bakker writes in *Droom van helderheid* (Utrecht, 2009, p. 137): 'Total Design's offer was disappointing. And in a short, accompanying letter, perceived as arrogant, the NS was presented as a fairy-tale "dragon" that had to change. In contrast, Tel Design's

quotation showed a focused plan of action. The concrete nature of this offer played an important role in choosing Tel Design.' In our review of the NS, PTT, and Simon de Wit house styles, we gratefully refer to Bakker's benchmark book and articles, which are the first to

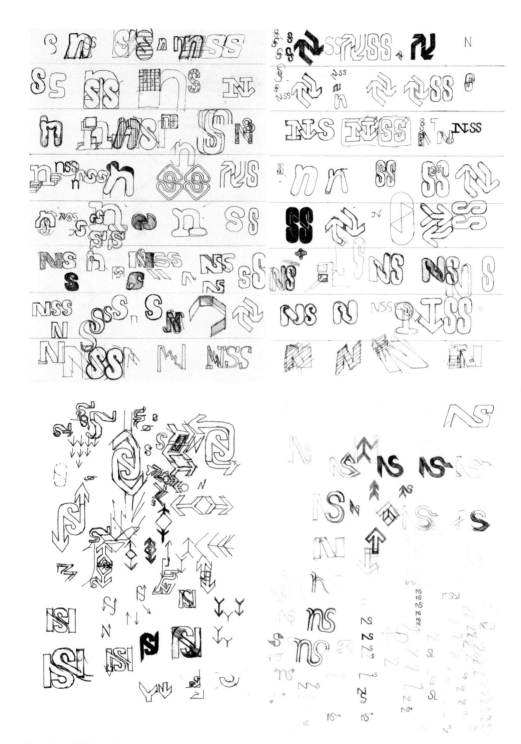

Sketches of NS logo (sketches: Gert Dumbar)

thoroughly describe and analyse the history of corporate
identity in the Netherlands.

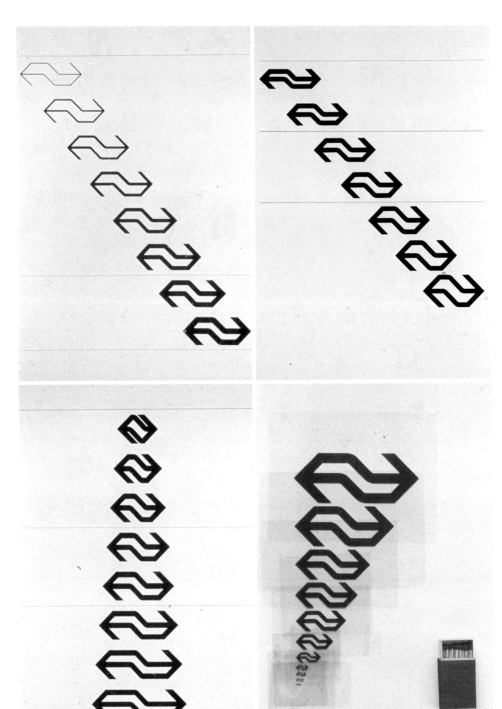

Sketches of various weights and proportions
of NS logo (design: Gert Dumbar)

Sketches of NS logo (sketches: Gert Dumbar)

Leuvelink would have a major share in developing the corporate identity for the NS, especially concerning the timetables. He had been educated at the AKI, the Bauhaus-inspired Academy of Art and Industry in Enschedé, and had worked for some time at the Staatsdrukkerij en Uitgeverij (SDU), the government agency that handled government printing and publishing. The experience with typography that he had gained there, as well as his more functionalist orientation, would be crucial in supporting Gert, who was 'more the man of the soft pencil,' according to Gertjan.[4]

Two conspicuous elements characterize the NS design, a colour scheme and the logo. The latter's point of departure was, according to the brief, 'a pictorial sign based on the letters NS'. From Gert's sketches, it is clear that he started off that way, exploring all possible and impossible ways of forging the two letters into one sign. At the same time, the use of arrows —a directional cliché one finds in countless railway logos around the world— was tested, including investigations into lines representing tracks. Gert: 'I couldn't let go. I was constantly busy, even at home during sleepless nights, or while shopping, developing ideas or making additional scribbles in the studio diary when I was on the phone.'

In the course of over 1,800 sketches it became clear that the two letters, N and S, were very hard to convincingly combine into one form, and gradually, they disappeared, or better: dissolved. The letterforms' characteristics —the angular N and the undulating S— inspired a free formal experimentation that suddenly locked into the final design, all but forgetting the original briefing: a simple track that goes into both directions, shifting along the way.

'Back and forth transport within a closed circuit with changing directions' is how Tel Design later described the logo.

NS logo 1969.. page from NS design manual (design: Gertjan Leuvelink)

Gert: 'One of the underlying ideas was that a letter sign would become obsolete sooner than an abstract sign. Moreover, an abstract sign crosses the language barrier more easily.' The logo became one of the longest standing brand icons world-wide — it is still in use virtually unchanged after almost sixty years. Gert's former teacher at The Hague Academy, Van Keulen, wrote about the vignette's development in news magazine *De Groene*: 'The design process followed by Tel Design is a textbook

---

4   Gertjan Leuvelink, interview, 2012.

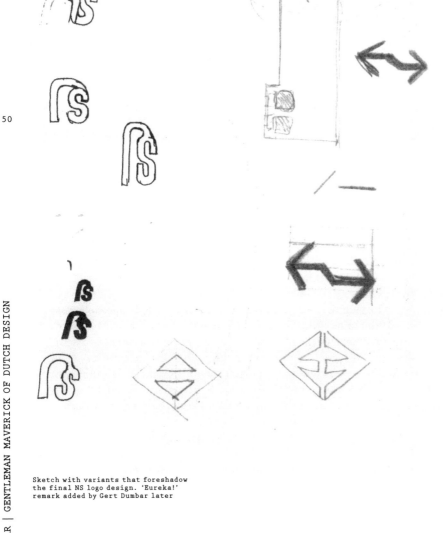

Eureka!

Sketch with variants that foreshadow
the final NS logo design. 'Eureka!'
remark added by Gert Dumbar later

Gert Dumbar photographing the first
application of his NS logo on the
yellow train

'A bright yellow line gliding through the
green landscape under the Dutch blue sky
— like a moving Mondrian'

example of how it grew, of slowly moving away from what was requested in order to arrive at the essence through detours, letting it prevail and then dropping the more or less accidental characters NS.'[5]

After defining the basic design, it needed to be detailed: proportions, line thickness, various sizes and widths were tested in dozens of series of sketches. In addition, the vignette was tested for its applicability and for remaining identifiable in rapid motion. Finally, photographs were taken to investigate whether it could be recognized under conditions of poor visibility. The vignette met all the requirements. It was an extremely thorough, structured and well-nigh

scientific method that also typifies the early development of the profession. Graphic design had yet to find its own identity, distancing itself a bit from its artistic roots and leaning more towards scientific argumentation.

THE YELLOW TRAIN

The other remarkable aspect of the new NS identity is its colour scheme. Its main colour, chromate yellow for the trains, caused quite a stir. It was considered daring and even too frivolous for a serious company like NS, and needed some intense argumentation with the client. Max Bruinsma described 'how Gert Dumbar

5   *De Groene Amsterdammer* magazine, 1968. Quoted in
Hefting et al., *Tel Design 1962–1992*, Amsterdam, 1992, p. 15.

6   Max Bruinsma, *IDEA* magazine, #255, 1996, 3.

talked the Dutch railways into accepting bright yellow as the colour for the trains. Dumbar's personal motive for this colour was mainly poetic. He says: "When a bright yellow train comes into the station, it's as if the sun rises in these dark and hollow caves..." or: "Wouldn't it be great to see a bright yellow line gliding through the green landscape under the Dutch blue

> *WOULDN'T IT BE GREAT TO SEE A BRIGHT YELLOW LINE GLIDING THROUGH THE GREEN LANDSCAPE UNDER THE DUTCH BLUE SKY - LIKE A MOVING MONDRIAN?*

sky — like a moving Mondrian?" This of course is not the kind of argumentation that would convince a board of government bureaucrats. So Dumbar argues: "The bright yellow will greatly enhance the visibility of the trains and thus improve safety of stations and railway crossings." Now the client sees that it is a sensible and friendly thing to do, and agrees to paint the trains bright yellow.' Bruinsma continues: 'This story exemplifies Gert Dumbar's rare talent of convincing traditional clients of unconventional solutions. ... But of course, there is more to it than mere argumentation. The work has to possess a quality that will communicate without explanation.'[6]

Gert recalls: 'Already at an early stage in the development of the corporate identity for the NS, I had the idea of doing something striking with the colour of the trains. Something that would deviate from the existing colour palette of the NS and the rolling stock of the government in the Netherlands in general — predominantly

black and grey and rusty red — which was rather dull and uninspiring. I took a cross-section of the NS with the corporate identity committee. Train trips, visits to an NS workshop, a shunting-yard, the main building in Utrecht, various conversations with station chiefs and engineers. I visited shunting-yards where shunters sat in wobbly shacks by a burning stove, I collected all kinds of NS forms that reminded one of the atmosphere of the war. The visit to the NS headquarters was an experience in itself. Managers proudly told me that it was the largest brick building in the Netherlands. It was

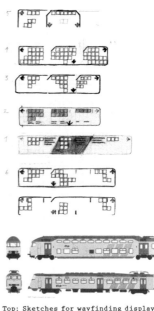

Top: Sketches for wayfinding displays
Bottom: Sketches for placing advertising in bands on the trains, in *Ontwerpen aan het spoor*, 1988

dark, musty and, with its heavy oak doors, felt like a Protestant monastery — the NS had a preference for Protestant employees at that time; Catholics would be better off working for the PTT, they thought. It was a huge challenge to bring some light

53

in there. The NS wanted to emerge in the future as dynamic, fast, non-official and I knew that, more than the logo, font, and typography, colour could play an important role. Henrion was already stressing the importance of colour for a corporate identity to us as students. And of course it was also a kind of provocation — to see if this could bring about a change in culture.'

'My starting point was a striking, positive colour that would light up NS stations and fit well into the Dutch landscape. Red and blue were discarded because these would quickly fade under the influence of UV rays. The colour yellow was less affected. However, its implementation did not go smoothly. There were protests from the NS workshop for "cost reasons", or so they said. But they sabotaged it, they did not want it. It was too modern. It was

decided to spray paint a test train set yellow and "dirt tests" were taken. The yellow

THE YELLOW COLOUR ALSO SPARKED PUBLIC SCORN — IT WAS THOUGHT TO BE TOO CONSPICUOUS. GERT WAS SEEN AS AN IDIOSYNCRATIC DESIGNER WHO SOUGHT OR EXCEEDED THE LIMITS OF THE BRIEF WITH THIS

remained powerful and highly visible under all conditions. In the end Siep Wijsenbeek, by the skin of his teeth, succeeded to convince the NS corporate identity committee of the importance of that colour.'

One of the first trains designed
by Gert Dumbar

7   Gertjan Leuvelink, interview November 2014.
8   Ibid.

Pages from NS design manual with Railway Station pictograms (design: Gert Dumbar)

The yellow colour also sparked public scorn — it was thought to be too conspicuous. Gert was seen as 'an idiosyncratic designer who sought or exceeded the limits of the brief with this'.[7] The corporate identity for NS received a lot of attention in the foreign press as well, generally stating that what was happening in the Netherlands was unprecedented. That such a large government company paid so much attention to graphic design and of all people engaged someone like Gert Dumbar, a designer with somewhat anarchistic traits. It was also a shock for the engine drivers union — the most conservative union in the Netherlands — who nicknamed the trains 'the banana' or the 'yellow parakeet'. Some train drivers initially refused to ride in it.[8]

In the final stage of the design process, the NS publicity department requested to apply advertising to the train sets, in an attempt to improve the company's financial position. Gert strongly resisted this at first: 'I envisioned one big smudge of aggressive commercial messages all over the train. That would become chaos, untidy, dirty. Then I came up with a system of slanted blue strips, in which advertising would have a secondary place. That's an example of a problem you can solve as a designer: ordering the disordered.'

WAYFINDING

A next step was the signage at the stations, with a pivotal role for a new set of pictograms. NS had already been making limited use of a set of 20 pictograms recommended by the UIC (Union Internationale de Chemins de Fer, the international association for railway companies) since 1965.[9] In Gert's view the existing pictograms were cluttered, with little consistency of visual language, and new ones had to be added. Thus, for the first time in the Netherlands on such a large scale, his team developed a new

Harry Beck-inspired railway map
(design: Gert Dumbar)

and coherent system of 33 pictograms for the NS to be applied in trains, railway stations, and timetables. Gert had become interested early on in the possibilities of an international sign language. At the RCA, Anthony Froshaug had drawn his attention to the pictograms of Gerd Arntz, designer of the symbols for ISOTYPE, the 'International System Of TYpographic Picture Education' devised by the Viennese sociologist and philosopher Otto Neurath. Based on Neurath's famous motto 'Words divide, images unite',[10] the system endeavoured to provide a pictorial language for conveying objective information to people, regardless of language or literacy — a kind of visual Esperanto that would break down language barriers, improve global communication and enhance international understanding. Arntz's

'signatures' as he called the more than 4,000 signs he designed for the ISOTYPE system, became one of the main sources of inspiration for all later pictogram designs world-wide.[11]

Gert became impressed by the idea that as a designer one could contribute to overcoming language barriers, 'and how in the process an idea could be visually reduced to its essence. But it will only work if the image is strong enough. The power of simplification, of getting to the essence. But it also resides in the artistry of the images — you recognize the artist Gerd Arntz in his pictograms'. Arntz, following Neurath, had moved to The Hague from Vienna a few years before Austria's Anschluss to Nazi Germany, and still lived there, continuing the work of 'visual statistics'. Gert would come to know him well. Arntz's work and the critical social commitment and political engagement of the man himself inspired him, and Arntz would later advise him on the design of the pictograms for Westeinde hospital in The Hague.[12]

The set for NS introduced a rather new visual language to the trains and stations, replacing the mostly text-based information used until then. Arntz's inspiration can be seen in many of them, for instance the sign for food vending machines, which uses a very similar hand as Arntz's sign for 'paying'.

But the main inspiration is the structure behind the visual language: the consistency of placing, spacing, line thickness, form and counter form, use of colour and symbolic detailing that Neurath and Arntz had worked out meticulously for their system. In rare cases, letters are used instead of pictures — the lower case 'i' for 'information' and capitals 'WC' for restrooms have both become pictograms in their own right.

9   The UIC pictograms were not always usable in the Dutch situation. The UIC pictogram for station buffet, for example, showed a wine glass while in the Netherlands at the time the glass stood for 'fragile,' handle with care. See also p. 128.

10   See Ed Annink, Max Bruinsma, *Lovely Language: Words divide, images unite*, Rotterdam, 2008.

11   See also Ed Annink, Max Bruinsma, *Gerd Arntz: Graphic designer*, Rotterdam, 2010.

12   See pp. 153–161.

treinnummer		317	1905	707	1906	705	⊡ 43	431	1937	709
Brussel Zuid	V	6 42	6 59	7 09	7 43	8 06	② 9 16		8 43	9 10
Brussel Centraal			6 43	7 14	7 47	8 10			8 47	9 14
Brussel Noord		6 49	6 53	7 20	7 55	8 20	8 26	8 44	8 53	9 20
Leuven	A		7 13	7 40	8 15	8 40			9 13	9 39
Liège-Guillemins	A	7 41	8 11	8 25	9 06	9 26	9 19	9 39	10 06	10 22
Liège-Guillemins	V	7 43	8 14	8 29	9 09	9 29	9 20	9 41	10 09	
Pepinster	A		8 43			9 49			10 24	
Pepinster	V			8 55	9 30	9 52			10 30	
Spa	A			9 13	9 46	10 14			10 48	
Pepinster	V		8 43	8 50		9 50			10 40	
Verviers Centraal	A	8 00	8 48	8 55		9 55	② 9 36	10 00	10 45	

treinnummer		799	⊡ 33	321	1909	7 11	1910	323		
Brussel Zuid	V			10 10	10 43	11 10	11 43	12 10		
Brussel Centraal				10 14	10 47	11 14	11 47	12 14		
Brussel Noord				10 20	10 53	11 20	11 55	12 20		
Leuven	A			10 58	11 13	11 40	12 13	12 37		
Liège-Guillemins	A			11 19	12 06	12 21	13 06	13 17		
Liège-Guillemins	V	10 26	10 57	11 22	12 10	12 25	13 22	13 20		
Pepinster	A	10 44			12 30	12 43	13 50			
Pepinster	V	10 57			13 03	13 03	13 57			
Spa	A	11 15			13 20	13 20	14 15			
Pepinster	V	10 45			12 38	12 44				
Verviers Centraal	A	10 49	11 14	11 39	12 43	12 48		13 37		

treinnummer		6934	1912	325						
Brussel Zuid	V		13 43	14 10						
Brussel Centraal			13 47	14 14						
Brussel Noord			13 55	14 20						
(Leuven)	A		14 13	14 30						

316
317

Alkmaar · Heerhugowaard (Stat. w.) · Den Oever · Harlingen (NS stat.) · Harlingen Haven · Franeker (Sorte) · Dronrijp · Leeuwarden (NS stat.)

Groningen (92a) / Akkrum (90b)
Terschelling/Vlieland (901a)
Sneek (NS station) · Heerenveen (NS station) · Meppel–Zwolle (90b)

106 a | > vervolg >

km	treinnummer		1154	3316	314	3368	520	1166	318	320	3324			322	324	4326	326	3332	4432	1130	4384	330	4334	3386	3434
0	Vlissingen	V	6 53	7 08	7 55			9 04	10 09	11 09		Vliss	12 09	13 09		14 09	15 09		15 46	16 02	16 21		17 01	
7	Middelburg	A	6 58	7 13	8 00			9 09	10 14	11 15		Mburg	12 14	13 14		14 15	15 14		15 52	16 07	16 26		17 07	
	Middelburg	V	7 00	7 15	8 02			9 10	10 15	11 17		Mburg	12 15	13 15		14 17	15 15		15 53	16 08	16 27		17 08	
11	Arnemuiden			7 19				9 14	10 19	11 21		Arn	12 19	13 19		14 21	15 19			16 12			17 12	
24	Goes	V	7 12	7 29	8 13			9 23	10 29	11 31		Goes	12 29	13 29		14 31	15 29		16 05	16 22	16 39		17 22	
	Goes	A	7 13	7 30	8 15			9 24	10 30	11 33		Goes	12 30	13 30		14 33	15 30		16 06	16 23	16 40		17 23	
30	Kapelle-Biezelinge			7 36				9 29	10 34	11 38		KapB	12 34	13 34		14 38	15 34			16 14	16 33		17 28	
35	Kruiningen-Yerseke	A		7 40	8 22			9 33	10 39	11 43		Kruin	12 39	13 39		14 43	15 39			16 16	16 33		17 33	
	Kruiningen-Yerseke	V	7 21	7 41	8 23			9 34	10 40	11 44		Kruin	12 40	13 40		14 44	15 40		16 16	16 34			17 34	
39	Krabbendijke			7 46				9 40	10 45	11 50		Krabb	12 45	13 45		14 50	15 45			16 39			17 39	
41	Rilland-Bath			7 50				9 44	10 49	11 54		Rill	12 49	13 49		14 54	15 49			16 43			17 43	
58	Bergen op Zoom	A		8 00	8 37			9 54	10 59	12 04		BoZ	12 59	13 59		15 04	15 59		16 32	16 53	16 59		17 53	
	Bergen op Zoom	V	7 38	8 02	8 39			9 56	11 00	12 05		BoZ	13 00	14 00		15 05	16 00		16 33	16 54	17 00		17 54	
67	Roosendaal	A	7 49	8 12	8 50			10 06	11 10	12 15		Rdaal	13 10	14 10		15 15	16 10		16 43	17 05	17 10		18 05	
	Roosendaal	V		8 24		9 09			11 28		✕12 28	Rdaal			• 13 28			16 28			17 09		✕17 26	18 09
81	Etten-Leur			8 34		9 19			11 38		12 38	Eleur			13 38			16 38			17 36		17 45	18 19
90	Breda	A		8 43		9 24			11 46		12 46	Breda			13 46			16 46			17 24		17 45	18 24
	Breda	V		8 45		9 25			11 47		12 47	Breda			13 47			16 47			17 25		17 46	18 25
99	Gilze-Rijen			8 53					11 55		12 55	Gilze			13 53			16 55				17 54	
111	Tilburg	A		9 02		9 39			12 03		13 03	Tilbg			14 03			17 03		17 39		18 02	18 39	
130	's Hertogenbosch	A		9 20		9 55			12 20		13 20	Bosch			14 20			17 20		17 55		18 19	18 55	
	's Hertogenbosch	V		9 34					12 33		13 33	Bosch			14 33			17 35		18 02		18 33	18 58	
145	Oss			9 48					12 48		13 48	Oss			14 48			17 50		18 16		18 48	19 16	
154	Ravenstein			9 55					12 56		13 55	Ravst			14 55			17 57				18 55		
161	Wijchen			10 02					13 02		14 02	Wijch			15 02			18 04				19 02		
169	Nijmegen	A		10 10					13 10		14 10	Nijm			15 10		② 18 12			18 32		19 10	19 32	
	Nijmegen	V		10 21			11 06		13 21		14 21	Nijm			15 21			18 21		18 34		19 21		19 34
179	Elst	A					11 10					Elst								18 39				19 39
	Elst	V					11 11					Elst								18 40				19 40
185	Arnhem	A		10 35			11 20		13 36		14 35	Arnh			15 35			18 35		18 49		19 35		19 49
	Arnhem	V		10 39			11 27		13 39		② 14 39	Arnh V			15 39			18 39		18 51	19 38		19 51	
187	Arnhem Velperpoort						11 29					Arnh V								18 54				19 54
189	Velp						11 34					Velp								18 59				19 59
191	Rheden						11 38					Rhed								19 03				20 03
197	Dieren-Doesburg						11 44					Dier-D								19 09		19 50		20 09
205	Brummen						11 50					Brumm								19 16				20 15
212	Zutphen	A		11 00			11 57		14 00		15 00	Zutph			16 00			19 01		19 23		20 00		20 23
212	Zutphen	V		11 02					14 02		15 02	Zutph			16 02			19 02				20 02		20 26
225	Deventer	A		11 13					14 13		15 13	Dvter			16 13			19 13				20 13		20 37
	Deventer	V		11 16					14 16		15 16	Dvter			16 16			19 16						
238	Olst			11 24					14 24		15 24	Olst			16 24			19 25				20 24		
241	Wijhe			11 30					14 30		15 30	Wijhe			16 30			19 51				20 30		
252	Zwolle	A		11 41					14 41		15 41	Zwol			16 41			19 43				20 41		
212	Zutphen	V		11 00					14 02		15 00	Zutph			16 02			19 02				20 02		20 26
225	Deventer	A		11 13					14 13		15 13	Dvter			16 13			19 13				20 13		20 37
	Deventer	V		11 16					14 16		15 16	Dvter			16 16			19 16						
235	Olst			11 16					14 16		15 16	Olst			16 24			19 25				20 24		
241	Wijhe			11 30					14 24		15 24	Wijhe			16 30			19 51				20 30		
252	Zwolle	A		• 11 41					14 30		✕15 41	Zwol			• 16 41			19 43				20 41		

ⓐ maandags op 2.1..8.IV. en 27.V.
ⓑ vrijdags en zzf
ⓒ maandags en op 2.1..8.IV. en 27.V. vrijdags en zzf

< slot <

Sketch and page for NS time table
(design: Gertjan Leuvelink)

Drawings by Grzegorz Marszalek. Centre left: a half
portrait of Gert. The main NS train model at the time
was called 'Hondekop' ('dog face')

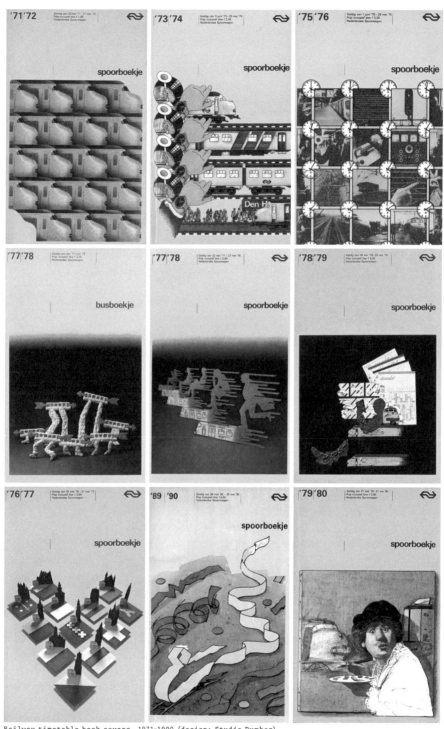

Railway timetable book covers, 1971-1990 (design: Studio Dumbar)
(Bottom right: design/drawing: Pat Andrea)

Gert's sketch for light boxes for The Hague Central Station, with Tel Design's 'pin-up'

In line with the total overhaul of the corporate identity, NS's traditional annual timetables needed a new design as well. Not just visually, but also in terms of content; the new booklets contained considerably more information than the old ones. More trains were deployed, the schedules were expanded and a lot of additional information had to be processed and organized in a more efficient way.

The first restyled timetable booklet appeared in 1970. Gertjan Leuvelink was responsible for the design and succeeded in accommodating the impressive amount of data in a clear structure that radiated a high degree of visual calm. Gertjan later stated that he 'was more strongly influenced than Gert by New Objectivity and Swiss typography', which shows in his care to detailing and balancing many layers of information — 'there must be no gap left between the joints'.[13]

Gertjan: 'There, too, you tried to push the limits. For example, I wanted the lines in the timetable booklet to be thinner. But since these had to be built out of lead at the time, that was difficult. Because of the material's mass you can't get thinner than a certain size. Gert saw the importance

Siep Wijsenbeek, ca. 1970

of this and immediately called Monotype foundry in London to ask whether they could make a slightly thinner lead line. They managed to do that. That was not just a detail. It was a real struggle to get it right and shape it as sharply as possible.'[14]

13   Gertjan Leuvelink, quoted in Jan Middendorp,
        Ha, daar gaat er een van mij, Rotterdam, 2002, p. 103.
14   Gertjan Leuvelink, interview November 2014.
15   See also p. 59.
16   Siep Wijsenbeek, interview, January 2010.

The timetable booklet was internationally acclaimed for its typographic clarity, allowing the traveller to plan his way easily and quickly.[15] Like the typography, also the railway mapping was completely redone, this time clearly inspired by Harry Beck's famous London Underground map. With its strict reduction of lines to horizontals, verticals and diagonals it had become

> *FINDING SOMETHING YOU WEREN'T LOOKING FOR BUT THAT YOU COME ACROSS DURING THE CREATIVE PROCESS, WHICH MAKES YOU TAKE A NEW PATH, CHANGING EVERYTHING THAT PRECEDED IT*

the international benchmark for such simplified maps. Another innovation was the change in tone of voice of the booklets, their editorial design — professional writers, often of literary work, were engaged for introductory texts that would both enliven and better clarify the information, and illustrators were brought in for the same purpose — to liven up the strict organization of data and make it more accessible, also on an aesthetic level. The booklets' covers are a case in point. While Gert and his team at Tel — and later at the newly founded Studio Dumbar — made the first covers, the covers for the booklets from 1980 onwards were done by invited artists. The first, for 1979/80, was created by Pat Andrea, a well-known Dutch illustrator and visual artist. He depicted Rembrandt, in the midst of immortalizing the yellow train on his canvas. The then 'President Director

General' of the NS could not appreciate the cover. The company was ridiculed with 'this horrible cover,' he felt.[16]

The timetable booklet was a turning point in the design of printed matter for government, aimed at better communication with citizens. In addition to the clear transfer of information, surprising elements were introduced: a striking use of images, controversial covers — not obvious elements in design for a state-owned company at the time. But they did foster greater recognition, 'unlike the old railway booklet which was drab, dull and unclear as if designed by a civil servant himself,' says Gert. The railway booklet was one of Holland's 'best designed books' in 1971 and later won an award from the British Designers and Art Directors Club, D&AD.

'For the realization of the NS corporate identity, the client was of great importance. In particular Siep Wijsenbeek played a critical role,' says Gert, looking back. 'He was totally dedicated to good design for the government. With tenacity and optimism, he eventually got everyone on board in the drab NS headquarters in Utrecht. He believed in the cause and dared to stick his neck out. And that was new within a bureaucratic public company like the Dutch Railways.'

61

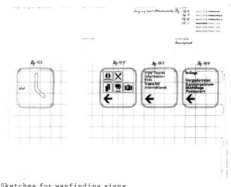

Sketches for wayfinding signs
at NS stations

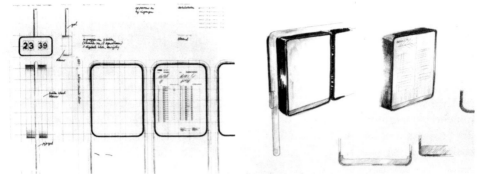

Sketches for wayfinding signs at NS stations

Gert later reiterates the importance of a good relationship between client and designer for the success of a good design: 'Every client, entrepreneur or government gets the graphic designer they deserve. As a graphic designer, you are as good as the client allows you to be. A good client tolerates something in us that in fact they can hardly allow: room for uncertainty, which both entrepreneurs and the government rather dislike. I'm talking about creativity, the leap into the unknown. And although the result of the creative adventure's ambiguity is often better than expected, this still remains a delicate aspect in the relationship between entrepreneur and designer.

WE ARE SERVICE PROVIDERS BUT ALSO WATER CARRIERS

Gert Dumbar

I like to connect that creativity to what's known as serendipity: finding something you weren't looking for but that you come across during the creative process, which makes you take a new path, changing everything that preceded it. Creativity, being open to the unexpected; it is the salvation of the profession in that it saves you from routine. Because

we shouldn't fool ourselves; the danger of routine and its consequences are always lurking in our trade. There is only a thin line between the originality of the design of the Bauhaus and the Swiss school and the sterile garbage that "consumer society" is now stuck with. It is up to us, as the eyes and ears of our clients, to always come up with something new. Because otherwise what follows is an unimaginable accumulation of bad and poor clichés: the disastrous end of any style that leads to mannerism. Or to use a metaphor, we must keep the wells from which we drink open. Otherwise, they dry up. We are service providers but also water carriers.'[17]

Gert incorporated a number of visual liberties into the functionalist design of NS's corporate identity. Wibo Bakker remarked: 'The good integration that exists between the house style and the signage at the stations developed in line with it is striking. This is rarely seen in railway companies in other countries and makes the NS house style —virtually unchanged since its introduction— unique.'[18] Or as design historian Frederike Huygen put it: 'The total overhaul of the image of the NS with its bright yellow trains, with the new signage and departure tables at the stations, the new well-ordered and more appealing railway timetable: the accessibility and

17   See also Gert Dumbar, 'Room for chance', in
        Vormberichten 4, 1994, p. 133.
18   Wibo Bakker, op. cit.
19   Frederike Huygen, interview June 2002.

unity in the transfer of information were unprecedented at that time.'[19]

Gert adds: 'It was the beginning of a new development of well-designed, more modern information communication by the government, ultimately culminating in the tax forms — traditionally a kind of jungle of difficult, unclear comments and questions — which were designed by design agency BRS in such a way that things became immediately clear to the citizen, with a clear structure and accessible language. The government had something to say and wanted to communicate it well.'

The house style for Dutch Railways celebrated its 50th anniversary with great pomp in 2018. The vignette in particular could have been designed today, NS thought — it has become a folk icon, 'which can certainly last another fifty years,' thus then acting director of the Railways, Roger van Boxtel.

Interior design and routing system (design: Gert Dumbar and others)
Bottom: First electronic time table display, The Hague Central
Station (design: Gertjan Leuvelink)

Display at Simon de Wit
grocery store

INFLUENCED BY POP ART

SIMON (DE WIT)

The success and publicity triggered by the NS identity spawned new large commissions for Tel Design from the private sector, often in direct competition with Total Design. In the case of the new identity for the Simon de Wit grocery chain, the job actually came to Tel Design after Total Design had turned it down — they were already working on a new house style for competing grocer De Gruyter, and advised Simon de Wit to go to Tel Design instead.[20] The two new corporate identities were launched at roughly the same time, in 1972, and it is interesting to compare and contrast them, as Wibo Bakker did in a critical article in 2006: 'De Gruyter's modernist corporate identity created by Total Design was a very clear design, which considered the 'critical consumer' through the product information on the packaging. In contrast, the corporate identity designed by Tel Design for Simon de Wit emphasized image and atmosphere

to create a cozy store. This house style is illustrative of a time when modernism was increasingly under attack in the design world.'[21]

69

Tel Design's argumentation for a retail 'philosophy of the future' is in hindsight visionary: 'Shopping will increasingly take place in the recreational sphere. ... when putting together the

Sketches for grocery store Simon de Wit logo (design: Theo van Leeuwen)

assortment, the leisure aspect will play an increasingly important role.'[22] Shopping as a pastime instead of buying groceries as a daily chore. Tel Design stressed their conviction that 'humour can be

20   Thus Total Design's Andrew Fallon, quoted in Wibo Bakker, 'Design in de supermarkt', *Jong Holland*, 2006–2, p. 20.
21   Wibo Bakker, op. cit., p.15.
22   Quoted in Wibo Bakker, op. cit.: 'Tel Design, "Verslag van onze ervaringen bij introduktie binnen Simon de Wit en

voorstellen betreffende een vruchtbare samenwerking",' Albert Heijn archive, 27 August 1971.

Grocery store Simon de Wit decorations and
vignette (design: Theo van Leeuwen)

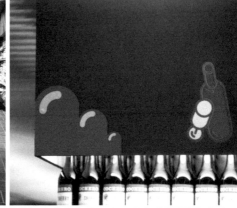
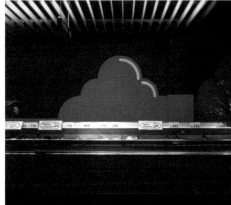

Simon de Wit interior
(design: Theo van Leeuwen and others)

an important positive element' in the communication with the customer, and incorporated it in a visual language that clearly harked back to Gert's sources of inspiration. 'We visited all kinds of supermarkets and I thought they were all fridges, with cold fluorescent light. We were able to design a really warm

THE IDENTITY FOR SIMON DE WIT IS ILLUSTRATIVE OF A TIME WHEN MODERNISM WAS INCREASINGLY UNDER ATTACK IN THE DESIGN WORLD

Wibo Bakker

atmosphere, with all sorts of totally weird stuff.'[23] Wibo Bakker: 'The visual language of modernism is marrying elements from Pop art and art deco.'[24] In the interior designs by Tel Design's Theo van Leeuwen, the decorations would at times 'adopt the appearance of clouds hanging from the ceiling, at other times of a sauce dripping over furniture. ... The round "cozy" character of the forms was reinforced by the use of warm colours in floor and ceiling'.[25]

Simon de Wit grocery store logo
(design: Gert Dumbar with
Theo van Leeuwen)

The 'sincere caring coziness of Simon de Wit' (thus Tel Design's 'Credo') was expressed in Frans van Mourik's rounded typography with cartoon-like highlights. Another innovation was the

use of pictograms instead of texts to indicate categories of merchandise above the store shelves. The illustrations were

simon de wit
A B C D E F G H
I J K L M N O P
Q R S T U V W
X Y Z
a b c d e f g h i j
k l m n o p q r s
t u v w x y z
1 2 3 4 5 6 7 8 9 0
[ ] ( ) ± ! ? : ; „ ‚
½ ¼ ¾ %

Simon de Wit font
(design: Frans van Mourik,
idea: Gert Dumbar)

done in a coarse grid reminiscent of Roy Lichtenstein. Bakker points to a certain kinship with Wolff Olins' 1969 design for the Bowyers meat company, with a similar rounded typography and cozy colours, and 'a tribute to Pop techniques'.[26] At any rate, it shows Gert's enduring connection with British and American design and popular culture from the 1960s. It was also one of the rare occasions in which Gert expressed his indebtedness to Pop art in a direct way. Although Pop art remained a profound inspiration, he mostly referred to it for its irreverent mentality, its way of combining 'high' and 'low' visual languages, rather than as an overt stylistic source. Gert: 'We did some revolutionary stuff with that shop and the house style. Totally Milton Glazer, you could say! It was so successful that Albert Heijn felt compelled to buy them.'[27]

Albert Heijn, Simon de Wit's main competitor, took over in 1972, and

23   Gert Dumbar: conversation, 29 April 2021.
24   Wibo Bakker, op. cit., p. 20.
25   Wibo Bakker, op. cit., p. 21.

26   Ken Campbell, 'Cases of corporate identity', in *Design*, 1969, p. 247, quoted in Wibo Bakker, op. cit., p. 21.
27   Gert Dumbar: conversation, 29 April 2021.

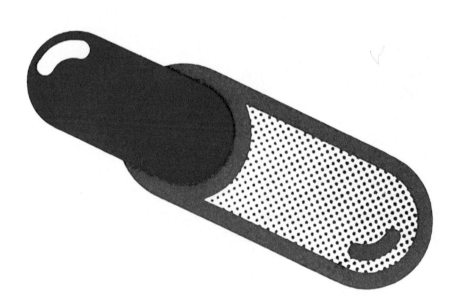

Top: interior design cash registers Simon de Wit store
Bottom: pictogram for cosmetics department

mobil oil / chevron

the
de wereld
van wim
en jet. &

krrrrr..... plop!
yrrr...... boem!
poeps? knal!

Simon de Wit font
(sketches: Frans van Mourik)

Simon de Wit decorations
(design: Theo van Leeuwen)

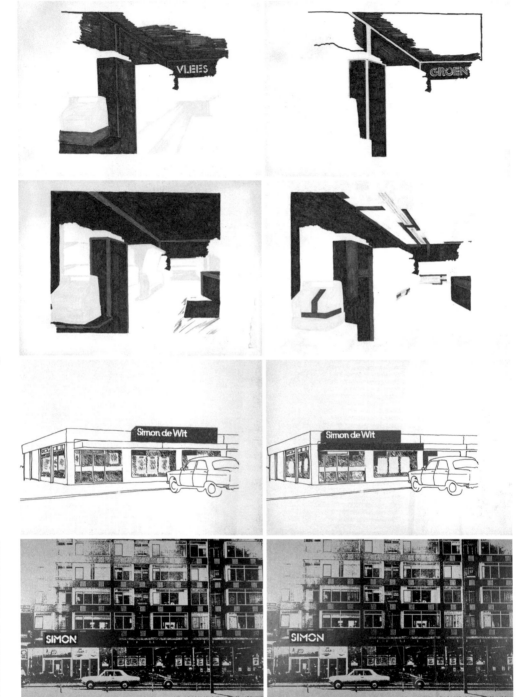

Sketches for Simon de Wit store
(sketches: Theo van Leeuwen, Frans van Mourik and
Gert Dumbar)

Various sketches by Gert Dumbar and others for
Simon (de Wit) redesign, 1972

Tel Design was tasked with a completely different brief that called for 'a simple interior in which the straightforward presentation of merchandise will be combined with custom decoration and atmosphere that ensures a certain coziness'. Nonetheless, 'to keep prices down, all unnecessary frills will disappear. All luxury in the stores will be removed'.

The result was a new design by the same Tel Design team, changing 'coziness' for a straightforward, more 'neutral' look: 'The cloud-like shapes were replaced by hard geometric patterns of dots and zigzag motifs. The rounded letters of Simon de Wit were replaced with Simon written in angular stencil letters, and the warm colours were replaced with red, green, and dark blue combined with white. The intention was for 'everything to exude efficiency.'[28] Skipping the chain's last name was suggested by Gert; one sees the argumentation for the name change growing in a series of sketches, where the last name 'de Wit' gradually dwindles to make room for the more lapidary, visually simpler, 'Simon'. In some of the sketches with lines and type fragments in primary colours one sees an echo of Jac. Jongert's designs for Van Nelle — icons of 1920s modernist graphic design.

Logo for one of HBG's brands

HBG (HOLLANDSE BETON GROEP)

Another client that came to Tel Design in 1969 as a result of the agency's success with NS was the construction holding Hollandse Beton Groep. A huge conglomerate of terrestrial and maritime building and construction companies, HBG needed a house style that would unify the visual identity of dozens of different companies. The result was a rather straightforward International Style logo and identity, although even this relatively conventional house style was seen as striking by Tel Design's competitors:

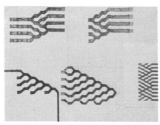

Sketch for HBG 'building block' vignette system

'With its voluptuous shapes and green-orange colour scheme, the new HBG identity was something of a shock to TD. ... Oh, how I wished I had been part of

that process!' Thus Andrew Fallon, at the time still working at Total Design. A few years later, Fallon got his chance: 'One evening in November 1975, Gert Dumbar of Tel Design phoned me: "I'm looking for a new staff designer. ... Can we talk about this?" That's how it started. ... Gert's enormous charisma was infectious and apart from there seeming to be no good reason I could turn down his job offer, I grew to wanting to take on the challenge. That curvy Tel Design work — in contrast to Total Design's restrained style — had become irresistible.'[29] The invitation was a consequence of Gertjan Leuvelink leaving Tel Design to start his own 2D3D studio. 'The gap had to be filled by someone like Leuvelink who had experience in system typography. That person was Andrew Fallon, an Englishman who had attended the RCA before gaining several years' experience at Total Design.'[30]

28   Wibo Bakker, op.cit. p. 23.
29   Andrew Fallon in *Roots* #51, [Z]OO producties and Wilco Art Books, 2019. Fallon would become partner at Tel Design in 1970.
30   Jan Middendorp, op. cit., p. ... (see note #13).

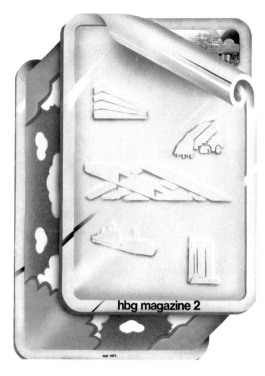

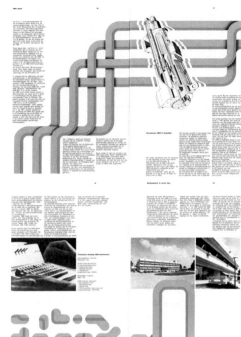

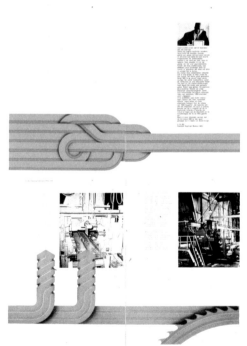

Top right & Bottom left: Pages from *HBG Magazine*, issue 1, 1970
(design: Theo van Leeuwen, Frans van Mourik)
Top left & Bottom right: Cover *HBG Magazine*, issue 2, 1971
(design: Theo van Leeuwen, Frans van Mourik)

Although Gert considers the HBG identity 'middle-of-the-road', it did provide institutional conglomerates that needed a 'house style generator', as Joost Roozekrans later termed the challenge for studio Dumbar's design for GAK.[31]

him with added experience in working on complex corporate identities for demanding commercial clients and large

Orange and green colour scheme on a machine of HBG's subsidiary company, road builders HWZ

31   See pp. 374–396.

hollandsche beton groep n.v.
rijswijk [z.h.] - holland

Back cover *HBG Magazine*, issue 1, 1970

'Mondrian' poster, 1972 (design: Gert Dumbar)

MODERNISM WITH A SMILE

In a now famous poster from 1972 highlighting the huge Mondrian collection at The Hague's Gemeentemuseum (now Kunstmuseum), Gert depicts the iconic Dutch modernist painter as a proud tinkerer. Mondrian is standing behind a table on which he has carefully arranged a series of coloured planes and lines in crude papier-mâché, apparently from the stock of materials behind him, piled up against the wall. The artwork is of a childlike simplicity and the viewer may assume from the stock in the background that this is not the end of the series. This ironic peek into the kitchen of modern art seemed to reduce the lofty ideals of Mondrian and modernism to a simple trick.[32]

The museum's director, L.J.F. Wijsenbeek, had asked four designers, including Paul Schuitema, to design a poster and in their designs Schuitema and the other two designers duly showed their respect to Mondrian. Not Gert. His ironic image of the painter evoked

vehement reactions. 'Has he lost his mind?' inquired the curator of modern art at the Gemeentemuseum in response to the poster. And Wim Crouwel moaned: 'Just when we had finally reached the point where the design profession was taken seriously, someone comes along and takes the whole thing down again.'[33] It seemed as if Gert wanted to undercut his childhood hero. But nothing could be further from the truth, Gert asserts: 'I chose that form of protest at the time, not against Mondrian himself, but against the exaggerated, almost religious reverence with which Mondrian was treated on posters and in publications. At the same time, it was a commentary on the modernist design rules prevailing at the time, which in my view were rigid and predictable.'

Even the lettering contains a commentary, both cultural and professional. For the word 'Mondrian', Gert used different typefaces for the three different language versions of the poster, inspired

83

32 See Leonie ten Duis, Annelies Haase, *The World Must Change: Graphic Design and Idealism*, Sandberg publication nr. 18, Amsterdam, 1999, p. 149.
33 Wim Crouwel, 'The relativity itself,' in *Behind the Seen*, 1996, p. 37.

by lettering images from 1920s Paris. One of them was taken verbatim from a sign with the inscription MODERN, in art deco-like letters, nickel-plated and pasted on a wooden base, which he found at a flea

Art deco sign bought by Gert in the 1950s at a flea market in Paris

market in Paris in the 1950s. 'I carried that sign with me everywhere. It evoked for me an image of the exciting Paris of the 1920s and 1930s, the Paris of jazz and abstract art, but also of the cheerful art deco lettering and inscriptions on facades, storefronts, cafés that were still recognizable everywhere in the 1950s, when I was there, and which must have surrounded Mondrian as he walked through the city as well. Everything came together in the Mondrian poster, my admiration for Mondrian, the image of a bustling Paris in the 1920s and a euphoric, hopeful zest for life.'

With his poster and its quirky typography, Gert was rocking the foundations of what was officially considered good design in the Netherlands at the time, based on modernism in content and form, with Crouwel as the most important representative. The anger the poster unleashed can only be fully understood if one realizes that it not just questioned a conception of graphic design — it challenged an entire belief system of ethical and social norms.

The foundations of the profession had been formed in the 1920s from modernist beliefs and an idealistic perspective: the goal was clear, objective, and neutral design, which would promote communication and result in a well-ordered, better society. This included a strict dictate of form — functional, clear, no embellishments — that was to express a new era. Form, commitment, and conviction grew into a trinity of a kind, and the underlying idealism became a hallmark for good design, expressed with pretty much religious zeal.

The line established in the 1920s was further systematized during and after the war by the Swiss or International School. Their functionalist, abstract design, based on a strict order perfectly matched the vision of Crouwel and Total Design. Like the Swiss, Crouwel believed that

Three 'art deco' variants of Mondrian's name for three language variations of the 'Mondrian' poster, 1972

communication could be objective. Based on analysis, systematization and grids, optimal solutions to design problems could be found and ultimately result in a well-designed and well-ordered society.[34] Crouwel: 'A social improvement in the interest of everyone through clear and sober designs as well as the professionalization of the trade, those were my expectations at the beginning of my career. When I started, I was really possessed with the idealism that design could play a major role. In graphic design, that meant, at least in my opinion, that it should play a subservient role and provide clear structures for information. ... The designer's job was to bring clarity

34   Leonie ten Duis, Annelies Haase, op. cit., p. 117.

84

Gert Dumbar's sketches for 'Mondrian' poster

to communication. That meant that the designer should not indulge in decoration, should not bother people with self-expression, should not propagate his own point of view, but remain invisible himself,

Wim Crouwel, 'Mondriaan' poster, Stedelijk Museum Amsterdam, 1975

as it were. You really had the idea that you could achieve something and educate the client.'[35]

It was a time of great debates around and on the social and cultural responsibilities of graphic design, which only came to the fore as a distinct trade and business since the mid-1950s. The austere visual languages of Josef Müller-Brockmann's and Armin Hofmann's Swiss functionalism became the dominant design doctrine. Their interpretation of the modernist credo 'form follows function' — an ideology that holds that any emotional interpretation by the designer is anathema — had great appeal for businesses that wanted to appear neutral and objective in the aftermath of the Second World War. The dispassionate 'Swiss' style, both in architecture and in graphic and industrial design, seemed an apt response to the devastating emotionality that had brought the world on the brink of annihilation. Post-war functionalism evolved into an 'international style' that has indelibly

marked the appearance of everything designed since, say, 1955, from train tickets to metropolises.

In the Netherlands, this cool professionalism was, as we saw, represented mainly by Crouwel and Total Design, although after Gert's departure, also Tel Design evolved towards international style functionalism. There were other smaller and larger design bureaus, such as BRS Premsela Vonk, who together redesigned the appearance of Dutch public institutions and the largest industries in the Netherlands in an ascetic International Style visual language that prompted comparisons with the flat, thoroughly gridded, Dutch polder landscape.

THE DESIGNER'S JOB WAS TO BRING CLARITY TO COMMUNICATION
Wim Crouwel

Gert was among the first to rail against this strict functionalist interpretation of modernism. He mocked its seriousness, the monotony and dullness of its products. He believed that the designer's thumbprint should also be visible in his work and rebelled against the cold rationalism of the modernists, the reduction of the image to

Gert Dumbar (l) with Piet Zwart, 1974

mere information. He wanted design to loosen up, to allow for emotion and humour. Gert advocated 'modernism with a smile'.

35   Leonie ten Duis, Annelies Haase, op. cit., pp. 115–117.

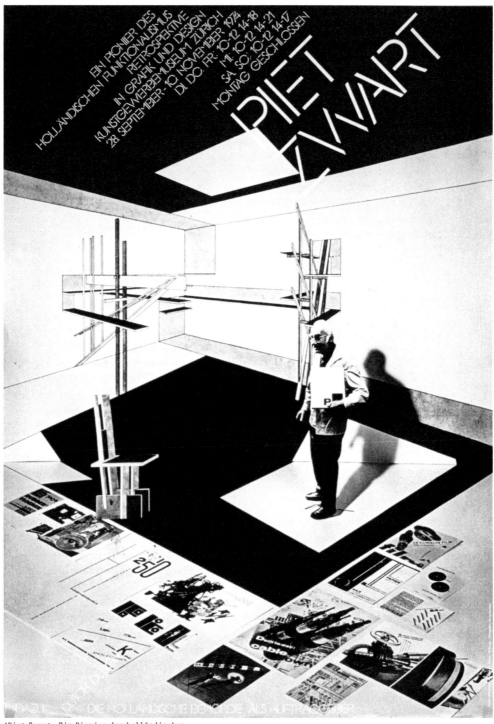

'Piet Zwart, Ein Pionier des holländischen
Funktionalismus' poster, Kunstgewerbemuseum, Zürich,
Switzerland, 1974 (design: Gert Dumbar)

'To keep communicating in an increasingly complex world, emotional aspects must also be allowed to play a role,' he said. 'The rational alone won't get you there. At some point design needs to switch off a too cerebral approach.'[36]

Two years after the Mondrian poster, Gert designed a poster for a retrospective exhibition of Piet Zwart at the Kunstgewerbemuseum in Zürich: 'Ein Pionier des holländischen Funktionalismus'. Just off-centre in the image is a cut-out photograph of Piet Zwart holding a book with his famous signature on the cover: a P with a black square ('Zwart' means 'black' in Dutch). He stands on a tilted

Piet Zwart, illustration for *The Book of PTT*, 1932

rectangle that is a negative version of his signature, surrounded by his designs for a chair and a trade fair stand for furniture company Bruynzeel. Spread out on the floor are posters and other work. The spatial impression of the scene is produced by adding a fold in the centre, creating a backdrop that matches the perspective of the Bruynzeel drawing. There stands the man, proud, with a smile, in the midst of his oeuvre. A highly visible, bent paper clip behind one of his feet further emphasizes that this is a staged scene, a construction.

'Was this our Piet Zwart, rummaging around among his work as the eternal artist?' wondered Wim Crouwel in despair this time.[37] Piet Zwart himself

Piet Zwart and *The book of PTT: A commentary*, by Paul Hefting, 1985 (photo: Lex van Pieterson; design: Linda van Deursen and Vincent van Baar)

could appreciate the poster, though. 'A proof,' said Gert, 'that modernism could take many forms.' Years later, Wim Crouwel would revise his opinion. Gert: 'I was reviled by art historians as a misguided rebel, but my good friend and colleague Wim Crouwel later stood up for me. He rightly saw my comments as an addition, not an attack. That was generous, to say the least.' To everyone's surprise, at the time of the Mondrian poster, both would collaborate in designing a house style, for the PTT — at that time one of the most important house styles in Dutch history.

Thirty years onwards, at the presentation of the Piet Zwart Prize to Gert in 2009, Paul Mijksenaar stated: 'Personally, I am of the opinion that Gert Dumbar is very close to Piet Zwart. ... The similarity could not be better demonstrated than in Piet Zwart's famous *Book of PTT*, for which Zwart also cobbled together all the spatial attributes himself. Both show the same "light-footed anarchy" toward a venerable client and unorthodox use of visual means, as long as they serve the purpose.'

36   Leonie ten Duis, Annelies Haase, op. cit., p. 150.
37   Wim Crouwel, 'The relativity itself', in *Behind the Seen*, Rotterdam, 1996, p. 37.
38   Inspired by the Enlightenment and the French and American Revolutions, the Dutch Patriots were opponents of Stadhouder (Viceroy) William V and the Orange Party.

They tried to instigate democratic innovations and rupture fossilized relations. These were turbulent times in which, similar to the 1960s, profound political changes took place. It is worth noting that also then pamphlets, posters, political prints and newspaper articles played an important role in supporting the political struggle.

COUNTER VOICES

Debates on what could or could not 'serve the purpose' pervaded the 1970s. Starting in the mid-1960s, a broadening range of 'counterdesign' approaches matched the growing 'counterculture' movements of a maturing postwar generation. Among them, the Provo movement most succinctly expressed the feelings of discontent in the Netherlands, embodying the anarchist spirit associated with it. Originating in Amsterdam in 1963, Provo was a catalyst for a new generation of dissenters (students, artists) who challenged established authoritarian structures. It rebelled against the system and its fossilized conventions, against the drabness of everyday life, the lack of imagination and the repressive attitude of the establishment of the time. Provo was small and unorganized, existed for only a short time, but its influence on society was relatively large because it received a lot of media attention — television in particular began to play an important role — which magnified seemingly trivial events. Provo's playfully anarchist actions, which drove authorities to despair, also inspired later protest movements, including the student revolters who would upset French political and cultural life in Paris in '68 with the battle cry 'L'imagination au pouvoir!' (Power to the imagination!).

This volatile period is sometimes compared to the era of the Patriots,[38] exactly two centuries earlier, because of the rejection of the old order, the opposition to existing structures of authority, the outburst of idealism. Gert refers to one of his ancestors, Gerhard Dumbar 'the younger' (1743-1802), historian and Clerk of the city of Deventer, and a well-known Patriot. When the Batavian republic was founded in 1795 after the Napoleonic invasion and occupation of the Low Countries, this

Dumbar was given an important post as Registrar of the provisional States of Overijssel. But in the ensuing internal struggles, Dumbar, 'whose powerful voice was feared', had to step down and was imprisoned at Honselaarsdijk Castle. Quite comfortably — he slept in a canopied bed and his wife and child joined his quarters to which he was, however, confined. During his detention, this headstrong Dumbar kept a diary from which a picture emerges of his striking imperturbability, non-conformism, adherence to his own values under all circumstances and his sense of humour. Gert likes to recognize himself in this ancestor.

PROVO CAUSED CONFUSION, HAD GOOD IDEAS. THEY EMBODIED A CREATIVE ENERGY THAT SEAMLESSLY DOVETAILED WITH MY IDEALS IN GRAPHIC DESIGN

Gert's own subversive attitude found fertile ground in the Netherlands of the late 1960s. Although still in England at the time Provo came up, he had closely followed developments via the media. 'Their ideas appealed to me, the different way they were trying to deal with authorities. Provo caused confusion, had good ideas. They embodied a creative energy that seamlessly dovetailed with my ideals in graphic design. Of course, I also liked the humour and fun that emanated from their actions. It kicked against ossified conditions. It was new and liberating.'

An active participant in Provo 'happenings' at the time was a young designer called Anthon Beeke, who, like Gert, would go on to 'plow like a mole

Dat is dus afgesproken: we geven de post bovenaan 4 cm vrij baan en plakken daarin **rechts boven in de hoek** de postzegel. Je brief kan daardoor vlugger behandeld worden.

Weet je waarom. Zelf? Neen? Zal ik je vertellen.

Heb je de post wel eens hooren stempelen? Vlug en regelmatig gaat dat, tikke, tikke, tikke, tik . . . . . **4000 per uur.**

Maar dan moet er ook niets onordelijks zijn in de brieven, die hij stempelt en dan moeten de zegels alle ongeveer op dezelfde plaats zitten: **rechts boven.**

Op de groote postkantoren worden de stukken gestempeld met een stempelmachine, die **40.000 brieven per uur** stempelt; dat roffelt alsof er erwten op de grond vallen rrrrrrr rrrrrrrrrrrrrrrrrrrrrrr rrrrrrrrrrrrrrrrrrrrrrrr

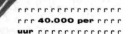

rrrrrrrrrrrrrrr rrr **40.000 per** rrrr **uur** rrrrrrrrrrrr

Dit machinale stempelen is echter alleen mogelijk als de **postzegel in de rechter bovenhoek** geplakt is; anders wordt de postzegel niet geraakt. Plak je de postzegel op ·een andere plaats, dan wordt bij het sorteeren je brief opzij gelegd en met de hand gestempeld, waardoor het soms onvermijdelijk is; dat je brief een post later wordt verzonden.

Piet Zwart, page from *Het boek van PTT*, 1932

through the raked lawn of Dutch design'.[39] Beeke was strongly influenced by the Fluxus movement in the visual arts, who, with disruptive happenings akin to Provo, rebelled against the existing arts system and bourgeois society in general. Art was taken out of the museum and integrated

I WANT TO MAKE A STATEMENT IN WHICH I WANT TO TELL OTHER PEOPLE WHAT THE WORLD IS LIKE AND WHAT THE WORLD OUGHT TO BE LIKE

Jan van Toorn

into everyday life, celebrating freedom and pluriformity. Likewise, the stage moved outside the theatre, and music was taken out of the concert hall. And similarly, some designers looked beyond the existing boundaries of their profession. Beeke, who regularly participated in the provocative actions of Fluxus, broke the codes of 'noise-free' modernism in his work, for instance by translating the gist of theatre plays into stark images that often caused more public debate than the plays themselves. His 1970 alphabet of carefully choreographed naked girls, for the squared publications of Steendrukkerij de Jong, was a direct answer to Wim Crouwel's experimental computer alphabet, published a few years earlier in the same series — a noisy response to what Beeke saw as the boring typographic prescriptions of the time. Beeke too advocated more space and freedom for the designer. But more than Gert, he also wanted to use this freedom to comment on his own time — in that sense he was true to his mentor Van Toorn: 'Every now and then I want to make a statement in which I want to tell other people what the world is like and what the world ought to be like.'[40]

Among the designers who provided a dissenting voice to the Dutch version of Swiss International Style functionalism, Jan van Toorn was the most outspoken one. A socially motivated graphic designer who saw it as a communicator's personal responsibility vis-à-vis the recipients of his client's messages to be transparent about the manipulative aspects of communication, Van Toorn was Wim Crouwel's perfect antipode. To him, what Crouwel had derogatively termed 'noise' was essential as a sign that the message was not objective, not neutral but informed — in a sense contaminated — by its cultural, social, economic and, perhaps most importantly, political contexts. On 9 November 1972, a debate was staged between the two in Amsterdam's Fodor Museum, on the occasion of an exhibition of Van Toorn's work. The debate became historic as the most elaborate representation of the two main currents in Dutch graphic design — the objective functionalist and subjective expressionist tracks, to summarize.[41] The Crouwel-Van Toorn debate has been a benchmark for discussions on the social and cultural use and responsibility of graphic design ever since, in the Netherlands and beyond. Gert was not impressed though. To him, both sides were stuck in their respective trenches, fortified with the kind of theoretical and political correctness that he loathed. They lacked humour, light-heartedness.

91

39   Interview in *art_i*, Maatschappij Arti et Amicitiae, volume 3 nr. 10/11, Amsterdam, October/December 1991.
40   Anthon Beeke, quoted in Leonie ten Duis, Annelies Haase, op. cit., p. 163.

41   Frederike Huygen (ed): *The Debate: The Legendary Contest of Two Giants of Graphic Design*, New York, 2015.

Staged photography by Gert Dumbar and
Lex van Pieterson in the latter's studio.
Set for Scarabee letterhead, 1979

STAGED PHOTOGRAPHY & PAPIER-MÂCHÉ

A barren concrete floor: scattered around the room are pieces of paper and cardboard, cut up, torn up, folded. There's an old iron tea trolley on wheels, a few sloppily painted chairs, a piece of iron wire, a dead bird. In a corner a box of eggs and a bag of overripe tomatoes, kindly donated by the greengrocer. Within reach a packet of paving chalk. At the centre of this chaos, theatrically lit, a table, on which two men are arranging an outlandish still life.

Location: photographer Lex van Pieterson's studio, a large, cluttered factory hall. He and Gert stand grinning at the scene, arranging camera, props, and lights. In this apparent chaos, they prepare for taking a photograph of a staged situation that will be the basis of a new poster.

Thus, in Gert's designs images — reduced to a shabby existence among the International Style functionalists and their reliance on typography — once again take centre stage. Gert's interest in staged photography dates back to the 1960s. At the Royal College of Art in London and influenced by Pop art, he made the first posters with conspicuously staged papier-mâché objects, still photographed by himself. Back in the Netherlands, Gert's collaboration with photographer Lex van Pieterson started with the Mondrian poster, which established his combination

Props and papier-mâché figurine for 'Mondrian' poster, 1972 (photos: Leonie ten Duis)

of staged photography and papier-mâché figurines as a kind of signature approach. The collaboration would last more than three decades. Their work harked back to the photo collages of Dadaists such as Raoul Hausmann or political activist

Staged photography set for Zeebelt poster, 1986
(photo: Lex van Pieterson; design: Gert Dumbar)

John Heartfield in the 1920s and '30s. They used cut-out photo fragments or staged scenes to create new images. A well-known example is John Heartfield's 'O Tannenbaum im deutschen Raum, wie krumm sind deine Äste!' published in the Arbeiter Illustrierte Zeitung (Workers' Illustrated Newspaper) in 1934. The

'Capitalist' papier-mâché figurine for the 'Poor : Rich = no balance' poster, 1972 (design: Gert Dumbar)

photomontage of a staged and manipulated —and rather barren— Christmas tree, with its branches bent to form a swastika, merged concept and form into a new image. Other avant-gardists, such as Alexander Rodchenko, El Lissitzky and Piet Zwart, all used photo fragments and staged objects in order to, as Gert would later state regarding his own work in staged photography, 'manipulate and/or intensify reality. It challenges our imagination and appeals to our associative capacity'. Gert and Lex developed a completely unique visual language over the years, with profound irony, but at the same time great confidence.

Gert, looking back: 'It went something like this: I had an idea and I worked it out in a few sketches. Based on these I manufactured one or more objects, usually from papier-mâché. I then made an arrangement of these, which Lex photographed as he saw fit. The idea came

from me, as did the cobbled-together ingredients, but when working it out, it could go any which way; Lex's input was essential. I gave the impetus and he ran with it, appending things, making suggestions. Precisely because it was in a sense unfinished, all sorts of things could still be added.'

Lex: 'I was inspired by things from the environment. My studio was set up for that. There was a lot of junk lying around. All sorts of things were brought into play. Often it is just coincidence what comes into view at such times. Gert gave me complete freedom. The end result was often unpredictable, but there was no doubt about the right image. We usually picked that out right away.'[42]

Gert later adds: 'It was about making something of high visual quality, capitalizing on the accidental; working with existing material and without general rules, creating something unique.' He compares it to the spontaneity of a child's drawing. An adventurous path where you don't always know in advance where exactly

John Heartfield, *O Tannenbaum im deutschen Raum, wie krumm sind deine Äste!*, 1934

you will end up. 'Unlike the "engineer-designer" who is focused on a fixed goal and brushes aside any accidental things he meets along the way, the "artist-designer" casts his net wide and instead makes use of what he encounters, which makes the result partly unpredictable. Another advantage of this working method is the speed with

95

which you can conjure up a different image each time you take a picture, simply by moving the objects, or taking a different viewpoint. By improvising on the spot,

'Poor : Rich = no balance'.
exhibition poster for the Institute
of Social Studies, 1972
(design: Gert Dumbar)

you often come up with surprising ideas. And staged photography allows for great complexity. The apparent excess of visual elements that sometimes results from this has a function, which is to hold the viewer's attention longer. The greater the complexity of the image, the greater the emotional attachment of the viewer. They have choices aplenty and in his process of perception they deduce the message of the image themselves. It does have to be carefully measured of course.'

FROM MISE-EN-SCÈNE TO MISE-EN-PAGE

In the early period, the images are still quite simple and unambiguous: papier-mâché figurines or objects, staged in a straightforward arrangement, and with a clear message. An example is the poster 'arm:rijk=geen verhouding' (poor:rich=no

balance), designed for the Institute of Social Studies in The Hague — the image leaves little room for doubt. Belonging to the generation that in the 1970s started to pay attention to the poverty of the Third

THE ZEEBELT POSTERS WERE THE STUDIO'S PLAYGROUND

World, Gert commented in this poster on the unevenly distributed prosperity in the world. The image has the acuity of a political print. But the images in his staged photography, mostly posters, gradually become more enigmatic and complex, resulting in technically sophisticated, staged scenes that are not always easy to fathom. Such opaque imagination culminates in the posters for Zeebelt, the experimental theatre, which Gert and friends had started in 1982, a few years after he founded his own Studio Dumbar.[43] Zeebelt would become the studio's experimental laboratory. Its lyrical posters depict an often enigmatic situation, a dream-like reality in which Gert could give

Staged photo for Zeebelt poster, 1988
(photo design: Gert Dumbar)

43   See pp. 253–287.

Staged photo for Zeebelt poster, 1990 (design: Gert Dumbar)

free rein to his penchant for absurdism. Heightened by Lex' lighting, the posters' theatricality gained an extra dimension when Gert would appear in them as actor himself. In some, we see his leg as he seems to flee from a barrage of eggs and tomatoes thrown at the stage, in others he sits quasi naked at a table or buried under the sand on a makeshift beach with a fish head masking his features. 'I could make my own theatre shows there — I was the director as well as the actor, designing the three-dimensional stage and then translating it

to the flat print surface.' Mise-en-scène turned into 'mis-en-page,' as Hugues Boekraad remarked. The orchestrated chaos of many of the Zeebelt images and other work Gert and Lex improvised together could not be further removed from Crouwel's idea of the 'invisible designer'. The experiments with staged photography, mainly applied to assignments within the cultural sector, would eventually work through to other assignments as well. Gert: 'The Zeebelt posters were the studio's playground for research

Gert Dumbar working with papier-mâché

and experimentation with image and typography in a way that was not possible elsewhere. But the creative processes that were set in motion there also bore fruit on other, more serious assignments later, such as corporate identities for the government.'

In advocating a free and unruly stance for designers, with a focus on the 'joy of creating', the visual power of images and expressive typography, Gert may seem to be closer to Beeke and Van Toorn than to Crouwel, but he stands apart in another respect. Both Beeke — famed for his own version of rehabilitating the image — and Van Toorn operated mainly in the cultural sector, which traditionally offered more space for subjectivity and experimentation, while Gert was keen on applying experimental approaches also within commissions for large governmental and commercial clients. Right from his start at Tel Design, he sought to break through the tight structures that such assignments required, eagerly looking for opportunities to find non-obvious solutions — to insert 'music boxes'. The NS corporate identity is a case in point. The 'free and expressive approach' — thus Hein van Haaren (see below) — to this large project, and the agency's ability to successfully manage and implement it, led to a new assignment for a public company: the development of a corporate identity for the Dutch national mail, the PTT.

Cover of Supplement to Campaign Issue of
Design & Art Direction, 11 October 1985
(image: Gert Dumbar)

Staged meeting of papier-mâché figurines for
'Mickery Module', 'Arm : Rijk' and 'Mondrian' posters.
The staging gives a good impression of the objects' scale

Staged set for 'Mickery Module' poster, 1985.
The 'Mickery Module' was a modular seating system
developed by Tel Design's Frans de la Haye for the
eponymous experimental theatre in Amsterdam
(design: Gert at Studio Dumbar)

Wisselende lettertypen, kleuren en typografieën
bij de PTT uit de voor- en naoorlogse jaren

24

Various logos and signs for branches
of the Dutch PTT, 1930s-1970s

PTT: DUTCH NATIONAL POST & TELECOM

THE RABBIT OUT OF THE HAT

Around 1970, the then state-owned PTT decided to adopt a new house style on the advice of the DEV (Dienst voor Esthetische Vormgeving), its 'aesthetic design department'. The assignment was initially awarded to Total Design, but it was soon found that a second agency was needed for such a large and complicated commission. At the suggestion of Hein van Haaren, art historian and then head of the DEV, Tel Design was chosen as the second bureau.

This was a remarkable decision. Cooperation between two bureaus led by two designers, Wim Crouwel and Gert Dumbar, who were diametrically opposed in terms of design views (the engineer vs. the artist) was not obvious. Moreover, they were each other's main competitors. At the DEV, on the other hand, they thought that the confrontation of Gert's free and playful approach with Total Design's strict functionalist method could produce unexpected results. They also assumed that a potential element of competition would benefit the final design. The aim was not only for a clear, functional house style, but also — fitting within the tradition of the PTT — a groundbreaking design.

Gert: 'Of course I was surprised when Hein proposed it. It took me a while to get used to the idea. Historically, it was an interesting thought; nothing like that had been done before. But I had mixed feelings about it at first. Total Design was a big agency, and much more formal than us. We were small and because of our attitude also much more vulnerable. To put it bluntly: Hein had an idea but the designers had to make it happen. You could say that both agencies were a kind of puppets for Hein and the DEV. I thought we could be branded the rabbit out of the hat, while Hein was the magician and Total Design was the hat. On the other hand: it was a bold idea and I wasn't afraid of taking risks.

And if I wanted to go on such an adventure with anyone it was with Wim —principled and a gentleman— even if our ideas were opposites. I did, however, nourish the secret desire, à la Van Doesburg, to draw a diagonal through Wim's grids and tie a knot here and there.'

THE ENGINEER VS THE ARTIST

While working from different design views, Gert and Wim respected each other's convictions. In this atmosphere, they were open to experiment, but also to compromise. Gert: 'We could put our own design opinions into perspective if necessary. We made concessions for the sake of cooperation. But mainly also out of curiosity about what would come out of such cooperation.' In 1971, they took off, 'Mr. Crouwel and the somewhat posh street fighter Dumbar', as they were called by DEV staff member Paul Hefting.

The PTT was not just any client. The state-owned company had a long-standing tradition in the field of good design. Parallel to the idea prevailing in (admittedly small) progressive circles in the 1920s that art and design could contribute to a new and better world, a policy had been initiated at the PTT, based on the idea that a large public company had a responsibility in that area. This was mainly due to Mr. J.F. van Royen, (1878-1942), top official and later deputy director-general of the PTT, who devoted himself like no other to advance good design, which would reflect the quality of the company and boost public confidence in the PTT's services.

Van Royen was early in awarding assignments in the field of graphic and interior design to progressive designers, artists, and architects such as Piet Zwart,

Paul Schuitema and Hendrik Berlage. After the Second World War, this task was continued and expanded in the DEV. Heads of the department included Hein van Haaren (1964-1976) and Ootje Oxenaar (1976-1994). The DEV was responsible for the design of all the company's industrial and graphic products, including all visual art commissions and acquisitions related to the PTT's buildings. The DEV developed into an important advocate and commissioner of good design in the Netherlands, open to innovation and experimentation.

THE HOUSE STYLE

Despite Van Royen's efforts, the PTT had never adopted a consistent house style, and in the mid-1960s this had resulted in a glut of forms and a chaotic accumulation of emblems, logos, colours, and lettering. The first plans to seriously pursue a corporate identity and a clear brand image originated in 1969 on the initiative of Hein van Haaren, not long after the house style for the NS was launched. The starting point was an aesthetically pleasing corporate image, grafted onto modern times; to 'show the visual identity of the company as a service organization engaged in communication on a large scale' and, following in Van Royen's footsteps, to be aware of its social task.

MR CROUWEL AND THE SOMEWHAT POSH STREET FIGHTER DUMBAR

Van Haaren: 'At the DEV I was able to propagate with my employees the conviction that art and design are forces that can make human existence richer and more profound within society — and not

Sketches for PTT logo by Tel Design

PTT Telekommunikatie

Tel Design

alongside it. Our creed is that art and design should naturally become part of economic thinking. After all, society benefits just as much from a cultural economy as, for instance, from an environmental economy.'[44] Gert: 'Hein and I operated from the same mindset. As mentioned earlier, one of my motivations for choosing

PTT Post

Tel Design

graphic design was precisely that it was a force — related to art — integrated into society, that everyone is confronted with in some form. And yes, a force that, if used well, certainly enriches life.'

All was not that simple. The PTT was to be seen not as formalistic but as 'technically and socially progressive' and 'modern'. 'To turn such an abstraction into a real visual presentation, into a corporate identity manifesting itself in all parts of the company, down to the smallest details, is an enormous undertaking,' as Paul Hefting remarked.[45]

Design started in 1971. It would be ten years before the final corporate identity was put into use. Both agencies met regularly to exchange ideas and sketches. In the early days, one vignette after another was fabricated, a kind of 'warming up,' says Gert. Both agencies each presented their own ideas and sketch proposals — surviving sketches from that time show the differences in approach. Both used grids and checkered paper, but Total Design's designs were more goal-oriented from the beginning, and, as Crouwel put it, 'restrained'. Tel Design had a looser touch, took a freer approach and 'fanned out' in

more unexpected directions. 'You shouldn't commit too quickly, but let your ideas run wild first,' says Gert. 'That gives a richer range of possibilities to choose from.' Total Design worked fairly directly towards an end result, while Tel Design kept the game open longer. Ootje Oxenaar, who had just joined the DEV: 'Gert was able to suddenly throw you off guard or turn the world upside down and say "this is how you could also do it." It had a great degree of liveliness to it.'[46]

Gert: 'If you look at those sketches of ours, unlike Total Design, we were more concerned with looking for an atmosphere, a mentality, an overarching idea. We were keen on developing something new from that vantage point. It is much more exciting to explore whether you can develop the idea of the corporate identity in a more narrative form, from an

WE WERE MORE CONCERNED WITH LOOKING FOR AN ATMOSPHERE, A MENTALITY, AN OVERARCHING IDEA. WE WERE KEEN ON DEVELOPING SOMETHING NEW FROM THAT VANTAGE POINT

Gert Dumbar

107

overarching idea or characteristic. From that thought, the idea emerged for us at a certain point to capture the identity in a red line, as a connecting element between all PTT expressions, a metaphor for communication with society. Imagine a line that recurs everywhere, running across buildings, across cars, recurring on the uniform, and so on, or a red wire letter, consisting of curved shapes with a constant

44   Hein van Haaren, quoted in Arnold Witte, Esther Cleven (eds), *Design is geen vrijblijvende zaak*, Rotterdam, 2006, p. 78.

45   Paul Hefting: 'Achtergronden, wordingsgeschiedenis en inhoud van de PTT-bedrijfsstijl', in *het ptt-bedrijf: denkbeelden methoden onderzoekingen*, The Hague, 1983, p. 26.

46   Ootje Oxenaar, interview, summer 2004. This would eventually come into its own in a later house style for the PTT — meanwhile KPN — from 1991, created under Gert's direction in his own Studio Dumbar, after taking over the house style for the PTT on leaving Tel Design in 1976.

line thickness. The red line that should connect everything, a recurring motif that would be visible everywhere in the environment.' The red line would be used as a motif alongside a letter vignette, and this idea was extensively elaborated by both offices, as Wibo Bakker shows in his book *Droom van helderheid* (Dream of Clarity), in which he discusses the development of the PTT house style in detail.[47]

A sketch by Total Design's Anne Stienstra shows how the red thread moves into the interior of a building where it could also serve for wayfinding. Tel Design's Theo van Leeuwen turned it into a system of agile straight and curved line fragment that could be combined at will to form undulating lines. Total Design then replaced the continuous line with a broken line consisting of elongated dots that moved as a straight line. This fractured line reappears everywhere. Although the designs sometimes seem interchangeable, here and there the differences in design conception are evident. Two images

Total Design (Anne Stienstra)

of a post office to which both designs have been applied clearly show this. Total Design places three dots in line on the side facade, while Tel Design makes the line move across the surface in unpredictable ways. Gert: 'We believed more in a line, fragmented or not, that goes with the object, with the building,

with the typography or goes against it. That line is almost irritatingly and unpredictably present everywhere. Total Design, as mentioned, was much more straightforward, goal-oriented.'

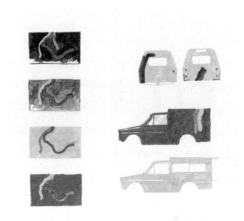

Tel Design (Theo van Leeuwen)

But a clear sense of purpose was also evident at Tel Design, as Wibo Bakker points out: 'The application of Tel Design's lines was distinctively presented in several sketches for post offices, where they ended in a signpost for the PTT. The effort to improve communication between citizens and government, and among citizens themselves, could not have been more clearly represented. The post offices became communication hubs that suggested an underlying system that connected all outlets. From each post office, the lines of communication literally extended into public space.'[48]

Colour played an important role in the corporate identity. The structure of the company, which consisted of three different departments, PTT mail, telecommunications and Giro/money, had to be clearly expressed in the corporate identity. This was conveyed through a colour scheme, for which the existing

47   Wibo Bakker, *Droom van helderheid*, Rotterdam, 2011, pp. 255–260.
48   Ibid, pp. 255–256.

left: Tel Design
right: Total Design

department colours were made brighter, with a new colour for the holding company. PTT's mail remained red, the money services kept their blue, and telecommunications, previously clerical gray, became bright green. The company as a whole — the group management — became brown. Each colour was merged

Total Design

with the name of the corresponding department. By using the logo together with the name of the department and the corresponding colour, one could recognize the different business units at a glance. The use of — for that time — bright colours ensured that the company became much more visible.

In the end, only the colour proposal was adopted. At Hein van Haaren's suggestion, a company logo consisting of the letters ptt in lower case Univers was chosen where previously capitals were

used. It resulted in an easily recognizable logotype that could be simply linked to the different services in the different colours. After all the above, the simplicity of the final logo is amazing to say the least — a simple, almost anonymous logo that works well but is hardly surprising. How does this relate to the initial, surprising choice of the two different agencies of which one had such high expectations? Wibo Bakker describes the context: during the design process, a changing of the guard took place at the PTT's board of directors. The main supporters of the house style retired, which brought the development of the design to a standstill. When finally, in September 1973, the house style proposals were brought to the attention of the board of directors, they were rejected. Drs. P. Leenman, the new postmaster general, felt that the development of house styles was a fashionable trend and past its prime. In his view, the public would see their introduction at the PTT as a waste of money.

The design process was not cancelled, however, and further elaboration of the corporate identity was handled by Total Design with Studio Dumbar, founded by Gert in 1976. After a trial period, the PTT officially introduced the corporate style in 1981. An experimental design

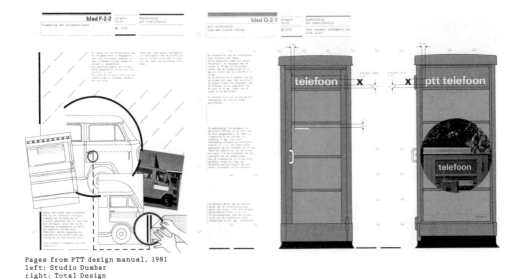

Pages from PTT design manual, 1981
left: Studio Dumbar
right: Total Design

process which was started with enthusiasm by the various parties fizzled out after a decade. The result is nevertheless a clear, uncluttered corporate identity, which in the end everyone agreed to. The final design more closely reflects Total Design's vision than Tel Design's, with the exception of the accompanying ptt design manual in which the sleek pages designed by Total Design alternate with the much more playful pages by (now) Studio Dumbar.

Both studios in the end were only too happy that the slow and tedious process was finally done. In hindsight, Gert ponders, 'Hein strategically thought that starting from a more cautious design, we could at least move forward with the corporate identity, hoping that in the future there would be more room for surprising solutions; which there was.'

In the run-up to the privatization of the PTT as KPN, in 1989, Studio Dumbar — this time without Total Design — was commissioned to develop a new identity for the company with the premise of maintaining as much as possible elements of the existing house style: the colours,

the letter, the rectangular shapes.[49] The studio designed a corporate identity in which there is room within certain basic rules to experiment. The starting point is a flexible system of visual components, 'cut up' as it were into a series of smaller form elements that can be linked in various ways, sometimes at random. This allows for an infinite range of applications that often lead to surprising results. A corporate identity with the greatest possible flexibility with regard to future changes, without compromising the recognizability of the ptt. More than in the previous house style, Gert's fingerprints are clearly recognizable here.[50]

49   See pp. 201–211.
50   Ibid.

PTT design manual, 1981
(design: Studio Dumbar and Total Design)

PTT visual identity
(design: Tel Design/Studio Dumbar/Total Design)

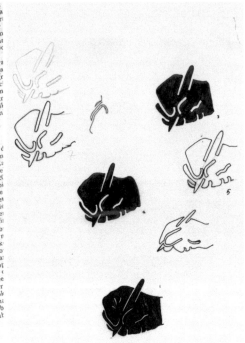

114

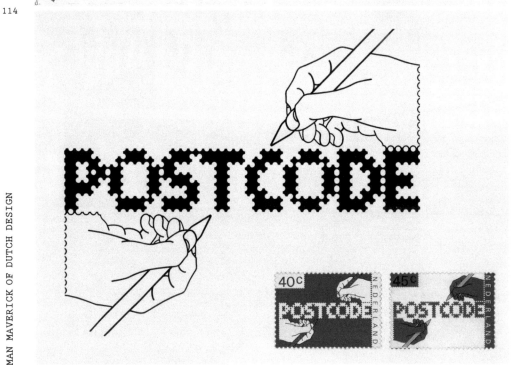

Sketches for Postcode pictogram and stamp, 1977
(design: René van Raalte)

GERT DUMBAR | GENTLEMAN MAVERICK OF DUTCH DESIGN

|16 |aug |9 77| snelheid"

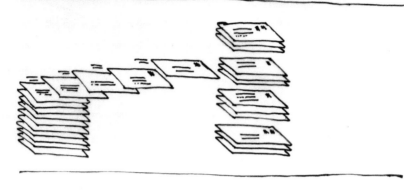

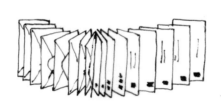

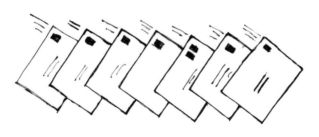

Sketches for Postcode brochure, 1977
(design: Gert Dumbar)

First 'Dutch Design for the Public Sector'
exhibition, 1974. Main construction made
from drain pipes (design: Gert Dumbar)

'DUTCH DESIGN FOR THE PUBLIC SECTOR'

The NS and PTT designs testify to a growing official and public interest in the importance of good design in the Netherlands — and Tel Design's significant role in this field. As we saw, Hein van Haaren, at the DEV one of the leading commissioners of design for public institutions, and Gert found each other in their conviction that attention to good design for government institutions represented a crucial public interest. And the Netherlands had been a flag bearer in this domain internationally for decades already. Thus Hein took the initiative to commission a traveling exhibition, propagating the Dutch achievements abroad. In 1973, Tel Design was tasked with designing the exhibition, titled 'Dutch design for the Public Sector'. In addition to his role of designer, Gert also co-curated the exhibition: 'Hein answered a request from the Danish cultural attaché whether one could do something with design in the Netherlands, instead of presenting the usual tulips and windmills. Hein and I worked it out and we introduced two other curators, Loek van der Sande and Benno Premsela, plus an official from the ministry of CRM (Culture, Recreation and Social Work) that funded the exhibition on Hein's request. I started the design with the packaging, trying to make it light and designing it so that two persons could set it up in one day, wherever.'

The exhibition showed corporate identities for national and local government institutions and companies, such as NS and the municipality of Rotterdam, printed matter for parliament and museums, forms, money, and all kinds of products issued by government institutions involved in communication, information, transport, and education.

The exhibition, which toured Europe, was followed up in 1978 with a sequel intended to travel the world over, designed again by Gert, this time with his team at his newly founded Studio

Dumbar. Because they had to travel, the guiding principle for both exhibitions was designing a system of crates containing

Poster, folded backside is information leaflet for first 'Dutch Design' exhibition, 1974 (design: Gert Dumbar)

lightweight exhibits that could be assembled in a straightforward manner in no more than two days by local staff, using simple instructions, without the assistance of Dutch stand constructors.

For the second exhibition, which was intended for countries outside Europe, materials were used that could weather tropical conditions. Still, getting the exhibition installed in a faraway country was not always easy. Gert: 'In Indonesia, the exhibition crates stood for far too long on the quay of the port of Jakarta, in all weathers and in the fierce tropical sun. The Dutch embassy refused to pay bribes to get the exhibit through customs quickly, thus dragging out the import of the crates.' The exhibit survived. Not a single item was affected.[51]

Both exhibitions were meant to set a benchmark for design in the public sector. In the information leaflet for the second exhibition, art historian Kees Broos wrote that 'the aim was to illustrate the various

ways in which Dutch authorities make use of industrial and graphic designers for the conscious and ingenious shaping of those numerous everyday objects and artefacts that make up the daily surroundings of a citizen of the Netherlands'.

Broos points out: 'Town, buildings, streets, bridges, trains, telephone booths, railway guides, postage stamps, all objects great and small have been given shape and form. And someone obviously determined what shape, which form. In the Netherlands the authorities have no small responsibility in the commissioning of design for the public sector; they provide both stimulus and critical appraisal and aid in the process of design through an exact definition of requirements. Above all, authorities should and do remain always open to new ideas and to criticism. ... The confrontation between citizens and government should be as pleasant as possible. That is one of the basic ideas underlying this exhibition.'[52]

First 'Dutch Design' exhibition, 1974 (design: Gert Dumbar)

To sum up the challenges involved in advancing design for public institutions, Broos quotes an art critic who wrote, 'One would think there was an article of the Constitution stipulating that the fittings of civil servants' rooms must be at least half a century out of date, and that thrift

51   See also pp. 125, 126, 128, 129.
52   Information leaflet, 'Dutch design for the Public Sector' exhibition, Rotterdam, 1978.

Poster, folded backside is information leaflet for
first 'Dutch Design' exhibition, Kunstgewerbemuseum,
Zürich, Switzerland, 1974. This poster is, also in
typography, a counterpart of the poster for the
parallel exhibition of Piet Zwart at the same venue
(design: Gert Dumbar)(see p. 87)

'Dutch Design' exhibition, 1974
(design: Gert Dumbar)

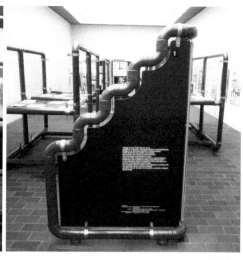

in every respect be regarded as the highest virtue. The dignity of the office usually means yellowish green or dirty brown smoke-grimed surroundings, bare walls, no fresh air, and a cheap hotchpotch of furniture containing, as curious reminders of better times, a few ancient pieces dating from sober but tasteful days.' Broos himself adds that the same goes for official documents, 'which should not look too attractive or even neat, for fear they would lose credibility. "Official printed matter is ugly, ugly, ugly; thrice ugly in lettering, typesetting and choice of paper," said Van Royen at the time, who was one of the first to try and change that and improve government printed matter.'

Luud Schimmelpennink's design for the 'Witkar' (white cart), a three-wheel electrical vehicle for individual public transport in Amsterdam. The prototype was introduced in May 1968

The exhibitions were a useful export product with which the Netherlands could distinguish itself abroad as a progressive country, open to innovation and engagement. Matching this, as part of the exhibition, was a private, not governmental initiative that made Amsterdam world-famous: the 'Witkar' (white cart). It was introduced in the mid-sixties as a small

white, non-polluting, electric city car that could be shared on a subscription basis and recharged at various points in the city. The 'Witkar' was a follow-up to the earlier 'witte fietsen' (white bicycle) plan, in

> *THE EXHIBITIONS WERE A USEFUL EXPORT PRODUCT WITH WHICH THE NETHERLANDS COULD DISTINGUISH ITSELF ABROAD AS A PROGRESSIVE COUNTRY, OPEN TO INNOVATION AND ENGAGEMENT*

which Luud Schimmelpennink and fellow activists connected to Provo collected a few hundred bicycles, painted them white and placed them unlocked in various places in Amsterdam for free use.

Thus, apart from the Dutch tradition of good commissioning exemplified by the PTT, the support for innovative design was related to the spirit of the times. Starting in the late 1960s, there had been a development towards a more open and less authoritarian society. And the government was gradually responding to this, although sometimes great cultural chasms had to be overcome — as late as the mid-1950s, for instance, the NS was a conservative bureaucracy with military traits; lowly workers such as engine drivers had to salute their chiefs, like soldiers obliged to salute their commanding officers. That was not a climate to foster innovative design. But Hein van Haaren was optimistic: 'Time was on our side because of the sometimes radical social changes. Partly because of this, civil servants were open to artistic adventures and were sensitive to modernizing their image.'[53]

53   See also p. 136.

Poster, folded backside is catalogue, for the second
instalment of the 'Dutch Design for the Public Sector'
exhibition, 1978 (design: Gert Dumbar and Tom Homburg)

Instruction book for the exhibition 'Dutch Design for the Public Sector'

Dutch Design

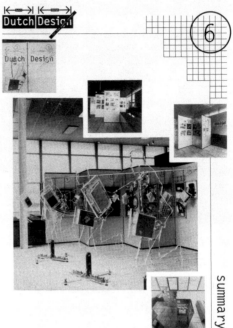

6

summary

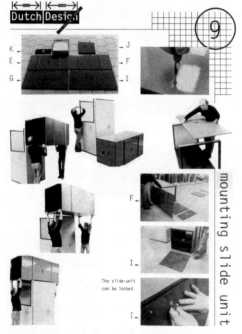

9

mounting slide unit

The slide-unit can be locked

12

packing chest no. 7/9

Make sure that the numbers of the panels correspond with those as indicated on the lid.

Canvas banner

Pages from construction manual for staging the 'Dutch Design II' exhibition, 1978 (design: Gert Dumbar). In the photos Gert Dumbar and Michel de Boer act as instructors showing only two persons are needed to set up the exhibition

'Dutch Design II' exhibition installed, former
Haags Gemeentemuseum (now Kunstmuseum The Hague),
1978. Above: the now empty crates serve as benches
(design: Gert Dumbar)

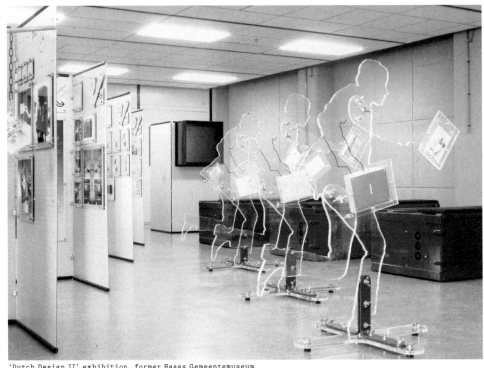

'Dutch Design II' exhibition, former Haags Gemeentemuseum
(now Kunstmuseum The Hague), 1978 (design: Gert Dumbar)

'Dutch Design II' exhibition installed, former
Haags Gemeentemuseum (now Kunstmuseum The
Hague), 1978. The now empty crates serve as
benches (design: Gert Dumbar)

Gert Dumbar (1) and René van Raalte,
early 1970s

LEAVING
TEL DESIGN

Tel Design Associated
Designteam

Emmapark 14 Den Haag
Telefoon 070-83 71 04
Telegramadres: teldesign

Postgiro 70 95 60
Algemene Bank Ned. NV
Bankrek. 51 87 11 080 P

+

+

131

Tel Design's stationery with the controversial
pin-up girl (design: Gert Dumbar and René van Raalte)

ALOHA

'We can't take this invoice seriously, and therefore refuse to pay it,' wrote the NS comptroller's department in 1972. The reason was Tel Design's new stationery on which the invoice was printed and which featured 'pin-up girls' in swimsuits in light pink, supported by an otherwise businesslike font and typography. The bill remained unpaid, whereupon Tel Design sent another invoice without 'girls'.

This Pop art-inspired pin-up girl was briefly Tel Design's mascot and, in addition to appearing on stationery, invoices, and so on, figured above the office entrance, in neon. The-well-to-do-neighbourhood requested that the flickering neon lights be turned off at night. After all, one might think that this was a massage establishment. This happened at a time when, except in Pop art, kitsch was seen as beyond reprehensible. 'Whoever produces kitsch is not someone who produces inferior art, he is not someone who is capable of little or nothing, [but] he is ethically reprehensible, he is the criminal who seeks what is radically evil,' wrote the Austrian writer Hermann Broch as recently as 1968.[54] So to go against that consensus was quite a statement at the time.

'That little woman in a bathing suit had fascinated me for some time,'

54   Quoted in Joost Zwagerman, *Alles is gekleurd: Omzwervingen in de kunst*, Amsterdam, 2011, p. 98.

Gert says, 'inspired by a Roy Lichtenstein painting, Little Aloha, and by my almost lifelong interest in kitsch. I first saw Lichtenstein's image in the early 1960s — the cliché of a Hawaiian girl in a bathing suit with those black locks of hair and red

Roy Lichtenstein, *Little Aloha*, 1962

lips. In a graphic way, Lichtenstein used the false sentiments of the comic strip and of Hawaiian culture, then popular, a kind of paradise, a distant land that evoked a vague longing. This single image summed up what I meant — that feeling of banality, of melodrama, expressed through the sentiments of the comic strip. At the same time, it greatly appealed to me because of the way it was graphically designed. For the sake of convenience, I then called my weakness for kitsch "Aloha" — my own interpretation of Pop art, which was close to kitsch.' The term covered a broad category, including postcards and saccharine pictures Gert had collected at the RCA, as well as Glenn Miller's music.

'The world of kitsch is a world of make-believe, of permanent childhood, in which every day is Christmas,' quipped philosopher Roger Scruton, to which Gert adds: 'It was meant to be provocative. In a protest-like intoxication, we applied that little woman, derived from a photograph from the 1940s, as a mascot for our agency, introducing Pop art at the same time. It was immediately picked up by my collaborators. It was a challenging gesture, but within the parameters of graphic

ART IS TO DO WITH JOY AND PLAY AND THE ABSURD

Iris Murdoch

design. René van Raalte then elaborated the image. Of course, it was also about the fun and enjoyment of making such a letterhead. It was hilarious. Stationery in those days was made in Helvetica. That was the norm, this letter was ubiquitous. In magazines, books, on forms, stationery.'

'I had the idea of doing something about that, breaking through something, kicking it a little bit.' Gert refers to a review by Joost Zwagerman of the exhibition 'Bad Painting-Good Art': '"Bad Painting"' is the wink that official and often deeply-serious modernism has never

Tel Design letterhead with pin-up (design: René van Raalte)

been able to show, never dared or wanted to show. "Bad Painting" is also perhaps the semi-legal reaching out to kitsch in times when movements such as surrealism, futurism … were on the rise, with a pretentious and radical urge for innovation that was never, ever to be downplayed. But "Bad Painting" is perhaps best regarded as a label that can be applied to diligently working painters who also wanted a time

55 Joost Zwagerman, 'Kliederen in Wenen, mooi slecht is niet lelijk', in *Vrij Nederland*, 21 June 2008.
56 Iris Murdoch, *The Black Prince*, New York, 1973, p. 414.
57 Gertjan Leuvelink, interview 2014.
58 Wibo Bakker, op. cit., p. 274.

Neon sign that adorned the entrance of
Tel Design's office

out from themselves; from the weighty
burden of their pretensions and lofty
ideals.'[55]

But there is more to it than just
taking a day off from the burdensome
pretensions of the profession. In England,
Gert had encountered the freedom, the
visual power, the unconventional thinking
spurred on by Pop art and, given the
chance, tried it out in his work. 'To say that
great art can be as vulgar ... as it pleases is
to say but little. Art is to do with joy and
play and the absurd. All human beings
are figures of fun. Art celebrates this,' said
Iris Murdoch, Gert's philosophy teacher
at RCA, which whom he would have long
discussions during his stay.[56] Murdoch's
quote can still serve as précis of Gert's
design philosophy. Just under the surface,
there's a little devil that can pop up at times
to undermine all too grand certainties —
'If you don't light a fire, it's no fun.'

A MORE BUSINESS-LIKE
APPROACH

This attitude eventually caused a
rift between Gert and Jan Lucassen, Tel
Design's founder and business director,
who wanted a more commercial approach.
Business was dropping in the mid-1970s,
after the boom caused by the international
success of the NS design, which had
attracted major clients such as Simon de

Wit, HBG, the PTT and Spaarnestad
publishers. Fearing for the agency's profit
margins, Lucassen initiated an efficiency
audit. He warned: 'Since we all have to
eat out of the same raffle, continuity is
very important for each of us.' The audit
resulted in a number of people being laid
off and the introduction of timesheets. This
was not well received by the firm's graphic
designers, and protests ensued. Gertjan
Leuvelink, who had worked as a designer
at Tel Design almost from the beginning:
'The limit was that the accountant, and
not the management itself, came to tell us
that we were not getting a salary increase
and that people were going to be laid off
because of necessary cost-cutting.'[57]

Lucassen, meanwhile, sought
continuity in a different direction,
hiring public relations specialist Ton
Haak to raise Tel Design's profile in
the market. An ally for Lucassen, Haak
wrote a communications plan in which
he remarked that Tel Design's image
had become too much associated with
'avant-gardism, relativism, causing
upheaval and confusion, which leads to
counterproductive results with the vast
majority of relevant audiences'. And he
advised: 'A somewhat dry, pragmatic
approach ... is the least dangerous and
probably the best way to go.'[58] In 1975,
the agency adopted a new structure, and
Haak became co-director, with industrial
designer Frans de la Haye who had become
partner the previous year, next to Gert and
Jan Lucassen.

This new structure met with much
resistance from the designers who had
been there almost from the start, René
van Raalte and Gertjan Leuvelink, and
who had greatly contributed to the growth
and reputation of the design firm, which
at the time was primarily relying on the
graphic design department for its turnover.

133

There, a unique climate and partnership had grown over the years between Gert and his designers and among the designers themselves. Gert — sometimes called an 'exceptional kind of group designer' — had gathered a special band of people around him to help him realize his ideas. Because he worked quite intuitively and 'artistically' (read: spontaneously), he needed solid backing. He had great aptitude in choosing the right people, a team of gifted designers who, like him, could think laterally. He didn't take this lightly and spent a lot of time recruiting talent. Gert: 'I discovered that I'm good at motivating people. It is important to create a pleasant environment in order to design well. This social side of the profession, the bedding in which designs can emerge, is never talked about by design historians, but it's tremendously important.' Gert's influence was clearly recognizable but equally vital were the diverse personalities of the young designers, who played a defining role in the design process.

This unique and gradually growing breeding ground for creativity, was a 'climate' that seemed severely endangered by the new structure, with its greater efficiency and hourly billing. Added to this unrest was René van Raalte's proposal to transform Tel Design into a cooperative with joint management and profit sharing. Both Leuvelink and Gert were in favour of this. Still, Gert's attitude was somewhat ambiguous. In part because he found it difficult to adopt the right attitude as director, he reacted in typical Dumbarian fashion. With a somewhat crude joke, he indicated the ambivalence of his own position — in solidarity with his employees but also as partner with the new management— by appearing at one of the meetings as 'a capitalist director' with a thick cigar in his mouth. 'He was a

bit laconic,' said Gertjan Leuvelink. This was not understood by all designers. Their impression was that Gert did not take a clear stand in confrontations between management and staff. He left the business decisions to Lucassen, who was not in favour of a cooperative. Gert: 'I did not take a clear position initially, that's true. But I did like the idea of developing the cooperative idea. To my surprise and without my knowledge, Lucassen suddenly, and without consultation, sent a letter to the staff saying: no cooperative. That was ultimately the main reason for me to leave Tel Design. Lucassen wasn't playing to play but playing to win.' Van Raalte and Leuvelink left in 1976. Gert, who had failed to convince Lucassen, followed shortly thereafter. Truijen had left earlier.[59]

GERT ALWAYS HAD ONE LEG IN THE OPPOSITION AND THE OTHER IN THE ESTABLISHMENT. HE INFILTRATED, AS IT WERE, FROM BOTH SIDES

In the ten years that Gert worked there, Tel Design had grown into a leading studio. It was an adventurous time for designers. The austere postwar years had gradually given way to a period of great economic boom, prosperity was growing. Graphic design gradually began to mature and the profession was expanding tremendously, while designers could still make an important contribution to its further development. New areas for graphic design were opened up: corporate identity, pictograms, wayfinding. The government took an interest in good graphic design, and the GVN (the Dutch professional association of graphic designers) began

59   After the NS assignment, Emile Truijen had spent much of his time developing the course in industrial design at Delft University of Technology. Here he was appointed professor in 1971. In 1974 he retired from the partnership.

60   Ootje Oxenaar, interview 2006.
61   Sagittarius, *Parlementaire portretten: de aftredende helft van de Tweede Kamer der Staten-Generaal*, Amsterdam, 1869.

Brand icons designed at Tel Design, in promotional brochure (design: Frans van Mourik) See also cover with pin-up (p. 42)

to increase awareness of the trade among potential clients. Technical changes such as new printing techniques also deeply affected graphic design and the associated industry. All of this took place in the midst of important social debates and cultural changes.

Characteristically, Gert always had one leg in the opposition and the other in the establishment. He infiltrated, as it were, from both sides. Gert had the gift of the word and the necessary powers of persuasion, but he also sowed confusion. 'I always had the greatest confidence in his vitality and his cleverness,' says Ootje Oxenaar. 'He didn't always recognize his limits and could sometimes sell incredible nonsense, including to companies. He could really talk bullshit, far off-topic. Also with jokes that he himself found incredibly

funny while absolutely nobody knew what he was talking about. But it always worked out. That's the strange thing about Gert, that you thought: oh Jesus, and then suddenly he could be extremely brilliant again. I think it's also an enormous sense of self-esteem, an enormous self-confidence, that you can let things go quietly because you know: "I'll catch up with that later." And it was ultimately about the work. That had the quality that convinced.'[60]

Gert, confronted with these remarks by Oxenaar again recalls, chuckling, one of his ancestors: also a Gerhard, former mayor of Deventer and from 1862 a member of parliament representing the district of Deventer. 'He was literate and educated, yet more or less an eccentric,' writes one Sagittarius (a contemporary) about him. And he then gives a description of the performance in parliament of this Dumbar, 'whose short sarcastic speeches bear witness to clear-sightedness, study and sagacity, which, often interrupted by a cough, put the assembly in good spirits and won them to his argument. This dryly comical tone does degenerate into sharp irony a few times and takes on the appearance of chasing eccentricity,' thus Sagittarius. 'But those who know Dumbar know that he is his own man and does not seek effect; his spirit is too independent to seek popularity outside the council chamber.'[61]

The Tel Design period was crucial in Gert's development as an 'independent spirit' and as a designer who had become intimately familiar with the demands of large institutions — including ways to influence them. Here the foundation was laid for what would later come to fruition at Studio Dumbar. Gert felt at home in his day and age, especially in the 1960s and '70s, when Dutch designers worked from a different, more hopeful attitude than today. Designers then thought they could,

135

through their work, make an important contribution to culture and society. They managed to convince clients of this as well and were not afraid of advancing strongly held beliefs. Designers were people with a mission.

Gert's 'mission', his commitment to helping large public and private institutions improve their communication with citizens and meanwhile put a smile back onto modernism's solemn face, can be seen as a fitting answer to the growing openness of 'officialdom' to experimentation that Hein van Haaren referred to. A distancing of institutional representation from the stern aesthetics of International Style modernism. Gert's success and popularity, therefore, arise parallel to a growing cultural question, to which he has a substantive answer: translating cultural metaphors into a visual language that perfectly matches how his clients see their place in the world.[62]

Gert Dumbar, Sketch of the garden of Dumbar's house in Pezuls, Dordogne department, France, circa 1980

62   See: Max Bruinsma, 'Prettig gebrek aan plechtstatigheid. Het handelsmerk van Studio Dumbar', in *Items* #2, March 1996.

STUDIO DUMBAR 1977–2003

MAX BRUINSMA

Studio Dumbar's team, 1978
(photo: Lex van Pieterson)

THE ATTIC STUDIO

In the early afternoon of June 1st, 1977, Gert Dumbar, 37, climbs up the stairs to the lofty attic of his home on Riouwstraat 26 in The Hague. Under the sloping roof, daylight pours in from a skylight and a row of small windows looking out over the quiet street. In the middle of the room a ping-pong table stands ready for play. Gert overlooks the space, which he has cleared of most of the stuff one usually keeps in spare rooms for lack of energy or courage to throw it away, and says: 'Behold our new studio!'[1] The young man next to him, his fresh intern Michel de Boer, 23, looks a bit puzzled. The only items on the table are two bats and a net. 'Well,' says Gert, following his new colleague's gaze. 'Let's do some shopping then.'

Michel de Boer is a young designer still working on his graduation at the Willem de Kooning Academy in Rotterdam. He had recently finished an internship at advertising agency McCann Erickson — a rather different corporate environment than the spacy but sparsely furnished attic, in which Gert has just pointed to the ping-pong table as 'your new desk'. Only days before, Michel had laid out his portfolio on the floor of Gert's living room, below. At McCann, he had had his first encounter with advertising for big brands like Coca Cola and General Motors, and with how agencies managed teams of copywriters and art directors. Now he wanted to experience a 'real graphic design studio' and his tutor had told him that Gert was looking for an intern. So there he was, crouched on the floor over sheets of cardboard and paper, with two young kids, Derk and Laurien, attentively following the conversation between their father and his guest. Michel was hired there and then.

'So we went to "Artificia",' he recalls, 'an art supply shop in the Hague, and I felt like a kid in a candy store! As an art student I knew the place but couldn't afford most of what they sold. Letraset,

1　All quotes by Michel de Boer: conversation, 15 July 2020.

Rotring pens, Ecoline — gosh, really expensive stuff! And Gert walked around, pointing at things like a veritable Santa Claus, and said, for instance: "Let's take some pen bowls too… you know what, take six — we're preparing for growth!" And everything in red, that was the chosen studio colour. If not available in red it was sent to the spray painter.'

GERT GRADUALLY DEVELOPED WHAT WOULD BECOME HIS SIGNATURE STYLE OF LEADING A TEAM; A SLIGHTLY ANARCHIC APPROACH TO ORGANIZING A DESIGN PROCESS

From these humble beginnings the newly founded Studio Dumbar would indeed grow to become one of the leading graphic design firms of the Netherlands — and internationally. The start was partly based on its namesake's ambition to organize a design studio in a different way than was usual at the time, and in part on some high-profile commissions he was able to take with him from his earlier employment as partner in Tel Design. There, Gert was hired ten years before as a junior designer himself, fresh from his post-graduate stay at the Royal College of Art in London. His first assignment, and the reason why Tel Design brought him in in the first place, had been a major corporate design commission, then still a rather new phenomenon in the Netherlands: the design of a new house style for the Dutch National Railways, the NS.[2] The logo and colour scheme he designed in 1968 became instantly iconic — and are used by NS to this day, making the vignet one of the longest surviving brand icons in Dutch design history. Another large commission was the design of the Dutch PTT's house style and logo, in collaboration with the other leading Dutch design studio of the period, Total Design.[3] The two bureaus, Tel Design and Total Design, were the very first in the Netherlands to embrace a business model for design studios that had been developed in the UK and USA — a full service model encompassing all aspects of design and communication for large corporations and equipped to manage complex multidisciplinary jobs.[4] At Tel Design, the young Gert Dumbar was engaged to set up the graphic design branch of the bureau, which until then had focused on jobs closer to its founders' background, industrial design.[5] As he became principal graphic designer and eventually partner of Tel Design, Gert gradually developed what would become his signature style of leading a team; a slightly anarchic approach to organizing a design process, with little attention to hierarchies, and a strong focus on playful experimentation and serious irony — characteristics that connect to a peculiar tradition of Dutch art and design while at the same time reinvigorating it, against the contemporary tendency towards corporate design — towards 'noise-free' communication of the client's message, as Tel Design's main competitor, Wim Crouwel, famously stated as Total Design's approach to the trade's core business.[6]

Gert's attitude and working method did not, however, fit well within Tel Design's organizational structure. Its founders, Emile Truijen and Jan Lucassen, favoured a rather more corporate leadership with clear hierarchies and matching scales of responsibility and remuneration. 'Jan cared about devising complex business structures and cash flow, and I cared about play,' says Gert. 'That went well for

2 See pp. 44–67.
3 See pp. 103–115.
4 Wibo Bakker, *Droom van helderheid: huisstijlen, ontwerpbureaus en modernisme in Nederland, 1960–1975*, Rotterdam, 2011.

5 Paul Hefting (ed.), *Tel Design 1962–1992*, Amsterdam, 1992.
6 Max Bruinsma, 'Official Anarchy: Dutch Graphic Design', in *The Low Countries, Arts and society in Flanders and the Netherlands. Yearbook, 1997–1998*.
7 Gert Dumbar: conversation, 6 April 2021.

quite a while — we flourished and got international attention, a good part of which was triggered by the NS design. So at some point I supported a scheme for profit sharing with the studio's designers — around thirty at that time, which was quite big for the Netherlands. Jan didn't like the idea. He said: "Then they should also share losses." That was clever, but also rather unsympathetic.'[7] Designers Gertjan Leuvelink and René van Raalte kept reminding Jan and the other partners they should discuss it, and they kept avoiding the subject, until it was decided that Tel would become a BV (limited liability company) with four shareholders instead of a corporation of all designers. One of the partners, since 1975, was writer Ton Haak, who was brought in as PR manager and conceived Tel Design's successful newsletter *Telwerk*. He remembers his time at Tel Design as a period, 'characterized not only by great joy but also by at least as great an unrest: these were the years of democratization, of revolution in the streets and at universities; we did not observe from the sideline, we participated, which meant that eventually more time and energy was spent in meetings and exchanges of dialectics than doing serious design. That stopped being fun, it led to cracks within the team and tears being wept, it terminated friendships. Gert Dumbar disappeared to tell his own story about what had happened and to continue a brilliant career under his own name.'[8] That, and other growing tensions — Gert recalls how Jan, who had no background in graphic design, would meddle with the designs of large house styles, forcing Gert to 'try and tell him in a delicate way that it looked terrible'[9] — in the end prompted Gert to start his own business.[10]

Easier said than done. As partner, Gert's finances and assets had become rather entwined with Tel's. He owned half of the studio's building, had a partners' stake in the profits and wanted to make sure he could take at least two of its most important clients with him, NS and PTT. Endless correspondence between lawyers and accountants followed, including negotiations on fees for taking over clients, which were eventually settled in court. That the divorce was strained, is clear from a letter by Gert to friends from December 1977, in which he summarizes the status quo as follows: 'My relations with bureau T. in G. are very bad, as you will have probably heard in all gory detail. I have meanwhile reached a state of adult acceptance of the fact that I've been in the direct presence of genuine assholes for a while. Amen!'[11]

TEAM BUILDING AND REPUTATION MANAGEMENT

Initially, Gert asked former Tel designers René van Raalte and Rik Comello to join him. Another former Tel Design employee was Kitty de Jong, a young temporary secretary who had made an impression as someone who could write correct letters to clients and produce coherent texts based on sometimes rather tangled input from Tel's partners, including Gert. 'At some point Gert asked me to type a letter — a pretty jumbled account, with references to Marcuse and what have you, but it boiled down to the message that he was leaving. So I was the first to know!'[12] Not long after, she was, in her own recollection, quite literally cornered by Gert with a proposal: 'One afternoon, on leaving Tel Design's studio, I was getting into my car with my boyfriend when Gert blocked the road with his car, got out and said: "What would you say if I asked you to start

8   Ton Haak, in *Dutch Graphic Roots*. Online: www.dutchgraphicroots.nl/en/ton-haak/ (accessed 7 February 2024).

9   Gert Dumbar: conversation, 6 April 2021.

10   See pp. 133, 139.

11   Letter to Thom and Gera Snels, 7 December 1977. 'T in G' means 'Tel Design in 's Gravenhage', the traditional name of The Hague.

12   Kitty de Jong: conversation, 26 March 2021.

a studio with me?" I was flabbergasted!'[13]
Kitty had meanwhile started to study
Dutch literature and took odd jobs to make
ends meet. It took some years before she
definitively decided to quit her studies
and her subsequent job and join Studio
Dumbar, in 1979, while in the meantime
assisting Gert in setting up business. An
account of a meeting on January 28th, 1977
puts Gert, Kitty, her friend André Smits
and René van Raalte in a room in Utrecht
with a gentleman named Ir. Provily. The
consultant introduces them to the pros and
cons of organizing a studio as a 'coöperatie'
or as a 'BV' (LLC) mainly in terms of
tax and employment law consequences.
Although it is clear from the account
that a BV is more profitable from a tax
perspective, the visitors' questions gravitate
toward the organizational and financial
characteristics of a cooperation. Bottom
line: every participant and employee of a
cooperation has a say on their own working
conditions and a voice in the company's
general policy. And they can share in
the studio's profit, which was a matter of
principle for Gert and René already at Tel

Gert Dumbar with Rik Comello at the
Riouwstraat 26 studio.
Photo in *Deoscoop*, Westeinde
Ziekenhuis, May 1978

Design and one of the reasons they left.
But ultimately the new Studio Dumbar
started as a business under his own name,
which only years later (in 1989) became

a BV. 'That was on the advice of our
accountant,' Gert summarizes. 'But we
shared profit right from the start — if there
was a profit. That all went very amicably.'[14]

René van Raalte finally decided not
to partner with Gert, and Rik Comello
kept a bit of a distance although he was a
frequent freelancer at the new studio, next
to Gert's half-sister Heleen Raue. And
right from the start, Kitty was there, as a
go-between in many guises. 'At some point,
René, who was a good friend, told me he
didn't want to partner with Gert, but left it
to me to tell Gert. That kind of became my
role, also later, between Gert and Michel
for instance.'[15]

Setting up a studio in the attic of
his home with Michel, a few freelancers
and interns, and Kitty in the background,
laid the basis for continuing existing jobs
and expanding towards new ones. Still,
Gert was adamant to establish his new
independence and secure his relationships
with clients whom he had worked with
while at Tel Design. From a perspective of
almost fifty years on, it is hard to imagine
the ways in which he and his collaborators
and competitors asserted themselves within
the small ecosystem of Dutch graphic
design. Clients, funders, designers, and
competitors would meet each other on a
very regular basis at pitches, presentations,
conferences, exhibitions, celebrations, and
other formal and informal gatherings in a
communal environment that was heavily
influenced by government investment, both
on a cultural and corporate level. Cultural
as a result of the Dutch government's
ongoing interest and investment in state-
of-the-art design since the early 1920s,
which reflected in high-profile and well
paid-commissions for innovative designers
and design studios by state-owned
institutions like the national railways
(NS), the national mail (PTT) and the

13   Ibid.
14   Gert Dumbar: conversation, 23 January 2023.
15   Kitty de Jong: conversation, 26 March 2021.
16   See pp. 116–121.
17   Letter to Gertjan Leuvelink, 24 January 1978.
18   Ibid.
19   Ibid.

national bank (DNB). By the 1970s, Dutch design for government institutions had been internationally exemplary and groundbreaking for decades. Thus, commissions like the NS and PTT were key in establishing a high profile within the Dutch design community — and towards clients who wanted to associate themselves with the cultural capital connected to the Netherlands' official commitment to innovative, high-quality graphic design. A reputation which Gert had helped to promote world-wide with Tel Design's traveling exhibition 'Dutch Design for the Public Sector' in 1974.[16]

SETTING UP A STUDIO IN THE ATTIC OF HIS HOME WITH MICHEL, A FEW FREELANCERS AND INTERNS, AND KITTY IN THE BACKGROUND, LAID THE BASIS FOR CONTINUING EXISTING JOBS AND EXPANDING TOWARDS NEW ONES

A telling example of Gert's commitment to upholding his own reputation is the correspondence between him and his former colleague at Tel Design, Gertjan Leuvelink, about claims to the authorship of the by then internationally famed NS design. Gertjan, who also worked on the NS at Tel, chiefly on the time tables that became internationally awarded, is reprimanded by Gert because apparently, he mentioned Tel Design projects as his own in his announcement of the start of his own new designers collective 2D3D in 1976. Gert is 'fairly irritated'[17] and reminds Leuvelink that he should not claim (sole) authorship

of things that were collectively designed at Tel, and that any graphic design that was produced by Tel Design anyway was made 'under my complete responsibility [and] supervision, as Tel's department director for graphic design'.[18] He reminds Leuvelink of the latter's irritation when his name was not mentioned in the colophon of the 'spoorboekje' (the NS annual time table — it simply stated 'Tel Design'), and writes that he will publicly announce the founding of Studio Dumbar shortly, adding: 'I don't rule out that this announcement will also mention projects, among others, which you have already cited as your own.'[19]

Such collegial irritation did not, however, cloud their relationship permanently. A good year later, in 1978, Leuvelink, then head of the graphic design course at AKI, invited Gert to give a lecture at the school. Gert accepted in a telephone call, but wrote the next day that he had been invited to come to Bandung, Indonesia, on the date agreed with Leuvelink. There, the second instalment of the traveling exhibition 'Dutch Design for the Public Sector' opened on September 24th and Gert was asked to address the attendees. This, of course, provided not only an opportunity to claim authorship and ownership of work that was initially developed by Gert and his team at Tel, but also to revisit Indonesia, the country of his youth.

Gert not only asserted his own authorship with respect to colleagues and the world at large. He also wanted to engage former clients of Tel Design for his new studio, although with some gentlemanly reluctance. Studio Dumbar's archive holds several letters from this period, which apparently have not been sent, but which give an interesting glimpse into the kind of concerns that absorbed an ambitious new independent contender in the field. In a letter drafted on 22 March 1977,[20] Gert reminds one of Tel Design's clients, the Dutch Dairy Bureau (Nederlands Zuivelbureau), of the fact that, with the exception of 'Ton Haak, a text writer', all of the collaborators that have worked passionately (and often in unpaid overtime) on a recent exhibition have meanwhile left Tel Design and that therefore the client will not find 'the atmosphere in which the exhibition was realized' at Tel anymore. Gert further remarks that his team has been worried that Tel Design would take too much credit for the creative work done by members in their own time, which, he writes, in hindsight is a plausible concern. He ends the letter by saying he'll c.c. it to Tel, 'for full disclosure'. In the archive, the letter is marked 'not sent'. In another apparently unposted letter, Gert informs the director of the Bernard van Leer Foundation, a charity devoted to early childhood development for which Tel Design designed stationery and newsletters, of the fact that he has left Tel Design 'for principal reasons',[21] adding that he would like to rekindle his previous contact with the Foundation, especially since he heard that they don't use Tel's services anymore.

GERT WAS CLEARLY CONCERNED TO ESTABLISH HIS AUTHORSHIP OF HOUSE STYLES THAT HE AND HIS TEAM HAD DEVELOPED WITHIN TEL

The correspondence and publications by and about Gert during this time of transition show that he was clearly concerned, if not anxious, to establish his authorship as graphic designer of house styles that he and his team had developed within Tel, and that had become internationally praised: the NS and the PTT, among others. Although his authorship of the NS logo is undisputed, some controversies over who did what for aspects of the house-style, for instance the 'spoorboekje', continue to this day, with René van Raalte and Gertjan Leuvelink asserting their roles in developing it. On the other hand, these documents also show how Gert sees his role — not only as individual designer (and 'author') among others in a team, but as 'director' leading, supervising, and taking responsibility for the end result. The experience of the transition from Tel Design to Studio Dumbar solidified Gert's ideas and practice of being quite transparent about which individual designers were (most) involved in specific projects, while at the same time establishing the overarching authorship of the Studio, which now bears his name.

INTERNATIONAL EXPOSURE

Amidst consultations on how to start a design business, Gert continued acting on the international stage of graphic design's discourses and platforms in which he had been an energetic participant since his start at Tel. Already in 1967 he figured among young models, media makers and advertising mavericks in youth magazine *TIQ* as representative of a 'cool profession', where he was described as 'one of those guys, who keep fantasizing endlessly during every conversation'.[22] In the following years, Tel Design's work is widely published, leading to invitations to present the work and take part in panel discussions and juries around the world. At a conference in The Hague in 1973, for instance, he

20 Letter to Nederlands Zuivelbureau, unsent, 22 March 1977.
21 Letter to Bernard van Leer Foundation, unsent, 18 August 1977.
22 *TIQ* magazine, August 1967, p. 36.
23 See also p. 55.
24 Summary of the talk given by Gert Dumbar of Tel Design Associated on October 5, 1973. (Ride conference, The Hague).
25 Szymon Bojko, 'Tel Design', in *Projekt Visual Art & Design*, #106, March 1975, pp. 58–65.

talks about Tel's design of the pictogram system for the NS.[23] They were based on the set that was issued in 1960 by the UIC, the international railways organization, as standard pictograms for railway stations worldwide. Gert is rather critical about the UIC set and quotes extended research he did with Tel Design in collaboration with visual perception scientists of Utrecht University and the NS to improve the design and legibility of the pictograms. Interestingly, he points out that scientists and designers have different perspectives, that may conflict, and, based on his experience with testing the NS pictograms, advocates that both designers and social scientists should compromise to achieve an optimal functional result: 'On the one hand the freedom of the designer was restricted, and on the other, there were limits set to the authority of the social sciences.'[24]

Already as a student of graphic design, Gert had eagerly explored the boundaries between the 'freedom of the designer' and the 'authority' that bound him to a commission, and felt he wanted to — and could — honour both. He embraced modernism's focus on a rational approach to a design's structure and content, but rebelled against the, in his view, narrowminded inference that a logical mindset would per se rule out playfulness in execution. An early signal that he was successful in reconciling the two opposed views — rational structure versus playful expression — that had haunted the avant-gardes ever since their inception in the early twentieth century, was given by Polish design writer Szymon Bojko. In an analytical essay in *Projekt*, the independent Polish magazine on art and design founded in 1955, Bojko writes that with the exception of pioneers like El Lissitzky and Piet Zwart, early modernism had left 'popular informative publications:

tourist guides, ... railway and airlines' time-tables, etc.' largely untouched and that the 'editorial activity' of the Ulm School of Design, headed by Gui Bonsiepe, was

ALREADY AS A STUDENT OF GRAPHIC DESIGN, GERT HAD EAGERLY EXPLORED THE BOUNDARIES BETWEEN THE 'FREEDOM OF THE DESIGNER' AND THE 'AUTHORITY' THAT BOUND HIM TO A COMMISSION, AND FELT HE WANTED TO HONOUR BOTH

the first in the postwar period 'to apply scientific semiotic methods in designing informative brochures'.[25] This is not an introduction that would nudge a Western reader towards thinking about Gert Dumbar. Still, Bojko continues that 'it is no wonder then that at the last Biennale of Applied Graphic Art in Brno everybody's attention was attracted by such prints, so rarely to be seen on similar occasions. These were annual time-tables of Dutch railways, prepared by the so-called Tel Design group.' He contextualizes the NS time tables within the Dutch tradition of government interest in good graphic design and remarks that Tel's NS booklets contributed 'to "humanize" railways'. What follows is an in-depth analysis of the encompassing design approach, not only by the designers of Tel, but also by the commissioner (in the person of Siep Wijsenbeek, head of design at NS and, like Gert, RCA alumnus) to all aspects of the railways as institution, from the logo and time-tables to the rolling stock and the train stations. He mentions the 'toilsome research' that went into the 'informative symbols' and reviews the time tables as 'extremely complicated and pioneering work'. He then offsets Tel's work for NS against that of their competitors and concludes: 'There is one aspect of this project that distinguishes Tel Design from the other similar design offices such as, for instance, Wim Crouwel's Total Design. ... The difference lies in showing equal respect for functional and non-functional factors. In other words, Tel Design fully allow for visual effects with all that it implies, with no detriment to the users' comfort. They introduce elements of game, surprise, and even humour.' It's an early acknowledgment of Gert's (who is mentioned as 'head of the team', together with Jan Lucassen) ability to create 'an amazing spectacle' without 'burdening the viewers with superfluous information'.[26]

I'm quoting Bojko at length because I think it's interesting to hear a voice from what was at the time a different culture — as sophisticated as Polish graphic design may have been since the 1920s, at the time of Bojko's writing it still took place in a depressingly bureaucratic communist country, across the 'iron curtain.' Interestingly, Bojko points to Gert's direct indebtedness to Modernism and simultaneously applauds his strategies to 'warm up' a space, a design, 'by a certain playfulness', while in the Netherlands the debate seemed stuck between mutually exclusive theoretical positions who each claimed to be modernism's true heirs.[27]

Perhaps triggered by Bojko's analysis in the leading Polish design magazine, Gert was invited to Warsaw the next year to present and discuss Tel's 'Dutch Design for the Public Sector' exhibition during the annual ICOGRADA conference — then one of the most significant international platforms for graphic design. At the time, he was already preparing his leave from

Tel Design and in the midst of setting up his own business, he travelled to Aspen, USA to speak at the prestigious annual International Design Conference and later to Paris to join the jury of the *European Illustration 1977/78 yearbook*. In a short text for the Dutch advertising trade journal *Adformatie* he summarized the jury's

Gert Dumbar (front, right) as part of the Jury of European Illustration 1977-1978, Paris

findings, which were quite critical of the industry's medium of choice at the time: 'The number of surreal, pompous, airbrush illustrations, whether or not hanging over a horizon, mountainscape, forest or sea, winged or not, floating, diving, with or without spatters, rising or exploding, rainbow or not, technically nifty but nonetheless superficial and nauseating, overwhelmingly abounded.' Instead, the jury chose to focus on 'the really original, simple work... so on to and back to new and old techniques, to wit: the pencil, the brush and the pen.' To conclude: 'The airbrush technique is running out of air.'[28]

It is an assessment of Gert's love of the pencil, but also of his skepticism of the new media of the day, which prompted his competitors to make huge investments in new technology that became obsolete within years. In the early 1980s Total Design, for instance,

26   Ibid., p.64. This remark is referring to Tel's design for the dairy pavilion at the Flevohof agricultural exhibition (1970). But it is clear from the text that this characterization is also meant for Tel's (basically Gert's) design approach in general.

27   Max Bruinsma, 'Points of View on Design Education', *Rietveld Project* #23, 1984.
28   Gert Dumbar, manuscript for *Adformatie*, 23 May 1977.
29   See: Frederike Huygen, 'Ontwerpen met de computer: TD en de Aesthedes', in *Total Design 1982–1996:*

invested an outrageous amount of money in acquiring no less than three 'Aesthedes' machines — 220 kilogram behemoths costing around 300,000 Dutch guilders a piece — which then represented the nec plus ultra of computer assisted design tools.[29] Such investments became all but annihilated by the advent of the Apple Macintosh computer only a few years later, and brought Total Design on the brink of bankruptcy. Although, as an ardent and skilled draftsman he was wary of computers during most of the initial decade of Studio Dumbar, Gert had already in his RCA days become interested in the imaginative qualities of the relatively 'old medium' of photography. Photo collage was a medium of choice for the modernist avant-gardes that had inspired him earlier, and Pop art's experimentation

> *STAGED PHOTOGRAPHY IS THE MANIPULATION OF REALITY, WHICH CHALLENGES OUR IMAGINATION AND APPEALS TO OUR ASSOCIATIVE CAPACITY*
>
> Gert Dumbar

and fascination with staged photography stimulated his own explorations in putting the medium to good use in graphic design.[30] In a newspaper publication on photography, Gert chose the well-known self portrait of El Lissitzky, an intricate black-and-white photo collage from 1924, as a constructivist inspiration: '… in a realistic and idealistic way, he expresses exactly what he stood for in his time: speed, dynamics and clarity.' On the facing page, Gert confessed his love for staged photography, not as a means to depict

'imaginary image worlds', but 'to entwine staged photography with graphic design. … For me, this form is the manipulation and/ or intensification of reality, it challenges our imagination and appeals to our associative capacity'.[31]

MAKING AND MOVING — STUDIO DUMBAR AT KANAALWEG

Meanwhile, practical matters demanded attention. Before long it appeared that maintaining a studio on the attic of one's family home was not ideal. Kitty's impression was that the family soon became rather fed up with the constant, and growing, traffic to and from the attic.[32] And so the search for a more apt and permanent studio space started. Various realtors and friends were contacted and several potential spaces were viewed and considered. A letter to Jan Snoeck, 25 March 1977, illustrates the frantic search for working space — and, in between, the vagaries of building a team and engaging partners: '… something has changed in the meantime: René is not on board for now, so I've started, with Kitty's help, in my own house, but I'm still looking for a suitable space' wrote Gert. Obviously, Snoeck was reluctant to let or sell his atelier, but Gert asked him to reconsider, stressing that he and Kitty will be 'nice, quiet neighbours'. Finally, on 23 February 1979, Gert acquired Kanaalweg 34b and c. They immediately start to refurbish it and engage interior architect Ben van Os to design and execute the plan. Van Os designed the new studio in state-of-the art 'high-tech' style, including a metal wall onto which over the years hundreds of polaroid images were pinned magnetically and a strip into which one could plug headphones and listen to music. The correspondence in

een ontwerpbureau in transitie, pp. 18–23, Stichting Designgeschiedenis Nederland, Amsterdam 2021. Download: www.designhistory.nl/wp-content/ uploads/2021/01/TD-Totaal.pdf (accessed 17 November 2022).

30   See for instance pp. 266–283.
31   Undated newspaper clipping, Gert Dumbar's personal archive.
32   Kitty de Jong: conversation, 26 March 2021.

Studio Dumbar's archive conjures up a rather chaotic and costly process, in which Gert alternatingly chaffs and chastises his architect. On 21 September 1977, he asked Kitty to write a letter to Ben, which she sent to him rather uncensored:

'Dear Ben,
Gert called me today from Zwolle, where he got a brainwave on the loo at restaurant 'De Postiljon', which he found so valuable, that he called me from the very same establishment about it. The assignment was as follows: 'Kit, draft a note to Ben van Os making it clear to him, that as part of an interior designer's customary promotional gift to the client, he is expected to install on the Kanaalweg, successively:
1. two sublimely designed ashtrays: one in the hallway of the toilet and one in the toilet area itself;
2. an equally sublime towel hook or rack;
3. as well as an extraordinary lined toilet bowl brush to remove the skid marks;
4. and to complete the picture, a strikingly beautiful soap dish.
Please write, Kit, that the costs involved in the purchase and installation of these items are estimated by us at about f 750 to f 1,000, so that Ben knows of what calibre these gifts must be.'
Well Ben, now what am I to do with that, or rather what are you to do with that? I'd say, whatever you want. Maybe as a fellow businessman in related industries you know if Gert is serious about this. To which I would like to add, to get you started, that 'jesting' is known in psychology as the way to express one's opinion (or one's wishes) in a non-committal way.
Gert can be reached all day Monday.
Greetings and I wish you a very pleasant weekend,

Kitty'

But a few days later, on 26 September, Gert's tone was more irritated when it became clear that many details have been overlooked or were sloppily executed. '… 6. The tiles at the end of the kitchen protrude to the left. Bah. You know that this adventure doesn't cost me a rib, but six ribs.' The refurbishment dragged on well into the next year, with ever-expanding lists of defects and deficiencies. Since Van Os had accepted the job on 'turn-key' basis, most of the extra and unforeseen costs ended on his plate — his omission, for instance, to organize permissions for the work caused considerable delay, and his decision to galvanize the heating pipes made them dysfunctional, triggering costly reparations — eventually causing his bankruptcy.

But gradually, Studio Dumbar was taking shape, both spatially and as a place where actual work is being done. And within a few years it turned out the space was too small. Gert bought a house in the vicinity and seduced the upstairs neighbours (who rented the apartment at 34b) to move. This provided two floors of extra space for the studio and a new commission for renovation, this time done by Opera. Within another few years, the neighbouring building was rented and connected to the studio. As Kitty recalls, all of this was 'really nice, but also very expensive'. At the same time it testifies to the steady expansion of the studio, which grew from a few to a dozen designers within a decade.

At first, alongside Gert, with Rik as frequent freelancer and Gert's half-sister Heleen Raue for the artwork and production drawings, new team members were engaged mostly as interns or freelancers. One of the first was Ko Sliggers, a fresh graduate from St. Joost Academy in Breda, where he received a

33   Ko Sliggers: Zoom conversation, 30 March 2021.
34   *Pro-fil*, mededelingenblad van het Staatsbedrijf der PTT tbv. Belangstellenden in de filatelie, 21 March 1978.
35   See also pp. 109–111.
36   Ibid.
37   Gert Dumbar: conversation, 9 April 2021.

solid grounding in typography by one of the grand old masters of Dutch type design, Chris Brand. Ko had called Gert asking for an internship, and Gert advised him to have a look at the second instalment

THE FIRST PERIOD OF STUDIO DUMBAR WAS MAINLY GERT AND KO, WITH RIK COMELLO ALMOST ALWAYS PRESENT AS WELL. MICHEL ATTENDED IRREGULARLY BECAUSE HE STILL HAD TO GRADUATE

of the 'Dutch Design for the Public Sector' exhibition, then at the Gemeentemuseum in The Hague. 'So I went and though it was totally cool with those cut-out Perspex figures with suitcases and all, and I showed my portfolio to Gert and he said: "You can come."' [33] In Ko's recollection, the first period of Studio Dumbar was mainly Gert and him, with Rik Comello almost always present as well. Michel attended irregularly because he still had to graduate. Ko immediately started work on the ongoing PTT commission, collaborating with René, who had taken over the 'Postcode' job, a separate project within the PTT's house style commission. In 1978, postal codes were introduced in the Netherlands to improve logistics for delivering mail. The Postcode design entailed a bespoke graphic identity and a campaign to familiarize the public with the new system of writing addresses — and persuade them to use it. The design attempted to reconcile the technological background of the codes and their human users with 'on the one hand a computer-like image and on the other, by means of its notable tearing edge, a

humane element'. In a publication by the PTT, Gert (who designed the cover for the Postcode book) and René stated that 'in the design a conscious choice was made for the 'friendly' sign of a writing hand, indicating that the reference to postal codes should not be limited to business use, but that eventually everyone who ever sends something by mail should mention the postal code.' [34]

Next to working with René on the Postcode design, Ko continued to work with Gert on the new corporate design for the PTT, which was fully implemented in 1981, with designers from Total Design. [35] Ko would come in from Breda in the morning, when Gert was already on his way to Amsterdam to discuss the latest designs at Total Design. Ko: 'One morning he came back and said, "I spoke with Jolijn [van de Wouw, principal designer at Total Design] and showed her your sketches. She decided on this version." And I said that was disappointing. So Gert asked which version I liked better and I told him. "Okay," he answered, "so get on the phone and call Jolijn." I was scared shitless, but I called and Jolijn said "okay, cool, then we'll take your preferred version." I think she appreciated the guts of an intern to call her. But it was Gert who made me do it. He was totally behind his designers.' [36] The collaboration resulted in a clear-cut corporate design, with at times rather hybrid outcomes, which found their way in the design manuals — internal instructions on how to consistently implement the house style: 'When you go through the manuals we made, you can easily see which page is from Total Design's Jolijn van de Wouw and which page is ours,' says Gert. 'Ko played an important role in that, in response to my wish to find a different, elegant and more playful approach to modernism.' [37]

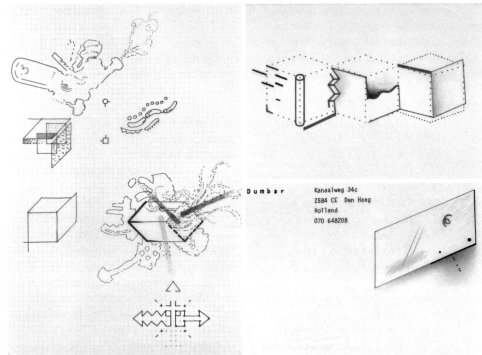

Sketches by Ko Sliggers for Studio Dumbar
stationery, 1980

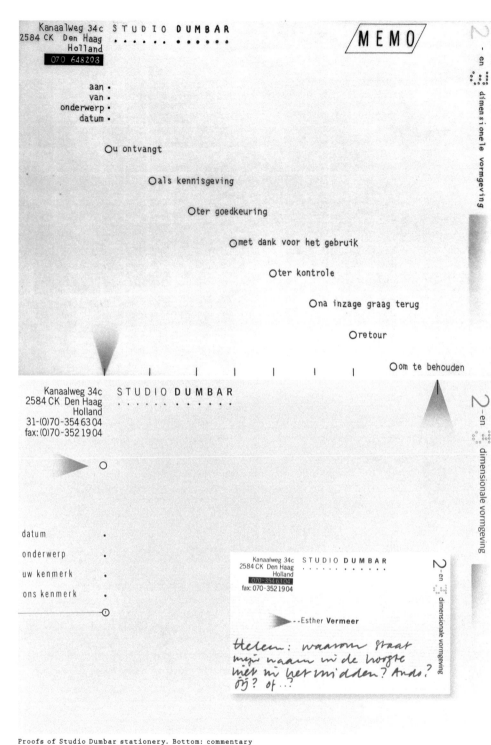

Proofs of Studio Dumbar stationery. Bottom: commentary
by designer Esther Vermeer: 'Why is my name raised and
not in the middle?'(design: Ko Sliggers)

Façade of Studio Dumbar at Kanaalweg 34b.
Note the shield above the entrance: a tweaked
ANWB recommendation sign, designed by Studio
Dumbar's Henri Ritzen (ANWB: see pp. 218-227)

Simultaneously, Ko was asked to redesign Gert's own temporary stationary and develop it into a house style for Studio Dumbar. 'Gert said "make something typographic",' Ko recalls, 'which was okay with me, because already at that time I had inexplicably complicated feelings about logos. So I started experimenting with the type News Gothic, with all kinds of graphic symbolics, with transfers and pencil shadings ... At some point I put dots under the two words — light ones under Studio and slightly fatter ones under Dumbar. Gert liked it a lot, don't ask me why ... But it felt special, the amount of trust you got, the space to explore. Gert basically said "surprise me". That of course was fantastic.'[38]

To design and develop stationary for a design studio has its complications; everyone using it will have their professional comments on the execution. In the archive, you'll find a hilarious collection of visiting cards for Studio Dumbar's designers that came back with critical remarks scribbled onto the proofs: 'lower a sixth of an inch', 'crooked!', 'too high', 'Why is my name raised and not in the middle?' Nevertheless, or in fact because of such scrutiny, the Studio stationary was kept virtually unchanged for almost two decades and was awarded Silver in 1980 at the British D&AD Awards. Ko recalls traveling with Gert to London to attend the ceremony — his first-ever flight: 'We felt a bit uncomfortable about the award event's seriousness, and Gert asked me, what shall we do? We thought up a small act to shake up the official atmosphere. When it was our turn to receive an award, Gert sat down on his knees, and I mounted him as a rider, on our way to the stage.'[39]

The growing international fame prompted requests and offers from various countries asking Gert to teach at design schools. In March 1980, he received a letter from the dean of design at Sydney College of the Arts in Australia, asking if he would be interested in accepting the position of head of the visual communication department.[40] Gert answered: 'I am of course very honoured and flattered by your proposition. But I cannot possibly even consider it seriously. I have a design studio in The Hague and my leaving for Australia would mean eight future unemployed people. Besides, as things work out right now I have no wish to start something completely different.'[41]

WESTEINDE HOSPITAL

While continuing work on jobs that were started at Tel, Studio Dumbar acquired an important new commission after a pitch against, among other bureaus, Total Design and a young Paul Mijksenaar: designing a brand-new house style for the newly built Westeinde hospital in central The Hague. In the hospital's own

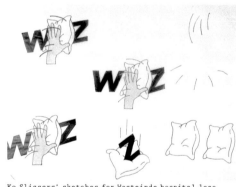

Ko Sliggers' sketches for Westeinde hospital logo

periodical, *Deoscoop*, Gert explains his points of departure, and his ambition: 'Many people come into a hospital quite suddenly. They see a lot of new things and don't feel comfortable. Those people want reassurance. With the visitors, it is

153

38   Ko Sliggers: Zoom conversation, 30 March 2021.
39   Ko Sliggers in Joost Roozekrans (ed.), *The Secret Bar*, May 2021. See also: www.the-secret-bar.nl

40   Barry Davis, Sydney College of the Arts, letter to Gert Dumbar, 14 March 1980.
41   Gert Dumbar, letter to Barry Davis, 14 March 1980.

154

Sketches for Westeinde hospital logo and
department illustrations: Ko Sliggers (top)
and Gert Dumbar (bottom)

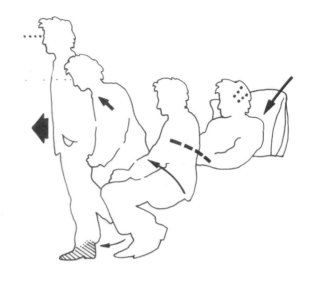

Sketches for Westeinde hospital logo
(design: Ko Sliggers)

Sketches for Westeinde hospital department
illustrations by various Studio Dumbar
designers

actually no different. They are part of the ailment. The signage system must restore peace and assurance. People must find their way around harmoniously. Therefore, the system must have something friendly. That is very important, that friendliness. I want to develop a system that in time can be applied nationwide in hospitals. A system that uses pictograms, because foreign patients also come to the hospital. A pictogram is the visual representation of a concept, with the intention of stepping over the language barrier, like the fork-and-knife symbol indicating "restaurant".'[42] He describes three stages of wayfinding: 'Where to go?', 'I'm on my way', and 'I've arrived'. This led to a layered wayfinding system that guides the visitor from start to end point via a path marked by visual 'bread crumbs' in an emphatically cheerful style. In addition to designing the logo, Ko Sliggers was tasked with finding the right symbolic language to differentiate the fifteen seemingly identical floors of the huge building. Gert suggested a direction, which Ko translated into a little ball: 'On each floor the little ball does something different, it bounces or almost disappears into a hole or it floats away like a balloon … well, fifteen variants which you'll meet across all floors, so you know, even without the number, 'ah, the ball that bounces into a hole: 10th floor!'. At some point we also placed them in the patients' rooms and on the toilets — it became a kind of benevolent virus.'[43]

Another challenge was to describe the many specializations and functions of the hospital in a visual language that would be understandable for all visitors, regardless of language or literacy. Gert has always had a fascination for pictorial languages, which he had honed at Tel Design in the pictogram designs for the NS.[44] Although that was already an extended set of

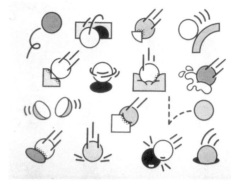

Variants of the 'ball vignette' identifying the fifteen floors of the Westeinde hospital (design: Ko Sliggers)

157

stylistically consistent symbols, governed by a stern visual grammar, the Westeinde set was even larger, and faced the added challenge of depicting sometimes rather outlandish medical specialities and departments. Not everyone immediately understands what 'hemodialysis' means. Like the previous set for the NS, the pictogram set designed for the Westeinde hospital was intensely researched and gained international acclaim.

Michel de Boer, who returned after his graduation to the studio to become its second official employee, after Ko, had missed the start of the design process, but vividly recalls its departure points: 'It typifies Gert, this "civil attitude" towards a hospital in the centre of the city, with many foreign nationals.' The 1970s had seen an influx of 'gastarbeiders' (foreign labourers)

42   *Deoscoop* magazine, Westeinde Ziekenhuis, May 1978, p. 11.
43   Ko Sliggers: Zoom conversation, 30 March 2021.
44   See also p. 55.

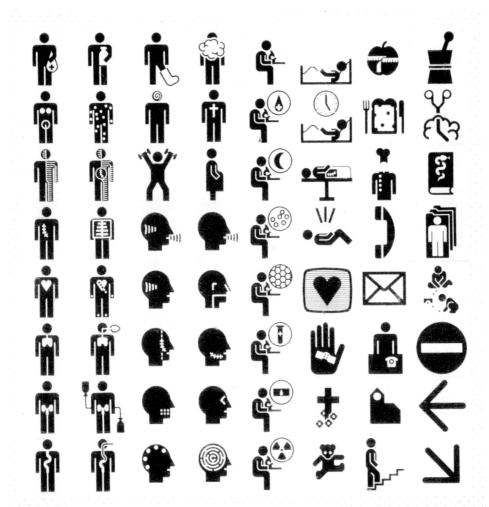

Westeinde Hospital
Top: pictograms (design: Gert Dumbar)
Bottom: application pictograms (design Ko Sliggers)
Right-hand page: signage (design: Rik Comello and
Gert Dumbar)

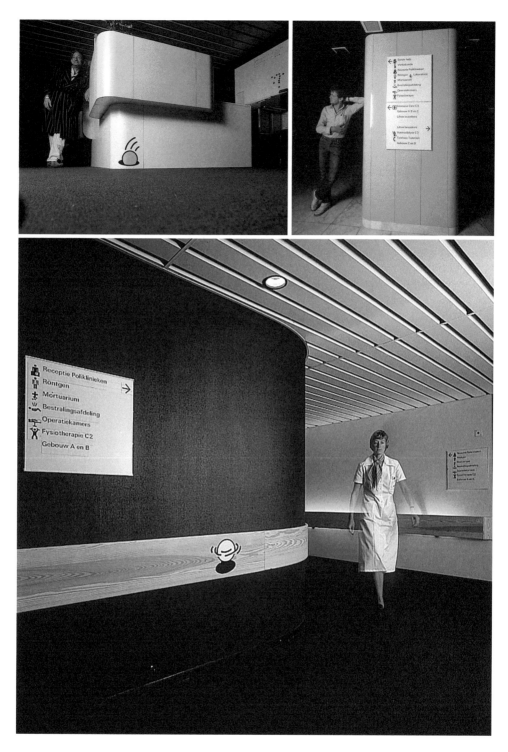

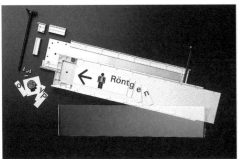

'CD-sign system' for signs indicating stations and departments within the hospital
(design: Rik Comello and Gert Dumbar)

from a variety of countries — Turkey, Portugal, Spain, Yugoslavia, Morocco — who could not be expected to be fluent in Dutch, but still should be able to 'read' the hospital environment in a language that could be understood by everyone. A detailed editorial structure was devised to warrant a seamless communication between hospital, patients, and visitors.

'Specialisms are the first line of communication with patients — they come to see an orthopaedic or an ophthalmologist or a paediatrician. So we designed a custom stationary for each unit within the hospital, with the pictogram for that specialism next to the general hospital logo, that also came in a variety of versions for the hospital's main sections. So the patient's correspondence with the hospital would prepare them for the visit also in visual ways; you could look for the same pictogram you saw in the letter and the wayfinding system would guide you to the right place.'[45]

One aspect of the wayfinding system, which was designed from scratch, were the signs indicating the location of each department or functional space. 'Hospitals are a dynamic environment; departments change or are expanded, new rooms are built for new disciplines, so we wanted wayfinding that could be easily adjusted by the hospital staff themselves. It's a kind

of old-fashioned letter box system, but with state-of-the art technology that was developed by the Koot brothers, a lettering firm in Rotterdam who liked the challenge of making something entirely new. They had a kitschy tile in their office, with a saying: "Business is like a wheelbarrow; if you don't push it, it doesn't move." That kind of typifies them.'[46] The 'CD Sign' system, as it was baptized using the initials of its inventors Rik Comello and Gert Dumbar, consisted of a modular set of injection moulded elements that could be magnetically fixed within a grid onto which pictograms and letters printed on magnetic rubber could be set, sealed with a removable Perspex cover. From today's perspective of digital screens that may be changed at a mouse click it looks like a rather elaborate Lego set, but the system of pictograms and signs was positively tested over a period of six months by hospital staff and foreign language visitors and analysed by psychology students from Utrecht University before being successfully implemented throughout the hospital. And it was favourably reviewed by trade magazine *Technische Gids voor Ziekenhuis en Instelling* (Technical Guide for Hospitals and Institutions) which, much to Gert's satisfaction, advocated its 'national acceptance'.[47] Michel was charged with the coordination of the implementation of the

45   Michel de Boer: conversation, 15 July 2020.
46   Ibid.
47   'Medische pictogrammen door duidelijkheid toepasbaar in elk ziekenhuis' (Medical pictograms applicable in every hospital thanks to clarity), in *Technische Gids voor*

Ziekenhuis en Instelling, 5 May 1980, pp. 171–173.
48   Michel de Boer: conversation, 15 July 2020.
49   Gert Dumbar quoted by Max Bruinsma: 'The Civilized Anarchy of Studio Dumbar', in *Graphis* vol. 52, no. 301, January/February 1996.

whole design, which marked the start of what would increasingly become a focus for him. 'Gert asked me to take care of that, so he obviously recognized my organizational side.'[48]

The intricate interplay between the design of various versions of the hospital's logo, the development of the pictogram set and the physical signs, and the visual markings of each individual floor were widely published and the Westeinde design won a D&AD Gold Award in 1982. All of this added to Studio Dumbar's growing international fame as a design firm that could handle complex communication challenges with a humanistic smile. To underline the humane aspect, Gert publicly announced that the pictogram set developed for the Westeinde hospital would be in the public domain, so every hospital in the world could use it for free. 'It's our UNESCO gesture', he would state later.[49]

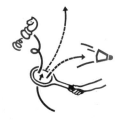

Ko Sliggers' sketch for Westeinde Hospital illustration

WHAT DESIGN IS NOT

Not long after the studio was internationally recognized for their heavily tested sets of pictograms, Gert published a glowing rant — against testing. Admittedly, his critique was directed at the members of his nemesis, the Dutch Advertising Society, during a lunch conference in Amsterdam and reviewed for the readership of advertising trade magazine *Adformatie*. In a lecture, written by Kitty, on 'Emotion as stylistic tool for visual communication', Gert admonishes his audience to quit 'pre-testing' designs and campaigns. 'Test results render the design or idea in cold, detached and often clichéd wordings. No idea survives such a treatment, unless it exclusively responds to market mechanisms.' He warns that pre-testing will 'test-out all emotion and intuition that designers invest in their work'.[50]

TEST RESULTS RENDER THE DESIGN OR IDEA IN COLD, DETACHED AND OFTEN CLICHÉD WORDINGS. NO IDEA SURVIVES SUCH A TREATMENT, UNLESS IT EXCLUSIVELY RESPONDS TO MARKET MECHANISMS

Gert Dumbar

It's a nice example of how Gert revels in provoking his audience, and of his perennial combat with advertising agencies and marketeers, whom he holds responsible for 'flattening' public communication and lacking the more profound design skills that are at the core of graphic design. In the case of testing, it is clear that Gert has high regard for seriously researching the legibility and user friendliness of designs for wayfinding or hard-core information design. If the public can't understand these well, the design has failed. But of course, design is about so much more than unambiguous information, or 'noise-free communication', to once again quote Crouwel. Gert often refers to a small 'music box' that should be there somewhere, even in the most serious designs. Since often

50   *Adformatie*, 27 November 1980, p. 33.

such playful additions, which season a design, are deemed superfluous in purely functional terms, they are the first to be 'tested-out.' In ranting against testing, Gert actually defends the cultural and communicative importance of 'music boxes'.

A year earlier, in a letter from July 1979,[51] Gert had elaborated on what he thought graphic design should not be. Answering a question from a student at AKI, the modernist art and design school in Enschede, in the East of the Netherlands, he states that he feels 'less attracted to a group of designers I would describe as overly balanced and with excessive self-control, the group that is emotionally at a very low ebb'. Reminiscent of his rant against airbrush, published in *Adformatie* in 1977, he criticizes designers who claim an almost 'scientific' attitude towards their trade and rely on technical means and research to achieve 'mechanical perfection'. 'Techniques,' Gert states, 'have a tendency to claim independence; ... Every technique therefore tends to erase the idea.' It is apparent that by 'technique' ('techniek' in Dutch) Gert mainly refers to modern technology and not to craft techniques and skills, which, 'if properly conceived, [are] almost everything'. But focusing on technology as primary means to approach a design and its intended recipients 'is doomed, and perhaps only useful to boring and coquettish professionals who need to mask their lack of imagination'.[52] Reading such lines, one cannot help thinking of Gert's colleagues at Total Design, most notably Wim Crouwel, who advocated a firm 'neutrality' of the designer vis-à-vis the commission, and whose bureau was, as we saw, an early adapter of computer technology. At the same time, his critique was directed at his favourite foe, marketing, which relies so heavily on 'techniques

of research in the field of "visual communication".'[53]

A THIN LINE BETWEEN WATER AND LAND

Conducting thorough research while adamantly defending room for play characterize the designs for one of Studio Dumbar's most steadfast clients since the early 1980s: the Dutch Ministry of Agriculture and Fishery. The first commission was the design of a permanent 'visitors centre' for the ministry's agricultural research department (DLO — Dienst Landbouwkundig Onderzoek) in Wageningen. The centre houses a variety of research institutes in areas such as environmental, bio-veterinary, plant, food safety and economic research. Although the institutes mainly focus on professional and scientific constituencies,

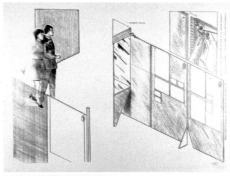
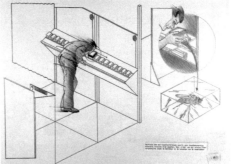

Sketches for DLO visitors centre, Wageningen, 1981 (design: Wim den Hertog)

51   Letter to Willem Boom, AKI student, July 6th, 1979, answering the student's question about 'a vision of my trade'. The text was later published in Willem Boom (ed.), *Het kader van grafisch ontwerpers*, Lecturis 10, Eindhoven 1980.
52   Ibid.
53   Ibid.
54   LNV House style manual, September 1997, p. 5.
55   Ibid.

the plan for the exhibition stresses the importance of also welcoming day trippers ('dagjesmensen'). The design consists of an open maze of panels with information and samples, drawn in lively colours with stylish accentuations.

HUMOUR AS COMMUNICATION STRATEGY HAS ALWAYS BEEN ONE OF GERT'S MAIN DESIGN PRINCIPLES

Around the same time, the ministry commissioned another exhibition, for the prestigious horticultural world exhibition 'Floriade', which was staged in Amsterdam in 1982 and attracted a total of 4.5 million visitors. The exhibition 'Energy saving in glass house horticulture' (Energiebesparing in de glastuinbouw), which Studio Dumbar designed for the ministry's contribution to the 'Floriade', combines in-depth agro-economic information with almost caricature-like illustrations of tomatoes and cucumbers, some of which were prominently staged as 3D objects in the exhibition space. 'Public education can be fun' seems to be the design philosophy. In the aftermath of the oil crisis of the 1970s, the need to save energy and focus on renewable resources is rendered in enticingly drawn diagrams and illustrations full of visual puns — humour as communication strategy has always been one of Gert's main design principles and it's used to good effect in this exhibition.

In the following years, the ministry tasked the Studio with designing a consistent house style that, in the words of Agricultural Minister Gerrit Braks, 'grants recognizability to the department across its full scope.'[54] The 1986 identity was, as usual in the Studio, developed through a

broad exploration of visual translations of 'atmospheric words that fit the ministry: flat, vast, land, water, landscape, space, control, ordering, organization, technology, research and its application.'[55] The gridded polder landscape, the contrast of land and water and the coastal line that separates the two — and protects the lower parts of the country from flooding— are tested for their iconic potential. In some

Cubic tomatoes for 'Floriade' exhibition, 1981 (design: Ruud van Empel)

163

of the sketches the solution surfaces in an abstracted rendering of Holland's characteristic coastal line, a curved line of dunes with a dotted string of islands to the north and the jagged outline of the Zeeland peninsulas to the south. Robert Nakata, who had tried out various approaches, takes a spin on Vincent van Baar's idea in a series of sketches. In other sketches Vincent further develops the outline into a finely detailed square vignette, in which the coastal line separates the sea's blue horizontal lines from the land's green verticals.

With that, he not only provided the ministry with a strong and highly recognizable logo, but also laid the foundation for a veritable visual language to be used for all the ministry's departments, with governance, supporting and executive branches, some of which

Sketches for 3D decorations,
'Floriade' exhibition, 1981
(design: Ruud van Empel)

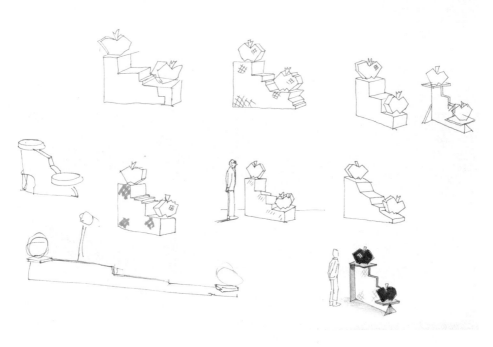

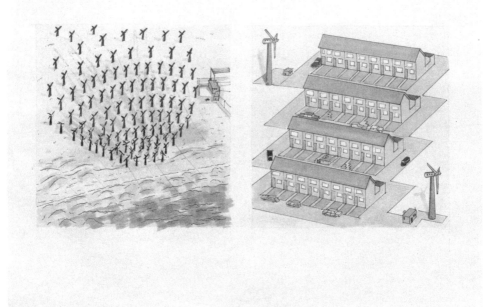

Sketches for 'Floriade' exhibition, 1981
Design: Vincent van Baar (top),
Ruud van Empel (bottom)

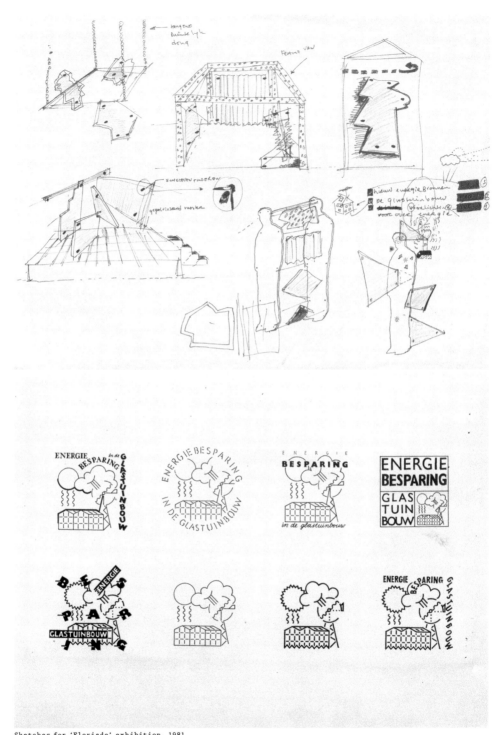

Sketches for 'Floriade' exhibition, 1981
Top: an early sketch for the exhibition
Bottom: sketches for exhibition vignette
by Vincent van Baar

'Floriade' exhibition, 1981
(design: Ruud van Empel and Gert Dumbar)

Robert Nakata's sketches for LNV
(Ministry of Agriculture and Fishery)
logo, with variations on Vincent van Baar's
'coastal line' idea

GERT DUMBAR | GENTLEMAN MAVERICK OF DUTCH DESIGN

Left: Various logos for Ministry of Agriculture departments, 1986
Top, right: Variations on 'coastal line' logo for Ministry of Agriculture (design: Vincent van Baar).
Vincent: 'I was often criticized for leaving out the fifth Waddeneiland, in the north, to make the drawing fit.
I'd always answer that the government had sold that island to the Germans to pay for this identity.'
Bottom, right: line sketches for Ministry of Agriculture logo (design: Bela Marady)

were more or less privatized semi-independent organizations. Together they formed, as the ministry stressed, 'one family'. With its tapered lines, the

THE HOUSE STYLE WAS UPDATED IN THE STUDIO SEVERAL TIMES IN THE FOLLOWING DECADES, ALWAYS FINDING NEW VARIANTS OF THE VISUAL LANGUAGE FORMULATED IN 1986

visual language of the logo is reminiscent of woodcutting or metal engraving and this provides a basic visual grammar that

in the following years was applied to an ever-expanding range of agricultural government institutes, from the wind-stirred tree of the National Forestry Administration (Staatsbosbeheer) to the leaf-eating caterpillar of the Department of Plant Pathology. The house style was updated by other designers in the Studio several times in the following decades, always finding new variants of the visual language formulated in 1986. Of course, the design was further developed for a plethora of applications, from letterheads, wayfinding, fleet lettering to invitation cards, brochures, flags and a steady flow of designs for special occasions such as Staatsbosbeheer's centennial in 1999.

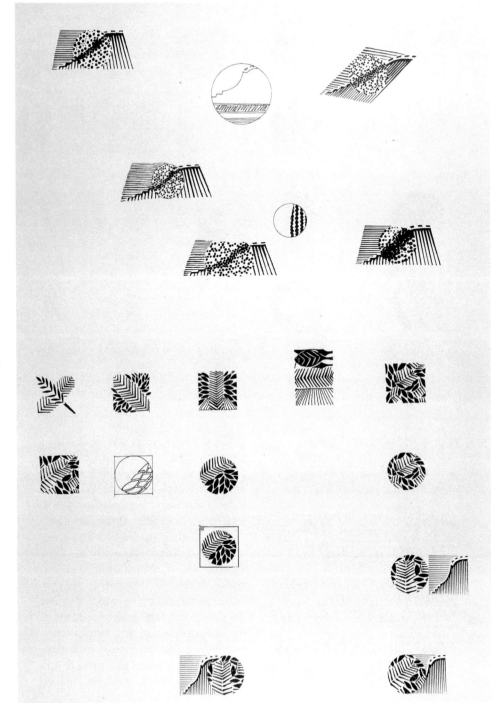

Various sketches for Ministry of Agriculture logos
(various designers)

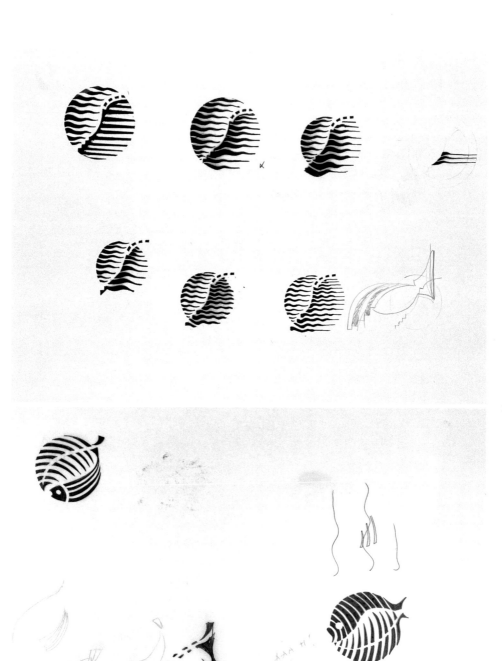

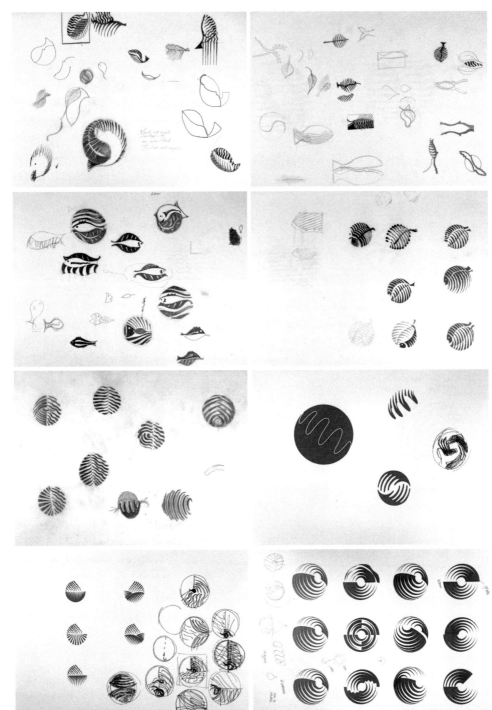

Various sketches for Ministry of Agriculture logos
(design: Vincent van Baar)

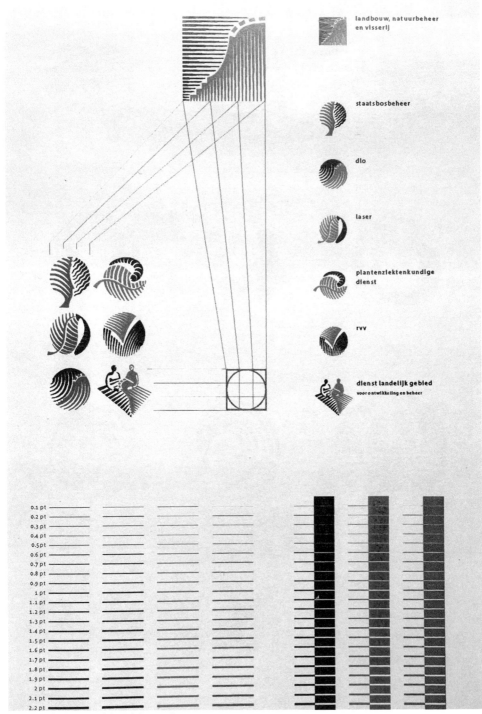

landbouw, natuurbeheer
en visserij

staatsbosbeheer

dlo

laser

plantenziektenkundige
dienst

rvv

dienst landelijk gebied
voor ontwikkeling en beheer

Page from design manual for Ministry of
Agriculture, with variants of the main
logo for various departments, 1994

GERT DUMBAR | GENTLEMAN MAVERICK OF DUTCH DESIGN

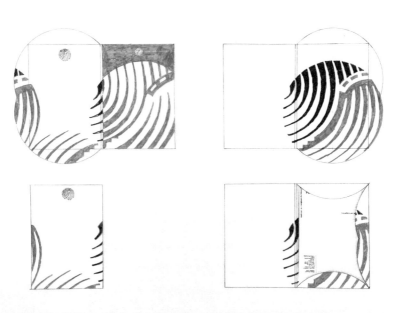

Sketches for Ministry of Agriculture logo, 1990
(design Ton van Bragt)

Various sketches for Ministry of Agriculture logos
(design: Vincent van Baar with Bela Marady)

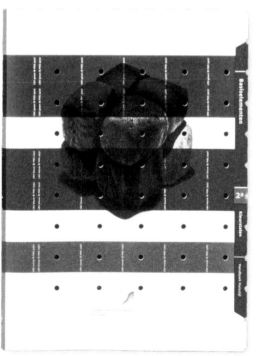

Pages from design manual for Ministry of Agriculture, 1997
(design: Maarten Jurriaanse)

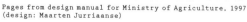

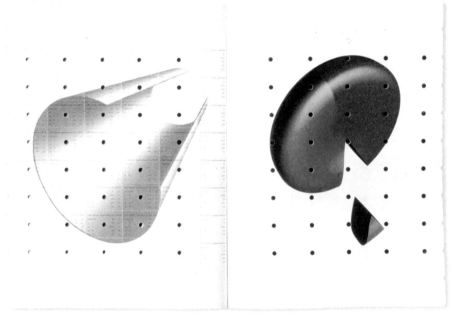

(design: Maarten Jurriaanse)

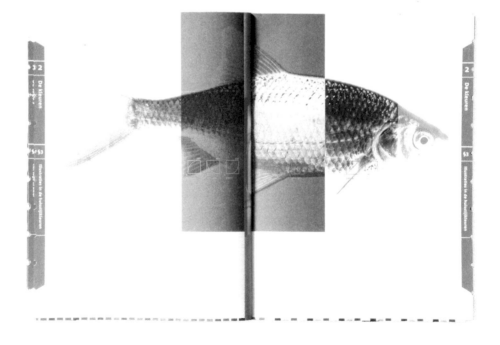

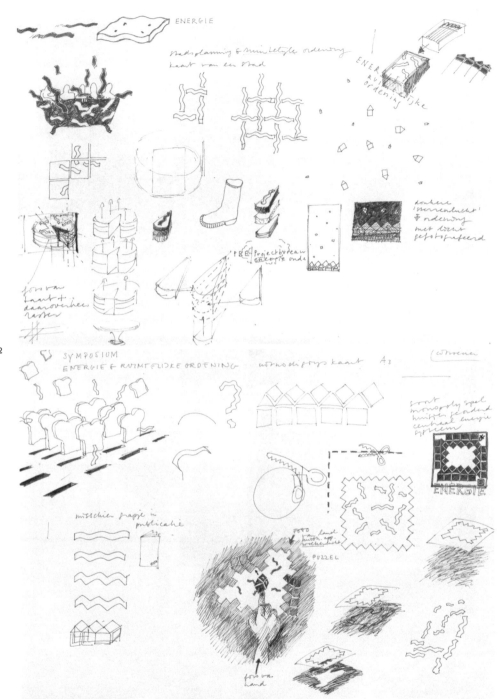

'Building for minimal energy use: the new building?', 1983
Sketches for a publication and poster (right page) for a
symposium on energy use in city planning, commissioned by the
government Energy Research Project Bureau, in collaboration
with writer Jan Noordhoek (poster design: Henk Hoebé)

Wim den Hertog (left), Ko Sliggers (middle)
and Michel de Boer (right) arranging the
figurine for Studio Dumbar's opening invite,
designed and jig-sawed by Gert, 1980

THE NEW ATMOSPHERE

On 2 May 1980, the new Studio Dumbar opened at Kanaalweg 34c in The Hague. The festive opening was announced in a folding card, with an invitation to raise a glass at the new studio and party on at Pulchri Studio, an art space in the city's centre. An elaborate design and photo session was staged for the invite. Several cut-out plywood figures of a man pouring wine and drinking it are photographed at Lex van Pieterson's studio and at the new work place, with countless polaroids testing it in various positions and against various backgrounds. The design, by Gert in collaboration with Lex, adds all kinds of details showing a talkative and at some point quite tipsy mood, which in the final print results in some funny and self-critical commentary, such as using the sign for showing the new place on the map also as a mark of inebriation by placing it on the figure's nose. On the inside, a small picture shows the now dysfunctional silhouette, unceremoniously dropped outside the studio. It seems to have subsided under the weight of too many bottles of fine wine. Apparently, they had a good time at the studio making the invite. But if you look at Gert's face in a few of the polaroids in which he is arranging the figure, together with his young daughter Laurien, one gets the impression he took the design quite seriously.

Such sincerity, however fun laden, paid off in the following years. Studio

185

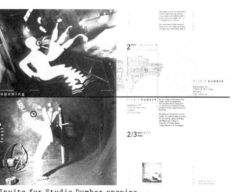

Invite for Studio Dumbar opening, backside of folding card, 1980

Dumbar is given the accolade of silver and gold awards at the British D&AD[56] — coveted recognition on one of the most prestigious platforms for communication

> *PURE VISUAL COMMUNICATION MIXED WITH HUMOUR AND SURPRISE IS A FAIR SUMMARY OF THE STYLE THAT TYPIFIES THE WORK OF THE DUTCH DESIGN HOUSE STUDIO DUMBAR*
>
> Design & Art Direction

design and advertising worldwide. In its September 1982 issue, D&AD's trade journal Design & Art Direction gave an explanation: 'Pure visual communication mixed with humour and surprise is a fair summary of the style that typifies the work of the Dutch design house Studio Dumbar.'[57] Gert is described as an 'infectiously ebullient personality' who adds his flavour to even such often boring publications like design manuals — an echo of the Polish praise some years earlier. The awarded manual for the new PTT corporate design 'abounds with photographs deliberately including things which are not supposed to be there, like a tiger suit and an old trestle table.'[58] In the article, Gert describes what he considers the core of his studio and his way of directing it, based on 'a philosophy of improvisation and intuition and spontaneous designing', deliberately keeping the studio small, to 'avoid the danger of hierarchies', with 'short lines of communications, small overhead and, most important, good contacts between the commissioner and the executive

186

Gert Dumbar and colleagues (and Gert's daughter Laurien) arranging the figurine for Studio Dumbar's opening invite, 1980

56   Gert went on to become D&AD's president in 1987/88.
57   Hillary McClaine, 'How to put the fun back into art', in *Design & Art Direction*, 10 September 1982, pp. 2–5.
58   Ibid. p. 2.

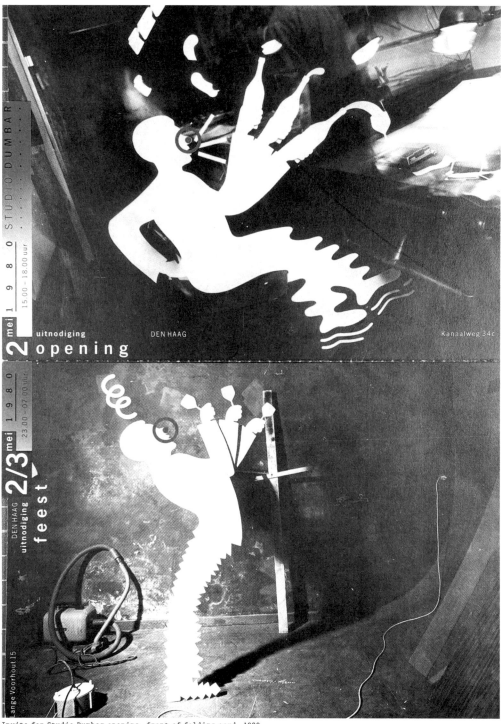

Invite for Studio Dumbar opening, front of folding card, 1980
(photo: Lex van Pieterson; design: Gert Dumbar)

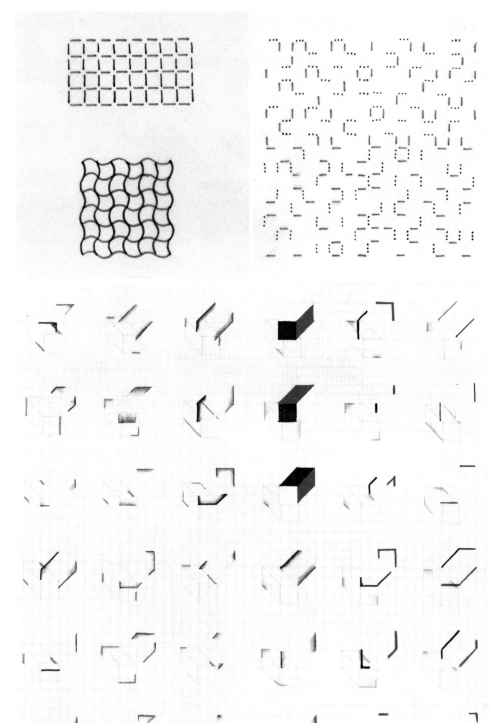

Sketches for '200 years USA-Netherlands relations'
identity, stamp and first-day cover, 1982. Modernist
structures in red, white, and blue turn into festive
confetti (design: Heleen Raue)

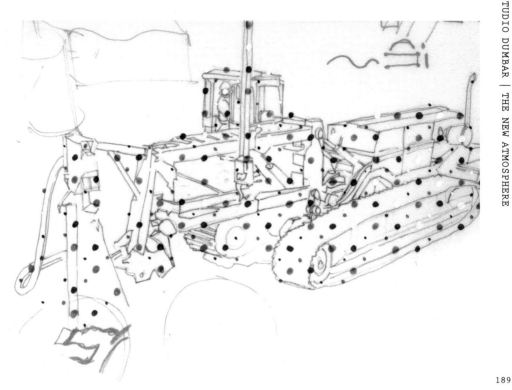

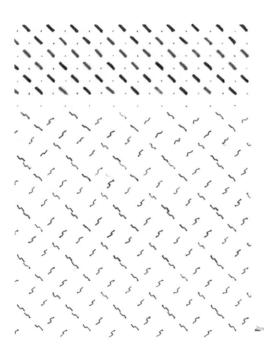

Nederland - U.S.A.
200 jaar erkenning
1782 20 IV 1982

EERSTE DAG VAN UITGIFTE·FIRST DAY OF ISSUE

Behorende bij de Amerikaanse
eerste-dag-kaart van 20 april 1982

'200 years USA-Netherlands relations' celebration poster,
1982 (design: Gert Dumbar; photo: Lex van Pieterson)

First-day covers for '200 years USA-Netherlands'
relations stamp
Top envelope: Netherlands (design: Heleen Raue)
Bottom envelope: USA (name American designer unknown)

designers.' Gert summarizes: 'By having to improvise very quickly, you create ... what I call the New Atmosphere. The success of the studio's formula is rooted in these innovative techniques: The why and why not ... concepts that change and are open-ended, this is very important to us. Often the process behind a project is more important than the final result.'[59]

One of the designs mentioned in the article with some amazement is the poster for the 'Dutch-American Bicentennial', commissioned by the Dutch Ministry of Foreign Affairs, which 'shows all the elements the brief demanded but also offended the establishment by including a crack in the wall, a table falling over and scratched paint.'[60] The poster's main image consists of an extravagant set photographed in Lex van Pieterson's studio, with a table that seems to topple over, pushed by the door opening behind it, a papier-mâché clad chair and paper-moulded figurines representing maps of the USA and the Netherlands staged as

cartoon figures, meeting and smiling. The small 'Dutch figure' seems to toss postcards of iconic Dutch products and artworks onto the rather shoddy table, all in all an image that could hardly be more removed from the solemn symbolics that usually accompanies diplomatic celebrations of long-standing friendship between countries and governments. The 'elements the brief demanded' are overprinted in plain sans-serif type in a rather dutiful manner, sharply contrasting the irreverent aesthetics of the background image. The crack in the wall may not have been the main cause for upsetting 'the establishment'. It remains unclear how the American side — establishment or not — would have appreciated the poster, which seems to present the 200 years of relations as a fairly one-sided affair, with its cliché summary of what Holland has offered the US and the world: windmills and Mondrians. Gert: 'The Ministry of Foreign Affairs

USA version of the '200 years USA-Netherlands' relations stamp, 1982
(design: Heleen Raue)

liked it — we made an entire house style for the event. Connected to it is the first instance ever of two countries issuing the same image on national postage stamps at the same time. It's a nice stamp, designed by Heleen Raue.'[61] While the stamp is the same, the first-day covers show the significant difference between the two cultures' dealing with historical events.

59   Ibid. p. 5.
60   Ibid. p. 4.
61   Gert Dumbar: conversation, 12 December 2023.

DE STIJL REVISITED

Playing with models, cut-outs, small papier-mâché sculptures and bric-à-brac of all sorts, was a design game Gert had already enjoyed during his time at RCA. At Tel Design he had used it in posters such as his now famous 1972 one for the Hague's Gemeentemuseum, in which he staged the iconic modernist painter Mondrian as a proud tinkerer in front of a tangled heap of papier-mâché blocks of various sizes in bleached primary colours.[62]

Gert Dumbar's 'very first sketch' for 'De Stijl' poster, 1982

Ten years later, Gert revisited the theme in a poster for a De Stijl exhibition in the Walker Art Center in Minneapolis, Minnesota, USA.[63] His 'very first sketch' depicts Stijl architect Gerrit Rietveld pondering a model of his famous 'Rietveld-Schröder house'. A few other sketches clearly hark back to the Mondrian poster from a decade earlier. Subsequent sketches enlarge the scene to a group portrait of De Stijl's artists and architects — Mondrian, Van Doesburg, Rietveld and others — hovering above an arrangement of rectangular shapes in various sizes as if floating in 'neoplastic space'. Gert explains: 'Neoplasticism was the term Mondrian and colleagues used for their art. It means that you can delineate any moment in space by horizontal and vertical lines or planes. I wanted to imitate that in a somewhat clumsy way — I can't cancel gravity.' Gert

decided to stage the photo for the poster in The Hague's municipal museum, home to a large De Stijl collection.

A series of polaroids by Gert shows how they placed a papier-mâché model of Rietveld at his neoplastic sideboard and leaning over his iconic red and blue chair. In one of the photos a young Michel is seen, sitting as stand-in for Rietveld. But the final composition took shape when they positioned Rietveld in front of a Van Doesburg painting, with a model of the Rietveld-Schröder house at his feet. Around him, coloured sticks are arranged on the parquet floor with its starkly contrasting diagonal pattern. 'It was a suggestion of roughly what they mean by "neoplasticity". So I set it up like that and then Lex (van Pieterson) could come the next day to make the final photo.'

The polaroids show how various angles were tested, all with Rietveld against the background of the Van Doesburg painting. Gert stresses the importance of that painting, because of its diagonal composition — a tinge of

Cut-out figures of De Stijl artists and architects; sketches for 'De Stijl' poster, 1982 (cutouts: Gert Dumbar)

irony referring to the dispute between Mondrian and Van Doesburg over the admissibility of diagonals in Neoplasticism — Mondrian had outlawed them. The poster's composition abounds with diagonals, from the painting to the slanted typography to the flooring's zig-zag, but the image still suggests the infinite space of

62   See p. 82.
63   'De Stijl: 1917-1931, Vision of Utopia', Walker Art Center, Minneapolis US, 31 January–28 March 1982.

Gert Dumbar, sketch for 'De Stijl' poster, 1982.
The figures represent central artists and architects
of the movement

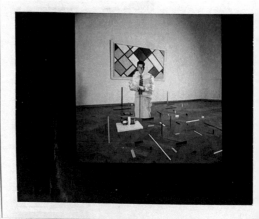
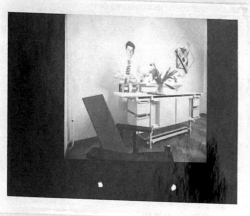

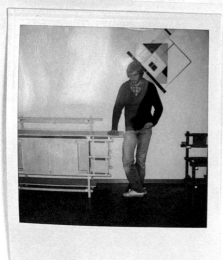
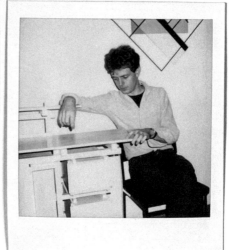

Polaroids taken by Gert, exploring various ways of staging the 'De Stijl' poster in The Hague's Gemeentemuseum, 1982. On the right: two shots of the final poster design

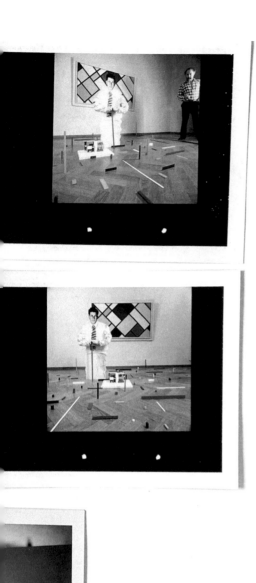

'De Stijl - Visions of utopia' poster, 1982
(design: Gert Dumbar)

Gert Dumbar, sketch for 'De Stijl'
poster, 1982

horizontals and verticals in the perspectival arrangement of the coloured sticks. 'I have overcome gravity, so to speak, to convey

Gert Dumbar posing with his 'Mondrian' poster and paraphernalia
Haagsche Courant, 10 March 1973, p.4

a message,' Gert concludes with a smile. Strikingly, he also overcame any qualms the museum might have had — all De Stijl props in the photo shoot are priceless originals from the museum's world-famous collection and the Rietveld maquette had to be separately insured before Gert could place it at the feet of the wobbly mock-up of its architect.

Not many of the papier-mâché figures have survived their purpose as props for a poster or other design. One of the very few is the figurine of Mondrian, which I encountered on my

Mondrian figurine and Gert Dumbar in his personal archive, 20 May 2020 (photos: Max Bruinsma)

first visit to Gert's own private archive almost half a century after it was used. Mondrian stands somewhat lost in a

corner gathering dust, and his jacket shows traces of unceremonious handling during transportation, but the fact that he's there testifies to his maker's fondness of the image. Apparently, a shared sentiment: the Mondrian poster became one of Gert's most reproduced designs.

Poster by anonymous student of Saint Martin's School of Art, London, announcing Gert's visit, 1981

CONFOUNDING THE RATIONALE

On a poster made by an anonymous student at Saint Martin's School of Art from early 1981, we see Gert Dumbar's face, looking confidently at his audience, pasted onto his famous Mondrian poster over the painter's features. His hand holds a small stack of NS time-table booklets (spoorboekjes) and on the table, in front of the original elements of the 'Mondrian' poster, are his 1974 UPU postage stamps, celebrating 100 years of the International Postage Union, the 'Dutch Design' poster and the related 'Piet Zwart' poster, and, for good measure, the original Mondrian poster at the bottom of the image. Some elements from other posters are displayed as well, with a papier-mâché 'capitalist' from the 1972 'arm:rijk' poster prominently at the right side of the table. The composition is framed by NS pictograms. The poster testifies to Gert's rising international fame — and to the fact that, at the time, it was still to a large extent based on work done at Tel. But his lecture at the illustrious London art school also shows he's a celebrity of a kind. And the selection of work on the lecture poster demonstrates that he's seen as a designer who combines rather contrasting sides of the spectrum of graphic design approaches, from the stern systematics of his pictograms to his tongue-in-cheek takes on cultural and social icons.

'I first saw Gert while I was studying graphic design at St Martins School of Art in the early 1980s. He had been invited to give a talk by our tutor and his fellow RCA student, Richard Doust. Until that point, nearly every talk we had been given by an external professional graphic designer had honestly been quite dull and un-inspirational. Graphic design at that time had become an industry with some companies employing hundreds of people. The work being produced in the UK seemed very conservative, unemotional and corporate.

At that time, I knew absolutely nothing about Gert or his work. So I sat there with my fellow students in a darkened projection room, preparing myself to be bored, with the possibility of even nodding off to the whirr of the slide projector. So I was very surprised when this man with longish hair and a Dutch accent started to project these dynamic images of integrated photography and typography onto the screen. I was mesmerized. He spoke about things with such humour and self-disrespect. It wasn't a graphic design lecture; it was pure entertainment. A true non-conformist that was somehow persuading his clients to go on these experimental journeys with him. I felt, at

last, I had met a designer with whom I shared a kindred radical spirit. The highlight of the talk was when Gert spotted what he described as possibly a pubic hair trapped in one of his 35mm slides and commented that it only improved the design layout.'

(Andy Altmann: Pub(l)ic speaking, posted 31 January 2021 on The Secret Bar)

This contrast not only appealed to students, but also to critics world-wide. As Hillary McClaine stated in her text in *Design & Art Direction*, quoted above, Gert shows us 'how to put the fun back into art'. In another newspaper publication of the period, a report on a design

THE ESSENCE OF GERT'S CREATIVE INTELLIGENCE AND OF HIS WAY OF EMBEDDING IT WITHIN THE PRACTICES OF THE STUDIO'S DESIGNERS: TO SYSTEMATICALLY UNHINGE THE RATIONALE OF A DESIGN

conference at York University, Canada, Gert is quoted as speaking of 'ways to relieve the oppressiveness of bureaucratic thinking'. The author (who consistently writes 'Dunbar') is positively amused by the 'graphic theme of a ball', bouncing across the floors of the Westeinde hospital where they 'appear in the funniest places — on doors, desk fronts, ceilings — and because they're so playful they humanize a cold environment and prevent stress'. She concludes: 'Dunbar made the only real contribution to the conference's theme of design process, showing all the pictograms as they evolved from concept to reality.'[64]

64 Adele Freedman, 'Design conference covers wide range' in *The Globe and Mail*, 19 January 1981.
65 Pierre Bayle, *Dictionnaire historique et critique*, 1697 (translation MB).
66 See pp. 201–211.

Gert's insistence on process — and the many anecdotes that come with it — often threatens to cloud our perception of the 'method in his madness'. But, as is clear from many remarks by Gert in interviews and conversations, his frequent references to open-ended processes as 'anarchy', 'improvisation', 'serendipity', and 'play' do amount to a methodical approach. Design, according to this method, is not a calculated, premeditated affair, but it does to a large extent rely on ratio or, more precisely, critical thinking. The kind of reasoning that French Enlightenment philosopher Pierre Bayle once described as the paradoxical cornerstone of scientific critique: 'Our reason serves only to confound everything, and make us doubt everything: it has no sooner built a work, than it shows you the means to ruin it.'[65] Gert, of course, would like to point to the last part of this thought, but what I find fascinating is that one needs a construction,

process — the exercise of constructing an argument, while deconstructing it in the very course of designing.

A perfect example of this might be the design of a decorative system around the ascetic logo of the Dutch PTT that was developed in 1989, after the recently privatized PTT had decided to continue with Studio Dumbar, without the collaboration with Total Design that had marked earlier stages of design for the PTT.[66] The client's briefing was very short: 'Make a new look based on the old logo and grid.' The aim was clearly to avoid having to adjust all outside lettering infrastructure such as light boxes. The logo itself, designed by Ton van Bragt, in three variants for departments or branches of the ptt (it was, already in the previous house style, consistently written in lower case Univers), was set within a strict grid that, visibly or invisibly, ruled everything around it.

Page from *PTT design manual*, 1989 (illustration: Berry van Gerwen)

before one can demolish it. A well-reasoned argument can be unhinged by the same reason that built it. It seems to me the essence of Gert's creative intelligence and of his way of embedding it within the practices of the Studio's designers; to systematically unhinge the rationale of a design. This, I think, is why he stresses

Based on this grid and the colours red, blue and green — the colours for the company's divisions — Studio Dumbar developed a grammar of lines and geometric shapes that enlivened the squareness of the system, indeed in many cases seemed to lead to it becoming undone. The decorative programme became

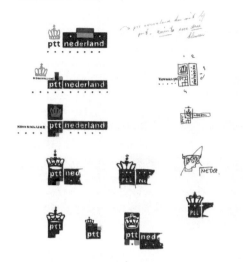

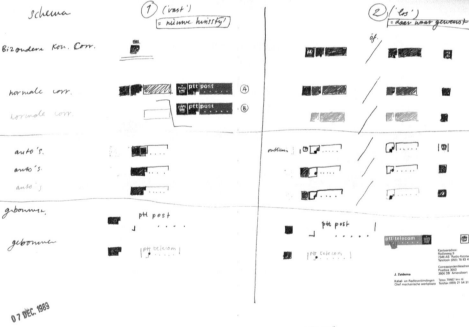

07 DEC. 1989

Sketches by Ton van Bragt for PTT identity.
Top left: Sketches for incorporating a crown after PTT
was awarded the 'Royal' predicate

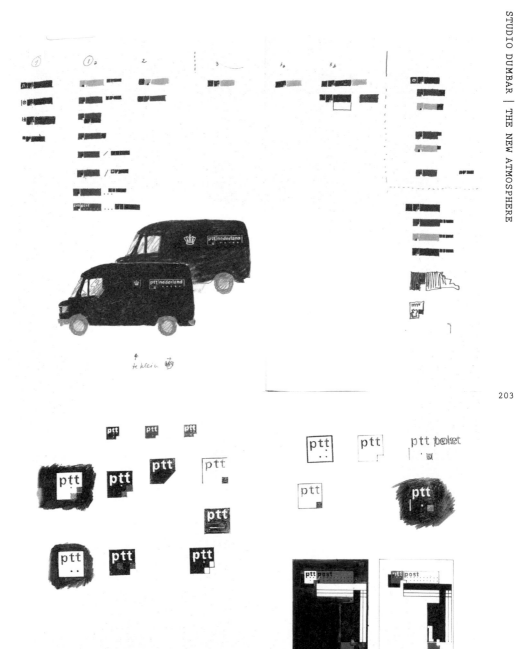

PTT design manual, 1989
(design: Eric Nuijten)

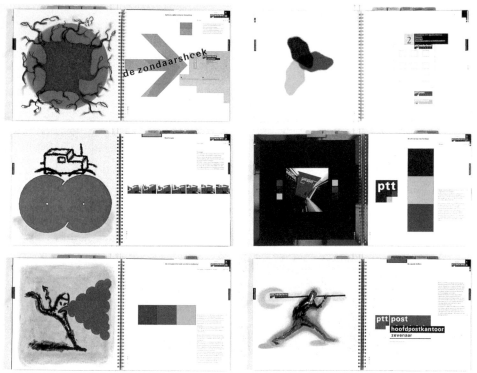

Pages from *PTT design manual*, 1989
Drawings by Berry van Gerwen
(design: Eric Nuijten, Hélène Bergmans,
Henri Ritzen and Ton van Bragt)

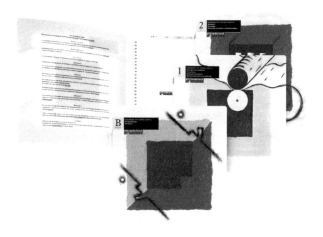

PTT design manual, 1989
(illustration: Berry van Gerwen;
design: Eric Nuijten, Hélène Bergmans,
Henri Ritzen and Ton van Bragt)

Top: PTT decoration on glass door
(design: Henri Ritzen)
Bottom: Gerard Hadders, *The Rise and Fall of
the House Style of the PTT*, art commission
for PTT's distribution centre, Terbregseweg,
Rotterdam, 1989 (detail)

a playground for other designers as well, who could use the elements and the rules of the grid in designing ornamentations for PTT products and buildings. Gert himself counts the way Gerard Hadders interpreted the system on the façade of a giant PTT distribution centre at the Terbregtseweg in Rotterdam among his favourites. Gerard judges Studio Dumbar's redesign of the PTT house style as 'one of the best graphic identities ever designed', and he enthusiastically embraced the 'graphic design adventure' to make his own 'episodic graphic novel' on the 100–metre long façade of the upper part of the building that housed its technical facilities. Titled 'The Rise and Fall of the House Style of the PTT', it could have been made as an illustration of the process of 'confounding a work's rationale' that I described above.

Starting with the logo's 'ptt' at the short side of the building, with 'post' around the corner, the logo gradually dissolves into a 'suprematist starry sky', including a light circle that mirrors the moon's actual

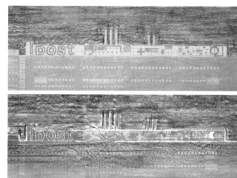

Sketch and overview of artwork on PTT's distribution centre, Terbregseweg, Rotterdam, 1989 (photo: Jannes Linders)

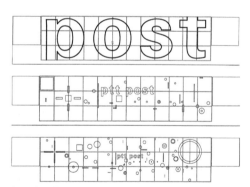

Gerard Hadders, designs for PTT's distribution centre, Terbregseweg, Rotterdam, 1989

position. 'It was a typical arts commission: no briefing whatsoever. So I came up with what you could call a suprematist explosion of the house style.'[67] Gerard was asked to renew the design several times, to align it with the changes in the company, which after its privatization changed its acronym from PTT to KPN to TPG to TNT within two decades as a result of mergers and takeovers.[68]

207

Reminiscent of Gert's mantra, one could call the decorative programme of the PTT house style a 'music box' that sounds a cheerfully quirky note over a minimal basso continuo, but I like to see it through Pierre Bayle's lens, as a system that demonstrates its own means to ruin it. Like another instance of a 'benevolent virus', the decorative scraps would scatter over anything ptt, from pens and coffee cups to boxes and printed matter to façades of multi-story buildings. In my own recollection, this seemingly marginal fall-out of a rather strict modernist design resulted in such a strongly branded aesthetic that one didn't need the brand name 'ptt' to recognize the PTT as the source or carrier of the message or object. In what feels like a reversal of Bayle's aphorism, the 'confusion' of the design's

---

67   Gerard Hadders: conversation, 17 November 2023.
68   A year after the privatization, in 1989, the PTT was awarded the predicate 'Royal' and changed its brand name to 'KPN' (Koninklijke PTT Nederland: Royal Dutch PTT). In 1998, the postal and telecommunication branches split and Post became 'TPG Post' (TNT Post Group, after

the acquisition of the Australian TNT express company) and in 2005 changed to 'TNT Post.' Hadders: 'You could say that the original artwork has gradually been defiled and degraded by the growing corporate needs of the client. But it was either that or destruction. In all, it sat there for more than fifteen years.' (email 17 November 2023).

Top: application of the corporate identity on the fleet of PTT
Bottom: PTT house style exhibition in Design Museum, London
(design: Gert Dumbar)

Gert Dumbar: 'The PTT crockery became the most stolen
tableware in the Netherlands!'

Left: PTT Telecom building (design: Gert Dumbar)
Right: PTT public telephone booth (design: Studio Dumbar)

rationale had become its very substance; the 'ruin' evoked the actual structure.

Throughout the 1980s such playful variation on an apparently rigorous system and grid became a kind of idiosyncratic

Rijksmuseum Amsterdam, exterior

feature of some of the more complex and elaborate designs Studio Dumbar produced. Another case in point is the house style developed since 1981 for the Rijksmuseum in Amsterdam, the most prestigious museum of the Netherlands. Home of world-famous paintings such as Rembrandt's *The Night Watch*, the museum is an internationally revered institution that radiates history and tradition, from its impressive nineteenth-century exterior down to the smallest sketches by the likes of Leonardo in the 'Prentenkabinet' (print cabinet). Studio Dumbar was chosen after Wim Crouwel had turned down the museum's invitation on the grounds that he didn't want Total Design to work for both of the country's leading museums — they already had the Stedelijk Museum, also in Amsterdam, as a client.

The gridded logo that was designed for the Rijksmuseum, with compartments that separate the two words of the name plus the location (Rijks / Museum / Amsterdam) already contains a minute 'music box' in the typography of 'MUSEUM' [69] — the two 'M's and 'U's in the word, set in Baskerville capitals, are mirrored, not only to mark a symmetry in the word itself, but also in reference to the symmetrical arcs in the famous

'bike underpass' that create a passageway through the building. The logo looks austere but it is used in remarkably flexible ways, treated rather as a grammar of possible inflections than as a static logotype. Thus, for instance, the double use of 'Rijks' for the Rijksprentencabinet (State Print Cabinet) at the Rijksmuseum is avoided by tilting the type of the logo and re-placing the name of the city.

Of course, the museum needed its own set of pictograms, which were designed in the abstract visual language of the international standards, but these were set on a background that played games with visitors' expectations and associations connected to the pictograms' mundane references. Details of the museum's revered stock of paintings were used as backgrounds, quasi forcing the viewer looking for the restrooms to ponder why the universally recognizable pictogram

Wayfinding sign in Rijksmuseum, Amsterdam (design: Gert Dumbar and Ruhi Hamid)

was placed over a seventeenth-century Dutch clouded sky? Some combinations could lead to an Aha-Erlebnis — I for one would have had difficulty in identifying the strange bended object held by a man in classic attire as a hearing aid, if

---

69   The logo was designed by Academy St. Joost's intern Hans Arnold.

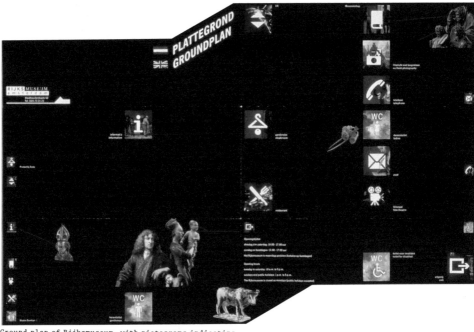

Ground plan of Rijksmuseum, with pictograms indicating
departments and services (design: Studio Dumbar)

213

the 'telephone' pictogram on top of the
fragment hadn't provided a clue. Angels
hovering behind the sign for the elevators,
the fork-and-knife pictogram embedded
in a detail of a copious still-life — if
Gert's idea of inserting a 'music box' into
even the most strictly informative designs
becomes crystal clear anywhere, it's here.
The fact that Studio Dumbar overcame the
opposition of some of the museum's staff
of art historians, who saw the decorative
use of details of artworks as sacrilege, is
another testimony to Gert's talents of
argumentation and seduction.

Likewise, the grid that organizes the
museum's wayfinding system (designed
in 1984) is used not only as an invisible
functional device, but is also exploited for
its decorative and referential potential as
well. The thin grid lines, printed in amber
colour on a dark-grey background, can be
read as a catalogue of a printer's variations

of dotted and dashed lines, or at some
points as an electronic circuit scheme.
The lines are occasionally interrupted by
the names of both famous and unknown
artists printed in tiny sizes — not omitting
several mentions of Studio Dumbar
and its designers — and throughout the
grid placement instructions are inserted:
measurements, proportions. The grid
contains its own design manual. From
a distance of a few meters — the usual
distance the viewer has to such signs —
all of this merges into a vague yellowish
checkered pattern that shimmers in the
background, anchoring the informative
text, gently breaking the blackness of the
background. The signs themselves clearly
hark back to the experience made with
Westeinde's 'CD-sign' wayfinding system: a
base onto which magnetic pictograms and
lines of text could be easily placed within
the grid, sealed by a removable Perspex cover.

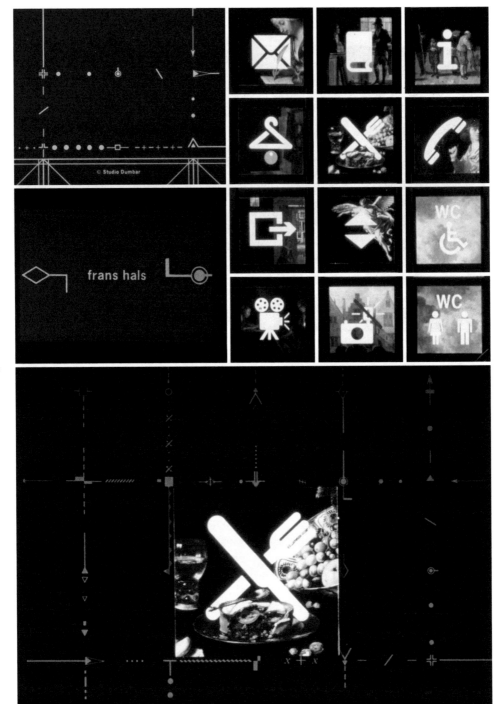

Pictograms for Rijksmuseum
(design: Gert Dumbar with Ruhi Hamid)
The Rijksmuseum identity was awarded several
individual D&AD pencils in 1990 and a gold pencil
for the signage programme as a whole in 1987

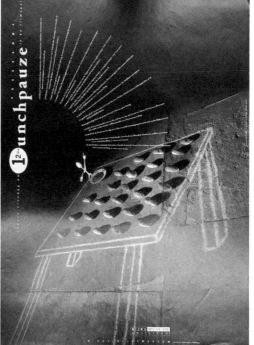

Top left: Rijksmuseum exhibition poster 'Kunst voor de beeldenstorm' (Art before iconoclasm) (design: Michel de Boer)
Top right: Rijksmuseum exhibition poster 'Prijst de Lijst' (Praise the Frame) on historic picture frames (design: Michel de Boer)
Bottom: Posters for lunch programme at the Rijksmuseum. Remarkably, Studio Dumbar reuses staged photography background images here, originally made for Zeebelt posters (see pp. 260, 263, 266-283)

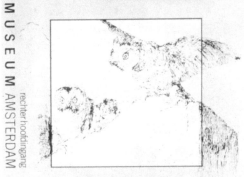

Posters for exhibitions at the
Rijksprentenkabinet (State Print Cabinet), 1981
(design: Ko Sliggers)

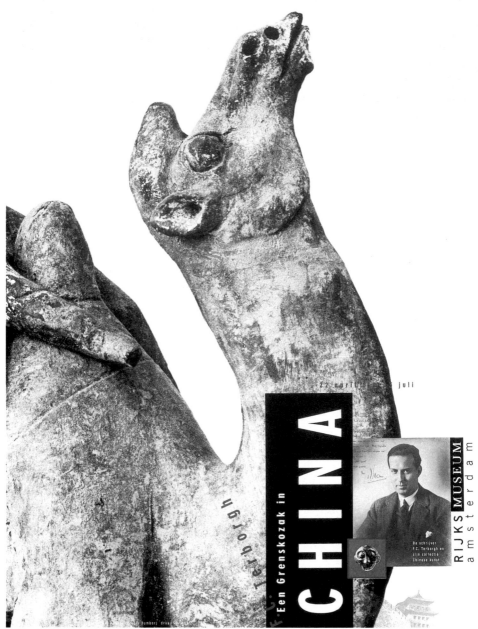

Rijksmuseum exhibition poster, 1989
(design: Robert Nakata)

WORKING APART TOGETHER
— THE ANWB SAGA

'Modernism with a smile',[70] is how Gert likes to call such play with well-ordered structural principles that anchor the design and, in a sense, regulate the room for improvisation without overtly dictating its rules. It's a characteristic that also pervades Studio Dumbar's persistent struggle with the grid for yet another complex commission, the new house style for ANWB, cultivating it into an inviting playing field rather than a strictly regulated school yard.

> *'MODERNISM WITH A SMILE', IS HOW GERT LIKES TO CALL SUCH PLAY WITH WELL-ORDERED STRUCTURAL PRINCIPLES THAT ANCHOR THE DESIGN AND, IN A SENSE, REGULATE THE ROOM FOR IMPROVISATION*

Arguably one of Studio Dumbar's less satisfying jobs, the new house style for the ANWB[71] was developed in a renewed collaboration with Total Design initiated by the client in late 1979. The Dutch motorist and tourist association ANWB was, and still is, deeply embedded in the country's governance of mobility —it had a monopoly on road side assistance and managed the Netherlands' official wayfinding system for roads and highways— while at the same time representing drivers' interests, lobbying for motorways, and advancing tourism. Its monthly magazine, *De Kampioen* (the champion) boasted the largest circulation of any magazine in the Netherlands,

Page from ANWB magazine *De Kampioen* showing the 65 degrees grid (design: Ko Sliggers)

simply because all ANWB members would automatically receive it. In the early 1980s, the ANWB counted around 2.5 million members, which earned the magazine the reputation of being the country's widest spread and least read periodical. Considering its huge reach, it is not surprising that the ANWB had its own well-developed design studio, called 'Bondspresentatie' (Association's Representation). It was responsible for its main magazine, but also for half a dozen offspring (such as the *Caravan Kampioen*, the *Motor Kampioen*, and so forth) and a vast output of informational brochures, advertising campaigns, wayfinding designs, and a plethora of forms.

In the fall of 1978, vice-director Backer of the ANWB thought it would be a good idea to have a specially designed vignette celebrating the organization's centenary in 1983. In response, the in-house studio proposed a redesign of the association's entire house style — in fact, to develop a house style to begin with. As with many large and traditional organizations, the ANWB sported an abundance of logos, vignettes and more or less heraldic signs, with no apparent (typo)graphic consistency. Moreover, the various departments of the organization

218

70 See pp. 86, 88.
71 Few people today still know that the familiar acronym ANWB stands for 'Algemene Nederlandse Wielrijders Bond' (General Dutch Cyclists' Association). Founded in 1883 as an organization to promote cycling and advocate cycling lanes, it evolved into a general interest association for all things rolling and moving, from cars to horse riders

to hikers. Since 1905 the association officially calls itself 'Tourist Association'.
72 See: 'ANWB huisstijl, meer dan stippels en ballen', in *Klapband*, #17, nr 5, 1987. The ANWB's in-house periodical devoted an entire issue to the new house style on the occasion of the introduction of the organization's design manual.
73 See p. 103.

operated rather independently, each maintaining their own styles. The ANWB studio organized a seminar on house styles, in which Siep Wijsenbeek (the design coordinator of the NS) and Ootje Oxenaar (head of PTT's DEV, Aesthetic Design Department) delivered 'illustrated lectures'.[72] It may be a coincidence, but both speakers were steadfast clients of Total Design, Tel Design and Studio Dumbar and good friends of Gert. Oxenaar's predecessor Hein van Haaren had been instrumental in bringing together TD and Dumbar in the earlier collaboration on the PTT.[73] So in hindsight it is not surprising that they advised ANWB to outsource the large and complex commission to develop a new corporate identity for one of the Netherlands best known public organizations to these two agencies.

It was clear from the start that the ANWB expected a similar synergy as was perceived with the collaboration between the two leading design studios in the development of PTT's house style, just a few years earlier. And it was also clear what was expected from Studio Dumbar. Vice-director Jan Barkhof wrote to TD's Loek van der Sande: 'We assume that in distributing tasks [for the design development] particular consideration will be given to our desired creative input on the part of Studio Dumbar.'[74]

It is unclear what exactly he meant by that, but quite obviously, the collaboration —with TD as main contractor— did not go smoothly from the get-go. Rumour has it that Gert characterized the collaboration as 'they'll water down the wine while we'll add wine to the water'. Although TD and Studio Dumbar focused on various parts of the commission separately, they both sketched designs for the association's new logo and

Page from ANWB magazine *De Kampioen* showing the 65 degrees grid (design: Ko Sliggers)

74   Loek van der Sande, quoted in Meera Dercksen and Frederike Huygen, 'TD en Studio Dumbar werken samen voor de ANWB, in Designhistory.nl, online, October 2020. www.designhistory.nl/2020/td-en-studio-dumbar-werken-samen-voor-de-anwb/ (Dutch only. Accessed 26 January 2022).

general points of departure for the house style. In Gert's recollection, that went well in general, but Michel, who coordinated Studio Dumbar's part, noticed differences of opinion and clashing characters right from the start: 'At Total Design, they worked with teams. We didn't, we just told everybody to come up with ideas and then went to TD and laid it all out on the floor. Gert likes to get people on their knees… That didn't work well at TD, especially with the team Wim tasked with the commission, that of Ben Bos. Now, if anyone is Gert's total opposite, it's Ben. So that didn't work at all.'[75] Initially, TD was represented by partner and co-director Loek van der Sande, who acted as 'traffic manager' and coordinator.[76] From the minutes of countless management meetings during the early 1980s in Studio Dumbar's archive, it seems Van der Sande's prime role was to stipulate that the cumbersome and time-consuming consultations between the designers and the client — and between the client's various departments — were also costly, and insufficiently budgeted.

The main obstacle in the communication with the ANWB, it seems, was the deep cultural chasm between the designers and their client. Even more than the PTT and the NS, the ANWB was a deeply hierarchical and bureaucratic institution, with a highly complex and layered management structure and several rather independent departments, of which the Wegenwacht (the ANWB's road side assistance branch and the most visible part of the association) was perceived as a separate kingdom. (Michel: 'That was off-limits for us. We tried, but didn't get access — they wouldn't let us change a dash!'). Matching bureaucratic schemes dominated the design process — a project planning from January 1982 lists no less than twenty-nine design phases and comes with an elaborate diagram of department heads, activity managers, steering group members, stakeholders and decision makers, not forgetting 'potential third-party supporters'.

But the collaboration between TD and Studio Dumbar was also bumpy. Michel recalls: 'At some point Wim Crouwel took Ben Bos off the job, because it was clear that that just didn't work. So, we got a new guy, Paul Mijksenaar. Now Paul is a wayfinding expert, but not an identity authority. I'll never forget that he came in one day and started to lecture us on the value of the ANWB brand in relation to society and design. And Gert got really angry, and began to bellow… Paul continued to state that he'd systematically researched the logo and presented a design as the one and only possibility. Well, killing for creativity!' Also Ko Sliggers, who worked with Ben Bos on the redesign of ANWB's *Kampioen*, recalls the incident: 'Paul started elaborating on type and brands and Gert completely exploded: "Do you think we're art school students or something?!"'

In the archive I found a letter in which Gert apologizes to Paul: '… I am sincerely sorry for stepping out of line. Disparities in professional principles and practices are in my view healthy for a dynamic and diverse trade … and therefore I'd appreciate if you'd come and visit us in The Hague and expound your vision and ideas on our profession.'[77] Paul replies, still irritated: 'I have accepted your apologies. … That does not mean, however, that I have given up my strong distrust with respect to your ideas. … That morning, I heard a bombastic story, replete with quasi-romanticism, dogmatic design principles, trendy 'hook-ups' and intolerance. … I don't doubt your sincerity, I'm merely afraid that losing sight of 'professional' warranties for usable designs for clients, will hamper

75 Michel de Boer: conversation, 15 July 2020.
76 Meera Dercksen and Frederike Huygen, op. cit.
77 Gert Dumbar, letter to Paul Mijksenaar, 7 April 1981.
78 Paul Mijksenaar, letter to Gert Dumbar, 17 April 1981.
79 Michel de Boer: conversation, 15 July 2020.

our profession's credibility'.[78] Still, Paul agreed to visit the Studio, hoping he won't be kaltgestellt after his first sentence. In hindsight, Gert downplays the incident: 'Paul gave a spirited analysis of how to make an identity for an institution like the ANWB. I was a bit irritated because, obviously, we had already done that way before he started to lecture us on it.'

'So that didn't go well either,' Michel continues. 'Thus, also Paul was taken off the assignment. Then came Anthon Beeke, who, like Paul, had just recently been hired at Total Design. He was the complete opposite. Gert, Anthon, and I had great

Sketch for ANWB logo, 1980

fun, but it didn't produce the kind of energy you need for a job like this — you need a plus and minus pole to produce electricity; with Anthon we were all just plusses. So Wim [Crouwel] again took control, this time himself, with Henk Hoebé as assistant. That worked better — now you had plus and minus poles. Mind you, ANWB never knew anything about all this.'[79]

In the course of 1980, the fundamental decision was made to stick to the typographic logo that had been in use for a while. The chosen Univers capitals

were slanted a bit more than the regular italic and, on Wim Crouwel's suggestion, were given a background striping derived

Sketch for ANWB logo, 1980

from the ubiquitous ANWB road signs on poles that were all marked by a blue diagonal 'banderol'. The slant inspired Gert to suggest a grid with 65° diagonals, which became the foundation of all ANWB designs. In contrast to TD, Studio Dumbar was not used to working with grids and in the studio's sketches the constant desire to 'confound' the grid is everywhere, albeit with endless variations and perversions of the 65° slant.

Another attempt to 'soften' the gridded structure was to introduce illustrations as a slightly anarchic, humorous element, and the use of fading colours and shadings. All to liven up the underlying construction — make it more friendly. The new house style was gradually implemented — the basic elements were introduced in the Spring of 1982, but it took a couple of years before everything was laid down in a design manual, which was presented in 1986. Meanwhile, the new slanted logo had been applied in all the very varied expressions of the large

Sketches for ANWB logo and illustrations, 1980
(sketches: Studio Dumbar)

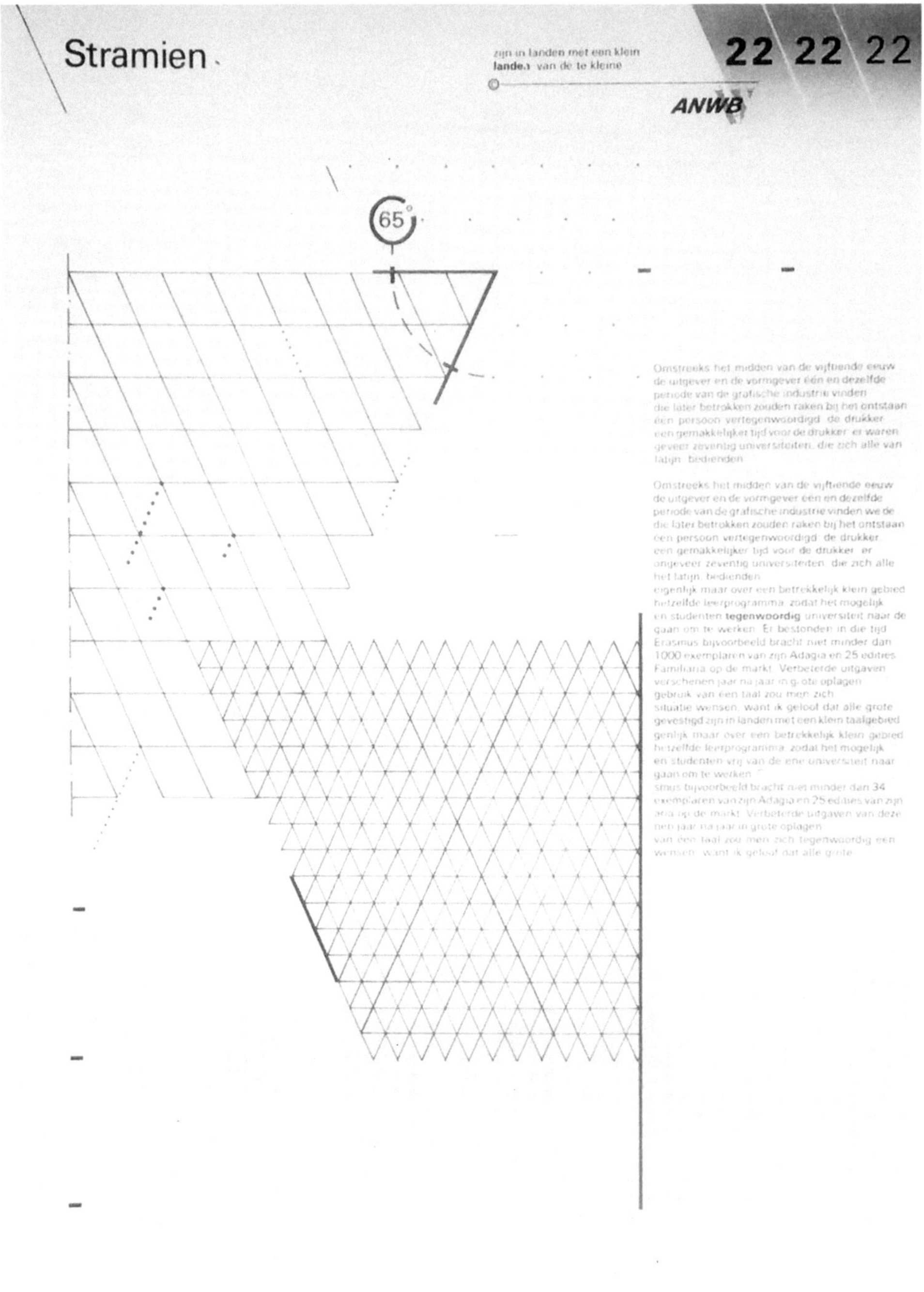

Page from *ANWB design manual*, 1987
(design: Ko Sliggers)

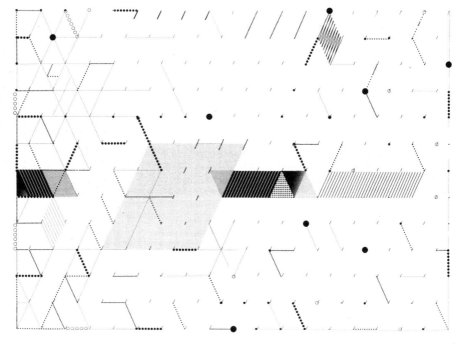

Grid design for house style ANWB
(design: Ko Sliggers)

Top: *ANWB design manual*, 1986
Bottom: pages from *ANWB design manual*
and ANWB wrapping paper

organization. As intern, the young Henri Ritzen worked on endorsement shields that would, for instance, state that a hotel or supplier was recommended by ANWB. 'I worked on that for an entire month, but had actually no idea what to do with it,' Henri recalls. 'But then Gert came along and said, indicating a break along a diagonal in the rectangular shield, "maybe do it this way". And that was the solution. But he first let you fiddle for weeks.'[80]

The *Kampioen* magazine was also redesigned. The first issues were done mainly by Ko Sliggers. 'I designed the basic lay-out and ANWB agreed that we'd make the first few issues. I worked on that with Ben, but also with Gert, who had quite outspoken ideas about whom he wanted to collaborate with for illustrations. Guys who could make clay-cars and fancy puppets. There was also a comic strip about someone having problems on the road. In the end it was handed over to the ANWB studio ...'[81]

In Ben Bos' words, that was done 'rather bluntly'.[82] To which vice-director Barkhof responded that 'the first issues in the new style gave abundant reason to hand over the lay-out to the in-house team starting with number 4'.[83] His colleague Van Iersel (head of the communication department) summarized that 'a clear formula that is supported by all parties is missing, that there is no planning over several issues, no proper collaboration and consultation between the disciplines involved and a conflict of interests between "careful creation" and "fast production".'[84] The directors announced they would 'further evaluate the issues at hand'. Meanwhile work on the design manual continued. But the board decided that the introduction of the new house style in all departments and sections of the large association needed more time than planned — and that further implementation

would be done by the in-house design department. So Barkhof proposed to end the collaboration with Total Design and Studio Dumbar.[85] Apparently, Gert and Loek succeeded in making the board change their mind, and in 1987 the design manual was finally presented in a special issue of the ANWB's in-house magazine.[86] It's an extraordinary object with a thick metal cover and ring-binding, the kind of sturdy manuals that one finds in factory

ANWB shawl and envelope

production places where the book can survive rough treatment, heavy impact, and other hazards of the workplace. Michel had found out such heavy-duty books were produced by a firm in Sweden and he was adamant to obtain them. Michel's father worked at KLM, the Dutch national airlines, so Michel could fly anywhere cheaply. He went to Sweden to have a look and ordered them.

The ANWB's new identity and its manual's design with its heavy cover and die-cut tabs was awarded 'best house style' by the Dutch Art Director's Club the next year. Public appreciation of the ANWB's new look was less favourable

80   Henri Ritzen: Zoom conversation with the author, 17 May 2023.
81   Ko Sliggers: Zoom conversation, 30 March 2021.
82   Ben Bos, quoted in minutes of a meeting of the 'stearing group "development ANWB house style"', 20 April 1982.
83   Ibid.
84   Ibid.
85   Letter J. Barkhof to Total Design, 27 August 1982. Evidently, the letter was c.c.-ed to Studio Dumbar.
86   *Klapband* no. 5, ANWB Huisstijl special, August 1987.

Dear Andrzej,

although we've
never met, I'm
looking forward
to do this
project.
This fax shows
the "mouse-hole
idea" integrated
in the earlier
suggestion.

Till next

HENRI RITZEN

228   Sketches by Henri Ritzen for a book on Polish
      illustrator Andrzei Dudzinski, 1983

SKETCHES FOR
DUDZINSKI BOOK

1983

The 'trawling suitcase' is Henri's take on
Dudzinski, 'who was constantly on the road, but never
really separated from his Polish roots. That's why
part of the suitcase, with the 'P' of Poland, seems to
stay put, while the rest stretches out following the
traveller'. He seems to walk towards a 'mouse hole',
symbolizing an unattainable home.

The sketches were made for a dummy of the book
to be presented at Frankfurt Book Fair. Based on his

own drawings, Henri made a cardboard model of the
suitcase, photographed at Lex van Pieterson' studio.
On the final cover design, Dudzinski would answer
with his version of the drawing, while the lower part
of the cover was reserved for Henri and Lex's photo.
The dummy did not, however, attract enough interest at
the Book Fair and the book was not realized.

GERT DUMBAR | GENTLEMAN MAVERICK OF DUTCH DESIGN

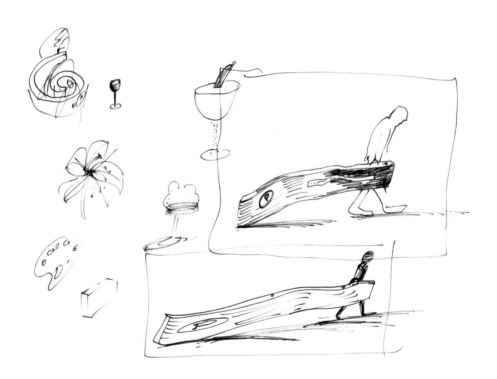

Sketches for Dudzinski book
(design: Henri Ritzen)

BAYER MEDICINE BOOKLETS

1983

Small booklets, inserted in the packaging of pharmaceuticals, explained the workings of the medicine in simple language, accompanied by humorous illustrations

Gert Dumbar: 'At Bayer, the informational leaflet accompanying the medicine was sacrosanct. It was not to be tinkered with and it was legally sealed.

So, to want to change that was totally weird for the Germans. I was seen as 'that artist Dumbar' who came to Düsseldorf with his strange ideas. It took a lot of talking before they agreed to add a little booklet to the medicine packaging, which in itself was pretty standard, like all medicine packaging in Europe. But the booklets were special — a friendly gesture, compassionately asking: "How are you?" The texts were written by a female doctor. It was commissioned as a brand loyalty device — and it boosted sales!'

Bayer medicine booklets, 1983
(design: Gert Dumbar and Armand Mevis)

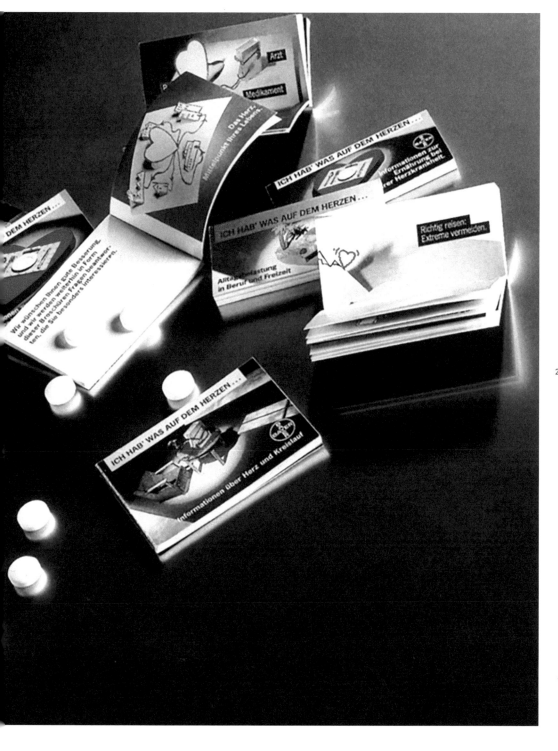

than that of the designers' peers. Especially the *Kampioen* was severely criticized for what was perceived as its chaotic lay-out and sloppy typography. In one of the Netherlands' largest newspapers, *de Volkskrant*, critic Hub. Hubben — the grumpy Dutch doyen of traditional typography — slashes the *Kampioen*'s design as 'pin ball machine typography' and 'typography for Neanderthals' and wonders 'how on earth anyone dares to shovel such junk to the printers?'[87]

> THE KAMPIOEN WAS SEVERELY CRITICIZED FOR WHAT WAS PERCEIVED AS ITS CHAOTIC LAYOUT AND SLOPPY TYPOGRAPHY. CRITIC HUBBEN SLASHES THE KAMPIOEN'S DESIGN AS 'PIN BALL MACHINE TYPOGRAPHY' AND 'TYPOGRAPHY FOR NEANDERTHALS'

In a remarkable column, the main designer at ANWB's in-house studio, Hans Martens, looks back on the new house style's saga and stresses the need to protect and maintain it: 'The introduction of the house style started in 1981 and to this day threatens to be crushed between a structural vision and department interests.'[88] He criticizes his superiors for not having a clear vision on what a corporate identity is and what it entails, and states that the house style as presented by TD and Studio Dumbar was accepted on dubious grounds: 'Like when you just closed the door and are left with a brand new vacuum cleaner you didn't want, because you couldn't resist the

shrewd salesman who went and had a nice diner off your money.'[89] Nevertheless, he wholeheartedly supports the new house style and warns that it needs a watchful eye to guard it, 'which today is still sleeping'.[90]

'It was a large commission,' concludes Michel, 'so you wouldn't just give it up, even if at times the collaboration with Total Design was quite explosive. But there was also mutual respect, and in the end, we were in it together and needed to solve it.'[91]

SKETCHING AS STRATEGY

A large commission indeed, but also one of many jobs for Studio Dumbar, which steadily grew in its first years. New designers were contracted and Kitty, who was appointed office manager in 1979, insisted that what she saw as imbalance in the studio's early staffing — a few freelancers, a lot of interns — was redressed. She realized that the way the studio had been organized until then amounted to a considerable risk, both concerning insurance and taxes: 'I said: no more than two interns per semester, and the rest all just go on the payroll.'[92] Although she had no background in accounting, she more or less invented her own way of administering a company, writing pitches, quotes, managing correspondence and sending invoices, with the help of a retired accountant for the financial bookkeeping. One thing that was regularly discussed was Gert's seeming neglect of time invested in projects. 'Gert would give endless space to designers to sketch on things,' says Kitty, 'so I became the one to insist on keeping hourly records, which was not always taken seriously — "there's Kit again with her time sheets". In the end, of course, our quotations were always leading. So you'll understand salaries could not be top, for

87   Hub. Hubben, 'Typografie van de flipperkast', in *de Volkskrant*, 22 September 1984.

88   Hans Martens, 'De problematiek van het vinden van de weg' (The problem of finding one's way). Typed manuscript in Studio Dumbar archive, marked 30 September 1985. It is unclear whether this text was published anywhere.

89   Ibid.

90   Ibid.

91   Michel de Boer: conversation, 15 July 2020.

92   Kitty de Jong: conversation, 26 March 2021.

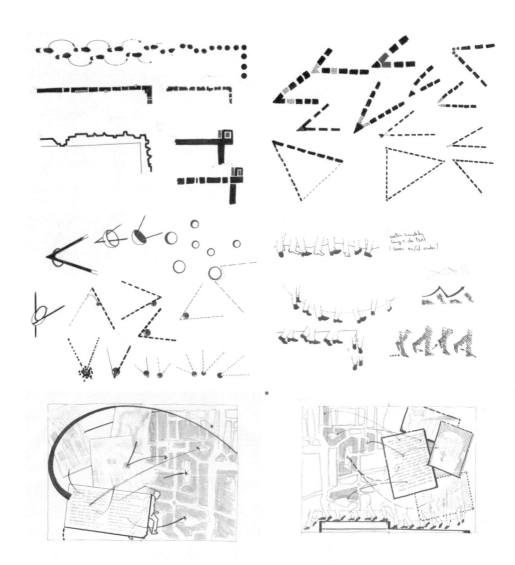

Sketches for architectural walks in and around
The Hague, Dr. H.P. Berlagestichting, 1981

anyone. Design was always done without time restrictions.'[93] Gert concurs from his perspective: 'You can't make anything with billable hours. Then it all becomes standard and baggy.'[94] 'We produced a lot,' Michel adds. 'Look, coming up with ideas in our view involved making a lot of sketches and having the guts to throw away a lot. That was our way. As creative directors, we stimulated the sketching process, but we were also responsible for making choices.'[95]

The relaxed stance on dealing with time at Studio Dumbar is evident from the sometimes gargantuan piles of sketches in the archive, also for less prominent jobs, such as a series of eight 'architectural city walks' in and around The Hague. The Studio's designers must have spent days

93   Ibid.
94   Gert Dumbar: conversation, 19 January 2023.
95   Michel de Boer: conversation, 15 July 2020.

Architectural walks The Hague, 1981
Designers who worked on the series are Ko Sliggers,
Ed Bax, Heleen Raue and photographer Arno Bauman

in researching and sketching an enormous variety of ways to depict walking in the abstract visual language of maps. Dozens of sheets show endless variations of footsteps, arrows, dashed route trajectories and orientation compasses.[96]

> *WE DEDICATED AN ENORMOUS AMOUNT OF TIME TO SNIFFING AT SOMETHING BEFORE THERE WAS A FINAL RESULT. WE DON'T GO TO THE CLIENT UNTIL WE HAVE SOMETHING BEAUTIFUL*
>
> Gert Dumbar

The guides became nifty folders, with a poster-size map on one side and information on the architectural highlights along the route on the other. 'We dedicated an enormous amount of time to sniffing at something before there was a final result,' Gert says. 'That was the challenging thing in the Studio — and I allowed time for that. The idea was: we don't go to the client until we have something beautiful. Clients liked that too, that we showed all those experiments — then they saw that work had been done. All those dull bureaucrats loved seeing how we had come up with a proposal.

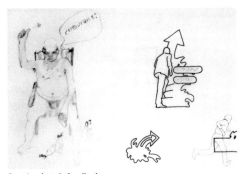

Gert's sketch for Kurhaus wayfinding, 1978

This way, they could suddenly imagine the function of a graphic designer.'[97]

Another early commission that triggered endless sketching was a wayfinding design for the Kurhaus, a hotel, restaurant, and casino at the popular Scheveningen beach, for which elaborate signage and construction designs were made in 1978. As in many of such sketches, a few of them hold rather churlish interpretations of the commission in playfully irreverent takes on the subject. In one of them, Gert drew a grumpy sunbather on the beach, looking slightly irritated because a passer-by disturbs his

Kurhaus wayfinding, 1978
(design: Gert Dumbar)

enjoying his fourth Grolsch beer by asking directions to the restaurant. The sunbather absentmindedly thumbs in the desired direction. The client will probably not have seen this caricature of wayfinding, but rather the more serious sketches — one of which is on the same page.[98]

Small jokes often start off the design process. In the first sketches for Paul Steenhuisen's stationary, in 1981, design intern Nicole van Schouwenburg freely associates on the client's name (literally: 'stone houses'), location (in The Hague, near the sea) and profession (copy writer) and notes: 'The waves ran high as houses, but Paul bravely stood his ground.' The desired impact of Steenhuisen's writing

96   Architectuurwandelingen Den Haag, client: Dr. H.P. Berlage Stichting, 1978–'82.
97   Gert Dumbar: conversation, 19 January 2023.
98   Kurhaus wayfinding, 1978–'79.

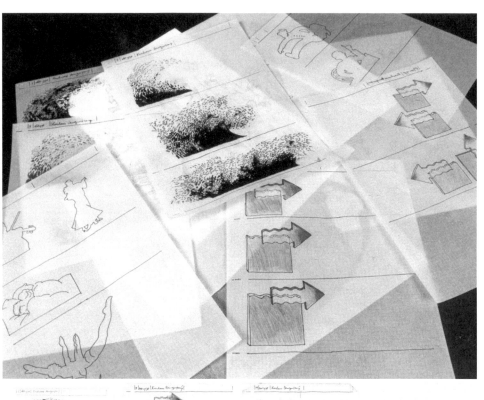

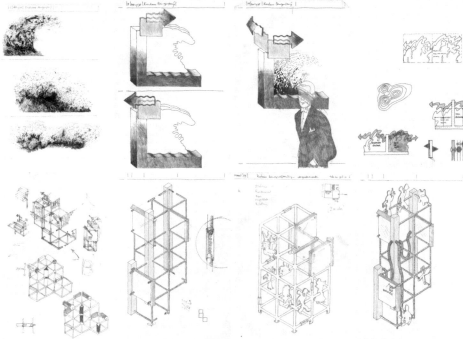

Gert Dumbar's sketches for Kurhaus
wayfinding, 1978

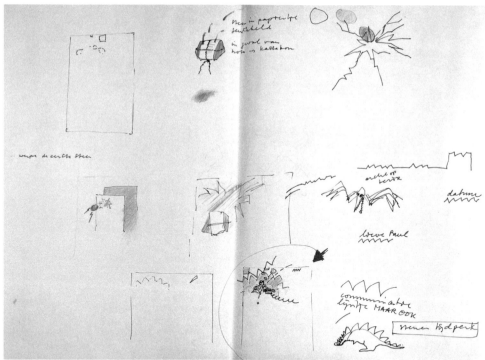

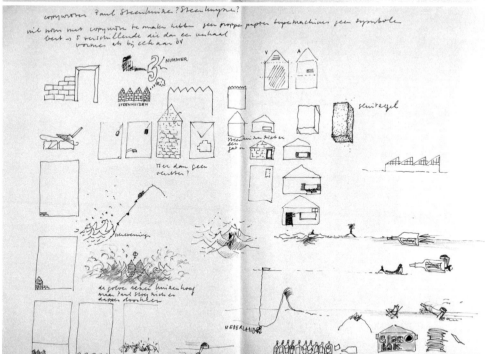

Sketches by Nicole van Schouwenburg for
Paul Steenhuisen stationery, 1981
The red markings in the top sketch are
by Gert Dumbar, suggesting irregular
contours

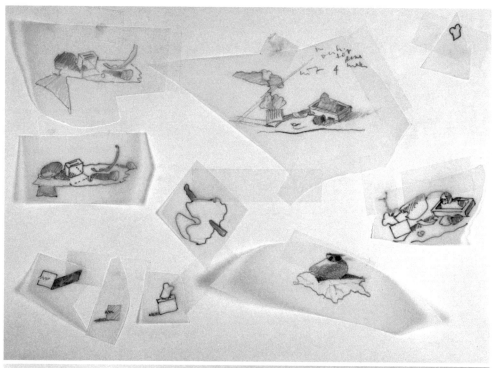

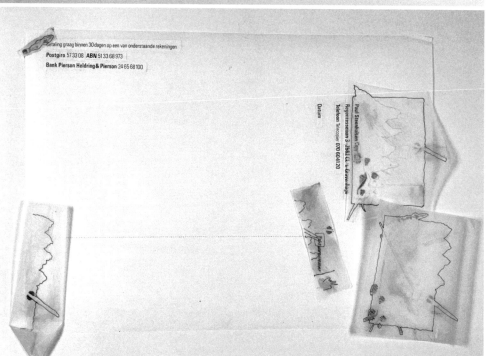

Sketches for image fragments for Paul Steenhuisen
stationery, 1981 (design: Nicole van Schouwenburg)

Paul Steenhuisen Copy
Regentesselaan 3   2562CL Den Haag
telefoon telecopier 070 604120
ABN 513368973 Postgiro 573308

Paul Steenhuisen stationery, 1982
(design: Gert Dumbar and Nicole van Schouwenburg)

Staged photography set for Paul Steenhuisen
stationery (design: Gert Dumbar;
photo: Lex van Pieterson)

is symbolized in stones thrown through windows while associations with the stone age are quickly discarded. In one of the sketches, a red marking by Gert indicates the direction of the final design: image fragments adorn the margins of the paper and a jagged line suggests what became the stationary's special feature, irregularly die-cut contours.

Also this relatively small job triggered an intensive process of sketching, probably in part because Paul was a good friend of Gert's and they had worked together. A few years earlier, Gert had engaged Paul for collaborating on a proposal for the Gasunie, the Dutch public-private conglomerate that operated the huge resource of the Groningen gas field. Gert had presented a well-developed design with Ko at the company's headquarters and was rather annoyed by the disinterest shown by its CEO: 'He kept us waiting while he was on the phone with his girlfriend.' On their way back Gert stopped to call the man at his home number. His wife answered the phone and said he was not available. Gert answered: 'Please tell your husband when he gets home that Studio Dumbar has decided not to work for him.' Since the job had come via the international marketing firm

J. Walter Thompson, who were obviously not amused, Gert and Paul decided to publicly apologize, not to Gasunie but to their colleague at the Dutch branch of JWT, Stephan Viegen. A full-page ad in *Adformatie* on September 6, 1979, simply read 'SORRY STEPHAN', signed by Paul and Gert. Only those who needed to know would know what it meant.

Paul Steenhuisen's stationary became a cause célèbre for quite another reason: its die-cut format and the rather opaque combinations of pebbles, objects, wads of paper and snippets of images that adorned it. The illustrations were staged in a by now vintage Dumbar and Van Pieterson take on throwing stuff on a table and photographing it in a manner that suggested that it had just landed there by pure chance. Such photo sessions remind me of the famous phrase by the French poet Lautréamont about the 'fortuitous encounter on an operating table of a

Paul Steenhuisen / Studio Dumbar

Gert Dumbar and Paul Steenhuisen,
advertising page in *Adformatie*,
6 September 1979

sewing machine and an umbrella'.[99] The phrase has become a kind of mantra for the surrealists, and Gert has throughout his career often worked in a very similar surrealistic vein — although he maintains he hates Surrealism. Fragments of the operating table for Steenhuisen — representing wealth and leisure, culminating in a mock-up of Paul in a swimming pool — were used in intricate combinations and minutely detailed in the

99   Comte de Lautréamont (Isidore Ducasse), *Les Chants de Maldoror*, Chant Sixième, I, 1869.

complex final designs for the stationary.

A rather mysterious set of sketches is devoted to Talking Heads, the band that represented the pinnacle of avant-garde pop in the late 1970s and early 1980s. It was a pitch brought in by Michel, but the material was never used by commissioner EMI, the British record company that produced and distributed Talking Heads of jury members that were designed for the *European Illustration Yearbook*, around the same time. The figures were staged by Michel in extensive sets in Lex van Pieterson's studio, in which they seem to be dancing against the backdrop of projected and cut-out text fragments.[100] Snippets of text suggest at least some of the photos are dedicated to the Talking Heads song

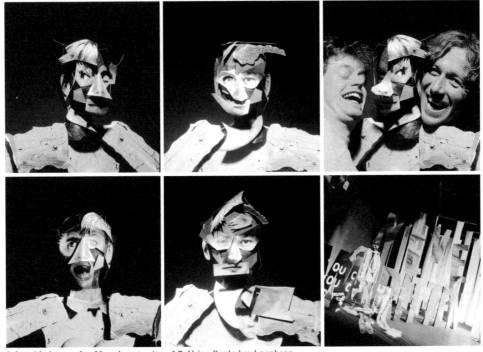

Polaroid photos of collaged portraits of Talking Heads band members
Photo top right: Michel de Boer and Lex van Pieterson
Bottom right: Staged photo in Lex van Pieterson's studio for Talking Heads album, 1979

albums in Europe. It's interesting also because portraits of the four band members' heads were constructed from fragments of photographs mounted on roughly chopped and painted body shapes. A kind of 'anamorphosis' that Michel and Studio Dumbar had used earlier in an artwork on the façade of a sports centre in Almere. The band members' portraits were also reminiscent of the collaged portraits 'Paper', which featured on their 1979 album 'Fear of Music'. Although the designs were not used, Studio Dumbar did get an invitation for the launch of the album in New York. Michel and Kitty went as studio representatives.

Gert and the Studio used a similar 'cubistic' way of staging portraits in the *European Illustration annual*. The 1982/1983 yearbook was the answer to publisher

100   Staged photos, designs for Talking Heads, 1979. Photos: Lex van Pieterson, client: EMI records.
101   Gert quoted in Joep Staal, 'European Illustration, boek dat geen boek is'. *Adformatie*, 14 April 1983, p. 34.

Edward Booth-Clibborn's, in his own words, 'utterly dangerous request to do something different with its design'.[101] The jury, including Dutch *Avenue*'s art director Dick de Moei, was depicted in Berry van Gerwen's 3D-collages of en face and en profil passport photos, interlocked as in a spatial puzzle. Ko Sliggers was brought in to illustrate the cover. He drew a map of Europe and the United States, highlighting — or so it seems — specific regions

THE BOOK FURTHER DISPLAYS WHAT GERT TERMS 'STYLIZED SLOPPINESS' IN SKETCHY TITLES AND STAGED PHOTOS OF SPATIAL COLLAGES MADE BY GERT FROM TORN SCRAPS OF PAPER

where there would be a concentration of work with airbrush, pencil, gouache or simply talent. 'Complete nonsense,' admits Gert, mocking the arbitrariness of such geo-mapping of intangibles. The

Cover of *European Illustration annual 1982-1983* (design: Ko Sliggers)

book further displays what Gert terms 'stylized sloppiness' in sketchy titles and staged photos (by Lex) of spatial collages

European Illustration annual 1982-1983, page with Vincent van Gogh's ear as 'easter egg'

243

made by Gert from torn scraps of paper. Throughout the book, Booth-Clibborn's logo reappears in places where it is completely dysfunctional, sometimes cut-off, irritatingly present nonetheless. 'It's about a benevolent smile; not provocative, but a friendly, coquettish design, showing "This is what you can do with a book like that".' Even the selected illustrations do not escape light-hearted satire. They are, of course, left untouched but details reappear on the same page, gently teasing the illustration's theme or inciting the viewer to find the seemingly trivial feature in the image itself. Thus, in the margin of the page devoted to Gottfried Helnwein's portrait of Van Gogh, we find the painter's cut-off ear. The book caused some alarm at the printer's, who started, grudgingly, to 'correct' what they saw as mistakes in the lay-outs: falsely placed register marks, skewed logos, stray lines that seemed not to

'Cubistic' portrait of jury members in
the *European Illustration annual 1982-1983*
(3D collages: Berry van Gerwen;
photos: Lex van Pieterson)

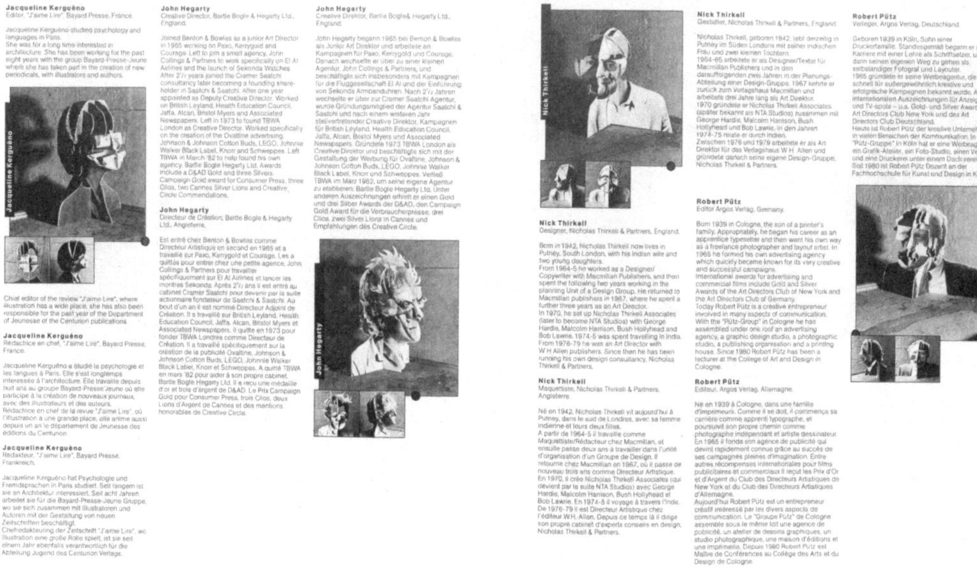

Jacqueline Kerguéno
Editor, "J'aime Lire", Bayard Presse, France.

Jacqueline Kerguéno studied psychology and languages in Paris. She was for a long time interested in architecture. She has been working for the past eight years with the group Bayard Presse-Jeune where she has taken part in the creation of new periodicals, with illustrations and authors.

Chief editor of the review "J'aime Lire", where illustration has a wide place, she has also been responsible for the past year of the Department of Jeunesse of the Centurion publications.

Jacqueline Kerguéno
Rédactrice en chef, "J'aime Lire", Bayard Presse, France.

Jacqueline Kerguéno a étudié la psychologie et les langues à Paris. Elle s'est longtemps intéressée à l'architecture. Elle travaille depuis huit ans au groupe Bayard Presse-Jeune où elle participe à la création de nouveaux journaux, avec des illustrateurs et des auteurs. Rédactrice en chef de la revue "J'aime Lire", où l'illustration a une grande place, elle anime aussi depuis un an le département de Jeunesse des éditions du Centurion.

Jacqueline Kerguéno
Rédakteur, "J'aime Lire", Bayard Presse, Frankreich.

Jacqueline Kerguéno hat Psychologie und Fremdsprachen in Paris studiert. Seit langem ist sie an Architektur interessiert. Seit acht Jahren arbeitet sie für die Bayard-Presse-Jeune Gruppe, wo sie sich zusammen mit Illustratoren und Autoren mit der Gestaltung von neuen Zeitschriften beschäftigt. Chefredakteurin der Zeitschrift "J'aime Lire", wo Illustration eine große Rolle spielt, ist sie seit einem Jahr ebenfalls verantwortlich für die Abteilung Jugend des Centurion Verlages.

John Hegarty
Creative Director, Bartle Bogle & Hegarty Ltd., England.

Joined Benton & Bowles as a Junior Art Director in 1965 working on Peau, Kerrygold and Courage. Left to join a small agency, John Collings & Partners to work specifically on D.A.Ashirea and the launch of Sekonda Watches. After 2½ years joined the Cramer Saatchi consultancy later becoming a founding shareholder in Saatchi & Saatchi when the year appointed as Deputy Creative Director. Worked on British Leyland, Health Education Council, Jaffa, Alcan, Bristol Myers and Associated Newspapers. Left in 1973 to found TBWA London as Creative Director. Worked specifically on the creation of the Creative advertising, Johnson & Johnson Cotton Buds, LEGO, Johnnie Walker Black Label, Knorr and Schweppes. Left TBWA in March '82 to help found his own agency, Bartle Bogle Hegarty Ltd. Awards include a D&AD Gold and three Silvers, Campaign Gold award for Consumer Press, three Clios, two Cannes Silver Lions and Creative Circle Commendations.

John Hegarty
Directeur de Création, Bartle Bogle & Hegarty Ltd., Angleterre.

Est entré chez Benton & Bowles comme Directeur Artistique en second en 1965 et a travaillé sur Peau, Kerrygold et Courage. L'en a quittés pour entrer chez une petite agence, John Collings & Partners pour travailler spécifiquement sur Et Al Ashirea et lancer les montres Sekonda. Après 2½ ans il est entré au cabinet Cramer Saatchi pour devenir par la suite actionnaire fondateur de Saatchi & Saatchi. Au bout d'un an il est nommé Directeur Adjoint de Création. Il a travaillé sur British Leyland, Health Education Council, Jaffa, Alcan, Bristol Myers et Associated Newspapers. Il quitte en 1973 pour fonder TBWA Londres comme Directeur de Création. Il a travaillé spécifiquement sur la création de la publicité Oraltine, Johnson & Johnson Cotton Buds, LEGO, Johnnie Walker Black Label, Knorr et Schweppes. A quitté TBWA en mars '82 pour aider à son propre cabinet, Bartle Bogle Hegarty Ltd. Il a reçu une médaille d'or et trois d'argent de D&AD. Le Prix Campaign Gold pour Consumer Press, trois Clios, deux Lions d'Argent de Cannes et des mentions honorables de Creative Circle.

John Hegarty
Creative Direktor, Bartle Bogle& Hegarty Ltd., England.

John Hegarty begann 1965 bei Benton & Bowles als Junior Art Direktor und arbeitete an Kampagnen für Peau, Kerrygold und Courage. Danach wechselte er über zu einer kleinen Agentur, John Collings & Partners, und beschäftigte sich insbesondere mit Kampagnen für die Fluggesellschaft El Al und der Einführung von Sekonda Armbanduhren. Nach 2½ Jahren wechselte er über zur Cramer Saatchi Agentur, wurde Gründungsmitglied der Agentur Saatchi & Saatchi und nach einem weiteren Jahr stellvertretender Creative Direktor. Kampagnen für British Leyland, Health Education Council, Jaffa, Alcan, Bristol Myers und Associated Newspapers. Gründete 1973 TBWA London als Creative Direktor und beschäftigte sich mit der Gestaltung der Werbung für Oraltine, Johnson & Johnson Cotton Buds, LEGO, Johnnie Walker Black Label, Knorr und Schweppes. Verließ TBWA im März 1982, um seine eigene Agentur zu etablieren: Bartle Bogle Hegarty Ltd. Unter anderen Auszeichnungen erhielt er einen Gold und drei Silber Awards der D&AD, den Campaign Gold Award für die Verbraucherpresse, den Clios, zwei Silver Lions in Cannes und Empfehlungen des Creative Circle.

Nick Thirkell
Designer, Nicholas Thirkell & Partners, England.

Born in 1942, Nicholas Thirkell now lives in Putney, South London, with his Indian wife and two young daughters.
From 1964-5 he worked as a Designer/Copywriter with Macmillan Publishers, and then spent the following two years working in the planning Unit of a Design Group. He returned to Macmillan publishers in 1967, where he spent a further three years as an Art Director.
In 1970, he set up Nicholas Thirkell Associates (later to become NTA Studios) with George Hardie, Malcolm Harrison, Bush Hollyhead and Bob Lawrie. 1974-5 was spent travelling in India. From 1976-78 he was an Art Director with W H Allen publishers. Since then he has been running his own design consultancy, Nicholas Thirkell & Partners.

Nick Thirkell
Maquettiste, Nicholas Thirkell & Partners, Angleterre.

Né en 1942, Nicholas Thirkell vit aujourd'hui à Putney, dans le sud de Londres, avec sa femme indienne et leurs deux filles.
A partir de 1964-5 il travaille comme Maquettiste/Rédacteur chez Macmillan, et ensuite passe deux ans à travailler dans l'unité d'organisation d'un Groupe de Design. Il retourne chez Macmillan en 1967, où il passe de nouveau trois ans comme Directeur Artistique. En 1970, il crée Nicholas Thirkell Associates (qui deviendra par la suite NTA Studios) avec George Hardie, Malcolm Harrison, Bush Hollyhead et Bob Lawrie. En 1974-5 il voyage à travers l'Inde. De 1976-78 il est Directeur Artistique chez l'éditeur W H. Allen. Depuis ce temps là il dirige son propre cabinet d'experts conseils en design, Nicholas Thirkell & Partners.

Robert Pütz
Verleger, Argos Verlag, Deutschland.

Geboren 1939 in Köln, Sohn einer Druckerfamilie. Standesgemäß begann er seine Karriere mit einer Lehre als Schriftsetzer, um dann seinen eigenen Weg zu gehen als selbständiger Fotograf und Layouter. 1965 gründete er seine Werbeagentur, die sehr schnell für außergewöhnlich kreative und erfolgreiche Kampagnen bekannt wurde. An internationalen Auszeichnungen für Anzeigen und TV-spots - u.a. Gold- und Silver Awards des Art Directors Club New York und des Art Directors Club Deutschland.
Heute ist Robert Pütz der kreative Unternehmer in vielen Bereichen der Kommunikation. In der "Pütz-Gruppe" in Köln hat er eine Werbeagentur, ein Grafik-Atelier, ein Foto-Studio, einen Verlag und eine Druckerei unter einem Dach vereint. Seit 1980 ist Robert Pütz Dozent an der Fachhochschule für Kunst und Design in Köln.

Robert Pütz
Editor Argos Verlag, Germany.

Born 1939 in Cologne, the son of a printer's family. Appropriately, he began his career as an apprentice typesetter and then went his own way as a freelance photographer and layout artist. In 1965 he formed his own advertising agency which quickly became known for its very creative and successful campaigns. International awards for advertising and commercial films include Gold and Silver Awards of the Art Directors Club of New York and the Art Directors Club of Germany.
Today Robert Pütz is a creative entrepreneur involved in many aspects of communication. With the "Pütz-Group" in Cologne he has assembled under one roof an advertising agency, a graphic design studio, a photographic studio, a publishing organisation and a printing house. Since 1980 Robert Pütz has been a lecturer at the College of Art and Design in Cologne.

Robert Pütz
Éditeur, Argos Verlag, Allemagne.

Né en 1939 à Cologne, dans une famille d'imprimeurs. Comme il se doit, il commença sa carrière comme apprenti typographe, et poursuivit son propre chemin comme photographe indépendant et artiste dessinateur. En 1965 il fonda son agence de publicité qui devint rapidement connue grâce au succès de ses campagnes pleines d'imagination. Entre autres récompenses internationales pour films publicitaires et commerciaux il reçut les Prix d'Or et d'Argent du Club des Directeurs Artistiques de New York et du Club des Directeurs Artistiques d'Allemagne.
Aujourd'hui Robert Pütz est un entrepreneur créatif intéressé par les divers aspects de communication. La "Groupe Pütz" de Cologne assemble sous le même toit une agence de publicité, un atelier de dessins graphiques, un studio photographique, une maison d'éditions et une imprimerie. Depuis 1980 Robert Pütz est Maître de Conférences au Collège des Arts et du Design de Cologne.

Dick de Moel
Art Director, Avenue, Nederland.

Dick de Moel hat an der Rijksacademie voor Beeldende Kunst in Rotterdam studiert. Zwischen 1965 und 1970 arbeitete er als Werbe-Grafiker und danach als Leiter der visuellen Projekte-Entwicklung der Marketing-Funktion für Elcoma-Philips Eindhoven. Seit 1970 ist er Art Direktor der Zeitschrift Avenue. Unter zahlreichen Auszeichnungen gewann er erste Preise des Art Direktors Club der Niederlande; den Dr. Erich-Salomon europäischen Preis für Zeitschrift-Fotografie; einen Silber Award und eine Reihe von Empfehlungen des Art Directors Club of New York. 1982 gewann er den sechsten Preis der Buchmesse in Stuttgart für seinen Buchuinschlag für "Die sieben Gesichter Chinas". Er hält häufig Vorlesungen in der Tschechoslowakei.

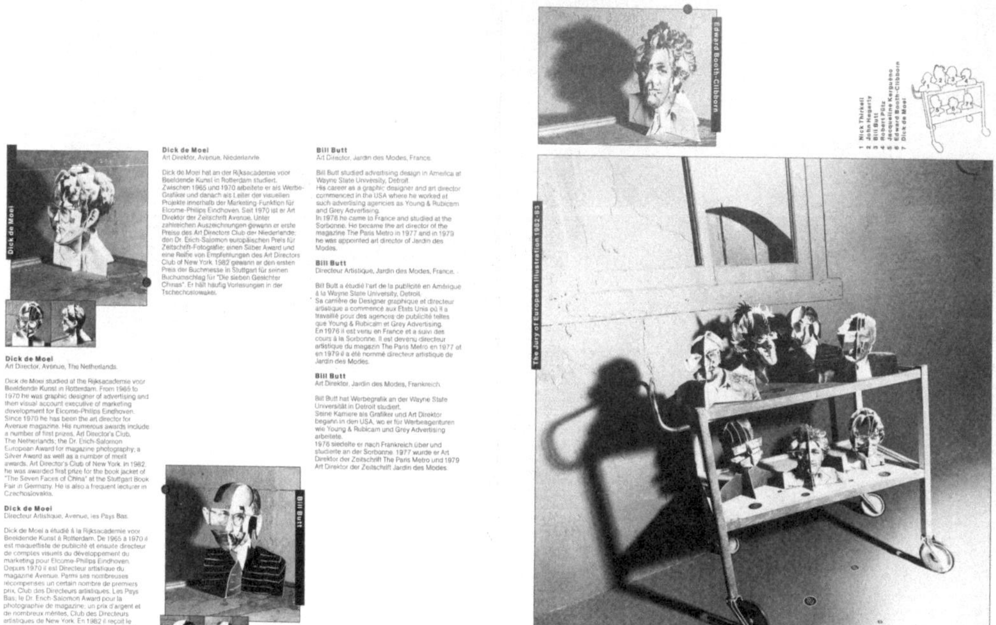

Dick de Moel
Art Director, Avenue, The Netherlands.

Dick de Moel studied at the Rijksacademie voor Beeldende Kunst in Rotterdam. From 1965 to 1970 he was graphic designer of advertising and then visual project executive of marketing development for Elcoma-Philips Eindhoven. Since 1970 he has been the art director for Avenue magazine. His numerous awards include a number of first prizes, Art Director's Club, The Netherlands; the Dr. Erich-Salomon European Award for magazine photography; a Silver Award as well as a number of merit awards, Art Director's Club of New York. In 1982 he was awarded first prize for the book jacket of "The Seven Faces of China" at the Stuttgart Book Fair in Germany. He is also a frequent lecturer in Czechoslovakia.

Dick de Moel
Directeur Artistique, Avenue, les Pays Bas.

Dick de Moel a étudié à la Rijksacademie voor Beeldende Kunst à Rotterdam. De 1965 à 1970 il est maquettiste de publicité et ensuite directeur de comptes visuels du développement du marketing pour Elcoma-Philips Eindhoven. Depuis 1970 il est Directeur artistique du magazine Avenue. Parmi ses nombreuses récompenses un certain nombre de premiers prix, Club des Directeurs artistiques, Les Pays Bas; le Dr. Erich Salomon Award pour la photographie de magazine; un prix d'argent et de nombreux mérites, Club des Directeurs artistiques de New York. En 1982 il reçut le premier prix pour la jaquette de livre de "The Seven Faces of China" (Les sept visages de la Chine) à la Foire du Livre de Stuttgart, Allemagne. Il donne fréquemment des conférences en Tchécoslovaquie.

Bill Butt
Art Director, Jardin des Modes, France.

Bill Butt studied advertising design in America at Wayne State University, Detroit.
He career as a graphic designer and art director commenced in the USA where he worked at such advertising agencies as Young & Rubicam and Grey Advertising.
In 1976 he came to France and studied at the Sorbonne; he became the art director of the magazine The Paris Metro in 1977 and in 1979 he was appointed art director of Jardin des Modes.

Bill Butt
Directeur Artistique, Jardin des Modes, France.

Bill Butt a étudié l'art de la publicité en Amérique à la Wayne State University, Detroit.
Sa carrière de designer graphique et directeur artistique a commencé aux États Unis où il a travaillé pour des agences de publicité telles que Young & Rubicam et Grey Advertising. En 1976 il est venu en France et a suivi des cours à la Sorbonne. Il est devenu directeur artistique du magazin The Paris Metro en 1977 et en 1979 il a été nommé directeur artistique de Jardin des Modes.

Bill Butt
Art Direktor, Jardin des Modes, Frankreich.

Bill Butt hat Werbegrafik an der Wayne State Universität in Detroit studiert.
Seine Karriere als Grafiker und Art Direktor begann in den USA, wo er für Werbeagenturen wie Young & Rubicam und Grey Advertising arbeitete. 1976 siedelte er nach Frankreich über und studierte an der Sorbonne. 1977 wurde er Art Direktor der Zeitschrift The Paris Metro und 1979 Art Direktor der Zeitschrift Jardin des Modes.

1 Nick Thirkell
2 John Hegarty
3 Bill Butt
4 Robert Pütz
5 Jacqueline Kerguéno
6 Edward Booth-Clibborn
7 Dick de Moel

European Illustration annual 1982-1983, double-page spreads, with 'cubistic' portraits and bios of jury members (design: Gert Dumbar)

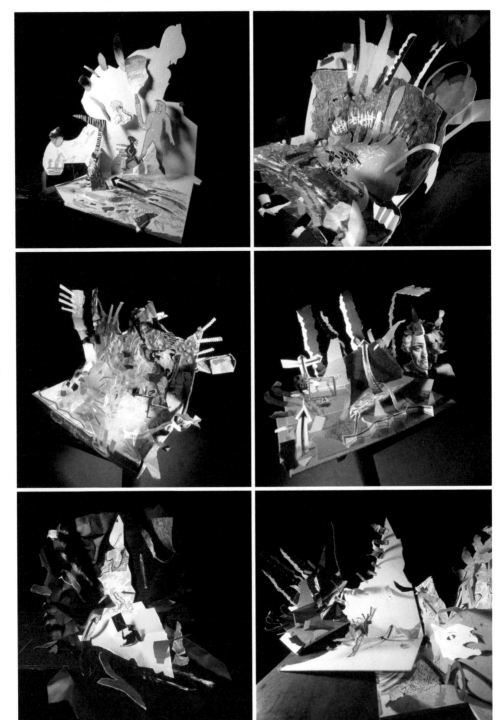

Gert Dumbar, 3D collages for *European Illustration
annual 1983-1984*, photos: Lex van Pieterson

EUROPEAN
the tenth annual
ILLUSTRATION

83/84

European Illustration annual 1983-1984, cover
(design: Gert Dumbar)

fulfil any function. ... Timely interference by the designers stopped the 'cleaning up'. Gert has a well-documented love for illustration, as a 'somewhat surreal image', which he mentions as inspiration for the design of the yearbook: 'That otherworldliness, we extended that line into the typography.'[102] Since the book also provided the information on the illustrations and their makers in a clear and unadorned typography, and the selection was contextualized in an 'excellent introduction by art historian Paul Hefting on the role of artists, illustrators and graphic designers',[103] publisher Booth-Clibborn was content and invited Studio Dumbar to also design the next yearbook.

PRAISE FOR EXPANDING THE DISCIPLINE

I FIND IT IMPORTANT TO INTRODUCE A CERTAIN ASPECT OF DOUBT. IN MY OPINION, YOU ALWAYS ACHIEVE MORE BY NOT BEING SO SURE OF YOURSELF

Gert Dumbar

In February 1984, the Amsterdam Endowment for the Arts (Amsterdams Fonds voor de Kunst) awarded its 1983 prize for outstanding graphic design, the H.N. Werkman Award, to Gert.[104] The jury[105] argued their choice by stating that they looked not only for excellent designers who 'work according to the prevailing views of typography and graphic design', of which they acknowledged there are many. Beyond general excellence, though, they looked for someone who 'stimulates and expands and integrates with other disciplines [and] works from another discipline,

using graphic techniques as an important visual tool'. In Gert, they found a designer 'who has given the broad and traditional discipline a striking expansion'. It was a remarkable choice, if one considers that Gert was the first 'design director' to receive the award in a graphic design culture that at the time still celebrated individual talent over 'running an agency' — Wim Crouwel shared the award in 1957 with three others, well before he started Total Design. Almost everything the jury formulates to argue their choice of Gert Dumbar amounts to a critique of the traditional Dutch graphic design establishment, and a rebuke of the kind of criticism Studio Dumbar had been receiving throughout its relatively short existence, which is why I quote the laudation at length here:

Dumbar's influence on 'government design' is characteristic of his views as a designer: appearance takes on meaning through the unexpected. Humour versus diligence. ...

The person Dumbar performs a remark-able function in the design world. In his view that 'anything goes', his use of techniques unrelated to graphic design, added to his tendency toward a certain extravagance, Gert Dumbar has become a pace maker for many young designers. He appears to have a nose for young talent, whose qualities he excellently brings out in a team context. In this sense, Dumbar is primarily a manager-designer. His inventiveness, aversion to dogmatism, agility, and improvisational charm lead to surprising results, also in his group.

Dumbar often adds pictorial figurations to his graphic work, more for the sake of expressiveness than to enhance readability, for example.

He scoffs at the proposition that everything should have meaning, takes seriously precisely what others do not take seriously, and despises analytical methods of

---

102   Ibid.
103   Ibid.
104   At the time, the H.N. Werkmanprijs (issued (bi)-annually, from 1945 till 2002) was probably the most prestigious accolade in the Netherlands specifically for graphic designers. The list of honoured designers reads like a

Who's Who of Dutch graphic design history. The award was installed in 1945, in memory of the graphic innovator Hendrik Nicolaas Werkman, who was executed by the Nazis in the last weeks of the war, in April 1945 he received the first Werkman Award posthumously.

105   The 'advisory commission' for the 1983 Werkmanprijs

measurement and so-called scientific research.

Regarding the introduction of a corporate identity, he says:

'I find it important to introduce a certain aspect of doubt. In my opinion, you always achieve more by not being so sure of yourself. ... You have to try to make (the client) part of an aspect of doubt. They should be able to put their own spin on it. You have to try to break through a rigid way of thinking.'

. ... With that alone, he seems to be causing a breath of fresh air in Dutch graphic thinking.

All of this reads like a polite critique of Gert's critics in the late 1970s and early 1980s, stemming from an — at root protestant— view of the morality of design as a purely or mainly applied craft in the service of public information and enlightenment.[106] Studio Dumbar has repeatedly been accused of 'graphic decadence',[107] which has been suspicious in the Netherlands ever since Paul Schuitema wrote off 'art' in favour of 'advertising' in a polemical text in the avant-garde magazine i10, in an echo of Adolf Loos' banning of

the gentleman maverick of Dutch graphic design — maverick because of his aversion to the standard ways of doing things, and being quite successful at showing how it can be done differently. And gentleman — well, after all, he quite effectively was and still is very much a gentleman from The Hague, or as locals would say: 'een Haags heertje'. Gentlemanly also, he decided to answer a tinge of unease among the studio's core designers with him being awarded individually, and not the studio collectively, by spending the award's money on a joint trip to New York together with Michel, Kitty, Heleen Raue and Henk Hoebé. Gert travelled on to deliver lectures at Cranbrook Academy and RISD, the art academy in Boston.[109]

> *GERT WAS THE FIRST 'DESIGN DIRECTOR' TO RECEIVE THE H.N. WERKMAN AWARD IN A GRAPHIC DESIGN CULTURE THAT AT THE TIME STILL CELEBRATED INDIVIDUAL TALENT OVER 'RUNNING AN AGENCY'*

decoration in the 1920s.[108] A ban repeated by Crouwel's much cited indictment of 'noise' in graphic design. To award Gert Dumbar the Werkmanprijs for 'causing a breath of fresh air in Dutch graphic thinking', amounts to anointing him as

---

consisted of Kees Endenburg (by virtue of being the winner the previous year), Gertjan Leuvelink and Abe van der Werff. The latter two were good friends and colleagues of Gert's. Abe was co-founder with Gert of Zeebelt Theatre in 1982.

106 See also: Max Bruinsma, 'Creative Civil Servants –

A Century of Dutch Design Education', 2017. Online: www.maxbruinsma.nl/DesignEducation.

107 See Richard Hollis quote, p. 292 [note 129].

108 Paul Schuitema, 'Reclame' in i10, #16, 1928, p.76 See also p. 26.

109 See p. 290.

HET UUR U

1983 (design: Gert Dumbar)

Martinus Nijhoff, *Awater / Het Uur U*. Bert Bakker publishers, 1983 (staging and illustrations by Gert Dumbar, photos by Lex van Pieterson, typography by Heleen Raue)

Awater is a classic of Dutch narrative poetry by Martinus Nijhoff, first published in 1934. Its protagonist looks for a travel companion in a dreamworld full of symbols, contrasts, and paradoxes. The poem contains the famous line: 'Lees maar, er staat niet wat er staat.' ('Do read, it does not say what it says.')

Gert Dumbar: 'This is the first time I experimented with torn paper. I kept it in black-and-white to match the atmosphere of the poem — it's more suspenseful without colour. The recurring cut-out figure is my interpretation of Awater's movements and actions throughout the poem'.

De kelner kent me. Hij weet wat ik voel.
Hij heeft mijn tafeltje al tweemaal gepoetst.
Hij blijft, met in zijn hand de witte doek,
geruime tijd staan zwijgen naast mijn stoel.
'De tijden' zegt hij 'zijn niet meer als vroeger.'
Ik weet dat hij ook aan mijn broer denkt, hoe
met zijn hond aan de ketting en zijn hoed
iets achterover op, hij binnenwoei
en 't hele zaaltje vulde met rumoer.
Hier ligt hetzelfde zand nog op de vloer,
dezelfde duif koert in zijn kooi als toen.
Oei, zei de wind, voort, voort! Zo is het goed.
Wie is dat? zeg ik daar 'k iets zeggen moet.
En hij, wetend terstond op wien ik doel:
'Iemand die voor het eerst de zaak bezoekt.'
Dan trekt hij van 't buffet het hekje toe.
In 't water worden glazen omgespoeld. –
Wat is 't dat in zijn zak Awater zoekt?
Het is een boekje van marocco groen.
Het is een schaakspel nu hij 't opendoet.
Awater's ogen kijken koel en stroef.
Zijn hand, op tafel trommelend, schenkt moed
aan het visioen dat door zijn voorhoofd woelt.
Een sneeuwvlok dwarrelt tussen droppen bloed.
Het spel wordt tot een nieuw figuur gevoegd.
Zijn glas, vóór hem, beslaat onaangeroerd.
De cigaret die in de asbak gloeit
maakt een stokroos die langs 't plafond ontbloeit.
Hij zit volstrekt alleen en ongemoeid.
Hij heeft wat een planeet heeft en een bloem,
een innerlijke vaart die diep vervoert.
Nu drinkt hij het glas leeg en sluit het boek.
Hij krijgt, nu hij stil voor zich kijkt, iets droevigs.
Hij kijkt mijn kant uit, zodat ik vermoed
dat hij mij roept als hij de kelner roept.

Anamorphous sculpture for Almere sports complex, 1984
(idea: Gert Dumbar; design: Ko Sliggers)

SCULPTURE FOR ALMERE
SPORTS COMPLEX

1984

Gert: 'One of my inspirations for this design was the first time I saw a seventeenth-century anamorphous painting, in the Louvre in Paris. That fascinated me. We marked a spot on the pavement in front of the sports building, from where you could see the image as intended. But actually, I liked the 'front view' better — these seemingly non-sensical forms, a completely abstract sculpture! Ko and I sketched a lot on this design, and Michel invested great effort in making sure the construction was storm-proof. The municipality at first didn't want it, because they were afraid it would come down in heavy weather. We had a space-agency construction bureau analyse the forces at play. When we presented the result — a thick report with insanely complicated measurements and calculations — the city finally accepted the plan'.

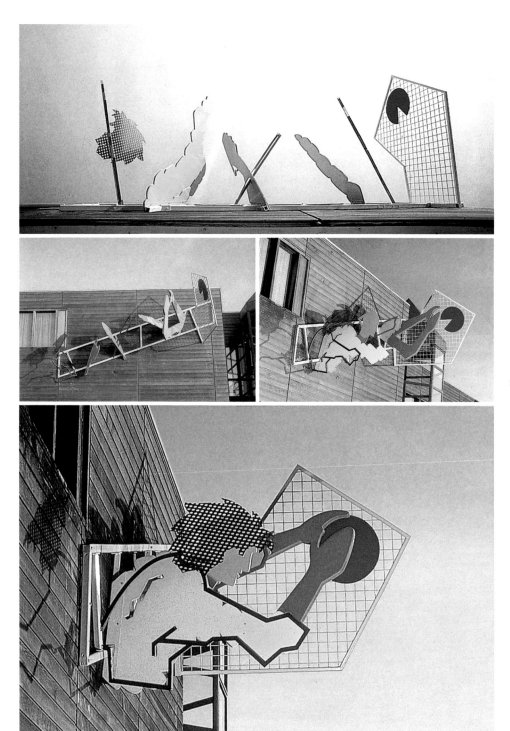

'Perfidia' poster, 1979
(design: Gert Dumbar; photo: Lex van Pieterson)

DUMBAR'S R&D DEPARTMENT

ZEEBELT AND BEYOND

Gert's motivation for engendering a 'breath of fresh air' in what he considered a stale design climate was his reason for doing design at all: experimentation, exploration, and the joy of surprising oneself. For years, the laboratory that provided Gert and the studio with the space and impetus for pandering to all of that was a small theatre and cultural centre in the Hague, the Zeebelt theatre. In 1982 Gert and DEV advisor Abe van der Werff[110] had taken over the venue that previously housed the experimental Studio Scarabee, of which both were board members, together with Hein van Haaren, DEV's chief at the time. Scarabee had been shaking up the Dutch theatre establishment since the mid-1960s with wildly experimental productions. The core aim of the group was to intensely mix visual art, theatre, music, and literature into new forms of performance and spectacle. They produced shows with the fine-fleur of the Dutch and international avant-garde in art and music — Lucebert, Bert Schierbeek, Woody van Amen, Otto Ketting, Bruno Maderna, François Morellet, to name a few contemporary celebrities. Jan van Toorn designed some remarkable objects for Scarabee, most notably a book for the 1969 'Poppetgom' production, that came with an inflatable cushion packed in a metal fuel can. The 'watch and television spectacle' Fata Banana, aired on national TV in May 1971, can be seen as an early instance of media art. In 1979 Studio Dumbar designed Scarabee's stationary, in another instance of using die-cutting. Studio Dumbar's poster for the 1979 theatre production of 'Perfidia' involves staged photo sessions with papier-mâché figurines and extensive sketching by Gert, featuring a 'cigarette girl' reminiscent of the pin-up he used as mascot for Tel Design.

Studio Scarabee went bankrupt due to its artistic leader Adri Boon's

---

110   Abe van der Werff (1940) studied art at the Vrije Academie, The Hague. He was secretary of several State advisory commissions in the 1970s, member of the Visual Arts and Exhibitions department of the Rotterdam Art Foundation (Rotterdamse Kunststichting) and advisor of PTT's Dienst Esthetische Vormgeving (DEV, Aesthetic Department). Later he was director of the art academy in Kampen and the Cultural Council of South Holland.

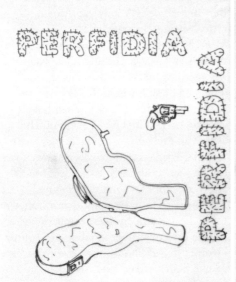

HOLLAND
STUDIO SCARABEE

Gert Dumbar's sketches for
'Perfidia' poster, 1979

Props for 'Perfidia' poster. Gert: 'I borrowed a real gun from the police for this shoot'

risky investments in future projects, with prospective funds that were not realized. Abe still vividly recalls the excitement that followed. When the bankruptcy was finally settled the next year, he went to the curator, who pointed to a bunch of keys lying on his desk. 'All that is left for me to do now is to return these keys to the rightful owner, the city of The Hague,' he said. 'Oh,' said Abe, 'I'm doing all kinds of things for the city and it so happens that I have an appointment this very afternoon with its department of real estate, so I could hand the keys to them.' 'Well,' said the curator, 'that saves me a tedious drive downtown. Here are the keys, and goodbye.' 'That was all made up on the spot, of course,' Abe confesses. Instead, he went straight to the closed and by now dilapidated theatre, opened the shoddy curtains and placed a torn-off piece of wallpaper in the window, on which he wrote: 'GEKRAAKT THEATER' ('squatted theatre'). He then called Gert: 'I have just squatted the theatre!' Gert: 'I'm on my way!'[III]

Thus, in a sense, Zeebelt Theatre was a continuation of Scarabee, now under the guidance of a group of cultural professionals who formed what founding member Gert calls 'a do-it-yourself board of governors.' Studio Dumbar would provide Zeebelt's posters and publications for years to come and actively collaborate on the programme — including financing it. Abe: 'Gert was brilliant at getting money. He would say, for example: "I have received a world-class assignment, from IBM in Paris, and they are paying ƒ 10,000 to Zeebelt as cultural sponsorship." And then he told me how he did it: "At the end of the meeting with the client, they asked if I had any questions. And I said that it was a little awkward that they didn't know. 'What don't we know?' 'Well, I hesitate, because I thought you also knew that big clients of Studio Dumbar always make a donation to the incredibly innovative theatre of which I happen to be

257

Staged set for Scarabee stationery, 1979

co-founder.' 'Oh, sorry, we really weren't aware of that. But no problem, how much shall we contribute? Is 10,000 okay?'" That's how he did it!'[112] In later years the concept became known internally as straf-sponsoring, ('penalty sponsorship'), a kind of friendly coercion of corporate clients and suppliers who would benefit as subcontractors from large jobs Studio Dumbar acquired. Similarly, most of the printing for Studio Dumbar's Zeebelt posters was sponsored via contacts of Gert and Abe.

III   Abe van der Werff: Zoom conversation, 17 May 2023.
112   Ibid.

Studio 7
Willemstraat 7
2514 HJ DEN HAAG
Holland
Telefoon 070 65 85 85
Bank Ned Credietbank NV
Rek. no 23 01 55 976
Postgiro 75 3175

Scarabee stationery, 1979
(design: Gert Dumbar)

'Grafische vormgeving in Oost Europa' poster, 1992.
(design: Robert Nakata and Gert Dumbar)

The Zeebelt theatre's projects ranged from experimental music and dance performances and art installations to conferences and debates on graphic design, literature, architecture, and cultural politics. The latter were mainly developed and organized by Leonie ten Duis and her colleague Annelies Haase, who travelled extensively to research and develop networks for conferences on Asian, Eastern-European and North-American graphic design. On one of those trips, through Japan and China, Leonie met prominent graphic designer Xu Wang in Shanghai, and thus laid the foundation

PRIX DE P WAS ONE OF GERT'S CHERISHED COMBINATIONS OF FUN AND SERIOUSNESS, A HUMOROUS WAY OF STIRRING UP THE DEBATE ON CITY DEVELOPMENT AND ARCHITECTURE IN THE HAGUE

of what eventually would become Studio Dumbar China. Wang would later publish the first Chinese book on Studio Dumbar.[113]

From time to time, Zeebelt staged special events such as the 'fly opera' of 1994, a miniature production with computer

music and live and dead flies in the starring roles — the audience was provided with magnifying glasses to follow the proceedings. Talented art students were scouted by the board and acknowledged with the annual Zeebelt Prize, while bad architecture was mocked with the satirical 'Prix de P' award for the building 'that most contributed to defiling The Hague's cityscape' (the 'P' stands for 'paardelul' (horse's dick) — both a genuine mason's term for a brick cut in half lengthwise and a popular invective). The award was one of Gert's cherished combinations of fun and seriousness — a humorous way of stirring up the debate on city development and architecture in 'the cultural desert of The Hague', as Gert summarized the state of

Prix de P... voor misplaatste architectuur

Prix de P...
(since 1991, designs: Gert Dumbar)
Top left: Prix de P... logo. The monkey who uses his crown for rather unofficial business stands for the architect, who thinks he's the crowning glory of the arts
Top right: Trophy for Prix de P...
Bottom: Newspaper clipping with a review of the 2000 'Awards'

affairs in his home town. 'The prize was theatre, in a term I learned from Pierre Bernard, mise en abyme — theatre about architecture as theatre. It was a bit Dada.'[114] Architects mocking architecture — most of the audience consisted of colleagues of the

113   Xu Wang, *Studio Dumbar: Graphic Designer's Design Life*, Beijing, 1998.
114   Gert Dumbar: conversation, 22 June 2023.

259

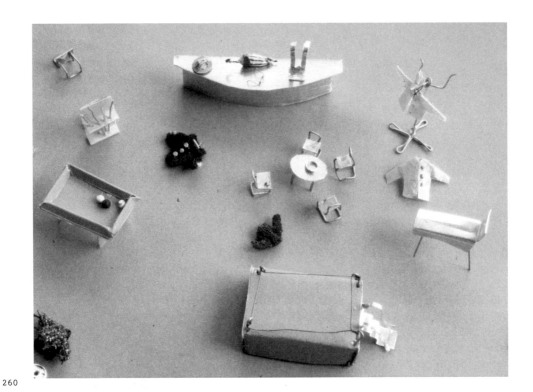

LIVING FLY OPERA

1992

The 'Fly Opera' started off as a mockery of the grand pretensions of the genre, but ballooned into a meticulously staged and extravagantly trimmed project, with music and sound performed by one of the first available computer-generated voices, developed by composers and technicians of The Hague's Conservatoire of Music. The flies' costumes were knitted by Studio Dumbar designer Bob van Dijk's sister (using tiny sewing needles), while the furnishings, including a snooker table, a boxing ring, and models of Marcel Breuer's cantilever chair were tinkered from paper and paper clips by Gert Dumbar and Bob van Dijk (top). The poster (below) is reproduced here in its actual size, matching the miniature dimensions of the entire production.

'Fly Opera' [Vliegenopera] tiny poster
(2.6 x 4 cm), 1992

Details from the performance
(design: Gert Dumbar and others)

Prix de P's 'winner' — eating 'architectural' cakes which Gert had made at 'a very posh patisserie in Noordwijk'.

Abe recalls 'much partying and much booze', but also how the board members' networks inspired and profited from the collaboration: 'Through my work at the DEV I made many studio visits, and I used that not only for the DEV, but also for Zeebelt. So that they could reinforce each other. For example, Floor van Keulen, the painter, once made an enormous painting of 3.5 by 2 metres, live in front of a breathless audience at Zeebelt. I was able to acquire that canvas for the PTT. So Zeebelt was an experimental environment also for the DEV and the PTT. Ootje Oxenaar, who succeeded Hein van Haaren as chief, also found that wonderfully interesting.' [115] The 'DIY board' consisted of a mixed group of professionals 'who like to think about essential matters,' as Gert once summarized: 'As a board we talk a lot; about what theatre is, in what ways design is related to it, things like that. There is an architect, a composer, Abe van der Werff is chair of the Cultural Council, there are two ladies who have studied literary history, there is an interior designer, and everyone brings their own profession and their own perspectives. So there's a strange group of people sitting there, sticking things together in perfect harmony. Those things are irrevocably reflected in the studio's work.' [116] But the board became increasingly distracted by their main jobs from actually running a theatre, so Hanna Boender was engaged as official manager, backed by the gentlemen and ladies of the board. She was assisted by Leonore van Prooijen and, later, Judith Schönefeld. The theatre expanded its reach by importing its own wine and issuing its own magazine, *Zeezucht*. The periodical was edited by Leonie ten Duis and Annelies Haase, with background reports, and analysis of Zeebelt's conferences and events. Gert and Lex designed its covers, with a masthead by Vincent van Baar, who also designed the Zeebelt logo. The sizable investment in time, research and resources dedicated to Zeebelt, its events, its magazine and other publicity channels shows the enthusiasm and seriousness of the endeavour — beyond acting as the Studio's R&D department, Zeebelt became a convivial vehicle to spread Studio Dumbar's ideas on graphic design and culture at large.

[117] Each year since the start of Zeebelt, Gert and Lex would lock themselves in the latter's spacious photo studio for a day, where after some brainstorming they'd start smashing dishes, playing with dolls and vegetables, or arranging hysterically dynamic still-lives on and around shoddy tables. At the end of the day there was an enigmatic picture that would remain a mystery because it wasn't meant to be clear. It wasn't intended to communicate a preconceived message either; it wasn't even finished. It was an idiosyncratic visual trope created by a designer and a photographer who liked to play. But it did have a purpose: the picture would reappear in a series of posters announcing Zeebelt's monthly programme. It was offset-printed in full colour in a large quantity as point of departure for a wildly disparate series of posters, which were designed by members of the studio for announcing the monthly programme. Each month new typography was silkscreened over the original image, disguising or sometimes transforming it almost beyond recognition.

Typography and image engage in a peculiar dialogue in these posters, inevitable perhaps when they have little in common. There is no question here of a preconceived relationship between the content of the image and the

115 Abe van der Werff: Zoom conversation, 17 May 2023.
116 Gert interviewed by Max Bruinsma, in Bruinsma 'Gert Dumbar – Er zijn geen wetten', *Items* #1, 1993.

117 The section on Zeebelt posters is an edited and updated version of: Max Bruinsma, 'Enigma variations', in *Eye*, Vol.5 no. 19, winter 1995, pp. 26-33.

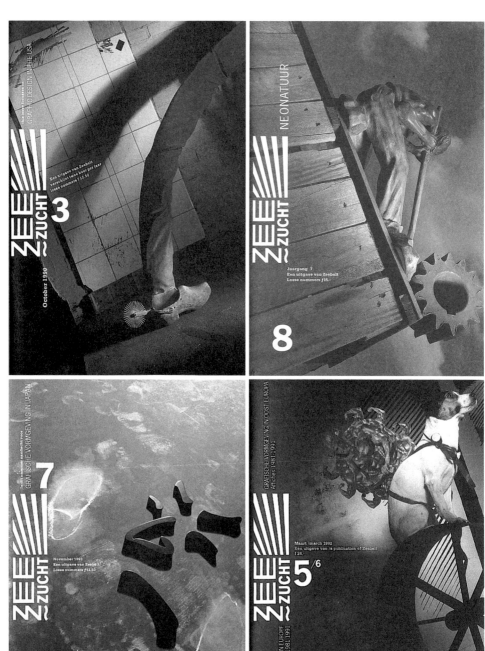

Zeezucht magazine, covers.
(design: Gert Dumbar; photo: Lex van Pieterson),
Zeezucht masthead: Vincent van Baar

announcement, rather they just happen to sit one on top of the other. Yet the images are too strong in their own right to be ignored. They act as an elaborate logo, highlighting the theatre's slightly anarchic image. The text supplies the concrete data. There are many ways to add text to an existing picture and in the case of the Zeebelt posters, the merging of two disparate elements into a single composition generally results in formal tension. They do not get along very well, the picture and the letters. You could even say that in many cases they engage in a mutually lethal competition — the typography murdering the image or vice-versa, the image ruining the text. Some of the more unhinged posters could be read as the enactment of a creative Oedipus complex with Dumbar in the role of the butchered father. But the tension between

image and typography is also stimulating — it effectively symbolizes the culture for which Zeebelt is a stage. 'We represent

THE POSTER SHOULD HAVE A STRONG CHARACTER, THEY SHOULD BE INSTANTLY RECOGNIZABLE, ALWAYS SLIGHTLY TONGUE-IN-CHEEK, GOOD HUMOURED

Gert Dumbar

a somewhat anarchic commentary on current events in the city,' says Gert. 'The posters should reflect this attitude — they should have a strong character, they should be instantly recognizable, always slightly tongue-in-cheek, good humoured. They emanate the energy of the friendly

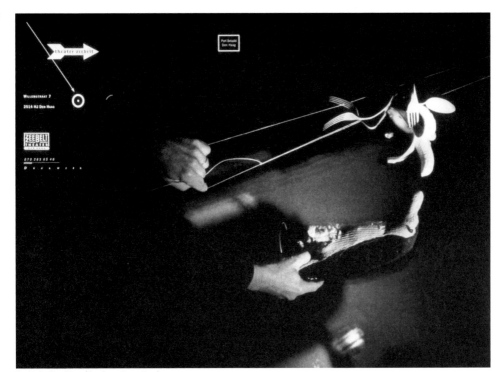

Zeebelt leaflet (design: Gert Dumbar; photo: Lex van Pieterson)

debating club that we are.' Friendliness may not be the first association for the viewer of these posters, but they do project the concerns and fascinations of civilized citizens who enjoy controversy as long as it is elegantly presented and accompanied by a good meal. As Gert remarks on the early posters: 'Please note that these images are mostly about food.'

Image for the cover of a *Zeezucht* issue devoted to 'mobility'. Gert: 'Bricks on wheels… At some point Lex kicked it over while taking the picture — that's how it became dynamic.' (design: Gert Dumbar, photo: Lex van Pieterson)

But for all their irony and playfulness, the posters also have an undertone of serious investigation into the possibilities of typography–as–image. In several instances the typography virtually overrides the picture, fragmenting it through the addition of solid blocks of colour or highlighting the structural aspects of its composition. In these cases, the photographic image is reduced to a series of two-dimensional forms that dissolve into the typographic composition.

For years, these posters have provided a prolific laboratory for the studio's designers to improvise freely with lines, boxes, arrows, and other typographic devices to create arresting compositions of layered and intertwined graphic material. And this approach fused with — and fed — Studio Dumbar's own tradition of staged photography and uninhibited use of typographic paraphernalia to become a hybrid form. 'We invest a lot of time and

concentration in these posters,' says Gert. 'They are a playground for the studio's designers, and they use it intensely.' It could also be called Studio Dumbar's R&D department, a special zone for experiments that would be too risky in most other assignments. And sometimes experiments from the Zeebelt laboratory had a direct effect on the studio's 'regular' output; the type-led posters for the theatre company Het Nationale Toneel are a case in point as are many Holland Festival posters. Usually, the playground's importance is more implicit. Zeebelt's small publicity budget meant that the posters had to be produced using limited technical means and function on different levels — folded in eight they acted as leaflets to be mailed to subscribers. This allowed for a flexible approach to readability and visual transparency: on the street the posters' main task was to remind passers-by of Zeebelt's existence, while the programme details could be read at closer range. As a result, body text could be treated as lines or blocks and used freely to structure the surface in an abstract way.

265

THESE POSTERS ARE A PLAYGROUND FOR THE STUDIO'S DESIGNERS, AND THEY USE IT INTENSELY

Gert Dumbar

This aesthetic rather than purely functional approach complemented the ironic and informal character of the theatre's eclectic programme. 'We are an intellectual Lunapark, not an institution,' Gert states. 'As soon as we notice any sign of becoming an institution, we will stop.' So the dramatic clashes of image and typography in the Zeebelt Theatre posters served a well-defined purpose: to prevent anyone becoming too settled or comfortable.

(1)

(2)

ZEEBELT THEATRE
POSTERS

1983-1990s

(1-3) The image on the Zeebelt Theatre posters for 1986 represents Gert Dumbar's attempt to make a 'postmodern still-life' that explodes the complacent intimacy of the genre. It's an ironic wink to Studio Dumbar's client the Rijksmuseum, home to the best examples of the Dutch still-life tradition.

The typography of the January poster (1 - by Ed McDonald) counters the desperate dynamism of the image with a rigid balance and self-conscious use of classical serif type. The brackets serve an almost protective function, fencing off the text from the forces of disintegration below.

At first sight the hand-scrawled lettering of the May poster (2) appears completely consistent with the centrifugal forces of the image, a rare example in the series of typography and picture designed in accord. But the enhanced dynamism of the design by

Linzi Bartolini, Esther Vermeer and Gert Dumbar — combined with the subtle positioning of illustrative elements — has a devastating effect on the photograph, depriving it of its depth and flattening it to the level of the typographic surface.

For the February poster (3 - by Robert Nakata) the typography echoes the brutality of the image but remains at odds with the composition. The hard-edged band of lettering forms an uneasily flat contrast with the three dimensionality of the photograph. The two heraldic logos belong to a fake organization ('Societé Internationale de la Culture, des Arts et de la Musique de la Ville Diplomatique La Haye'), mocking the bourgeois provenance of the still-life genre and of established high culture in general

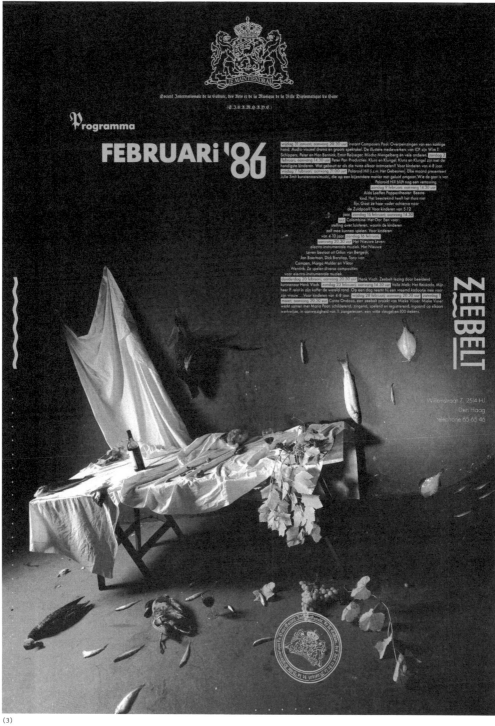

(3)

Postcards announcing lecture series at Zeebelt
Theatre, early 1990s. Gert Dumbar: 'I made these after
hours, at home… that's why our family cat "Dummetje"
makes an appearance'

In de maanden maart, april en mei zal in Theater Zeebelt en aantal beeldend kunstenaars, vormgevers en architecten over hun werk praten. Naast het eigen terrein zullen onder meer de 'tussengebieden' van vormgeving en beeldende kunst, architectuur en muziek aan bod komen. Hierbij nodigen wij u van harte uit bij deze lezingen aanwezig te zijn.

Two Zeebelt leaflets (design: Gert Dumbar)

Left: Zeebelt Theatre monthy posters in 1995. Front design by Bob van Dijk and Rieme Gleijm, Photography by Lex van Pieterson. Back of the poster: November programme announcement, designed by Renate Boere. The popular studio's Dog - Beer - was frequently used for experimental posters at the Zeebelt Theatre.

Right: 'Grafische vormgeving in Oost Europa' poster, 1992. Designed by Robert Nakata, poster announcing four exhibitions and a symposium on Eastern European graphic design organized by Zeebelt Theatre, with a *Zeezucht* publication edited by Leonie ten Duis. The lines of French text that criss-cross the poster evoke the 1789 'Declaration of human rights' — they seem to catch the upside-down figure in a maze. With the mirrored type of the names of the countries involved in the exhibition, Nakata seems to comment on the lack of human rights in these former communist countries during the then recently ended Cold War. The central image by Gert mocks Lenin as failed communist, with the Studio's dog carrying a multi-armed body-builder as a symbol of the oppressed workers. For good measure, Robert added a communist sickle. The dog-with-body-builders reappears on the cover of the *Zeezucht* magazine devoted to the subject (see p. 263, bottom right)

Poster for a symposium 'Overzeese visies', on American
graphic design, October 1989 (design: Robert Nakata)

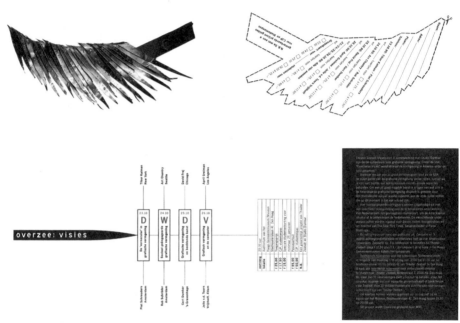

Flyer for a symposium 'Overzeese visies',
on American graphic design, October 1989
(design: Robert Nakata)

Poster and flyer for a symposium 'Overzeese visies', on American graphic design, October 1989. Designer Robert Nakata: 'The typography is done with a discarded typeface designed for the American highways; so, not Interstate, but a letter the Americans rejected. The Dutch bought it after the war, cheaply, for their highways. So for me, that was a good typeface for the theme of Dutch-American relations in design, even if I thought no one's ever going to know that thing.' Nakata vividly recalls the making of the background photo for the poster: 'We had been fooling around in Lex's studio for a day and I'd been thinking about the poster's theme of Dutch-American relations in design, so I had set up this Dutch wooden clog and an American cowboy spur, and Lex had been throwing water all over and we'd made a lot of pictures. ...

Because of the way we photographed it, the clog was looking like a fish with its mouth wide open, and I wanted to make a fin for it.
... A thin sheet of metal was lying around and I took a cutter to make a crazy fin-like thing. I made that on the spot. At some point — we were already taking the set down and removing filters and lights and stuff — this thing was just standing there, mounted on a pole, dripping with water. And I looked at it and thought it kind of interesting, so I asked Lex to photograph it like that. He didn't like it, also because we had done so many other things that day. But for whatever reason, this thing seemed more compelling to me, even though I couldn't verbalize it, even to myself. To his credit, Gert managed to convince Lex, like, okay, this is going to be the thing'

Left: Poster for Zeebelt symposium 'Visie op visie' [visions on television], 1990. The three-day symposium brought together designers for television graphics from various European countries to discuss 'the seemingly boundless poss ibilities of the graphic computer', and debate whether 'in this brilliant uniformity the personal style of the designer threatens to eventually get lost.'

Background image by Gert Dumbar and Lex van Pieterson. Shown is a basic poster on which the actual information still needs to be silk-screened (design: Gert Dumbar; photo: Lex van Pieterson, with parts from a destroyed tv set stuck to the wall)

Right: Zeebelt posters, December 1986 and May 1987 (design: Gert Dumbar; photo: Lex van Pieterson)

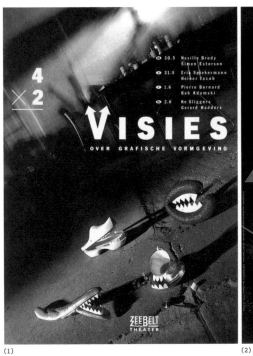

(1)

(2)

The posters for a series of Zeebelt Theatre debates 'visions on graphic design' in 1989, which brought together practitioners with contrasting methods and aims, opening the debate rhetorically by offering alternative typographic approaches. The image simultaneously suggests both 'having a bite' and the hoped-for animation of verbal debate

(1 and 3) Typography by Robert Nakata on alternative versions of Gert Dumbar's and Lex van Pieterson's photo (poster design 3: Gert Dumbar)

(2) Typography by James Mason of Cranbrook Academy of Art

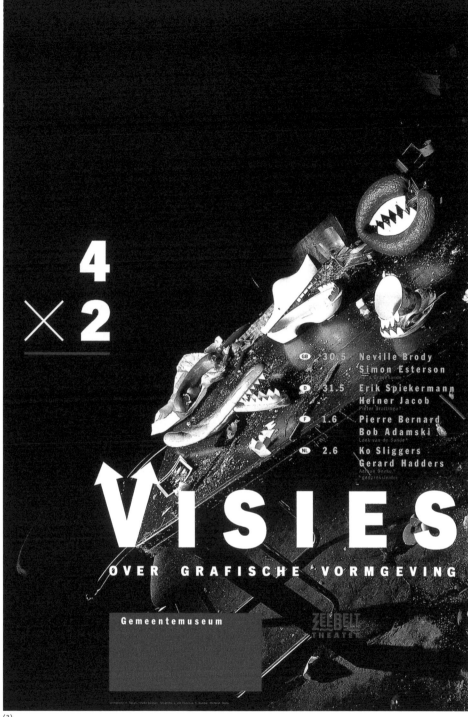

4
× 2

GB 30.5 Neville Brody
           Simon Esterson
           Graesande

D   31.5 Erik Spiekermann
           Heiner Jacob
           Pieter Brattinga

F   1.6 Pierre Bernard
           Bob Adamski
           Loek van de Sande

NL   2.6 Ko Sliggers
           Gerard Hadders
           Aanon Beeke
           gespreksleider

VISIES

OVER GRAFISCHE VORMGEVING

Gemeentemuseum

(3)

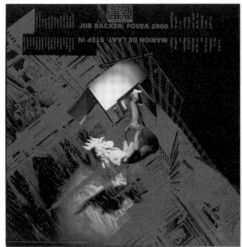

Zeebelt Theatre monthly posters. The enigmatic rooster woman in the series for 1992 looks strangely at ease, as if watching television. Most of this image is covered in the February poster (2 - Robert Nakata) by silhouettes of a businessman with a briefcase grouped around the rooster's head. Is the cloned executive dancing around a vain idol of power and splendour? Or is the configuration a dig at macho corporate culture? Both interpretations conform with the theme of the 'coveted profile of western culture' announced in the poster.

The typography of the April poster (3) reinforces the enigmatic character of the image with seemingly random symbols. Here the encircled rooster's head becomes a graphic sign, as flat as the hand, cross, plane and heart. Small letters scattered along the dotted lines read: 'go where ... ever before.' The poster is an apt accompaniment to the video festival and Beckett plays it announces

(1)

(2)

(3)

(4)

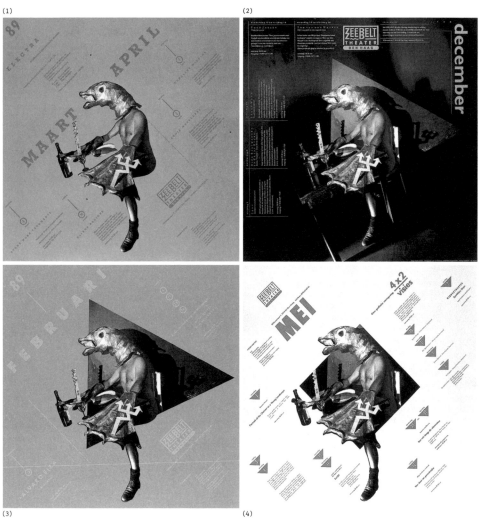

Zeebelt Theatre monthly posters. Fish is a recurrent theme in the posters — The Hague is near the sea and fresh seafood is much appreciated. In the December 1988 poster (2 - Ming Tung) the fish first seen buried in a previous poster reappears as the head and fins of a naked Gert Dumbar indulging in an apostolic meal of fish and wine. At this stage the typography still maintains a modest distance from the images. In later posters in the series most of the image is overprinted, reducing the photograph to the seated figure. Deprived of its pictorial context, it becomes another pictogram representing Zeebelt's culture of 'eat, drink and talk'

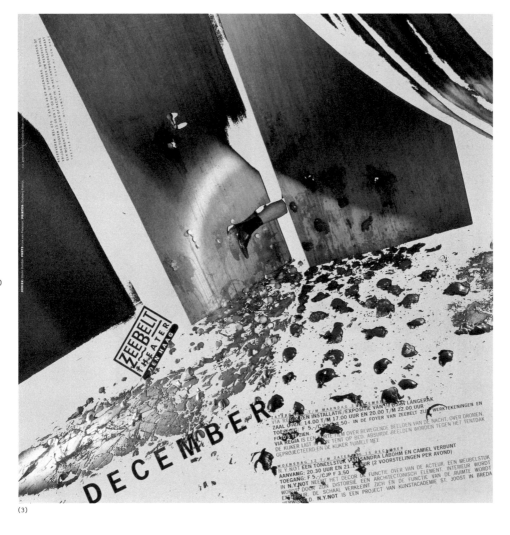

(3)

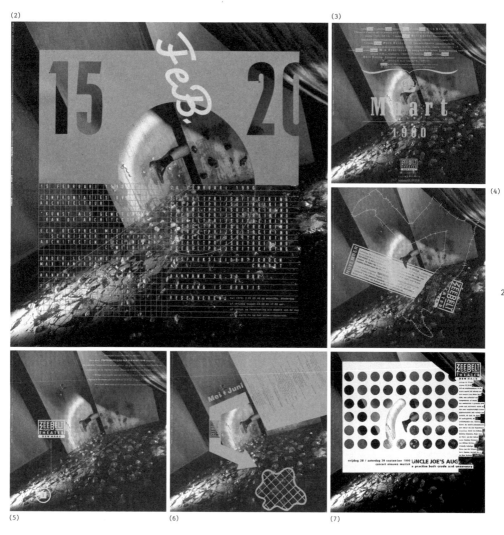

(2)

(3)

(4)

(5)

(6)

(7)

Zeebelt Theatre monthly posters. The base image for the 1990 series is characteristic of Gert Dumbar's ideas about 'controlled chaos'. The scene suggests an actor who has to take refuge from a bombardment of eggs and tomatoes. The stage is littered with smashed projectiles, but a closer look reveals that all the eggs have landed to the left and all the tomatoes to the right of a straight line. The December poster (1) accentuates this line by bleaching out the background. The September poster (7) highlights formal elements of the image, more or less ignoring its content

(1)   (2)

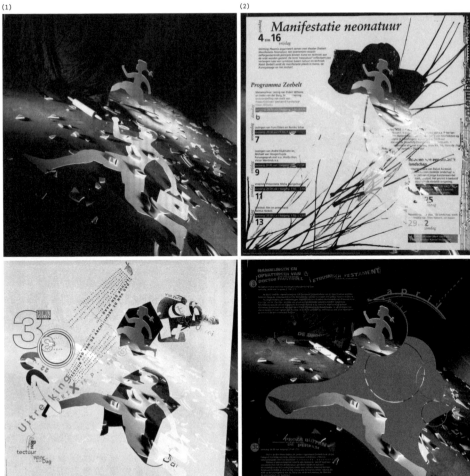

(3)   (4)

Zeebelt Theatre monthly posters. Smashed dishes surround the silhouettes of a running boy and girl — a familiar pictogram from the road sign warning drivers to watch out for children at play. In the basic photo for 1993-1994, the warning seems to have come too late, as the children seek refuge from what looks like a serious domestic brawl (1 - photo by Lex van Pieterson, staged with Gert Dumbar). In Martin Venezky's version (3) most of the original image is covered by a light blue layer over which the typography is printed in black and gold.

Fragments of the boy and girl become elements in a new composition around the gold text announcing the 'Prix de P…', the award for the most blatantly ugly building in The Hague. Date and place can be detected somewhere on the poster, but easy readability is clearly not the main concern. The design plays freely with typographic and photographic fragments and is replete with insider jokes and ironic commentary. The BNA (Union of Dutch Architects) logo in the lower left-hand corner, for instance, suggests that the 'Prix de P…' is supported by the Dutch architectural

(5)

establishment, which is not the whole truth.

Although the orange surface that covers most of the boy and encircles the girl in the April 1994 poster (4) suggests a map of the Netherlands, this is not in fact the theme. Once again, the design is a free interpretation of the formal qualities of the image beneath it.

The October poster (5) all but ignores the pre-existing image. Its typography would work well on a clean sheet of paper, but here it clashes badly with the background. A series of thin lines connects small encircled pictograms to the boy and girl, suggesting a relationship that exists only on a formal level. Japanese characters announce the symposium on Japanese design

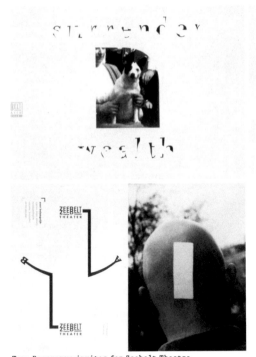

Top: Programme invites for Zeebelt Theatre
(design: Marc Shillum)

Bottom: Direct mail asking whether the recipient wants
to keep receiving mail from Zeebelt. The 'yes' and 'no'
options are mirrored, causing the happy smile to become
a sad grin when answering 'no'.
(design: Marc Shillum)

Invite for greenhouse party (design: Undine Löhfelm)
Gert. Dumbar: 'In Amsterdam there was a plant nursery, which
had an entire alphabet of boxwood trees outside. During
a conference on typography in The Hague, Studio Dumbar
organized an excursion to the nursery's greenhouse for a party
for the conference's delegates. The invite refers to 'topiary',
the practice of pruning trees into specific shapes

Two posters for a series of debates on
'The Creation', focusing on the creative process
in literature, design, theatre, art, music and
science, 2000 (design: Chung Yew Kee)

Works from Studio Dumbar displayed
on the gallery of Cranbrook Academy
of Art, 1980s

CRANBROOK & POSTMODERNISM

Gert's almost innate inclination to, politely but unyieldingly, question a design's argumentation and indeed its points of departure as expressed in the briefing by the client — including when he is the client himself, like in the Zeebelt posters — can be seen as his own internal brand of Baylian design critique. 'Don't listen to the client!' is one of Gert's famous aphorisms, and he has never tired of explaining why it is necessary to take apart a client's brief to the point where one can formulate a new one based on the original's ruins. There is in my view a strong connection between such testing of a design's or brief's internal logic — or lack thereof — and the vogue for 'deconstructivism' in graphic design that arose in the 1980s, especially at three leading art schools in the United States: CalArts (California Institute of the Arts), RISD (Rhode Island School of Design) and Cranbrook (Academy of Art).

In 1983, Katherine McCoy, then co-chair of Cranbrook's design department took a sabbatical that she spent in the Netherlands to study Dutch graphic design. American graphic designer and critic Michael Rock documented her recollections of that trip years later, in 2010. McCoy remembers: 'Here was a body of work built on the same Constructivist foundation [as Swiss Modernism] but with an entirely different expression.' To which Rock adds: 'While Swiss design morphs seamlessly into the modular requirements of corporate identity, Dutch work offers an alternative way to interpret modernism.'[119] McCoy tells Rock that her visit to Studio Dumbar was 'transformational', not only because of the quality of the work she encountered there, but also for the method of working: 'Studio Dumbar is like a grad studio, a real atelier.' Rock points to the similarities in her description with the ateliers of her own students at Cranbrook — no wonder Gert is invited to lecture there. In a letter to Gert, McCoy suggests that he present the Studio's work 'as a basis

---

[119]   Michael Rock, 'Ameridam: The Dutchification of America', 2010. Online: www.2x4.org/ideas/2010/ameridam-the-dutchification-of-america (accessed 21 December 2021). This essay was written for a planned monograph on Anthon Beeke, which was not realized.

for a discussion of your design philosophy and process and your personal development and influences as a designer'.[120] She also invites him to 'assign our group a short-term graphic design project and critique the results'. The visit (the first of several) fell on fertile ground — Studio Dumbar in turn welcomed quite a few Cranbrook alumni in the following years.

> *'DON'T LISTEN TO THE CLIENT!' IS ONE OF GERT'S FAMOUS APHORISMS, AND HE HAS NEVER TIRED OF EXPLAINING WHY IT IS NECESSARY TO TAKE APART A CLIENT'S BRIEF TO THE POINT WHERE ONE CAN FORMULATE A NEW ONE BASED ON THE ORIGINAL'S RUINS*

When Tom Ockerse, a former Dutchman who became chair of Rode Island School of Design's graphic design department, heard of Gert's invitation to Cranbrook, he wrote to him and suggested to combine that trip with a visit to Boston and RISD. As a result, in the fall of 1984 Gert visited two of the main design schools that at the time were, in the words of Michael Rock, '"theorizing" the implication of the [Dutch] work, because Dutch design at this point seems to happen in an almost theory-free zone — Van Toorn being the notable exception'. While Cranbrook was oriented on French theorists such as Barthes, Derrida and Deleuze, Ockerse at RISD focused more on the new interpretations of modernism that came out of the Basel school of design, mainly through the work of Wolfgang Weingart (and his American pupils April Greiman

and Dan Friedman), and on the semiotics of American 'pragmatist' philosopher C.S. Peirce. Van Toorn became a frequent visitor at RISD, along with a steady stream of visiting lecturers from the Netherlands — in addition to Van Toorn and Gert, Ootje Oxenaar, Anthon Beeke and Gerard Hadders in the first semester of Ockerse's 'Visiting Designers' programme. Rock writes: 'The impact of the Dutch contingent is powerful and immediate. Each visitor brings an alternate model of critical practice: Van Toorn, a probing investigation of social conditions and a strong affinity with Lissitzky; Oxenaar, a long tradition of illustrative modernism and design for the Euro-modern state; Hadders, a brute visuality and refreshing DIY sensibility; and Beeke, a parodic, hyper-sexualized image-based production that seems outside of the Dutch compositional tradition. In the studio their critique is rough, crude, sub-lingual. As a foil to the hyper-intellectualism of coolly rational Ockerse, the young Dutchmen offer a highly seductive, sometimes juvenile, always passionate model of design-by-sensation.'[121]

I am citing Rock's view from the vantage point of 'a distinctly American attachment to European design'[122] at length for the same reason I quoted Polish design writer Szymon Bojko earlier — because it gives a view from a different culture. Dutch graphic design, Rock suggests, became so popular and influential in the US because the new generation of graphic designers at schools such as CalArts, Cranbrook and RISD — the latter had been one of the main representatives of the cool Swiss International style — interpreted the manyfold formal freedom they saw in the Netherlands as a new thesaurus of visual languages for their recent theoretical understanding of language and (visual)

120   Katherine McCoy, letter to Gert Dumbar, 14 December 1983.
121   Michael Rock, op. cit.
122   Ibid.
123   Max Bruinsma, 'The aesthetics of transience', in *Eye* #25,

Summer 1997, pp. 40-49. This was my first essay as chief editor of *Eye* magazine.
124   Jean Baudrillard, quoted by Mike Gane in 'Ironies of Postmodernism: Fate of Baudrillard's Fatalism', in *Economy and Society* 19 #3, 1990, p. 331).

communication. A mix of European postmodern interpretations of semiology and a fresh interest in American vernacular graphic culture spawned a 'decon' graphic design that I summarized in 1997 in 'The aesthetics of transience:'[123] 'Heavily influenced by postmodern thinkers like Derrida, Lyotard and Baudrillard, a view of graphic design has evolved that evaluates every visual communication in terms of the underlying code systems. ... There has emerged a new ordering aesthetics that is not, as it traditionally was, concerned with the hierarchical division of clear-cut meanings, but one that challenges the idea of ordering — and meaning — itself. An aesthetics that by composition and typographic manipulations consciously points to the fact that this is one of a myriad possible ways of presenting the material, of telling the story. And that it is a temporary way. The premier task of this aesthetics of transience is to show not so much the simple message as well as the complexity of possible connotations,

> *THERE HAS EMERGED A NEW ORDERING AESTHETICS THAT IS NOT, AS IT TRADITIONALLY WAS, CONCERNED WITH THE HIERARCHICAL DIVISION OF CLEAR-CUT MEANINGS, BUT ONE THAT CHALLENGES THE IDEA OF ORDERING*

allusions and meanings that is implicit in the message. ... The message is in the complexity. More and more we seem to accept that this is the way information works: chunks of possible meaning with no apparent connection other than

their synchronicity whirl through our environment like a flock of seeds in a spring breeze. Then they settle on a page or a screen, and flower for a fleeting moment...'

Though much of the above was referencing designs made in the second half of the 1990s, I think one can safely say that the terrain I described was richly fertilized by students who were experimenting at Cranbrook, RISD and CalArts in the mid-1980s and by the designers who inspired them, among whom Gert figures prominently.

DIFFERENTIAL TRACES

When, in many conversations, Gert insists he is 'allergic to the term "postmodernism"', he seems to repeat Baudrillard's remark 'I have nothing to do with postmodernism',[124] seen by many as a strategic move away from being incorporated into what is commonly considered a systematic critique of modernism. Away from '-isms' altogether. But Gert's entire œuvre — and 'praxis', to use a term that gained new currency in postmodernism's discourse — is consistent with quite a few concepts that are generally understood as central to postmodern philosophy, especially where it concerns aesthetics. Take the importance given to irony, which Linda Hutcheon sees as a postmodern strategy to resist all ideological positions, and which, as we have seen, is an adamant stance of Gert.[125] Or Lyotard's rejection of 'Grand Narratives' in favour of more situational and provisional 'mini-narratives'. This, one could see as a philosophical echo of Gert's insistence on 'music boxes', the kind of signifiers that undermine or put into perspective the main 'narrative' of a design. The same Lyotard, who firmly grounded the term in his

125   See: Linda Hutcheon, *The Politics of Postmodernism*, New York, 1989, and *Irony, Nostalgia and the Postmodern*, Toronto, 1998. See also: Max Bruinsma, 'Nostalgia for a future past', in *De Gids*, vol. 175, 3, 2012.

1979 book *The Postmodern Condition*, later famously stated that 'A work can become modern only if it is first postmodern. Postmodernism thus understood is not modernism at its end but in the nascent state, and this state is constant'.[126] Correspondingly, Gert's adherence to modernism, while at the same time constantly critiquing its rigidities and false pretences of universality, can be understood as a postmodern strategy to continue modernism's project. Or consider Derrida, who sees authorship as a 'differential trace', and states that a work does not, strictly speaking, have an author. On the contrary, the name of the author is a signifier linked with others.[127] If Gert's praxis proves anything, it's the indeterminacy of authorship. His authorship as designer and creative director of Studio Dumbar is as undeniable as that of the many designers who worked there — it is in the linkage that all signatories become opaque and the Studio emerges as 'author' of vastly differing outcomes. 'Our style is that we don't have any', is one of Gert's maxims and it resonates postmodernism's insistence on the transience and situatedness of any utterance, be it a design or a philosophy. His distaste for postmodernism prompts Gert to suggest an intermediary term: 'modernism with a smile'.[128] A rather ironic stance towards modernism, which, I'd say, seems to cheerfully balance both discourses.

Not all critics were as tolerant, though. Comparing Studio Dumbar's design of the new edition of *The Faber Guide to Twentieth-Century Architecture* from 1985 with Frutiger's architectural guide of 1961, design writer Richard Hollis — also a firmly traditional typographer — concludes in a classical defence of modernism: 'By animating the page, using fragments of photographs out of place, the designers have had a lot of fun.

Visual entertainment is a large part of New Wave. But using symbols gratuitously and maps as decoration, to make a fantasy of functionalism, is not. To promise function and not deliver is a slide into graphical decadence.'[129]

The 'decadence' of Studio Dumbar proved to be a magnet for Cranbrook students. One does wonder, however, how they felt so at home in the 'theory-free space' that Gert had carefully carved out from the bedrock discussions on design's social and political responsibility in the Netherlands and the international discourses on the instability and complexity of visual language games like graphic design. 'Cranbrook was a community dedicated to exploring things,' says Gert. 'I don't fancy Derrida and the like, which they all had to read there — nonsense, come on! — but I was impressed by what students did under McCoy's guidance,

CRANBROOK WAS A COMMUNITY DEDICATED TO EXPLORING THINGS. I DON'T FANCY DERRIDA AND THE LIKE, WHICH THEY ALL HAD TO READ THERE BUT I WAS IMPRESSED BY WHAT STUDENTS DID UNDER MCCOY'S GUIDANCE, SO THAT CLICKED

so that clicked. They were all dedicated postmodernists by their own admission. Sometimes a bit extreme, in my view. One of them, David Frej, designed a manual for the ministry of Agriculture, and when I showed it, the client said: "Now you're going a bit too far, Dumbar!" But in general, it was a seamless fit. What I

126   Jean François Lyotard, 'The Postmodern Explained to Children', in Lyotard, J.F. *Answering the question: What is the postmodern?* Sydney, 1992, p. 79.
127   See: Gary Aylesworth, 'Postmodernism', in *The Stanford Encyclopedia of Philosophy* (Spring 2015 Edition),

Edward N. Zalta (ed.). Online: www.plato.stanford. edu/archives/spr2015/entries/postmodernism/ (visited 26 February 2023). Derrida focuses on text, but his characterization is applicable to 'authorship' in the context of 'language games' in any medium.

found most important was their explorative mentality. Students from St. Joost academy in Breda had a similar trait, albeit in a very different way — the explorative mentality, the sketching.'[130]

THE 'DECADENCE' OF STUDIO DUMBAR PROVED TO BE A MAGNET FOR CRANBROOK STUDENTS

Also Rick Poynor, in his 2003 book *No More Rules: Graphic Design and Postmodernism* acknowledges the link between Cranbrook and Studio Dumbar in the dissemination of 'decon' design: 'If deconstructionist design in the 1980s was a semi-underground, seemingly rather subversive activity, carried out in the insulated 'hothouses' of the academy and viewed by professionals with deep suspicion, in the early 1990s deconstruction was primed for popular assimilation. In Europe, one of the channels by which this would occur had been opened in 1985 when Katherine McCoy asked Gert Dumbar, Dutch founder of Studio Dumbar, to lecture at Cranbrook. Dumbar did not share the students' theoretical agenda, but he was interested in their inventive and expressive approach to form and, from the mid–1980s onwards, a stream of Cranbrook students — among them Jan Jancourt, Edward McDonald, David Frej, Robert Nakata, Allen Hori and Martin Venezky — became interns at Dumbar's base in The Hague, where their work helped to redirect the studio's output, especially for cultural clients.'[131]

Vincent van Baar, who had started as an intern and was hired in 1983, recalls the arrival of Cranbrook interns from 1985 onward: 'We shared a mentality — that design was not just a profession, but a passion. Gert saw that common mentality and had initiated the exchange. There was an arrangement with Cranbrook, which resulted in a constant influx of interns, who all stayed for half a year, or just stayed on, like Robert Nakata.'[132]

Although as Vincent states they shared a mentality, the growing number of foreign designers — some came from England as well, mainly Saint Martin's and RCA — did change the studio. Vincent, who acted as mentor for quite a few interns: 'Of course it meant that we spoke English with them. I didn't learn to speak English in secondary school so much as at Studio Dumbar — and acquired an American accent in the process.'[133] The other way around was a bit different. In many sketches of designs for Dutch clients one recognizes the hand of foreign designers in misspellings or misunderstandings of Dutch words. And the American and English collaborators would be introduced to the decidedly French-styled joie de vivre that Gert cherished. Vincent recalls how 'Gert would come in at the end of the day and ask "Who's going to the grocer's?" We knew that meant someone had to go to the shop across the street where they sold Chablis, and pick up a few bottles. Over drinks, we talked about all kinds of stuff, but I don't recall heavy design theoretical discussions. Of course we talked about proportions, composition, typography but also, and I'd say mainly, about just the events of the day ...'[134]

Although Cranbrook is seen as a 'school' representing a design philosophy and style, this did not mean that its output was uniform. Vincent describes vastly differing characters: 'Robert Nakata, a Canadian with Japanese roots, designed entire systems before doing anything else. He made notes in a handwriting

293

128   See pp. 86, 88.
129   Richard Hollis, 'Life after Helvetica', in *Blueprint* 19, July, August 1985.
130   Gert Dumbar: conversation, 19 January 2023.
131   Rick Poynor: *No More Rules: Graphic Design and*

Postmodernism, New Haven, 2003, pp. 57–58.
132   Vincent van Baar: conversation, 9 February 2023.
133   Ibid.
134   Ibid.

that looked like a 6-point semibold Helvetica. And he worked day and night ... Occasionally we lost sight of him and found him somewhere on the floor, taking a "power nap". And then he just went on — he was, in his own lingo, "intense". His work was meticulous, to the tenth of a millimetre. That really was new to us, that kind of precision and attention to proportions. After Robert came Ed McDonald, also from Toronto. A completely different personality — boisterous and immensely self-assured. He was utterly dedicated to Cranbrook's "deconstruction" principle, which adamantly avoided the notion of a design

THEY FOUND AN OPEN PROPOSITION AT STUDIO DUMBAR BASED ON THREE PRINCIPLES: TRUST IN THE INDIVIDUAL DESIGNER; EVERYONE ELSE IN THE STUDIO IS AVAILABLE FOR COLLABORATION; AND IT IS UNDERSTOOD THAT THE CLIENT IS NOT GOD

being a 'whole'. Ed drew that strange Holland Festival logo, with the swoosh. Then came David Frej, in 1986, who was trained as an artist, and he came with completely different forms. All of them were interns, and together with us they shaped the Studio. Perhaps for Gert it was a logical step, but for the young designers it must have seemed like a trip to Mars. They came from a culture of a highly compartmentalized and consolidation-oriented design practice, and found an open proposition at Studio Dumbar based on three principles: trust in the individual

designer; everyone else in the studio is available for collaboration; and it is understood that the client is not God.'[135]

FOR THE YOUNG DESIGNERS IT MUST HAVE SEEMED LIKE A TRIP TO MARS

The first international acknowledgment of the links between Cranbrook Academy and Dutch graphic design came in 1988 with the publication of a special issue of Emigre magazine devoted to the exchange. Emigre was founded by Dutch expat graphic designer Rudy VanderLans four years earlier and had meanwhile established itself as one of the leading conduits for 'New Wave', computer-based graphic design and typography. In issue #10 'several designers' exchanged interpretations of each other's designs focusing on 'cultural and cross-cultural stereotypes, experiences, and

Esther Vermeer,
Emigre #10, 1988

expectations'. A letter from the issue's Cranbrook organizers, Kathy Holman, Glenn Suokko and Kathy McCoy, argues the collaboration: 'The interaction between Studio Dumbar and Cranbrook has historically been an enlightening experience. It will be interesting to see the results of this particular collaboration documented in one publication devoted to the influence of cultural exchange.'[136]

135 Ibid. with added written commentary, February 2023.
136 Letter from Cranbrook Academy, 1 February 1988.

Although the issue was not exclusively devoted to the exchange with Studio Dumbar, the participation of the studio's designers and its (ex–and future)

Ed McDonald, Jan Jancourt,
Emigre #10, 1988

Cranbrook interns was large. Esther Vermeer, Hélène Bergmans, Vincent van Baar, Ed McDonald, Jan Jancourt, featured among Dutch designers such as Rick Vermeulen (Hard Werken) and innovative type designer Max Kisman — at the time living in the US and Spain, respectively — and American experimental designers such as Jeffrey Keedy, Ed Fella, Andrew Blauvelt and future Dumbar intern Allen Hori. McDonald and Jancourt proudly presented their Studio Dumbar designs for Holland Festival and Artifort, while Jancourt summarized the mood he experienced as intern in the Netherlands: 'The current

Vincent van Baar,
Emigre #13, 1989

Dutch design scene reminds me of a birthday party for a ten-year-old. It's full of surprises, humour, and good wishes. ... The design community is supported in their

efforts to reflect a humanistic spirit that is Holland.'

The Cranbrook/Dutch issue as a whole was simmering with graphic fun and wit, and at the same time testified to the new spirit in design described above, that considered play, open-endedness, complexity and stirring up the old rule book the central concerns of its designers. A few issues later, in #13, 1989, Vincent van Baar took a more deadpan look at cultural stereotypes in his 'map of Holland', which sketched the country's position as a neatly raked field with some neighbouring patches — the rest of the world.

DIE-CUTTING AND THE MEASLES

One of the reasons Studio Dumbar was known and admired in the US to begin with was the big roll of posters that Katherine McCoy brought with her from her trip to the Netherlands. Added to it was the first series of posters for Artifort, a small but upmarket furniture company, with a solid modernist background since Kho Liang Ie became its design director in the late 1950s. Elementary, though sometimes rather complex, organic forms characterized the brand. McCoy's husband, industrial designer Michael McCoy, was a regular freelance designer of furniture for Artifort, and advised the brand to go to Studio Dumbar for a redesign of their public campaigns. It was one of the first times that Gert chose to use die-cutting for posters, after discovering its aesthetic potential in the design for Paul Steenhuisen's stationery. The first series, presented in 1984, was still more or less rectangular, with parts of the edges 'gnawed away', but the second series, a year later, was completely free form. The poster for Jeremy Harvey's 1978 die-cast aluminium

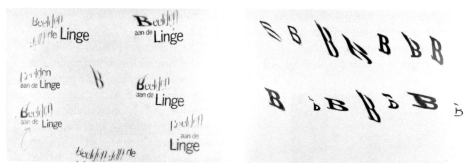

Gert Dumbar's pencil drawings (left) based on his photo-copy experiment with distorting letters for 'Beelden aan de Linge' exhibition

'Hello There' chair (hailed as one of the first Dutch postmodern furniture designs) was die-cut as a painter's pallet. The design was by the first Cranbrook intern, Jan Jancourt, and used the 'O' in the brand name's logo as the pallet's hole. Another poster from the same series echoed the title and the forms of McCoy's 'Quadrio' chair's more geometric shapes in overlaying square and rectangular formats, with some painterly effects on the sides. Vincent still marvels at the freedom of form it offered — and the effort it entailed: 'Imagine, Gert not only demanded that it be perfectly printed, but then about half of it had to be cut away by means of a giant cutting die, which must have cost a fortune.'[137]

Die-cutting became a feature at Studio Dumbar for a while, ever since Gert found out it wasn't as costly as many people thought. He used it again in 1984 for another poster, for the 'Beelden aan de Linge' sculpture festival. That poster's design started with distorting type by photocopying bent sheets with lettering.

It is one of Studio Dumbar's many designs that in a sense prefigure the age of computer design with technology that was made obsolete or redundant after the introduction of the Apple Macintosh in 1984. It was done by other designers as well at the time, such as Neville Brody in England, Tibor Kalman's studio M & Co in the US and Hard Werken and Wild Plakken in the Netherlands: all used stencilled and photocopied type and pasted copied photo fragments from a wide variety of sources in free-plan compositions — harking back to the 1920s avant-garde's experiments with collage, notably Dada's. Like Gert, none of these designers worked with computers, but from today's perspective it seems that they in a way made the invention of the new tool necessary — to cater to a stylistic craving that had been viscerally present for quite some time. Ever since the 1960s, a counter culture had grown to

'Beelden aan de Linge', poster, 1984 (typography: Gert with Ton van Bragt)

offset the smooth institutional aesthetics known as International Style Modernism with rowdy mixtures of pop culture, 'bad typography', grainy press photos and low-

137   Ibid.

Die-cut poster displayed for photography
at Lex van Pieterson's studio

brow dissemination tools like photocopiers, faxes, and stencil machines. From Pop art to punk, such countercultural aesthetics had been prominent in youth culture and political activism for a while already, as a decidedly irreverent answer to 'officialdom', and by the 1980s it gradually pervaded design's more experimental practices, as by

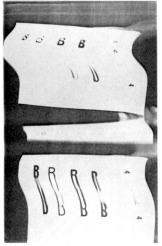

Gert Dumbar's photo-copy experiment with distorting letters for 'Beelden aan de Linge' poster

osmosis — Gert's work is a good example of filtering the aesthetic potential out of unlikely sources and incorporating it into the craft of design. The 'Linge' poster is a case in point: after exploring a variety of distortions the coarsely photocopied letters are finely drawn in Gert's pencil sketches, with the final choice roughly rasterized for printing. 'Then you leave it,' Gert recalls, 'and on seeing it the next morning, you think: you could go one step further.' That's when a serendipitous association with the sculpture exhibition leads to the idea of die-cutting the poster — to add one more sculptural object to the show.

At roughly the same time as the Cranbrook interns started to arrive at Studio Dumbar, a new cultural commission

kindled new criticism of what Hollis called 'graphic decadence'. In 1986 Studio Dumbar was chosen by the new director of the Holland Festival, Ad 's-Gravesande, to redesign its house style and public presentations.[138] The festival logo, designed by Cranbrook intern Ed McDonald, prompted Hub. Hubben to suggest that its blind designer had probably left his guide dog outside tied to a pole. Other critics remarked that it seemed to plagiarize a painting by Kandinsky[139] (quod non), which to Gert would not have been a problem at all, by the way. As he stated in the same year, interviewed on the relationship between graphic design and art in Dutch art magazine *Kunstschrift*: 'We try very explicitly, when a commission affords it, to copy the same feelings that artists have already crystallized for themselves, to simply nick things out of that, and bring them into applied design.'[140]

GERT'S WORK IS A GOOD EXAMPLE OF FILTERING THE AESTHETIC POTENTIAL OUT OF UNLIKELY SOURCES AND INCORPORATING IT INTO THE CRAFT OF DESIGN

Director 's-Gravesande was content, though. The logo's flexibility allowed all manner of variation in a seemingly endless range of colour combinations. 'That did it,' said 's-Gravesande, 'that variability, and the fact that Studio Dumbar, although a very established agency, work with a very young crew.'[141] McDonald, who had already returned to the US after his internship ended when Studio Dumbar was chosen from a pitch with six other bureaus, was brought back to finish the job. In

138 Since 1947, the Holland Festival is the annual Dutch celebration of international experimental theatre, dance, and music, taking place mainly in Amsterdam. The design of its publicity and posters is a coveted commission in the Netherlands, with Dick Elffers, Anthon Beeke, Benno

Wissing, Gielijn Escher, Metahaven (Kruk en Van der Velden) and Thonik as prominent designers besides Studio Dumbar, who held the job from 1986–1989.

139 *Het Parool*, 1 June 1986.

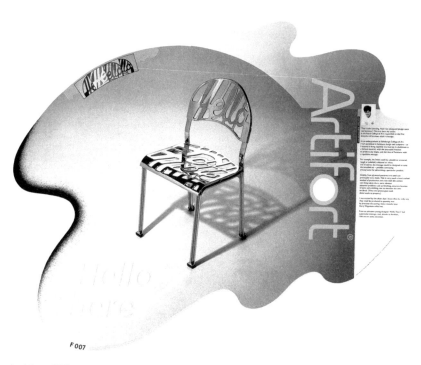

Posters for Artifort, 1985
(design: Gert Dumbar with
Jos Stoopman and Jan Jancourt,
Cranbrook intern, bottom)

140   Paul Hefting, 'Grafisch vormgevers en beeldende kunst:
Studio Dumbar', in *Kunstschrift* 2, 1986, p. 54.

141   Ad 's-Gravesande quoted in 'Vignet even dynamisch als
het Festival', in *de Volkskrant*, 14 March 1986.

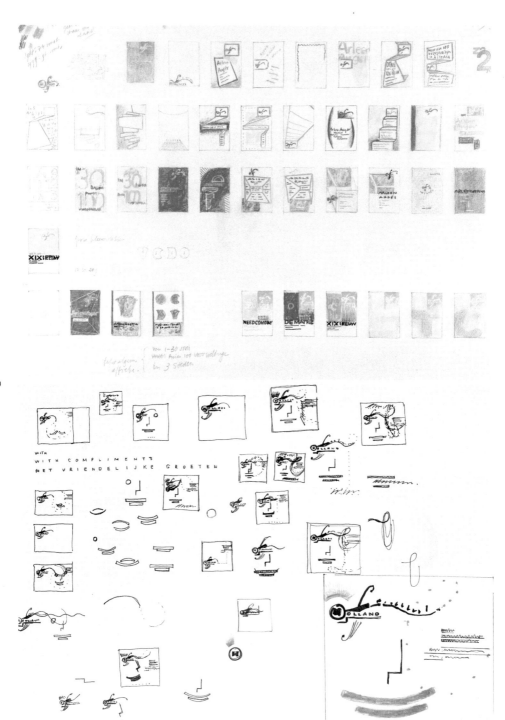

Sketches for Holland Festival, 1985-1986
Top: poster sketches by Vincent van Baar
Bottom: sketches for 'with compliments'
card by Robert Nakata

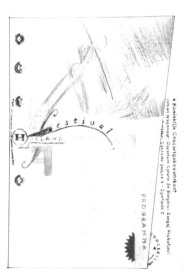

Sketches for Holland Festival
programme brochures, 1989

1 till 30 June **1987**

Holland Festival

Programme

KLM Flying the world to the Festival that's Holland

Free
Order now!
Order tickets by the
bookingform
till 9 may.
From Day to Day.
Bookingform
at page 38.

Gratis
Bestel nu!
Schriftelijk bestellen
tot 9 mei.
Van Dag tot Dag.
Bestelbon
op pagina 38.

Opera
Concert
Theater
Dance

Holland Festival programme magazines, left 1987, right 1988
(design: Gert Dumbar and others, with miniature musical
instrument models by Derk Dumbar)

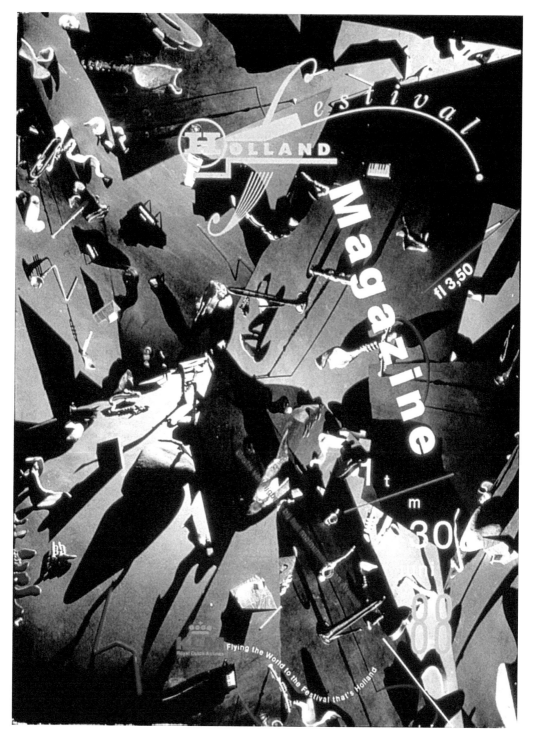

HOLLAND FESTIVAL
MARC WIELAERT ←

304

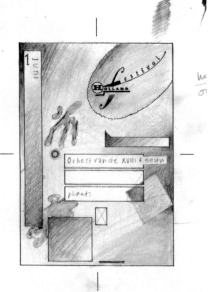

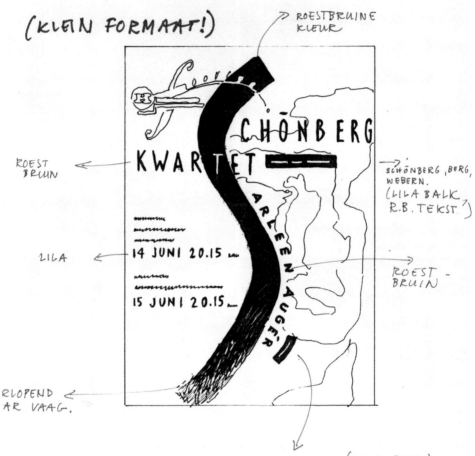

HOLLAND FESTIVAL
AAN → MARC WIELAERT

VAN ESTHER VERMEER, STUDIO DUMBAR

(KLEIN FORMAAT!)

→ ROESTBRUINE KLEUR

CHŌNBERG

KWARTET

ROEST BRUIN ←

LILA ←

14 JUNI 20.15

15 JUNI 20.15

ARLEE NAUGER

SCHÖNBERG, BERG, WEBERN. (LILA BALK R.B. TEKST.)

→ ROEST-BRUIN

RLOPEND AR VAAG. ←

SOPRAAN (LILA BALK).

MARC: KAN DIT IN GROTE
→ LIJNEN ZO UITGEVOERD WORDEN? (BEL!).
DAN KAN IK ZETWERK BESTELLEN.

IK HOOR WEL VAN JE
GROETEN.

— esm

305

(5)

Sketches for Holland Festival posters
and leaflets, 1988
1, 2, 5 Typography: Esther Vermeer
4 Typography: Ton van Bragt

(1) (2)

(3) (4)

(5)

Holland Festival posters, 1988
3, 4 Typography: Ton van Bragt
2, 5 Typography: Vincent van Baar

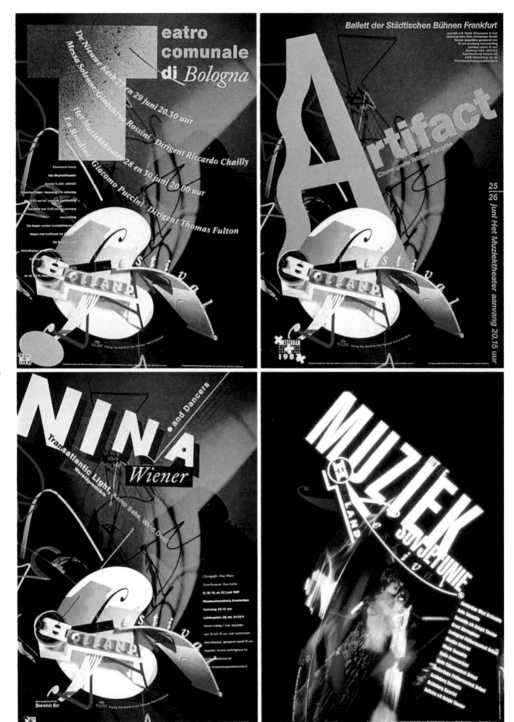

Holland Festival posters, 1987 (3D logo: Robert Nakata,
idea: Gert Dumbar; photos: Robert Nakata and Lex van Pieterson;
typography: Ton van Bragt)

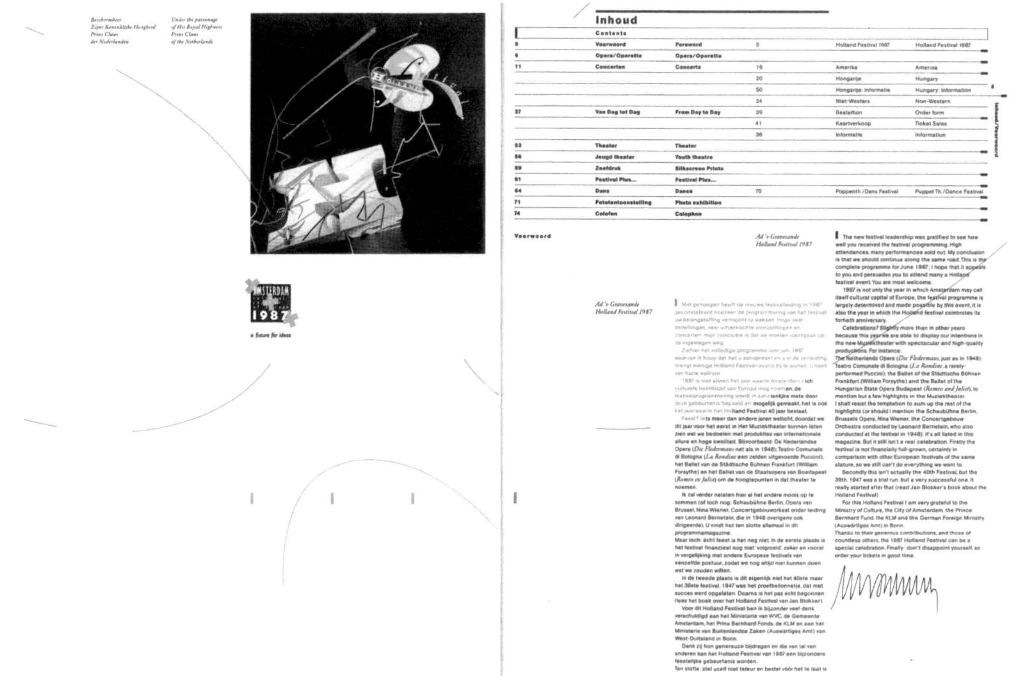

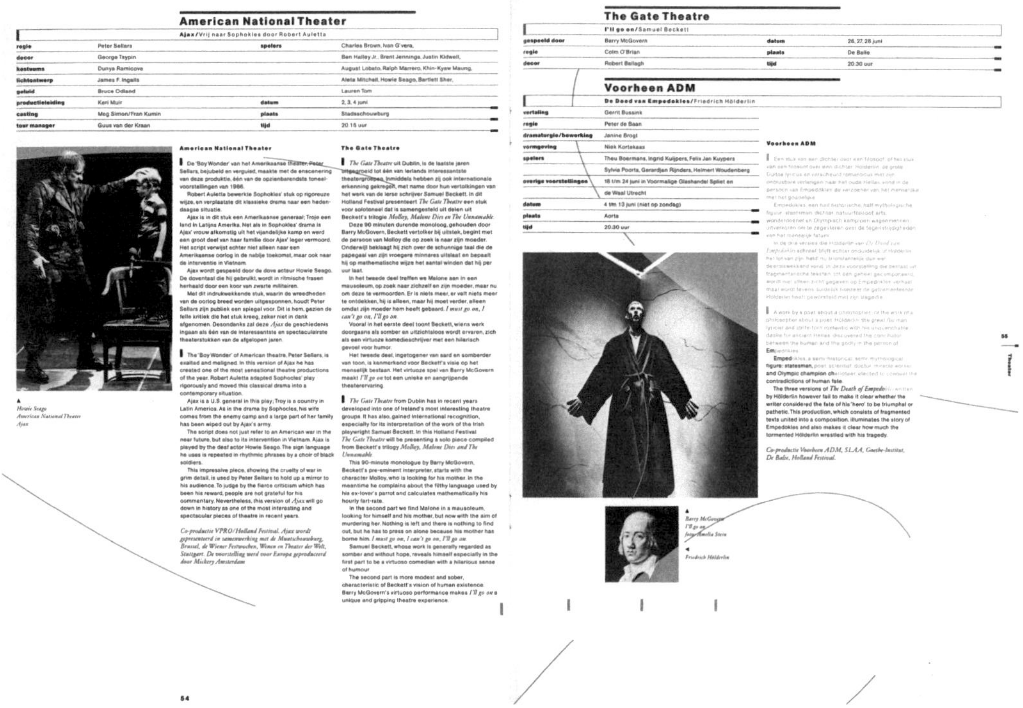

Inhoud

Contents

Voorwoord

Ad 's-Gravesande
Holland Festival 1987

[Dutch text — illegible at this resolution]

Ad 's-Gravesande
Holland Festival 1987

The new festival leadership was gratified to see how well you received the festival programming. High attendances, many performances sold out. My conclusion is that we should continue along the same road. This is the complete programme for June 1987; I hope that it appeals to you and persuades you to attend many a Holland festival event. You are most welcome.

1987 is not only the year in which Amsterdam may call itself cultural capital of Europe, the festival programme is largely determined and made possible by this event, it is also the year in which the Holland festival celebrates its fortieth anniversary.

[English text continues — partially illegible]

American National Theater

Ajax/Vrij naar Sophokles door Robert Auletta

regie	Peter Sellars	spelers	Charles Brown, Ivan G'vera,
decor	George Tsypin		Ben Halley Jr., Brent Jennings, Justin Kidwell,
kostuums	Dunya Ramicova		August Lobato, Ralph Marrero, Khin-Kyaw Maung,
lichtontwerp	James F. Ingalls		Aleta Mitchell, Howie Seago, Bartlett Sher,
geluid	Bruce Odland		Lauren Tom
produktieleiding	Karl Muir	datum	2, 3, 4 juni
casting	Meg Simon/Fran Kumin	plaats	Stadsschouwburg
tour manager	Guus van der Kraan	tijd	20.15 uur

[Body text about American National Theater — partially illegible]

Howie Seago
American National Theater
Ajax

The Gate Theatre

[Body text — partially illegible]

The Gate Theatre

I'll go on/Samuel Beckett

gespeeld door	Barry McGovern	datum	26, 27, 28 juni
regie	Colm O'Brian	plaats	De Balie
decor	Robert Ballagh	tijd	20.30 uur

Voorheen ADM

De Dood van Empedokles/Friedrich Hölderlin

vertaling	Gerrit Bussink	
regie	Peter de Baan	
dramaturgie/bewerking	Janine Brogt	
vormgeving	Niek Kortekaas	
spelers	Theo Boermans, Ingrid Kuijpers, Felix Jan Kuypers	
overige voorstellingen	Sylvia Poorta, Gerardjan Rijnders, Helmert Woudenberg	
	18 t/m 24 juni in Voormalige Gisterhandel Spliet en	
datum	4 t/m 12 juni (niet op zondag)	
plaats	Aorta	
tijd	20.30 uur	

Voorheen ADM

[Body text — partially illegible]

Barry McGovern
I'll go on
Joan Sheila Stern

Friedrich Hölderlin

Pages from Holland Festival programme book, 1987
(design Robert Nakata, with decorative lines echoing
Gert Dumbar's bent rebar lines from that year's base
Festival image — see facing page)

Adformatie, he states that 'purely providing information is irrelevant' for graphic design these days. His logo design puts 'Holland in the centre, static, with everything around it loose and dynamic. Holland has always been there. What's moving is the

Left: Holland Festival logo, 1986
(design: Ed McDonald)
Right: Poster with Kandinsky's *Hommage à Leger*,
Centre Georges Pompidou, 1981

festival'.[142] Movement is one of the more prominent features in the poster series for Holland Festival. Dotted lines, curved and oblique strings of text, seemingly random placed boxes and assorted ornamentations in stark colour accents further dynamize the already vibrant background picture in many of the posters. Such feverish vigour firmly established the Studio's reputation of spreading 'the measles' in graphic design. Although the term was meant derogatively, the associated 'style' proved to be contagious — Studio Dumbar's decorative use of typographic paraphernalia became widely copied.

Over the next few years, the Holland Festival posters and program booklets would seasonally stir up dust in the press, while providing a passionate playground for the studio's designers, most notably Robert Nakata, who had stayed on after his graduation. He recalls the process of making the basic poster for each festival as very similar to a strategy that had been developed and tested in Zeebelt: a general offset-printed semi-finished background, including the Festival logo, onto which specifics could be silkscreened. Robert

made the three-dimensional version of Ed McDonald's logo and photographed it with Lex. 'And then we'd improvise with what was laying around in Lex's studio. As long as the Holland Festival name was there. ... It was a cooperative thing, with Lex, the gist of which was that it's a celebration, a cultural festival. And then another designer would do their thing on top of that.' Partly this was done for budget reasons, because while the Holland Festival is one of the most prestigious events in the Dutch cultural calendar, its budget was tight. Robert: 'It was always a struggle to get the printing done. So Gert would leverage this with printers, like he always did with smaller-budget cultural jobs, and say, like: "Can you do this stuff for the Holland Festival, or for Zeebelt, because we get you this work for ministries or other big clients."'

SUCH FEVERISH VIGOUR FIRMLY ESTABLISHED THE STUDIO'S REPUTATION OF SPREADING 'THE MEASLES' IN GRAPHIC DESIGN. ALTHOUGH THE TERM WAS MEANT DEROGATIVELY, THE ASSOCIATED 'STYLE' PROVED TO BE CONTAGIOUS

Apart from tight budgets, making a basic poster and then adding to it was also done because the actual information on the Festival's concerts and performances often came in at a very late stage in the production. Time pressure and tight budgets had their effect on the Festival's programme booklets too, 'one of those really dense informational things', as Robert remembers. The budget caused

142   Ed McDonald quoted in *Adformatie*, 7 March 1986.

Programme folder for Holland Festival, 1989
(design: Eric Nuijten)
This booklet was blasted by critic Ron Kaal
as '42 pages unreadable!'

Page from programme brochure, 1989
(design: Eric Nuijten)

strict limits to the number of pages and colours to be used in the print work, and Robert recalls warning the booklets' editors that there was too much text to leave any room for images. To which they replied: 'Can't you do something with the typography?' 'Well,' answered Robert, 'if you want people to read 3-point typography, sure, I can see what we can fit in. But I want to make it readable, so you really need to edit it.' [143]

In a column in *HP* magazine, design critic Ron Kaal — not considering the risks of an excess of copy within a limited page count — slashes the lay-out of the 1989 Holland Festival programme brochure designed by Eric Nuijten as '42 pages unreadable'. He imagines Gert whispering to his stooge about 'the postmodern strategy of illegibility', and concludes that 'not a soul can decipher what's on the

programme, or order tickets … thanks to studio Dumbo, from The Hague'. [144] In Gert's personal archive the magazine's copy has a post-it on this page with a scribble in his handwriting: 'splendid!'

THE SECRET BAR — PROFESSOR DUMBAR AT THE RCA

Not long after Katherine McCoy equated Studio Dumbar to a 'grad studio' like the one she taught at Cranbrook, Gert started teaching at his old graduate school, the Royal College of Art in London.

THE UNIQUE THING ABOUT OUR COURSE IS NOT THAT WE'LL POLISH UP STUDENTS' SKILLS, BUT THAT WE'LL STRIP AWAY THE POLISH. WE WANT STUDENTS HERE TO REDISCOVER THAT EVERYTHING IS POSSIBLE

Gert Dumbar

'We went there almost every year on studio trips in a couple of cars on the ferry,' Gert recalls, 'to see final exams of the RCA. So I did stay informed. At one point I was asked to stop by the new director, Jocelyn Stevens. Would I want to become head of the graphic design department, he asked. So I went for an interview and Stevens said that the department was all in shambles and asked if I felt like reviving it. I replied that I did.' [145]

In October 1985, Gert started as the new head of the department, commuting a day each week. One of his first official acts was to merge the two separate departments under his responsibility, Graphic Design

143   Robert Nakata: conversation, 16 April 2021.
144   Ron Kaal in *HP*, 29 April 1989, p. 37.
145   Gert Dumbar: conversation, 17 March 2023.
146   Ibid.

147   John Thackara, 'A Royal revolution', in *Creative Review*, March 1986, p. 32.
148   Ibid.
149   Gert Dumbar: conversation, 17 March 2023.

and Illustration, and put students from both sides next to each other: 'We are not used to that here in the Netherlands, but illustration is very important in England. The collaboration between designers and illustrators was very fruitful, the two inspired each other. I didn't know that beforehand, but I thought, let's try that cross-pollination.' Gert's interest in connecting illustration and graphic design has always been clear — and is indeed in a sense 'un-Dutch'. Now, like in the Studio, it became part of the programme at RCA. Together with Liz McQuiston, his newly hired 'head of department', Gert developed a new curriculum, which highlighted the students' freedom to choose their own projects: 'It's a post-graduate course, so they knew what to do. And then we discussed those projects in class and everyone could comment. That was very much appreciated by the students.'[146]

In an article by John Thackara in *Creative Review*, Gert is quoted stating that 'the unique thing about our course is not that we'll polish up students' skills, but that we'll strip away the polish. We want students here to rediscover that everything is possible'.[147] Thackara remarks that Gert's educational ideas make 'a fascinating contrast to Stevens, the hard man preaching relevance to industry'. Gert, on the other hand, is cited with rather 'un-Stevens-like pronouncements' such as that he will teach students to 'ignore the clients and concentrate on themselves for this short period'.[148]

Gert's demeanour at the RCA mimicked his working method in the Studio: 'It's about giving people freedom, not being obstinate, not being authoritarian. Then you can bring out the hidden potential. And yes, sometimes it's rubbish, but I never say that! There is always, somewhere in those sketches,

often without anyone seeing it themselves, something that I do see. Then, by talking about it, I can give them a nudge. Like a kind of design psychiatrist! Then I say, for example, 'turn it around, it will be more interesting.'[149,150]

Upside — down
Posted January 31, 2021

Then
Me: Showing Gert some sketches.
Me: Proud of my achievements considering the complexity of the project.
Gert: Yes, great thoughts; very good.
Gert: Rotating the printouts by 180 degrees, looking at them upside-down.
Gert: Even better, now continue your explorations.
Me: Baffled and somewhat pissed.

Now
This was probably the most significant lesson I learned as a designer. Keep exploring, be adventurous and don't settle for the obvious. Thank you, Gert.

Michael Lugmayr

Backed by Stevens, Gert dismissed two unproductive teachers and hired new ones, keeping on present teaching staff such as typographer Margaret Calvert,[151] who together with Gert's former teacher at RCA Jock Kinneir designed the UK's road signage and Rail Alphabet fonts, and Ken Garland, the graphic designer who wrote the 1964 'First Things First' manifesto. Meanwhile he initiated a 'secret bar', promising his students that if they arranged a refrigerator and some furniture in the attic of the school's building, he'd keep it filled. The informal atmosphere paid off, says Gert: 'Of course they had to work. We also attracted external commissioners

---

150   Michael Lugmayr, 'Upside-down', posted 31 January 2021 on The Secret Bar. Online: www.the-secret-bar.nl
151   Calvert was appointed head of graphics after Gert left in 1987, and held the position until 1991.

with a penchant to experimentation and our students started to win awards. So that went well.'[152] One of his students, Hannah Tofts, recalls his appearance at RCA as 'a beguiling presence, exotic from Europe! Completely not Heritage British, a relief'. She goes on to describe one of Gert's assignments, with a 'wretched brief, "describe how the internal combustion engine works, so even your grandmother can understand." Us breakaways wrote a script, made costumes and a set to perform the process, I was a fuel inlet-outlet valve; truly a piece of brilliant theatre!'[153]

GERT'S POSITION AT RCA LASTED LESS THAN TWO YEARS, BUT AS RICK POYNOR OBSERVES HE 'HAD A MARKED IMPACT ON A NUMBER OF STUDENTS, MOST NOTABLY DAVID ELLIS AND ANDREW ALTMANN, WHO, ON GRADUATION IN 1987, FORMED WHY NOT ASSOCIATES

In 1986, Stevens asked Gert to commission his students with making a vignette for the RCA's upcoming 150th anniversary. One of the students, Doug James, produced an 'insanely clever design' and Stevens seemed content. But it turns out that he had meanwhile also asked the very established design firm Pentagram to do the job. Students felt betrayed and complained, and Gert backed them. This did not amuse Stevens, who in December decided not to renew Gert's two-year tenure. In Gert's recollection, it was a clear instance of professional envy: 'The department was running like clockwork, and I think Stevens was just jealous of that.

He couldn't take it that I was getting so much attention — we won one award after another in several design competitions. Then nasty things started to happen. At one point the toilets in my department were no longer cleaned.' Students vented their anger in the design press and journalist Jane Dickson assessed 'the mood at the college'.[154] She concluded it was gloomy. In the article, as elsewhere, Stevens insists that Gert, although an excellent designer and remarkable teacher, did not devote enough time to the College's administration and long-term strategy by not attending staff meetings. Gert, on the other hand, puts the termination of his tenure down to 'personal differences' and adds: 'The basic problem is that artistic and administrative policies should not be made by the same person. Jocelyn is very good at administering buildings ... but he doesn't know how to run a design school. ... He has turned my department into a design concentration camp, and as usual in this sort of situation it is the students who suffer. I am angry and ashamed that this business should have to be fought over the backs of my students, who are extremely talented and highly motivated designers.'

Infuriated by these comments, Stevens did not wait to retaliate. Gert was summoned to the Rector's office and recalls that 'for the first time in my life, I saw a man —literally— foaming at the mouth. He was in a rage and I was sacked effective immediately'.[155]

Gert's position at RCA lasted less than two years, but as Rick Poynor observes he 'had a marked impact on a number of students, most notably David Ellis and Andrew Altmann, who, on graduation in 1987, formed Why Not Associates. Where Cranbrook design had been steeped in theory and sometimes made these ideas the subject matter of the design. ... Why

152   Gert Dumbar: conversation, 17 March 2023.
153   Hannah Tofts, 'Exotic from Europe', posted 31 January 2021 on The Secret Bar. Online: www.the-secret-bar.nl
154   Jane Dickson, 'Angry Dumbar hits back at Stevens', in *Direction*, May 1987.
155   Gert Dumbar: conversation, 17 March 2023.
156   Rick Poynor, 2003, p. 59.
157   Student Hannah Tofts, quoted in Michael Evamy, 'When Worlds Collide', in *Design*, October 1992, pp. 11–13.

Not's commercial projects of the late 1980s and early 1990s employed superficially similar visual devices for largely aesthetic effect.'[156] Another critic, Michael Evamy,

Design Week cover, 10 April, 1987

noted that virtually the whole class landed well, despite Stevens' remark to students demanding an explanation of Gert's sacking that they 'were not making a commercial product, and that they were all unemployable'.[157] In the next years, Gert's class spread out to large design and advertising firms such as Cartlidge Levene, Wolff Olins and Newell & Sorrell, and design departments of CBS records in New York or the BBC in London. Evamy concludes: 'The class of '87 students have proved the rector wrong.' In 1992, Stevens left RCA to become director of English Heritage, administering buildings such as Stonehenge.

In the same year Gert was sacked, Studio Dumbar received the most prestigious British design award for their wayfinding design for the Rijksmuseum. A news item in *Design Week* wryly noted that Dumbar won D&AD's only Gold Award in 1987, 'just weeks after being controversially ousted from his visiting professorship at the Royal College of Art', and adds that 'there was a triumph

too for RCA graphic design students, fresh from their humiliation at the hands of Rector Jocelyn Stevens who recently rejected their work on a new college logo and commissioned Pentagram instead. The students scooped two of the twelve Silver Awards — for best catalogue and best poster design.' Gert featured beaming on the issue's cover, with the byline reading 'Dumbar bounces back with D&AD gold after RCA snub'.[158] Later that year, Gert is elected president of the D&AD — the first non-British designer on that distinguished post.

The secret bar
Posted 31 January 2021

In the mid-1980s Gert Dumbar was appointed Professor of Graphic Design at the Royal College of Art in London. He was only there for two years, but luckily for me, this coincided with my time there as a student. The graphics department was based in a large rambling building opposite the Natural History Museum on Cromwell Road.

In his first week, Gert climbed the stairs to the very top of the building where several of us had set up our desks. He enquired whether we had a fridge. When we said no, he replied that he would fill it with alcohol if we acquired one. By his next visit the following week, we had, of course, found a second-hand fridge from somewhere and true to his word, he gave us the cash to fill it with beer.

Andy Altmann

EXPANDING THE STUDIO

The international success of Studio Dumbar naturally prompted thoughts of expanding the studio beyond the Netherlands. An opportunity arose when

315

158   *Design Week*, 'D&AD gold award for Dumbar', 10 April 1987.

Gert, then still professor at the RCA, met the chair and major shareholder of WHSmith, Simon Hornby, who suggested Studio Dumbar to design a new corporate identity for the big firm. Gert realized that this would be a huge and ongoing job — WHSmith is an immense conglomerate in publishing and distributing books and newspapers world-wide — which would necessitate opening a Studio Dumbar branch in London. After consultation with the studio in The Hague, he decided against it: 'I didn't really fancy it. We had so much work, and with a new agency in London, the charm would go away, the fun. To me, it was all about the fun. And I wasn't ready yet, business-wise. It would mean flying up and down and managing, while we were doing such cool things here, with Zeebelt and so on. I found that much more interesting.'[159]

IN ADDITION, THERE WAS THAT MARKETING THING, THAT CAME UP SO PROMINENTLY IN DESIGN, I HATED THAT. HUMBUG, NONSENSE! IT KILLS THE ORIGINALITY OF THE DESIGN

Gert Dumbar

There were more opportunities — several leading design and advertising agencies wanted to collaborate or even take over Studio Dumbar. One of them, Minale Tattersfield, a big design agency that worked for prominent international brands, suggested a merger, which was seriously discussed. Michel remembers that Marcello Minale was keen on Studio Dumbar's 'special niche', which Michel translates as a 'creative niche' that larger and more marketing-oriented agencies

coveted but missed.[160] Kitty recalls Minale visiting in The Hague, admiring the stately studio façade, and exclaiming 'I can see the name "Minale" up there already!'[161] Gert also remembers the reciprocating visit to their London headquarters: 'They had an immense office, with a kitchen with cooks, you know. That was not my world. In addition, there was that marketing thing, that came up so prominently in design, I hated that. Humbug, nonsense! It kills the originality of the design. That was a turbulent world, where I would end up in London, and I didn't particularly have a taste for that.'[162]

Expanding the studio did remain a theme, though. An option that was seriously considered came after Studio Dumbar had designed the identities for two Dutch broadcasting companies in two consecutive years: the NOB and NCRV. The two commissions triggered thoughts to open a Studio Dumbar branch in Hilversum, the capital of the Dutch broadcasting system. The NOB[163] job landed at Studio Dumbar after a pitch in 1988. Robert Nakata was tasked with designing the identity. The starting point

Nederlands Omroepproduktie Bedrijf nv

NOB logo, 1988 (design: Robert Nakata)

was not so much branding the name as branding the function. 'Unlike in North America, the NOB is this meta structure that provides all of the facilities, because the independent broadcasters like NCRV, VPRO etcetera don't have the scale or size to have all that infrastructure. So the

159   Gert Dumbar: conversation, 17 March 2023.
160   Michel de Boer: conversation, 15 July 2020.
161   Kitty de Jong, email, 16 August 2023.
162   Gert Dumbar: conversation, 17 March 2023.
163   NOB ('Nederlands Omroepproduktie Bedrijf' –

the Dutch Broadcasting production Company) was founded in 1988 as an independent faciliatory company providing broadcasting facilities (studios, recording equipment etc.) to the various broadcasting organizations within the Dutch government-funded public media system.

visual idea of the three circles and the three circles inside was based, in a very abstract form, on two strains: there is the NOB

NOB plastic bag for records

providing the facilities, and then there is the programming that is coming from the independent broadcast organizations. So it was about the semi-completion of different strains of development and technology. I don't know how much I actually overtly verbalized that or how much the NOB understood it… But they liked it.'[164]

Unlike most other identities developed by Studio Dumbar, the design was limited to the broad outlines and basics, the logo, and its application on the major carriers of the house style. It was further implemented by NOB's in-house design studio, assisted by a concise style manual.

A year later, in 1989, one of the five original broadcasting associations of the multifaceted Dutch public radio and TV landscape, the NCRV,[165] came to Studio Dumbar for a redesign of their identity. The new logo was designed by American/Swiss intern Adrienne Pearson. The vaguely Christian associations in her interpretation, such as the 'C' that seems to embrace a centre point (representing the world), did

not stand in the way of a remarkably up to date illustration programme, that emanated from the logo in animated 'idents'. The design represents one of the first instances of the use of computer-generated graphics in Studio Dumbar, and an entry into the realm of animated graphic design. It earned Studio Dumbar a pencil at the D&AD awards in 1990. From the letters of the name emanate rays of image fragments, Paintbox-distorted photos of eyes, ears, people, landscapes. Pearson explained: 'I started from the idea that the most successful logos are the ones composed of letters. … I wanted to do something with them which, without destroying their legibility, would have a symbolic relationship to what the company stands for. We knew we didn't want any flying logos, any laser beams, but what was the alternative? The alternative was that there should be people and landscapes. It was a real departure.'[166]

NOB broadcasting truck
(design: Robert Nakata)

Michel designed the screen work (leaders, idents), opting 'for a natural rather than a high-tech imagery'.[167] Contrary to the contemporary fad of animated, moving 3D idents, Studio Dumbar chose a two-dimensional approach — the central ball was the only 3D element in the sequences Michel made. Gert declares: 'All these extremely expensive computer programs are based on 3D space. That makes them so boring. Everybody is falling into the same trap today: because there are

---

164   Robert Nakata: conversation, 16 April 2021.
165   NCRV (Nederlandse Christelijke Radio Vereniging: Dutch Christian Radio Association) is a broadcasting organization founded in 1924 to provide evangelical information to the reformed-protestant 'Christian

segment of society'. In the 1980s it had evolved into a mildly Christian broadcaster catering to a general middle-class audience.
166   *Broadcast News*, October 1989, pp. 24–27.
167   Ibid.

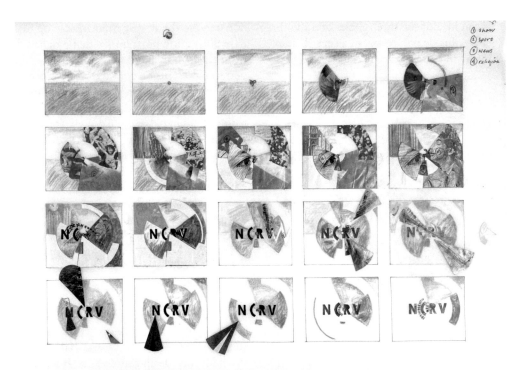

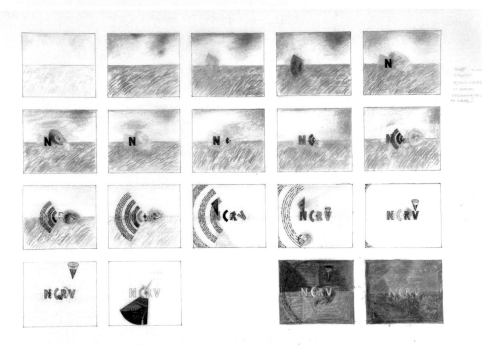

Storyboards for NCRV leaders, 1989
(design: Michel de Boer)

three dimensions, they think they have to use them. We brought it back to two dimensions. ... We used computers in a way they hadn't been used before. What we did was anti-slick, anti all that.' To which Michel adds: 'At Studio Dumbar

Still image for NCRV to be shown during interruptions of broadcasting: 'One moment please'

we tend to change our minds even at the printing stage. With all this expensive equipment it's very different.' He points to the fact that designers for this medium are dependent on operators who need clear instructions, building the animated design layer by layer. 'It's impossible to go in with a completely open mind and try to sketch with the computer. Immediately you see the limits of working with a computer. You realize how important it is not to become a slave to this stupid machine.'[168] Which is quite a remark, coming from the only designer in the Studio at the time who used computers at all.

The two new identities triggered further ambitions in media-city Hilversum. Michel: 'With the NOB and NCRV identities we had a foothold in the television world as designers, and NOB came to us to discuss their creative studio, which they thought needed a boost.'[169] The NOB's in-house design department was a provider of graphics and animated leaders for most of the individual broadcasting organizations, and although at the time other, external companies and designers were starting to compete, the NOB studio

was for many programme managers the first place to go for TV idents and leaders. Michel recalls that 'many talks were held, and at one point it seemed to be a done deal: Studio Dumbar would open a second studio, a television unit in Hilversum. It was pretty much settled — we had already opened a bottle of champagne. I was going to be there for a good part of my time.' The merger of the NOB creative studio with a new Studio Dumbar branch in Hilversum — called 'NOB Dumbar Videographics b.v.' — would be a 50–50 partnership, with a heavy legacy from the NOB. The 'Intentional Agreement' proposed in March 1995 clearly shows the NOB's concern

> *AT STUDIO DUMBAR,*
> *WE TEND TO CHANGE*
> *OUR MINDS EVEN AT*
> *THE PRINTING STAGE*
> Michel de Boer

to keep their share in the broadcasting business as 'preferred partner' of the various broadcasting organizations, as owner of an extensive technical infrastructure and as employer of a significant workforce of technicians and managers. In a letter to the advising consultants of the merger, Gert on the other hand stresses the value of his Studio's brand name and stipulates

NCRV crockery

168   Ibid.
169   Michel de Boer: conversation, 15 July 2020.

that 'Studio Dumbar typically does not remain in the shadow, but has from its start aimed for a position in the avant-garde. We are prudent with our name and cherish our culture'. He and Michel emphasize the importance of 'vision, intuition and fingerspitzengefühl', clearly as a contrast to the perceived bureaucratic culture of the NOB and its focus on commercial success — 'next to striving for profit, the contents of the business plan should also warrant the potential for "enjoying the job." So rather less result and more satisfaction than a high turnover and a bad mood in the company.'[170] Michel: 'In the end it fell through with the workforce. The NOB basically said: "Michel, here is the team of twenty people, which you'll have to take over." Well, hello, then it remains to be seen if that works. Because what is most important for a successful design studio is your human resources.' A good part of the 'legacy' Michel is referring to consisted of people within the NOB's creative department 'in white lab coats' who were good studio operators and technicians, but

> ## STUDIO DUMBAR TYPICALLY DOES NOT REMAIN IN THE SHADOW, BUT HAS FROM ITS START AIMED FOR A POSITION IN THE AVANT-GARDE. WE ARE PRUDENT WITH OUR NAME AND CHERISH OUR CULTURE
> Gert Dumbar

not necessarily creatives. Michel: 'In the end, I think it was good that it didn't work out. But I thought it was an interesting idea — moving images were becoming increasingly important!' Gert had already

made a similar statement in an interview a few years earlier: 'Those crazy things you see on MTV, all of a sudden something is happening there that is diametrically opposed to film, or parallel to it, as a completely independent medium. That is where I see a great future and that is what we are kind of working on. The design of video and television programmes, 'station calls', the question of interactive media, 'virtual reality'... after all, somebody has to make the pictures for that.'[171]

INTIMATE COLLABORATION

A remarkable collaboration, which at the same time testifies to the closely-knit graphic design scene and industry in the Netherlands, was the joint authorship of Studio Dumbar, Hard Werken and Anthon Beeke Associates in the 1988/'89 calendar for Mart. Spruijt printers in Amsterdam. For decades, Spruijt's calendars had been an annual feature celebrating the industry's craftmanship and its support for innovative graphic design in the Netherlands. Jan van Toorn used the commission for the Spruijt calendars as his early laboratory for image editing and visual narrative. Other printers —De Jong & Co, Rosbeek, Lecturis, Thieme— also commissioned designers to experiment; De Jong's 'Kwadraat-Bladen' were famed for their often strange or provocative designs. Such publications cemented relationships across the trade, between publishers, designers, printers, and cultural institutions. Simon den Hartog, former printer at De Jong and later director of the Gerrit Rietveld Academie, sketched the climate: 'We all had our own area and the market was big enough, so we could afford, so to speak, to see each other not as competitors but as colleagues. .... Each had his own clients, and they were very loyal in

170   Letter to Hoek Geers Rapmund & Velding consultants, signed by Gert and Michel, 12 January 1995.
171   Gert interviewed by Max Bruinsma: 'Gert Dumbar – Er zijn geen wetten', in *Items* #1, 1993.
172   Simon den Hartog, 'Printing is a mentality', in *Cor*

Rosbeek, een leven in druk, liber amicorum, Nuth, 2008, pp. 101–102.
173   Ian Horton, Bettina Furnée, *Hard Werken*, Amsterdam, 2018, p. 316.

those days — the 1960s and 1970s. As were the designers, for that matter. Designers had a one-to-one connection with the people who did their printing; those were really collaborative relationships. So you didn't go to another printer because they happened to be cheaper. As a designer, you chose the printer who knew what you wanted.'[172] This was the ambiance in which Hard Werken's Rick Vermeulen could approach the printer's director Frans Spruijt with a proposal to collaboratively design the next calendar with Studio Dumbar and Anthon Beeke Associates on a potentially controversial theme: erotica. As Ian Horton and Bettina Furnée described, 'the main aim of the calendar was to subvert the clichéd sexist imagery of the Pirelli calendar by infusing it with truly erotic content ...'[173] My own review of the calendar found it had 'distinct garage appeal'.[174] Gert, Anthon, and Hard Werken's Gerard Hadders set the tone in the opening image (week 25), a wink to Rudolf Koppitz's 1925 *Bewegungsstudie*, a decidedly less suggestive study of the female body's movement in dance.

The project was managed and in part inspired by Helen Howard, a designer who had previously worked with both Hard Werken and Anthon Beeke. Howard explicitly states that six images in the calendar were 'maximal realizations' of her own erotic fantasies, which pivoted around voyeurism and exhibitionism. In one image, by Hadders, the two fetishes merge, with Howard, naked except for her mask, being casually watched by a man in business attire (week 44). In another, Gert casts her as a stray Dalmatian dog, rummaging around a nightly back yard (week 5, photographed by Lex van Pieterson). Howard describes Gert's approach as 'funny and surprising'. The original association with Pirelli's infamous

calendars only surfaces once, in Michel's and photographer Maarten Laupman's staging of a girl whose chest barely rises above the stack of tires she's standing in

Week 5 page from Mart. Spruijt calendar, 1988 (design: Gert Dumbar with Helen Howard; photography: Lex van Pieterson; typography: Studio Dumbar; model: Helen Howard)

(week 35). The design and typography of the calendarium were divided over the three teams in more or less random order. Thus one finds Hard Werken designs on pages with photo ideas from Dumbar, Howard or Beeke and vice versa. The calendar is an interesting historical document for a variety of reasons: the abovementioned spirit of collegiality is one, but the publication also demonstrates the 'permissiveness' of the 1970s and 1980s concerning erotic and sexual expressions, which today is becoming increasingly anathema again. Beyond the modest erotic contents of the images — and the fact that quite a few of them represent an explicitly female perspective — the real lustful delight was reserved for designers with a heart for print quality. 'Look, four colours black!' sighed one afficionado at the calendar's presentation, eying its seemingly monochrome cover with moist eyes. 'Hot printwork!'

It is interesting to compare and contrast the use of staged photography by Hard Werken and Studio Dumbar in this calendar. At the time, the approaches of

174   Max Bruinsma, 'Verantwoord bloot' (justifiable nudity), in *Items* #27, August 1988, p. 45.
Online: www.maxbruinsma.nl/items/Items27_1988-c.htm

Mart. Spruijt 'Erotica' calendar, 1988

both studios were quite similar — both used spatial arrangements of a great variety of theatrically lighted props, with live models in masks or quasi-sculpted costumes. And both worked in close partnership with their photographers — Pieter van der Meer and Lex van Pieterson, respectively. But there are marked differences, especially in the early period, in the 1970s, when Gert started his collaboration with Lex. Central in these staged images are Gert's papier-mâché objects and figurines.[175] Horton and Furnée mark a shift in Studio Dumbar's use of staged photography in the early 1980s when it 'became aesthetically similar to the Staged Photography used by Hard Werken, with lighting used to create intriguing and spatially ambiguous images'.[176] Hard Werken's 'greater exposure' may have played a role in their mutual inspiration, but it is clear that both groups harked back to 'a Dada-infused spirit of absurdity' that had been a fixture of the more expressionist strand of Dutch graphic design ever since Piet Zwart started tinkering with paper puppets.[177]

A marked difference in the approach of staged photography between Studio Dumbar and Hard Werken can be seen in another collaboration between the two groups a few years earlier: the 'double A-side' single 'Angelique / Ohrendierenbaby'. It was released as a kind of spoof on traditional Christmas songs, performed live at Zeebelt on December 20, 1984 and successively aired on national radio by the experimental broadcasting association VPRO. The initiative came from Hard Werken's Rick Vermeulen, who invited Gert and his crew to fill the other A-side. Both studios staged an outrageously garnished set for their respective sides of the record cover. Gert and Lex topped a pinball machine with an

abundant choice of sausages and cut-out figurines of a male body builder and a topless (though censored) female figure for their side, titled 'Angelique'. Again, erotic inuendo and Pop art references meet, this time in a burlesque take on sentimental French love songs, performed by Gert as a wannabe Serge Gainsbourg. Other members of the makeshift band, called 'Cru Bourgeois', are 'Michel de Bour' on 'batterie au ordinateur' (computer percussion) with painter Willem van Veldhuizen and composer Kees Went on synthesizers and backing vocals. Horton and Furnée remark: 'This constructed collage of found elements virtually parodies Richard Hamilton's 1959 artwork *Just what is it that makes today's homes so different, so appealing?*[178] Although Gert maintains it was not a conscious reference, I'd say it follows Hamilton's composition quite literally, with the prominent body builder and the beaming pin-up — up to the comic strip figure in the background. Hard Werken's side of the cover is rather different: 'Willem Kars, dressed as Father Christmas with his beard perched awkwardly on top of his head, towers above the others as the leader of the group, whilst driving a sleigh across an arctic landscape made of broken polystyrene sheets. The designers Hadders, Van den Haspel and Vermeulen are the reindeers being steered by Kars, dragging Kees de Gruiter behind them as a sleigh deliveing girls wrapped in ribbons as presents.'[179] One of the nude 'girls' is Helen Howard, then designer at Hard Werken. The music on both sides is very different as well; Cru Bourgeois' song is a pastiche of contemporary French synthesizer pop, without the slightest pretension of professionalism (although Went is an experienced and prolific musician), while Hard Werken engaged the experimental band Nieuw Hip Stilen — at

---

175   See pp. 93–101.
176   Ian Horton, Bettina Furnée, *Hard Werken*, Amsterdam, 2018, p. 247.

177   See also pp. 88, 90.
178   Horton, Furnée, 2018, p. 306.
179   Ibid.

Left: 'Ohrendierenbaby' cover (design: Hard Werken),
middle: 'Angelique' cover (design: Studio Dumbar)
Right: Richard Hamilton, *Just what is it that makes
today's homes so different, so appealing?*,
mixed media, 1959

the time a well-known underground act in the Dutch music scene. Their improvised electro-acoustic track, engulfing Willem Kars' spoken word narrative, is vintage 1980s indie-new wave.

SCISSORS, POLAROIDS, AND THE COMPUTER

Apart from some experiments with computer graphics in the idents for NCRV, most of the images and typography in Studio Dumbar's work until the late 1980s were done by drawing, sculpting, moulding, staging, photographing, copying, cutting, and pasting — without computers, that is. Which is amazing, considering the fact that Studio Dumbar worked for three of the world's most successful computer manufacturers throughout the 1980s: IBM, Apple, and Wang. In 1983 IBM, through Gert's London contacts, commissioned Studio Dumbar to develop the showroom identity and product display design for a European network of retail outlets, which IBM was planning at the time. A sizable job — the total quote was ƒ 360.000 — that was shared with Opera Studios, the design bureau of former Dumbar freelancer Tom Homburg, for their interior design expertise. IBM had a rather strict design

policy, developed under the supervision of Paul Rand who had designed its world-famous blue and white striped logo. The dossier on the commission in the archive features IBM's design manual, clearly as a mandatory reference. But Gert recalls that they tried hard to 'break out of that mould', while rebranding IBM in Europe. 'They wanted a string of outlets throughout Europe with their computers and branded office supplies, which we needed to design, including the shops' interiors. So I introduced a new slogan: "Beating the system." Paul Rand liked it and called it a "beautiful dream". I think he meant that both ways — both positively and negatively.'[180] The system that Studio Dumbar wanted to beat included, of course, IBM itself. The customer-oriented interior design for the outlets was a marked difference from IBM's supplier focus, and the red dot that prominently features as a marker for the stores seems at times to gnaw at Rand's sacrosanct logo.

To contemporary eyes, the IBM Product Centers look remarkably like today's Apple stores — predating them by almost two decades — with their prominent display of computers on pedestals and tables and ample space for information and advice.

180 Gert Dumbar: conversation, 19 April 2021.
181 Gert Dumbar: conversation, 19 January 2023.
182 Apple briefing to Studio Dumbar, 21 February 1990.

But in the end, 'the system' decided differently: although the designs were generally liked and approved, IBM's board changed their mind regarding a focus on retail and the project was cancelled.

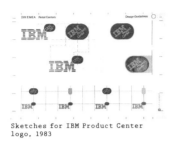

Sketches for IBM Product Center logo, 1983

'We were invited to a weekend in Paris in compensation,' Gert recalls, 'where we were housed at the Ritz and had a copious dinner in a very expensive restaurant with someone from the IBM board. He again said he liked our plan and confided that we had been considered inexpensive as well. I said, "what if we would have added a zero to the bill?" He answered without blinking, "Oh, we would have paid that too."'[181] Perhaps that was why they did not hesitate to generously donate to Zeebelt, as related above.

> *WHAT IF WE WOULD HAVE ADDED A ZERO TO THE BILL?" HE ANSWERED WITHOUT BLINKING, "OH, WE WOULD HAVE PAID THAT TOO*
>
> Gert Dumbar

A year later, in 1985, Apple's European marketing department turned to Studio Dumbar for designing their European management meetings. These were sumptuously staged events to be held annually in various European cities, meant to boost the local resellers' morale

and of course for establishing a sound base on the European continent. The three-day events pivoted around 'The Channel', Apple's network of retailers, an outsourced 'sales force', which is key to Apple's connection with most of their customers. The management meetings were staged to 'have a more concrete interconnectivity & commitment to the channel'.[182] The briefing listed the need for three identities: 'a flexible meeting 'look', a more specific meeting concept [per venue] and a location logo'. This led to an extended list of specifics, including invitations, letterheads, hotel tags, brochures, note pads, badges, banners, delegate gifts, signage, and lavish stage designs. Michel, who headed the account for Studio Dumbar, remembers it as a big job for a demanding client: 'They

Designs for IBM Product Center, 1983

had their visions and missions and targets, and Gert said, "Michel, that's something for you." That's how we often did it, quite naturally. We had different views on how to arrive at a result, but we were always on the same page where it concerned its creative relevance and quality of design.' One of the more marked differences between the

Interior designs for IBM Product Center, with Opera Studios 1983

Interior designs for IBM Product Center,
with Opera Studios 1983

two men is Gert's and Michel's stance on technology. Gert still today shuns computers when he can — Vincent recalls Gert stating on several occasions that 'the computer has a million colours, none of which is nice'. Michel on the other hand was, to all accounts, an early adapter. He had bought a Commodore Amiga, which was used mainly by interns as an experimental playground. He remembers — still with boyish enthusiasm— how

Digital tools such as brushes and scissors returned to their analogue references. Designs for Apple's European Management Meeting by Ming Tung

the Apple account introduced the first Macs at Studio Dumbar: 'Apple gave us three, and a printer. I got a small one, an Apple Macintosh SE, with a modem and AppleLink, a precursor of email. Email didn't exist at the time, 1988, 1989 — this was a telephone link to their own network so I could directly communicate with the client in California. It produced one problem: I am dyslectic as heck, so typing at a keyboard was not fun — there were no spell-checkers at the time. Usually, I'd go to Kitty when I needed something typed out and simply said "these are the ideas" and she would write a perfect letter. She was great at writing.'[183]

Other studio members, however, recall that Michel was more or less the

only one using the Apple, apart from Kitty, who received one of the Macs for administrative and organizational work. A few, Michel and Henri Ritzen among them, followed a course in Apple's lay-out program PageMaker, making odd designs for Apple and the Rijksmuseum. But most

IN THE SURREAL ENVIRONMENT OF THE DESIGN, THE COMPUTER TOOLS ARE MOVING FROM THE 2-DIMENSIONAL WORLD INTO THE 3-DIMENSIONAL WORLD

sketching for the Apple account was done by hand drawing and staged photography. A remarkable instance of trying to link the digital world to tangible reality by analogue means is a series of sketches, in which the concept is stated as follows: 'With the increasing use of computers many tools such as a brush or a pair of scissors will be used less because of the capabilities of the

computer. ... In the surreal environment of the design, the computer tools are moving from the 2-dimensional world into the 3-dimensional world. ... The 2-dimensional imaginary world will conquer the 3-dimensional world.'[184]

Here again the brand's iconic logo was to be respected throughout, but as we

183   Michel de Boer: conversation, 15 July 2020.
184   Concept description, undated (1990).

saw, that didn't deter the studio's designers from freely associating on Apple's — and computers'— new roles in contemporary

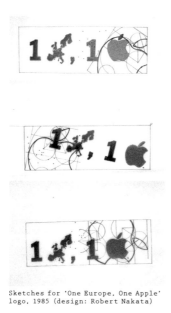

Sketches for 'One Europe, One Apple' logo, 1985 (design: Robert Nakata)

culture and society. Old biblical memes were sketched until likely someone at the studio will have remarked that referring to the apple in Adam's and Eve's expulsion from paradise was probably not a good metaphor. Still, the god-like aspects of digital tools — you don't really see what's going on, but something does get created — and all manner of visual associations on mice, waste bins, brushes, scissors and other analogue organisms and objects that have been turned into digital appliances and software were explored in sketches for the meetings' identities. 'God created the world with the aid of a computer, because the computer is a device that incorporates a lot of other devices. These objects are not tangible, however.' Thus one of the designers noted their first ideas in a brainstorming sketch for the meetings and a European corporate brochure.

Interestingly, one sees the European Union grow in the logo that Robert Nakata designed for the overarching theme '1 Europe, 1 Apple'. Like the brand name, the word 'Europe' is rendered visually, as a schematized map of the EU (including, for convenience's sake, Switzerland). In the late 1980s, East Germany was still not an EU member, but Austria is already incorporated in the logo — it didn't join the EU until 1995. In these early variants, Greece is more or less represented by the comma in the logo — a serendipitous accident. In 1990, after the German unification, the logo was adjusted, also to include Russia, which from the vantage point of Cupertino (Apple's headquarters) had become part of Europe after the collapse of the USSR. That, of course, resulted in an area too big for the

329

'One Europe, One Apple' logo, 1985

2D-rendering of the first '1 Europe' logo. Robert found the clever solution to render it in 3D, as a globe with the vast expanse of Russia more or less suggested over the curved horizon.

One of the meetings of the European 'Channel' is to be held near the company's hometown of Cupertino, in San Francisco in October 1989. It was scheduled to open, it turns out, only a few days after a major earthquake hit San Francisco and the surrounding Bay Area. The 17 October 'Loma Prieta' earthquake of magnitude 6.9 and a death toll of 67 was one of the most powerful and destructive quakes ever to hit a populated area of the

The other way to get things done

(Top right and bottom) Pages from Apple's European corporate brochure *The other way to get things done*, 1988 (design: Henri Ritzen and Ton van Bragt). The staged 'desert' sets are by Gert Dumbar and Lex van Pieterson. Gert: 'The set was quite shallow, but we succeeded to bend the perspective in the way we arranged and lit it, so it looks like a vast space. It was another instance of anamorphosis.' A version of the 'Europe map' sets (top left and facing page) was used as illustration in the programme book for the 1988 Monte Carlo meeting

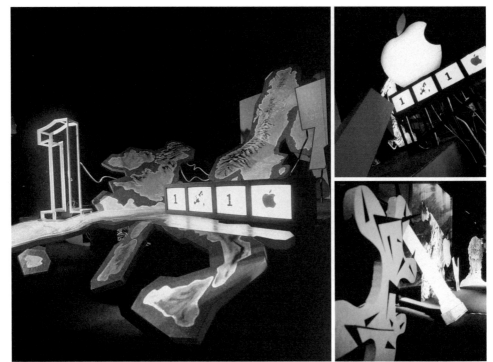

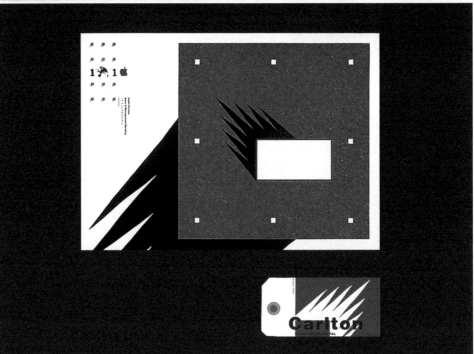

'One Europe, One Apple'
Top left and right, top: stage set for 1989 Munich meeting
Right, middle: stage set for 1989 Geneva meeting
Bottom: Envelope and tag for 1990 Cannes meeting
(design: Ming Tung)

GERT DUMBAR | GENTLEMAN MAVERICK OF DUTCH DESIGN

Event style for Apple's European Management Meeting,
Cannes, 1990

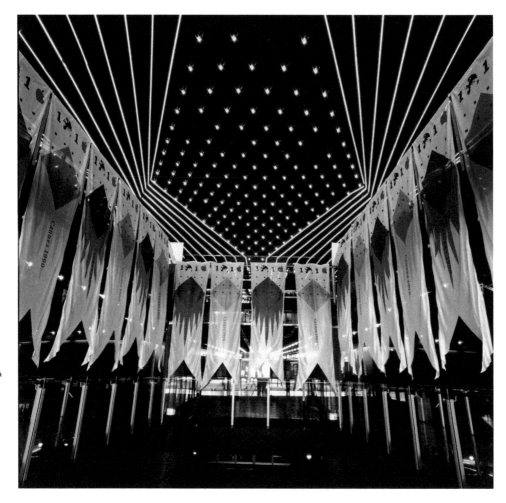

United States — and Michel and other team members were in the middle of it, preparing for the Apple event. Gert and Kitty remember the nervous moments spent vainly trying to contact Michel while all communication with the area had broken down. The meeting, of course, was cancelled.

While it survived an earthquake, the Apple account ended with a war. Michel recalls that the first Gulf war, in January 1991, 'made Apple decide to retreat to their headquarters in Cupertino, California — that's where their main marketing department was. The European branch was just terminated, and that had been our commissioner for years. So that weird war put an abrupt end to it.'[185] In Michel's recollection, it added to an already strenuous time: 'We were just starting the Police account, we still dealt with the aftermath of the Apple account and we were in the middle of moving the studio to a new place, at Bankaplein in The Hague.'

185   Michel de Boer: conversation, 15 July 2020.

'One Europe, One Apple'
Event style for Apple's European Management Meeting.
Cannes, 1990

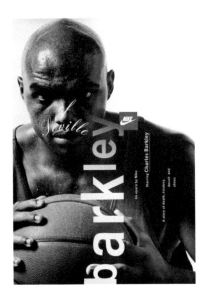

NIKE POSTERS

1993

Gert Dumbar uses the posters as an example to counter the idea that 'advertising agencies have taken over the role of graphic designers'. The suggestion is made by the director of the PTT museum, Ben Koevoet, in a press release for the 1997 'graphic seducers' exhibition, which also contains work by Studio Dumbar for PTT. Gert replies by sending an image of a Nike poster, stating that advertising agencies don't 'take over'— they just 'neatly copy' what Studio Dumbar did years before

SDR

opera by Nike

NIKE

quincy

Starring Olympic Champion
Quincy W

INTERNATIONAL

A story of infidelity,
betrayal
and shoes

Nike posters, 1993
(design: Robert Nakata)

Logo object Het Nationale Toneel
(design: Gert Dumbar)

ESTABLISHED REBELS

STUDIO DUMBAR AT BANKAPLEIN

The move in 1991 to a new location was a major change and a tell-tale sign of success — the studio had outgrown its already expanded base at Kanaalweg. The new venue was a rather posh place, situated on the edge of a small square with a fountain in the middle in a quietly bourgeois residential neighbourhood in central The Hague. As if to underline the fragile balance between the much-advertised classlessness of Dutch society and economic privilege, Gert was quite amused when a nouveau-riche client got a ticket for sloppily parking his Rolls Royce in front of the building. And every week, the Royal Guards would pass by on their training round, on horseback in full ceremonial finery with gleaming helmets, pulling noisy cannons. Intern Martin Brown recalls that Gert would each week rush to the window to watch, 'like it was the first time he'd ever seen them. His

excitement never diminished — week in, week out, he'd rush to see and beckon you to join him.'[186] The move to the new three-story office triggers new renovation plans, again with Opera designers. The sizable investment is sharply monitored by Kitty, reminiscent of the seemingly uncontrolled renovation processes at their previous address. In a letter outlining the procedure in great detail, Kitty stresses that she is 'adamant to know in all respects where we stand financially'.[187]

Emphatically branding Studio Dumbar as a laboratory and a playground for design rebels, had been key to the studio's international success. But internally such characterizations increasingly grew at odds with a design agency that had been growing over the years into an established purveyor of corporate identities and visual communication for large commercial and institutional clients, including the government. While Studio Dumbar's cultural clients —Holland Festival,

186 Martin Brown, 'The Queen's Guards', posted 11 February 2021 on The Secret Bar. Online: www.the-secret-bar.nl
187 Kitty de Jong in a letter to Erik Vellekoop, the renovation supervisor, 11 December 1990.

Rijksmuseum, Zeebelt and many others — were carefully showcased as proof of the studio's experimental, avant-garde outlook, less publicized but large corporate commissions — which provided a sound financial base — necessitated changes in the internal organization. The studio was booming and large jobs such as the identities for the Ministry of Agriculture, Aegon, the Rijksmuseum, PTT, recently privatized to KPN, required a different account management than the more or less open and shared approach that had been the studio's organizational DNA

THE MOVE TO BANKAPLEIN MORE OR LESS NATURALLY REORGANIZED THE STUDIO, WITH SEPARATE TEAMS ON SEPARATE FLOORS, EACH HEADED BY A LEAD DESIGNER

since the start in 1977. Harking back to his experience as an intern at McCann Erickson, where he worked with account managers, Michel had meanwhile developed a more 'agency-like' approach to handling big design jobs. 'Account managers, or account leads, are the link between creatives and client. But they are actually often seen as extensions or representatives of the client, and that caused for some enmity between the two, creatives and account. But there's a healthy aspect to that as well.'[188] What he means is that dedicated teams, with a clear lead designer as reference for the client, can work more efficiently than the studio's standing practice of having the collective team come up with ideas and then gradually develop those towards a result — a process that, as we saw, was shared

with the client insofar they were always presented with several options instead of a single direction. Michel recounts that he 'saw problems arise in managing the business', and after some discussion the studio adopted a new business structure, with Michel and Kitty as new minor partners and co-directors. A holding company and three BVs (LLCs) were created as vehicles for the three partners in the studio.

Increasingly, Gert and Michel started to focus on different accounts, or on aspects of accounts, with Michel gravitating towards the organizational side of large corporate commissions: 'We were growing fast and had a portfolio that was big enough to necessitate a division of tasks.'[189] The move to Bankaplein more or less naturally reorganized the studio, with separate teams on separate floors, each headed by a lead designer. 'It was necessary,' Kitty says, 'because the studio had grown to a size in which the three of us could not oversee all projects in detail anymore. And by adding lead designers — Henri and Joost at first — to our weekly gatherings, we institutionalized these meetings, minutes, and all.'[190]

Animated figure displayed by led lights on the façade of Renzo Piano's Rotterdam KPN tower

One of the designers who gradually grew into a managing role was Henri Ritzen: 'I discovered that I could coordinate things and lead, and I liked that. It started with the new PTT identity. We developed that — Ton van Bragt designed the cubic logo — and in addition to

188 Michel de Boer: conversation, 15 July 2020.
189 Ibid.
190 Kitty de Jong, email, 28 August 2023.
191 Henri Ritzen: Zoom conversation, 17 May 2023.
192 Ibid.
193 In June 2023, Aegon introduced a new logo designed

by Total Design, rendering the brand name in lower-case and disconnecting the square that accentuated the ligature. The change was due to Aegon's growing focus on the US as primary market and led to, in Gert's words, 'a logo designed by marketing pigs'. In the Netherlands the original logo is still in use.

KPN headquarters 'Toren op Zuid', Rotterdam, 2000
(design: Renzo Piano)

designing I helped organize and implement it, mainly the designs for buildings and vehicles, while someone else did stationery and forms.'[191] Henri and other lead designers also represented the studio at presentations for clients. 'Gert only went along when things became complicated.' The more agency-like approach was also a response to tightening budgets and schedules enforced by big clients. Henri: 'That was a new phenomenon for Studio Dumbar: that we were fined by the client if we didn't deliver on time.' The PTT had ordained a fine of ƒ 400 per day delay, mainly in connection to the delivery of the design manual, which they wanted on time. 'So each Friday an older manager from the PTT came by with some collaborators to see how far we were and pick up the pages that were due. That was hard work, but I liked to organize the steady flow — we were not going to pay a darn fine!'[192]

Besides the ongoing work for PTT, later KPN, a typical example — although originating much earlier, in 1983 — of the kind of commission that increasingly became the focus of Michel was Aegon, the merger of two Dutch insurance companies that resulted in one of Europe's biggest firms and a world player in its field. The logo may not look

Led lights mounted on the façade of KPN tower

particularly sensational, but it has been in use for forty years, virtually unaltered since 1983[193] and generations of Dutch citizens will recognize it instantly. Such

KPN headquarters 'Toren op Zuid', Rotterdam, 2000 (design: Renzo Piano). The led wall was an idea of Henri Ritzen, who recalls he 'overdid it a bit'. 'In the end the wall contained about 960 led lights, slightly protruding from the façade's grid. It's a special kind of led light that you'll find only in Swiss tunnels because they need to last for a ridiculous number of hours. I got five minutes to sell the idea to Wim Dik, KPN's CEO. He asked "what does it cost?". I said "about a million". He looked at my sketches, thought for a second and said: "ok". Then I went to Paris to convince the architect, Renzo Piano, that it was a good idea. He liked it. We were standing in his studio next to a model of the building, with a similar "screen" wall also at the back. After seeing my plan, he literally tore off the back wall from the model and said "Then I only want to have it on the front side." So the backside of the building is actually the result of that light wall plan! And then of course, Piano meticulously detailed it aesthetically and technically.'

'I wrote the briefing for the animations to be shown on the light wall and stipulated it shouldn't become a mere advertising wall. So I advised KPN to collaborate with the art academy and cultural festivals in town to program it, which they did. Art students could simply code it on their laptops' 'sustainability' has been a central concern for Gert in designing corporate identities — indeed, many of the logos that were

MANY OF THE LOGOS THAT WERE DESIGNED FOR BIG CLIENTS IN TEL DESIGN AND STUDIO DUMBAR UNDER GERT'S DIRECTION HAVE SURVIVED DECADES OF CHANGES IN THE MARKET

designed for big clients in Tel Design and Studio Dumbar under Gert's direction have survived decades of changes in the market. It is therefore interesting to see that for this job too countless sketches of variants were made. Starting with rather obvious experimentation with the classical Æ-ligature, the designs explore a wide range of possible connections between the two initial letters of the brand name, which after all are pronounced as one sound. Henri Ritzen, who also worked on the

Aegon's board in the 1983 annual report (photo: Lex van Pieterson)

logo, recalls that it was another example of 'intimate collaboration in the studio. We literally passed sketches amongst each other, saying "have a look, see if you can

solve this" or "I wouldn't do this, but that one works".'

With some excursions into building the capitals from distinct bands or patterns and shadings, gradually the diagonal of the right side of the A that is basically covered in the traditional ligature reappears as a line overlapping with the E, optically reinstating the ligature. This

Sketches for Aegon logo, 1983
(top: design for light boxes,
Henri Ritzen, bottom: final logo by
Henk Hoebé)

design, by Henk Hoebé, seems to be the crystallization moment when earlier sketches with decorative lines and colour blocks find a new raison d'être in the word image: the accentuation of the A, dynamizing the otherwise rather lapidary word. Interestingly, setting off the A leaves 'EGON' as a two-syllable sound, which in fact is exactly how the Dutch would pronounce the brand name ('eygŏn'). The A and the blue block behind it are then rendered in countless sketches to find the right balance of block, A, E and the underlining which holds the Dutch word for insurances, 'verzekeringen'. In a rare document Hoebé, the designer of the final logo, explains in great detail why no

343

less than 13 variants of the logo are not as good as the one chosen. The definitive design is then applied to anything from letterhead to towels to huge 3-dimensonal signs on the company's headquarters and local branches. The tilted square, in turn, finds a place of its own as expression of the company's identity as sponsor of the national ice-skating team in sports attire. The international success of the Dutch skating champions proliferates the Aegon identity on TV-screens all over the world.

Studio Dumbar continued to work for Aegon in the decade after the first design, with award-winning annual reports that sometimes seemed to playfully mock the strict hierarchies of a multinational

Holland Dance Festival posters, 1995
(design: Bob van Dijk)

SUCH CAREFULLY CHOREOGRAPHED PHOTO SESSIONS ALSO IN A WAY SYMBOLIZE GERT'S TALENT IN SEDUCING HIS CLIENTS TO PLAY ALONG AND JUMP WHEN HE WANTS THEM TO

company's board of governors. In one of them, the chairman seems to hover above the floor while his lesser colleagues are planted firmly on the ground. In Lex van Pieterson's photos, all of them cast long shadows, an apt metaphor for their influential positions. Such carefully choreographed photo sessions also in a way symbolize Gert's talent in seducing his clients — up to the highest level — to play along and jump when he wants them to.

Still, cultural commissions remained the more publicly discussed products of the studio, and Gert was increasingly asked to advise and contribute as board member of cultural organizations. In 1993,

he was invited to become part of the board of governors for the new foundation for the Holland Dance Festival. That year the Holland Festival separated from its former dance branch, which continued as independent biennial. Gert is invited to the new board as 'PR/design and advertising expert'. Not coincidentally, for the next festival, in 1995, Studio Dumbar acquires the commission to redesign the festival's identity and publicity. In a marked departure from the studio's colourful earlier work — and Gert's consistent stressing of the importance of colour — Bob van Dijk designs a series of black-and-white posters, with dancers, some naked, who seem to hover in a white space against an abstract background with fragments of musical notation. The undulating black lines, a reference to the festival's theme of 'Music for dance', seem to echo

'Holland Dance Festival' posters, 1995
(design: Bob van Dijk)

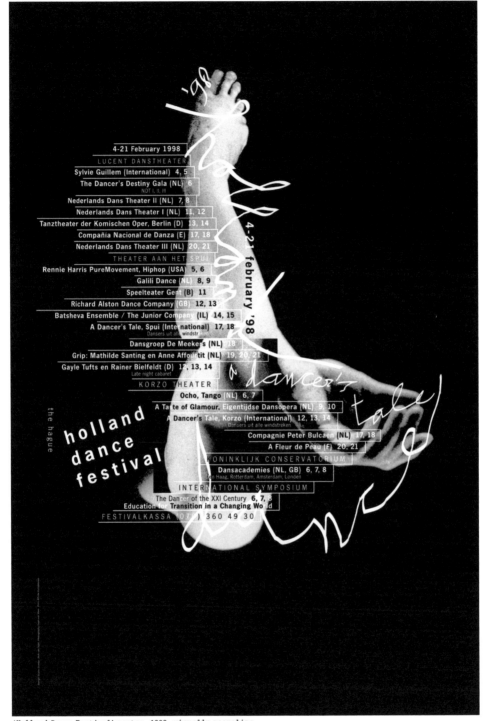

4-21 February 1998

LUCENT DANSTHEATER
Sylvie Guillem (International) 4, 5
The Dancer's Destiny Gala (NL) 6
NDT I, II, III
Nederlands Dans Theater II (NL) 7, 8
Nederlands Dans Theater I (NL) 11, 12
Tanztheater der Komischen Oper, Berlin (D) 13, 14
Compañia Nacional de Danza (E) 17, 18
Nederlands Dans Theater III (NL) 20, 21

THEATER AAN HET SPUI
Rennie Harris PureMovement, Hiphop (USA) 5, 6
Galili Dance (NL) 8, 9
Speelteater Gent (B) 11
Richard Alston Dance Company (GB) 12, 13
Batsheva Ensemble / The Junior Company (IL) 14, 15
A Dancer's Tale, Spui (International) 17, 18
Dansers uit alle windstreken
Dansgroep De Meekers (NL) 18
Grip: Mathilde Santing en Anne Affourtit (NL) 19, 20, 21
Gayle Tufts en Rainer Bielfeldt (D) 12, 13, 14
Late night cabaret

KORZO THEATER
Ocho, Tango (NL) 6, 7
A Taste of Glamour, Eigentijdse Dansopera (NL) 9, 10
A Dancer's Tale, Korzo (International) 12, 13, 14
Dansers uit alle windstreken
Compagnie Peter Bulcaen (NL) 17, 18
A Fleur de Peau (F) 20, 21

KONINKLIJK CONSERVATORIUM
Dansacademies (NL, GB) 6, 7, 8
Den Haag, Rotterdam, Amsterdam, Londen

INTERNATIONAL SYMPOSIUM
The Dancer of the XXI Century 6, 7, 8
Education for Transition in a Changing World

FESTIVALKASSA (070) 360 49 30

holland
dance
festival

the hague

'Holland Dance Festival' poster, 1998, visually recycling
fragments of photos made for the previous festival
(design: Bob van Dijk with Zuzana Lednická)

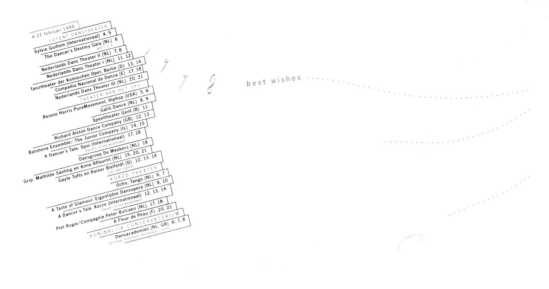

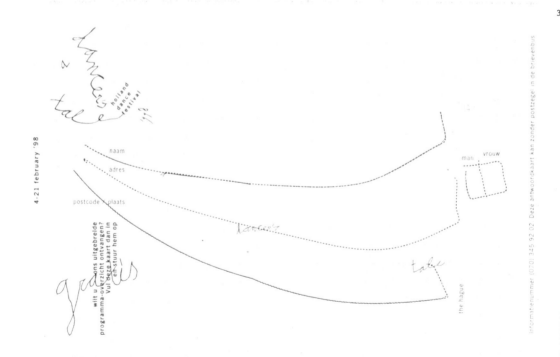

Holland Dance Festival postcards, 1998
(design: Bob van Dijk with Zuzana Lednická)
Bottom: reply card for receiving information by mail.
Gert: 'the strange bent lines were an association on
dancers' movements, but also a bit of a mockery of
bureaucratic procedures. We were quite amazed that many
people filled in their information by meticulously
following the crooked lines!'

or answer the frozen movement of the dancers' bodies — like dancers answer or follow the music. This dynamism is both

Het Nationale Toneel logo, 1993
(design: Gert Dumbar)

balanced and contained by boxed type for the dates and slanting titles. The series won the Netherlands' most prestigious design accolade, the Rotterdam Design Award, the next year. Jury chairman John Thackara applauded the posters as 'strong signs in the urban landscape, with a dramatic, artistic expression and an ambitious, personal quality'. The jury report further remarked: 'The old ideal of integrating typography and photography has been realized again in these designs, in a new and unusual way. They are a powerful proof that the poster has not, as many argue, exceeded its shelf life in our culture.' An international acknowledgment came when the posters graced the walls of the New York Museum of Modern Art's restaurant.

A bit earlier, Studio Dumbar acquired another prestigious cultural client, Het Nationale Toneel (the National

Theatre). Here too, the designer dared to ignore Gert's perennial emphasis on colour. Gert thought Catherine van der Eerden's posters and general identity for the theatre company were beautiful but wondered 'if she couldn't add some colour to it?' To which she bluntly replied: 'No, absolutely not.' The posters and programme booklets were, however, often printed on various coloured backgrounds, but the stark contrast — in both photos and typography — was always kept, heightening the dramatic effect of the images. For the logo,

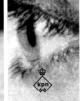

The 'KPN tear' on Nationale Toneel posters

designed by Gert, the company's name was printed in Akzidenz-Grotesk on a block of transparent Perspex, casting a shadow in front of it. It aptly represented the idea of theatre as 'shadow play', as a dramatized reflection of life, sometimes resulting in a mirror image. The 3D-aspect of the logo — also symbolizing the space of the stage, with actors projecting their performance toward the audience — allowed for extremely flexible use; it appeared in all kinds of angles and perspectives on posters and other publications, including the company's huge trucks.

While condoning the lack of colour, Gert did insist on another thing, he recalls. The main sponsor of the theatre company, KPN (formerly the PTT, who had meanwhile become 'royal': Koninklijke PTT Nederland) needed their logo on each poster and publication. For designers, it's always an awkward thing, having to

Het Nationale Toneel poster, 1995
(design: Catherine van der Eerden)

Het Nationale Toneel posters, 1996, 1995
(design: Catherine van der Eerden)

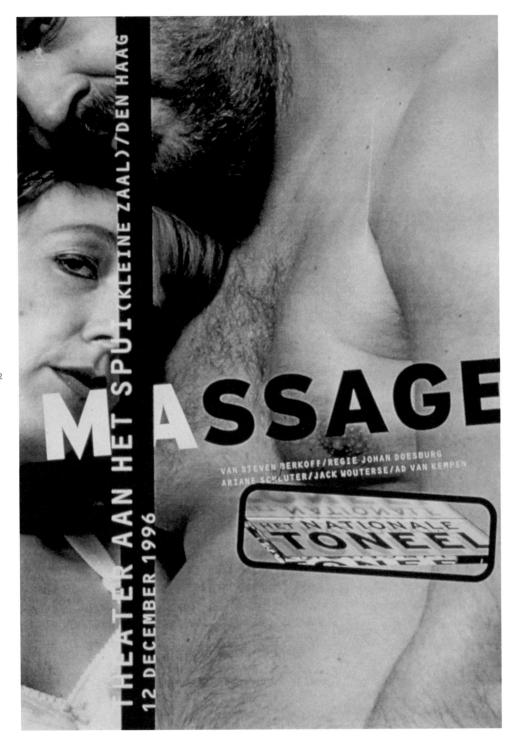

MASSAGE

THEATER AAN HET SPUI (KLEINE ZAAL) / DEN HAAG

12 DECEMBER 1996

VAN STEVEN BERKOFF / REGIE JOHAN DOESBURG
ARIANE SCHLUTER / JACK WOUTERSE / AD VAN KEMPEN

HET NATIONALE TONEEL

Het Nationale Toneel posters, left 1996, right 1994
(design left: Catherine van der Eerden ; design right:
design: Bob van Dijk and Catherine van Eerden)

incorporate company logos that generally ignore or counteract the publication's design. Gert: 'Since almost all National Theatre posters included a face in the image, I suggested to Catherine to use the KPN logo as a small tear, coming from an eye in the picture. It was a way of doing what the client asked, but bend it in a different direction, albeit an absurd one. Luckily, KPN saw the humour of it.' It might even have enhanced the company's visibility — once you've noticed the strange placing of the company logo in one poster, you start to look for it in others.

CIVIL HOUSE STYLES: GRONINGEN MUNICIPALITY AND DUTCH NATIONAL POLICE[194]

In his introduction to their new house style for the municipality of Leeuwarden, in 1991, Total Design's Ben Bos observed that 'house styles for local authorities are a growing phenomenon' — and he was quite right. This 'growing phenomenon' was the manifestation of a form of social evolution evident from the 1970s onwards: a tendency towards a more people-centred, and later more business-

Masks for 'Mr and Mrs Groningen' figures who playfully
introduced the new municipal identity
(design: Dirk Behage)

194   The section on the Groningen municipal and Dutch police identities uses edited and updated versions of: Max Bruinsma, Carel Kuitenbrouwer, 'Het zondagse spiegelbeeld', in *Items* #30, June 1989, and: Max Bruinsma, 'A Civil house style – Studio Dumbar's restyling of the

Dutch National Police.' in *Politievormgeving*, Ministerie van Binnenlandse zaken, June 1997.
195   See also pp. 316, 355, 373, 403, 404.
196   Memorandum House Style Management, Groningen Municipal Council, 1988.

like presentation of the government and governmental services communicated in conspicuous changes to word and image. The government learned to address the citizen as a 'client', and to refer to the 'market' for governmental service provision. In short, the language of the marketing manager made its entry into the world of officialdom.[195]

In addition to this marked restyling of political and administrative jargon, the outward appearance of government institutions was also subject to change: ministries, municipal authorities and local and national services adopted new institutional logos, clearly inspired by the business community. Throughout the 1970s and 1980s, the old, handed-down symbols of Authority were cleared: one after another, the awesome clawing lions and eagles, the coats of arms and banners, the swords and stars disappeared to make way for more friendly or entirely abstract images. Take Studio Dumbar's house style for the city of Groningen, in 1989. The city council labelled the traditional double-headed eagle in Groningen's crest 'a green bird of prey' and told Dumbar to forget this obsolete heraldry. Studio Dumbar produced a house style like many others of its time, its most important aim being: to give the impenetrable government machinery a coherent, clear, progressive and, above all, friendly face. Studio Dumbar were commissioned to design 'the identity, that is to say the 'image', the brain position, the impression the firm wanted to make', as the municipal managers stated in vintage marketing lingo.[196]

The design (by Heleen Raue, mainly, with Dirk Behage, who had recently graduated from Minerva Academy in Groningen) answers with abstract associations on the city and its role as provincial capital. The word

Provisional design manual for Groningen municipal identity, 1987

355

'gemeente' (municipality) rests on an arched line, which is also an extension of the city's capital G. It's easy to interpret the embracing gesture as a sign of care and protection, which are seen as central characteristics of a modern and approachable government. The ellipse is not closed, which suggests openness and flexibility, while at the same time hinting at the central role the city plays for its 'ommeland' (the surrounding areas of the eponymous province). Meanwhile, the commissioner stressed the importance of the new house style for the internal coherence of the administration: it's 'a lubricant, a crow bar for a change of culture within the municipal organization; it brings together people who would otherwise not meet'. Such cringeworthy language, however, was wasted on Gert who dismissed interpretations that the

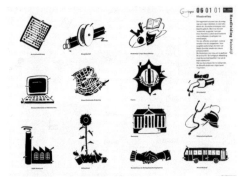

Vignettes indicating Groningen
municipal departments
(design: Valentine Edelmann)

years.'[198] The individual identities of the
municipal departments and institutions
are stressed in the design by Valentine
Edelmann's 'watermark' drawings, cartoon-
like cheerful vignettes that adorn the

*ONE AFTER ANOTHER,
THE AWESOME
CLAWING LIONS AND
EAGLES, THE COATS OF
ARMS AND BANNERS,
THE SWORDS AND
STARS DISAPPEARED
TO MAKE WAY FOR
MORE FRIENDLY OR
ENTIRELY ABSTRACT
IMAGES*

half G and the open ellipse represented
development and open-mindedness: 'No,
we don't think like that. We don't apply
such symbolism or heraldry. We try to
make a clear, striking thing. It's just nicer if
you leave that arch open, more playful, and
design-wise it's just better not to give the
text inside and outside the ellipse the same
colour. I chose the red — and I said so at
the presentation — because I think it's a
nice colour, nothing else. That colour stands
out. In the council, that colour almost
caused a political riot. The city government
was blamed for overemphasizing the
municipality's political signature. That
does indicate the level of Dutch municipal
politics.'[197]

Charlotte Lemmens, the city's
project manager, agreed with the focus on
aesthetics: 'Dumbar came here about three
or four times and spread out dozens of
design drawings and told wonderful stories
to go with them. In the process, it turned
out that we didn't want that sleek, neat,
businesslike look; that was already running
out of fashion, anyway. The symbolism of
the design is inescapable (centre position,
emanating to the 'ommeland'), but the
symbolism is not that important; more
important is that it is beautiful, appealing
and that we'll get by with it for about eight

departments' stationary and 'in a subtle,
playful way reflect their individuality,' as
Gert stated at the presentation. Here too, a
new symbolism replaced the old crests, in

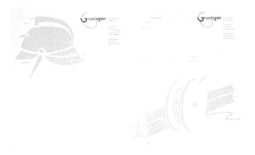

Groningen municipal stationery
(design: Heleen Raue)

a manner that foreshadowed the approach
for the redesign of the identity for the
Dutch national Police, in 1993.

Initially, the 'trend' of replacing a
severe, authoritarian imagery by a more
accessible, friendly design that Ben Bos
was referring to was a case of restyling the
old city arms and heraldic symbols with the
kind of logos that could be found in trade
and industry. Total Design's checkered

356

197   Max Bruinsma, Carel Kuitenbrouwer, 'Het zondagse
       spiegelbeeld', in *Items #30*, June 1989.
198   Ibid. In 2008, after 21 years, a mangled redesign of the 1987
       city logo was introduced, which is still in use to date.
199   See p. 80.

200   Gert Dumbar, quoted in Max Bruinsma, 'Prettig gebrek
       aan plechtstatigheid: Het handelsmerk van Studio
       Dumbar', in *Items #2*, March 1996, p. 39.

octagon for the city of Groningen from 1970 or their honeycomb pattern for the municipality of Rotterdam from 1975, echo abstract company logos like Schrofer's Hoogovens logotype from the late fifties. Gert's own HBG logo from 1970,[199] when still at Tel Design, is also a good example of corporate logos that found eager emulation in restylings of public institutions, such as BRS's 1976 logo for the Dutch Ministry of the Interior. At that time, clarity, openness, and modernity were all-important — fairly vague but highly appealing concepts, which were quite clearly missing in the old symbols of power. But gradually this new, in essence rational abstract design, in its turn came to be associated with an authoritarian mood, which has been suspect in the Netherlands since the late 1960s, when Dutch civic culture became allergic to the harsh, authoritarian aspects of governing a complex society. 'Friendliness', later evolved to 'customer-friendliness', became the code word in the 1980s for a generation of public servants who ten, twenty years earlier had challenged the arrogance of power — with devastating effect. Studio Dumbar has provided that generation with a visual language that perfectly suited the needs of powerful institutions at a time when power had become a cultural embarrassment. Dumbar's slightly anarchic cheerfulness and his ability to put things into perspective, added to the studio's artisan solidity, held enormous appeal for a culture that didn't want to take itself too seriously, without incidentally abandoning all claims to entitlement and decency. Gert: 'It's incredibly Dutch, that questioning of authority. You find that in a lot of Dutch graphic design; irony, humour, a smile, humaneness. In big cultures that is much harder to achieve — the political interests there are also much stronger, much greater.

There is a pleasant lack of pomposity in Dutch graphic design.'[200]

In the post-Cold War period, in which one traditional institution after another was declared 'dead', and in which concepts such as 'ideology', 'truth', and 'authority' were interred in the museum of bygone misconceptions, there arose a cultural craving for symbols that were staunchly contemporary, but at the same time represented at least a semblance of continuity and constancy. Visual signs that would work just like pictograms in computer programs: once clicked on they reveal a coherent world.

'PROBABLY THE WORLD'S HIPPEST LAW ENFORCERS'

WE HAVE TRIED TO CHANGE MILITARY HERALDRY INTO CIVIL SYMBOLISM
Gert Dumbar

357

The design commission for the police identity was a perfect testing ground for such social-cultural considerations. It was necessitated by the merger of two longstanding Dutch police forces, the National (Rijkspolitie) and Municipal (Gemeentepolitie) police. The challenge was to find a design that two amalgamated and highly traditional organizations could still identify with. However, no less important were the social and cultural contexts described above, which needed to be taken into consideration. As usual in Studio Dumbar's practice, many possible answers were explored, including designs that only remotely echoed the standard iconography. Three designs were presented to the clients, the Dutch Ministries of the Interior and of Justice. The explanation

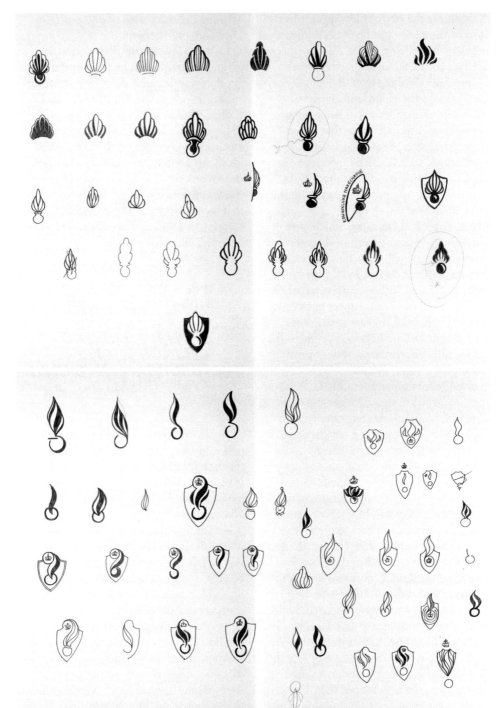

Sketches by Joost Roozekrans for a new vignette for
the Koninklijke Marechaussee (Royal Dutch military
police). The design was not realized

GERT DUMBAR | GENTLEMAN MAVERICK OF DUTCH DESIGN

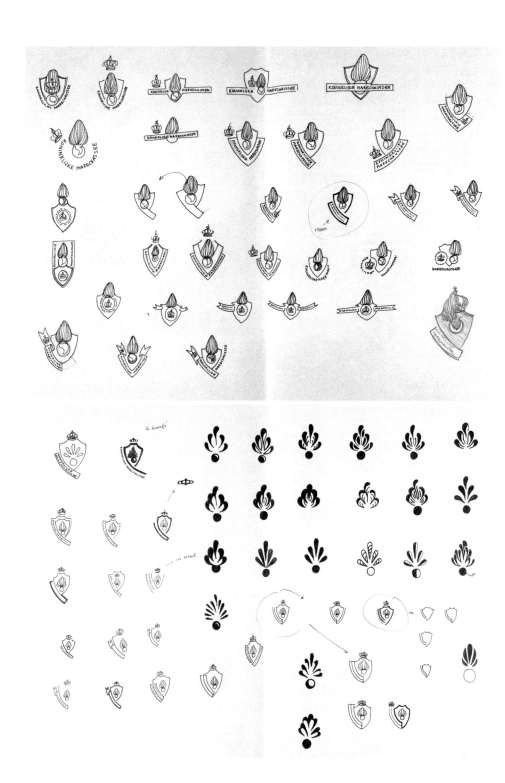

for 'Logo C', by Robert Nakata, clearly sums up the social context for which it was designed: 'The logo expresses the two seemingly contradictory facets of police work: on the one hand, the police help the public and bring them together and on the other, by contrast, they will sometimes have to be separated and kept at a safe distance from each other. The helping hand

Police identity, proposal B (design: Henri Ritzen)

Police identity, proposal B
(design: Henri Ritzen)

prevails in both situations ... although the excessive display of authority is generally rejected.' The typographical rendering of this argumentation may have been a bit too literal, though.

In variant 'B', by Henri Ritzen, the design takes a spin on the eight-pointed star that traditionally adorned the vignettes of police forces, not only in the Netherlands but also internationally. The star becomes a 'rosette'— or a friendly toy windmill.

All variants were presented with digitally printed stationery, elaborate mock-ups of the identities on uniforms, cars, and buildings, seductively photographed in the studio or mounted on photos of existing buildings. For that, Gert made clever use of Studio Dumbar's extended

network of suppliers, from printers to sign makers to car fleet managers — they would provide advice and prototypes for free, with the perspective of becoming part of the vast production phase that would follow a successful pitch. Meanwhile, the presentation to the client looked as if the designs had already been implemented.

The design, by Joost Roozekrans, that was chosen best represented the mentality that triggered Gert's remark at the final presentation of the identity in 1993: 'We have tried to change military heraldry into civil symbolism.' Like the other two proposals, it's a 'pictogram' which clicks onto a new interpretation of the whole

Police identity, proposal C
(design: Robert Nakata)

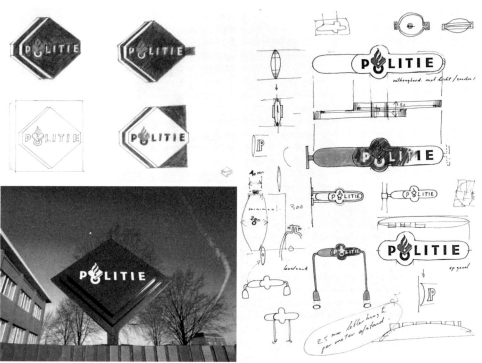

Sketches for police station sign (top left: Joost Roozekrans; top right: Gert Dumbar; bottom left final sign: Joost Roozekrans)

cultural programme 'police' — an effective solution in more than one way. It is of course intrinsically pleasing that elements of both merging police organizations were incorporated in the new symbol: the law

the sword or grenade from the old crests? Why not think up a new symbol, in order to indicate that it really is a new organization, with new duties, as suggested by variant 'C'?

The two traditional vignettes for the national (left) and municipal police (middle), merged into Joost Roozekrans' design (right)

book from the Municipal police and the beacon — formerly exploding grenade from Napoleonic times — from the National police. But this is only half the story. Why these two elements in particular and not the others, like the star in variant 'B', or

Joost Roozekrans' design is indeed staunchly contemporary, but the two pictorial elements from the old vignettes also argue how the new organization continues to be anchored in the old institute. That, of course, happens anyway

by making the word 'POLITIE', in a slightly modified Frutiger capital, the basis of the logotype, and by the use of blue

Poster (design: Henk Bank)

and gold, two colours that were already used by the police in the nineteenth century. But the 'special detail' in that word picture — the 'pictogram'— shows how the organization has changed. The law book is no longer defended sword in hand, no longer surrounded by a shining star, elevated above the ranks of mortals. Instead, it has become a collective agreement, which must be protected — vigilance is imperative: a luminous beacon in uncertain times, if you will. Another advantage of integrating the word politie and its pictorial representation is international recognizability: the word looks similar in all languages in Latin script. The special detail added to that word by means of the symbol with the law book and the beacon is thus a national application of an international concept. The design process, by the way, followed an opposite course, as Joost remembers: 'For a long time I focused on the visual part, on making a vignette, indeed a kind

of pictogram. That ended up with the combination of the law book and the flame. Only in the last instance, when I presented it in the studio, Gert said: "You need to incorporate the word 'politie', then it will become meaningful."'[201] Gert recalls he also advised Joost to 'do something with the flame — just not that elated Napoleonic way'. Joost came up with a sketch and in the studio, someone noted a striking resemblance to the flame used in the logo of the Spanish bank Santander. So that was changed. The final combination, with the vignette and the lowered 'o' of 'politie', was later described by Ootje Oxenaar, chairman of the advisory board for the commission, as 'a stroke of genius': The image can be used without the word, but the typography of the word, with the lowered 'o', can never be used without the vignette.[202]

Top: illegal copying of police striping by a private security company
Bottom: official police striping
The photos were taken as evidence of copyright infringement

Being visible to the public eye was of great importance in the updated interpretation of police duties. Therefore, special attention was devoted to developing the 'striping' of police cars, which greatly

201 Joost Roozekrans: conversation, 14 April 2021.
202 Ootje Oxenaar, interviewed by Albert Roskam, in *Politievormgeving*, Ministerie van Binnenlandse zaken, June 1997, p. 73.
203 Joost Roozekrans: Zoom conversation, 14 April 2021.

204 Kitty de Jong, email, 30 August 2023.
205 Letter Gert Dumbar to G. Herkemij, direction Fire Department, Ministry of the Interior, 20 April 1999.
206 Ibid.
207 Kitty de Jong, email, 30 August 2023.

enhanced the awareness of the police's presence in public space. To Joost, the development of the striping was at least as important as that of the logo: 'It looks amazingly simple, but it took a lot of research. The police, the 25 new regional police departments in the Netherlands, had a total of 140 different types of vehicles. And they all had their own way of marking them. There was no central buying department. So first of all, we figured out that the one colour that all these cars had in common, as off-factory standard, was RAL 9003 signal white. Now white is highly visible, so we took that as basis for the design of the striping. That saves a lot of money: you don't have to spray paint new cars; you just order them in standard white. Then we studied the placement. At first it was at the back. But when we tested that, we realized that not all cars in the fleet had four doors, while we had also seen that with the doors open, the striping functions as an extremely effective road block. So, we moved the striping to the front, so it could be identical for all vehicles. Then we researched the colours. We started with the traditional blue and gold, but decided for a specific fluorescent red, which tests showed to have the greatest visibility at daytime, and a retroreflective blue, which is most effective at night. Then we added reflective dots along the entire contour of the cars … We tested everything and in the end came up with a super simple 'one-size-fits-all' system: basically a bundle of plastic stripes and logos, with which you can turn any white car into a police car and a moving traffic sign within two hours.'[203] The striping was widely adapted for many mobile government services, such as ambulances, the military police (Marechaussee) and the fire brigade. Some of these adaptations were done by Studio Dumbar, for the Marechaussee and

the fire department, for instance. When, during a visit to the Secretary General of Justice, Gert learned that the Ministry of the Interior had opened a pitch for a new identity for the fire brigades, he mentioned that it had to a large extent been done already. It shows how well-connected Gert was, with easy access to high-ranking government officials, but at the same time it demonstrates how precarious such connections were; his intervention caused

WE CAME UP WITH A SUPER SIMPLE 'ONE-SIZE-FITS-ALL' SYSTEM: BASICALLY A BUNDLE OF PLASTIC STRIPES AND LOGOS, WITH WHICH YOU CAN TURN ANY WHITE CAR INTO A POLICE CAR AND A MOVING TRAFFIC SIGN WITHIN TWO HOURS

some irritation at the other ministry, that of the Interior,[204] especially after Gert had written a rather critical letter to the fire department's head in which he stated that the striping 'in fact already constitutes the onset of a new house style. … For another design bureau there actually is very little to be gained by designing a logo for a house style that to a large extent has been put into place already'.[205] He mentions the bewilderment of one of the bureaus who responded to the announcement of a European tender. They called Gert, asking 'if he could explain why there is a competition initiated for the remaining element of the house style?'[206] Kitty: 'As a result, we were not invited to tender for the ƒ 300,000 job, which went to another bureau; our striping was kept.'[207] When Joost was working on the striping for the

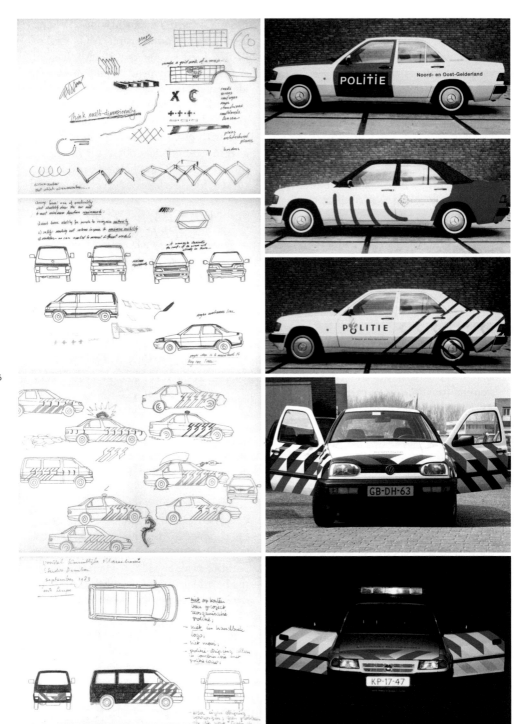

Left: Various sketches for striping on Dutch Customs
(top three) and Marechaussee (bottom) cars
Right: mock-ups of variations of police car striping

Bankaplein 1
2585 EV Den Haag
Holland
070-354 63 04

S T U D I O **D U M B A R**
. . . .

voor Joost.

datum ·

onderwerp ·

uw kenmerk ·

declaratie ·

geheel wit

geheel blauw.
Kon March.

voorstel ①

geheel wit

geheel blauw
Kon. March

voorstel ②

geheel wit.

geheel blauw.
Kon March.

voorstel ③
(is verreweg de mooiste)

Bankrelatie: Algemene Bank Nederland, Den Haag
ten behoeve van rekeningnummer: 51 85 17 225
postgironummer ABN: 7112 te Den Haag

Studio Dumbar bv
Inschrijving Handelsregister
K.v.K. 's-Gravenhage nr. 91102

Telefax 070-352 19 04

Gert Dumbar's comments on Joost Roozekrans'
proposals for striping on Koninklijke Marechaussee
cars: proposal 3 'is by far the nicest'

Marechaussee, he suggests a redesign of the force's vignette as well. Considering the stature of the military police — changing its official look would require royal consent — he wrote to Ootje Oxenaar, who had warm ties with the court: 'If they like our proposal, does that mean that the Queen should be informed? If so, could you please arrange that contact?'[208]

Initially, several local police forces were reluctant to embrace the new house style. In Studio Dumbar's design the 'service provider' was unequivocally distinguishable from the others, the traffic warden, the security officer, and the private security guard. The fact that they are so clearly distinguishable was seen by some in the police force as a threat — which shows that the new culture had not sunk in in all layers of the firm. For the managers, however, nation-wide support for the new house style was also a matter of efficiency, and the cars were a major argument. With the new remarkable striping, even different kinds of cars looked quite similar. As Michel recalls, '... all of a sudden, everybody saw the same cars everywhere. Together with the standardized uniform and logo, that gave the public the impression that there was more "blue on the street". Research by the ministry showed that

people thought there was more patrolling, while in fact there were less police cars on the road than before. So that's return on

Striping applied to various police, ambulance, and fire brigade vehicles

investment in a uniform house style!'[209] Return on investment also in the studio's own reputation; Gert once remarked that 'our portfolio is on the street'.

OUR PORTFOLIO IS ON THE STREET
Gert Dumbar

Studio Dumbar interpreted the word politie as a brand name, in consistency with the developments described above, and made a contemporary logotype that is instantly recognizable to Dutch citizens and to visitors from all over the world. The corporate identity built up around this visual image, with its various applications and effects, and extra features like the remarkable striping on police cars, however, also gave rise to recriminations from the design field and other commentators. The Amsterdam chief of police likened the 'law-book-cum-flame' to a gas fitter's logo and stated that the fact the designers thought it necessary to attach the word 'politie' to it was proof they had no confidence in the logo's recognizability. That the eight-pointed star in both old vignettes was discarded is lamented throughout the police force, but it was done for a very practical reason: the

208   Joost Roozekrans, fax to Ootje Oxenaar, 14 September 1993. The Marechaussee did not adopt Studio Dumbar's proposal.
209   Michel de Boer: conversation, 15 July 2020.
210   Kitty de Jong, email, 30 August 2023.
211   Mijksenaar and Kuilman quoted in 'Nieuw beeldmerk levert altijd gedonder op', in de Volkskrant, 15 January 1993.
212   Vormberichten #3, 1993, pp. 20-21.
213   Ibid.

authoritative star had become adopted by private security branches as well and could not be copyrighted — the new logo and striping could, and was. 'The resistance the logo evoked was beyond compare in my experience,' states Kitty. 'We received threatening letters, anonymous of course, and were pounded by the press. But the striping became the ambassador of the whole style. The police were so enthusiastic about it that they applied it to anything, including speeding cameras, which thereby became quite easy to avoid by drivers.'[210]

A remarkable criticism came from Studio Dumbar's two competitors in the pitch for the commission, Paul Mijksenaar and Dingeman Kuilman (of Anthon Beeke's studio). Mijksenaar

thought it missed a chance to make 'something different', and Kuilman complained that Dumbar did not stick to the briefing, which in his view favoured the traditional star that encircled both old vignettes.[211] In a reconstruction of the pitch in Vormberichten, the periodical of the Dutch designers' association, however, Anthon Beeke states that the briefing stipulated that the old symbols should not be used, and criticizes Studio Dumbar for ignoring that brief. Together with Paul Mijksenaar — who judges Dumbar's design a 'political compromise' — he files an objection with the client.[212] Notwithstanding, Ootje Oxenaar, chairman of the client's supervisory committee, concludes that 'Dumbar had made the

most of the presentation, with photos of the logo on uniforms and all. He also presented three designs, where the other bureaus each showed only one'. The committee almost unanimously chose Joost Roozekrans' design, as Oxenaar affirmed,

because of 'the good alliance between logo and image. Those two elements are also easy to separate. Further, the sentiments for the old logo played a role as well. It is a sturdy, useful logo'. Kuilman's design was deemed too scant. Oxenaar again: 'I expected something more surprising from Studio Anthon Beeke.'[213] In a review in trade magazine Billboard&Sign Gert downplayed the commotion around the new police identity as part of the game: 'It fosters the process of acceptance. Give it half a year and they can't do without it.'[214] He was right. Thirty years onwards, the police vignette and the broad institutional identity are still in use. The uniforms have been redesigned, but although the striping has been adjusted —broader, with muddier colours and generally less conspicuous— it still echoes the design argumentation of the original.

The police style triggered a new wave of publications, and not only in the Netherlands — it inspired several international police forces to follow suit and adopt a uniform house style. When Pangea Design in Stockholm, for instance,

214   Marc Vlemmings, 'Nieuwe huisstijl moet 50 jaar mee gaan', in Billboard&Sign, Vol. 4, no. 1, 1993, pp. 32-36.

was asked to 'update the corporate identity of the Swedish National Police', they approached Gert because 'it is our belief that we could have a great deal to learn from the Dutch Police example'.[215] Together with Ootje Oxenaar's bank note designs, the police identity became exemplary for what many commentators saw as design heaven. The Southern German newspaper *Süddeutsche Zeitung* started off ironically by stating that 'a veritable design hysteria rages through the country. Cities, offices, and government have fallen prey to a bunch of Schöngeister (design aesthetes)', but ultimately admired the police restyling as Studio Dumbar's 'most spectacular coup'. It turned 'the mice-grey uniformed troupe into probably the world's hippest law enforcers'.[216] The Malaysian newspaper *The Star* sketched 'the breath of Dumbar's influence on design, particularly in his homeland', as 'truly remarkable. The postal authorities, the railway system, the telephone booths, even the country's social security organization [GAK], all bear the inimitable design stamp of the Dumbar Studio'.[217] And a Dutch design special in the German weekly magazine *Der Spiegel* concluded

TOGETHER WITH OOTJE OXENAAR'S BANK NOTE DESIGNS, THE POLICE IDENTITY BECAME EXEMPLARY FOR WHAT MANY COMMENTATORS SAW AS DESIGN HEAVEN

that Holland is 'Fast ein Paradies' for design. Gert is introduced as 'a colourful chap, who collects French motor cycles. His main occupation is star-designer'. The magazine confronts him with the fact that the police design was given an award

by the staunchly conservative American trade magazine *Law and Order*, and notes that 'Kafka-fan and bureaucracy-hater Dumbar sees this as a mere testament to his subversive potential as a designer in government service'.[218]

KAFKA IN TIMES OF PRIVATIZATION

Any Kafka-fan would recognize the public-private bureaucracy of the GAK with familiar horror — the name alone, 'Common Administration Office', looks like it's straight from a Kafka novel. Founded in the early 1950s, the organization was tasked with administering the Dutch welfare state, which had been built up in the Netherlands after the war on the foundation of its booming economy. The GAK was a typical exponent of the Dutch 'polder culture', headed by a 'tripartite' board of governors with members representing the State, trade unions and employers' organizations. It managed the administration and payment of unemployment and disability benefits to entitled employees on behalf of a dozen business associations, organized by their branch of industry, with taxpayers' funds. With a central office in Amsterdam, twenty–five local branches and a number of support centres throughout the country, the organization employed thousands of civil servants. And in 1995 it was in the eye of a bureaucratic storm that raged through the Netherlands — as it did in Europe and most of the rest of the western world, ever since Ronald Reagan and Margaret Thatcher redefined the role of government in economic life as 'leave it to the market'. After the National Railways, the National PTT and the National Broadcasting organization — all with Studio Dumbar identities, by the way — the national social

215   Letter from Orjan Nordling, partner of Pangea Design, Stockholm, 10 November 1997.

216   Mark Spörrle, *Süddeutsche Zeitung Magazin*, 14 July 1996, p. 40.

217   Sheila Murugasu, 'He's got the eye', in *The Star*, 9 April 1998, pp. 2–16.

218   Stefan Scheytt, 'Form-Vorbild Niederlande', in *Der Spiegel*, no. 6, 1995.

219   Tom Dorresteijn, 'En dan nu de echte verandering' (And now: the real change), GAK communication strategy paper, May 1985.

insurance was also to be privatized, and dynamized by the invisible hand of the market. In addition to its task of managing the government's social security policies and funds, the GAK needed to enter the free market of service providers in social insurance, advice, information technology and employment services. In short, it needed a marketable look and a matching corporate identity.

IT WAS A WONDERFUL OPPORTUNITY TO HELP THE BUREAUCRACY, THROUGH DESIGN, TO BECOME MORE STRAIGHTFORWARD

Gert Dumbar

In a strategy paper from May 1995, GAK's communication manager Tom Dorresteijn outlines the challenges: 'Something changes fundamentally and critically by the addition of market activities and in its wake the introduction of mindsets and behavioural patterns belonging to private enterprise.' He goes on to state that the GAK's public image is rather negative — it is perceived as an impenetrable, sluggish, bureaucratic behemoth and therefore its communication is in dire need of 'a commitment to real change' with 'boldness and decisiveness'.[219]

It seems the job landed more or less effortlessly at Studio Dumbar, after an informal pitch, without elaborate presentations. Kitty remembers a first meeting with the GAK team, which 'clicked without a sliver of hesitation or suspicion'.[220] One of the members of the young GAK team explained the job, its context of privatization and the challenges that it entailed, and then introduced a 'quite handsome thirty-something next to him as the leader of the team'. Tom

Dorresteijn had left the introduction of the sizable commission to one of his juniors, which in Kitty's recollection was very rare. It indicated the match between the two teams — also Gert and Michel often made space for their juniors to present a design. Considering his allergy to bureaucracy and marketing — two worlds that coalesced in the GAK job — it is not a surprise that Gert was not very much involved, leaving the dealings with the client to Michel and Kitty, assisted by Joost. 'That's my innate repugnance to government bureaucracy. But that's also why I thought it was an interesting assignment,' Gert recalls. 'It was a wonderful opportunity to help the bureaucracy, through design, to become more straightforward. I once had a desire to redesign the military, which didn't happen, but this came close.'[221] With Michel, Gert did oversee the initial creative explorations in plenary meetings in which all designers involved would gather around the central meeting table at the studio and discuss approaches. Gert: 'The GAK was basically an unguided projectile — and our job was to help steer that in the right direction.'[222] In Joost's recollection it was a typical project for Michel: 'He ran the show: systems thinking, long haul, high energy — he was the locomotive. Without Michel such large and long-term projects would have been impossible for Studio Dumbar.'[223]

It is clear from the archive that a good part of the studio's designers provided first ideas and sketches for the logo and variants, with Joost emerging as lead designer, although none of his early sketches were chosen to be developed further. Kitty: 'Joost played a central role in the sketching and became the leading act in implementing the very elaborate house style, from the stationery to the last piece of porcelain in the canteen. With the

---

220 Kitty de Jong, email, 15 June, 2023. Representing Studio Dumbar were Michel de Boer, Kitty de Jong, Joost Roozekrans and Henri Ritzen.
221 Gert Dumbar: conversation, 22 June 2023.
222 Ibid.
223 Joost Roozekrans, email, 19 June 2023.

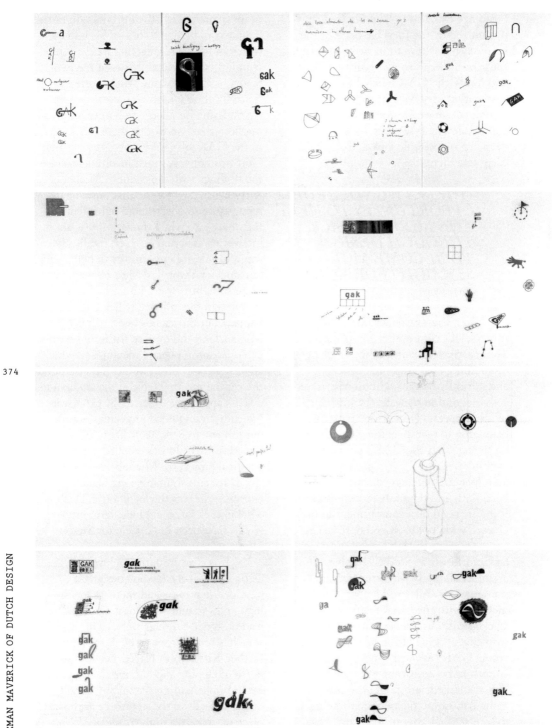

Sketches for GAK (Common Administration Office), 1995

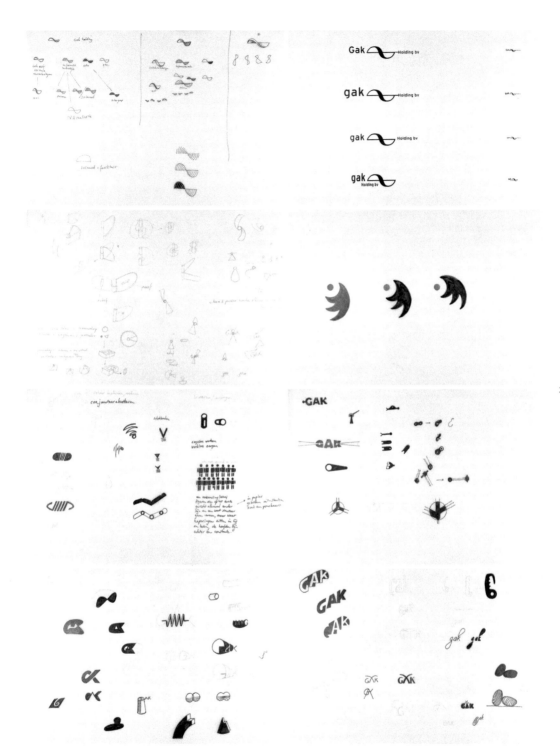

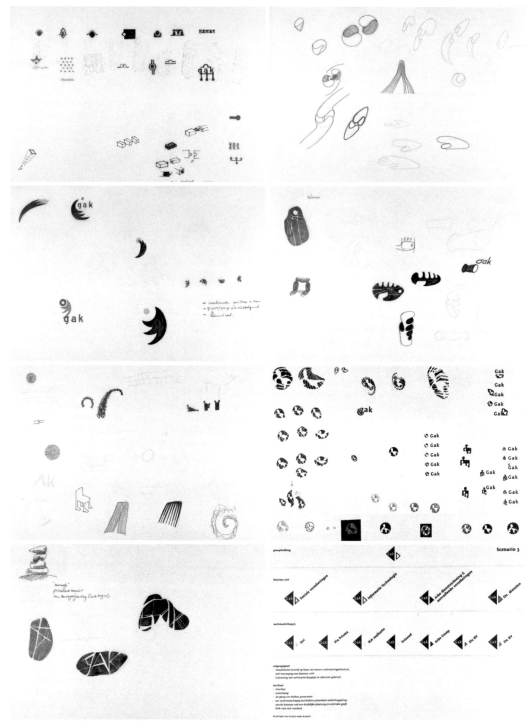

Sketches for GAK (Common Administration Office), 1995

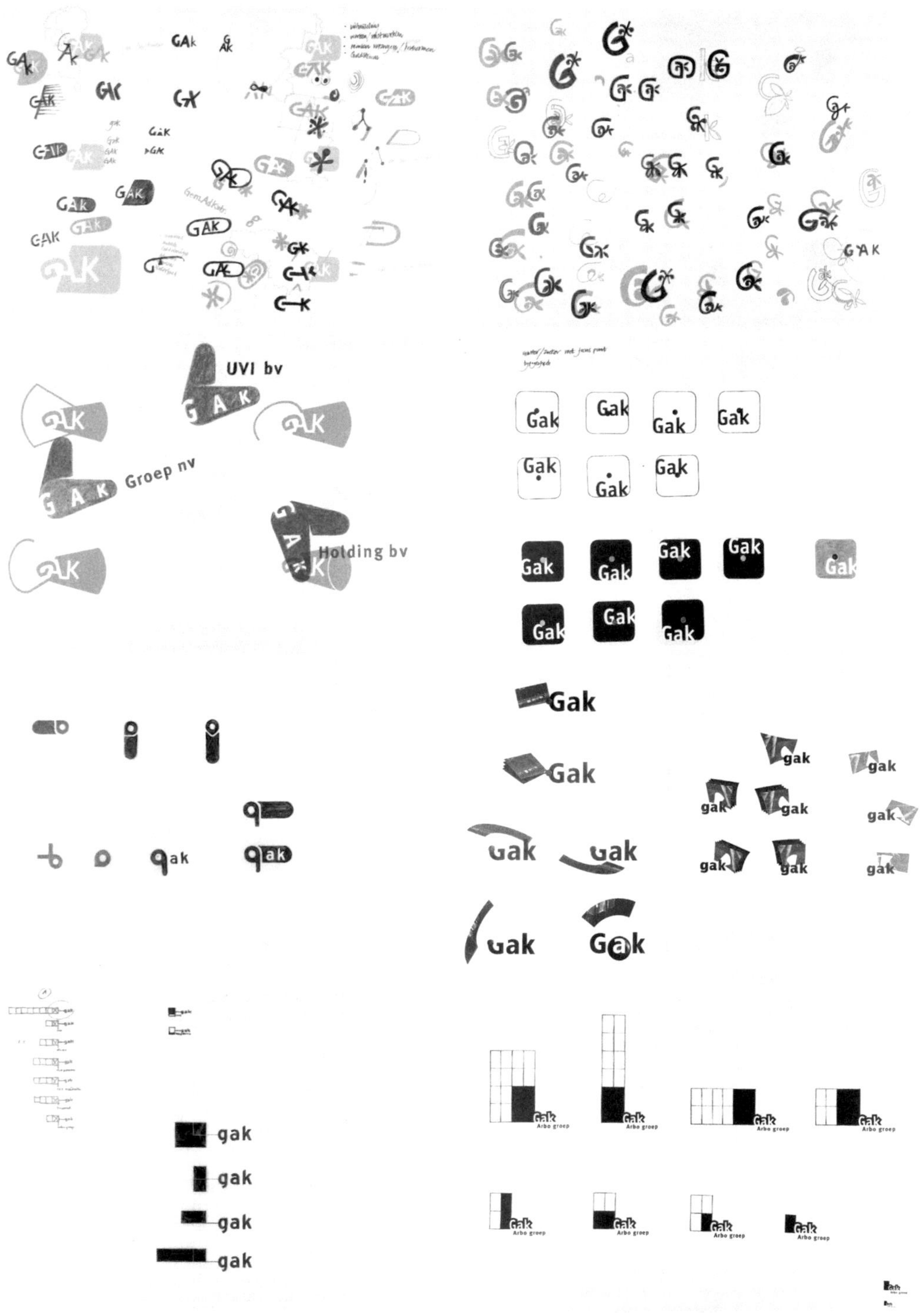
UVI bv
Groep nv
Holding bv
Gak
gak
Arbo groep

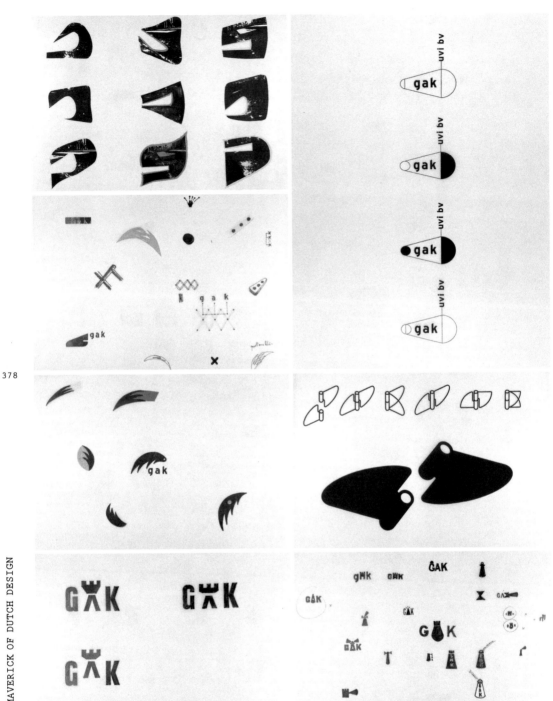

Sketches for GAK (Common Administration Office), 1995

GERT DUMBAR | GENTLEMAN MAVERICK OF DUTCH DESIGN

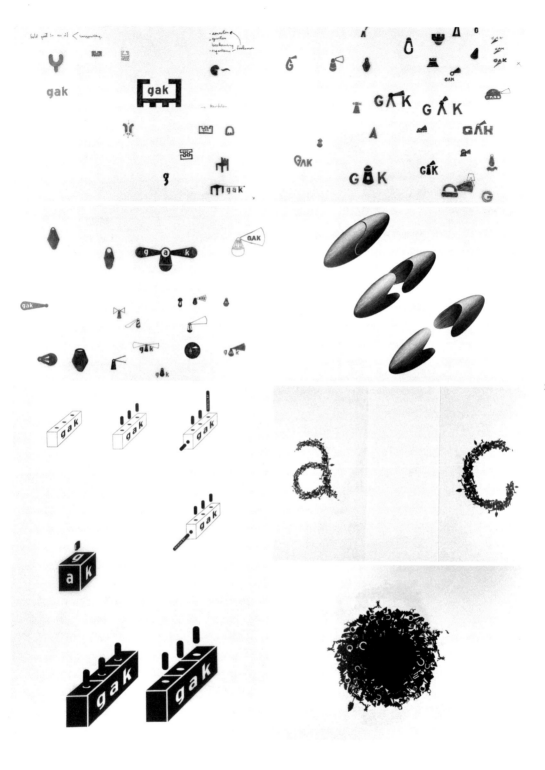

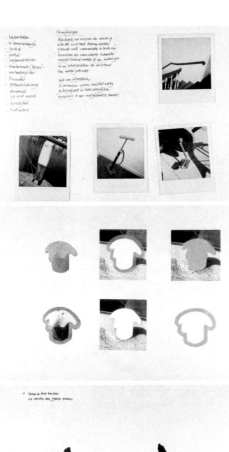
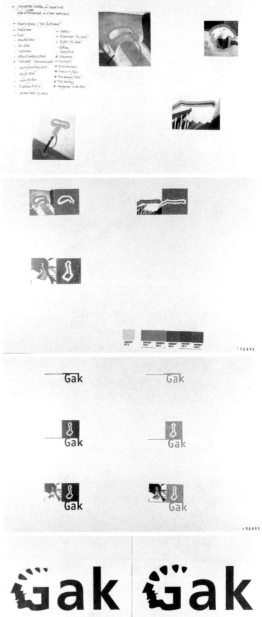

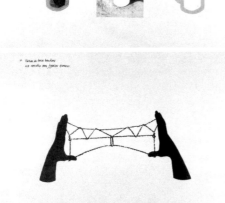

Sketches for GAK (Common Administration Office), 1995
This page top two images: Joost Roozekrans' polaroids
and sketches for Tom Dorresteijn's stationery. The
two images below show Joost's variations on the theme
for GAK

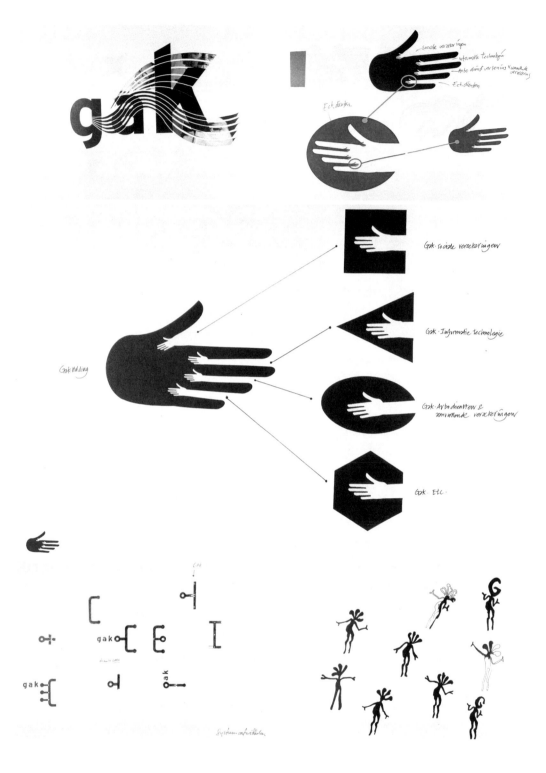

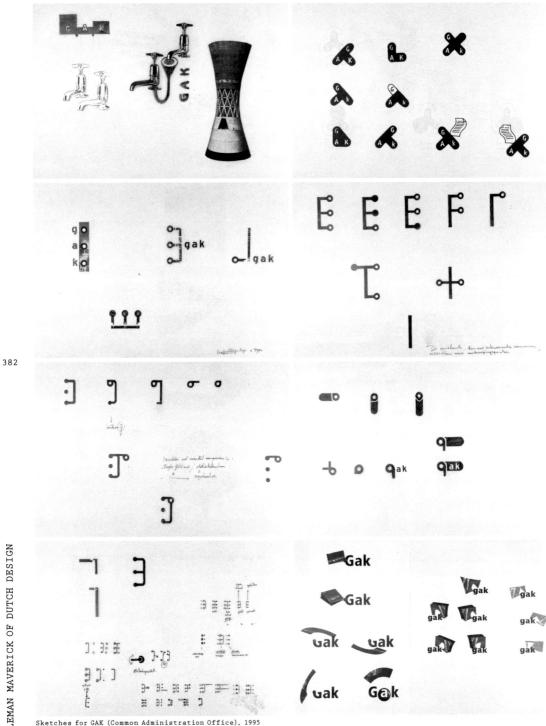

Sketches for GAK (Common Administration Office), 1995

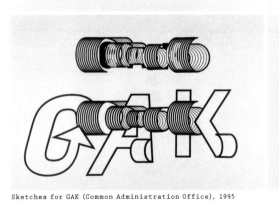

Sketches for GAK (Common Administration Office), 1995

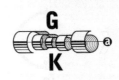

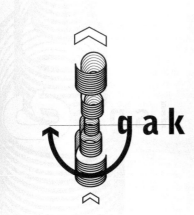

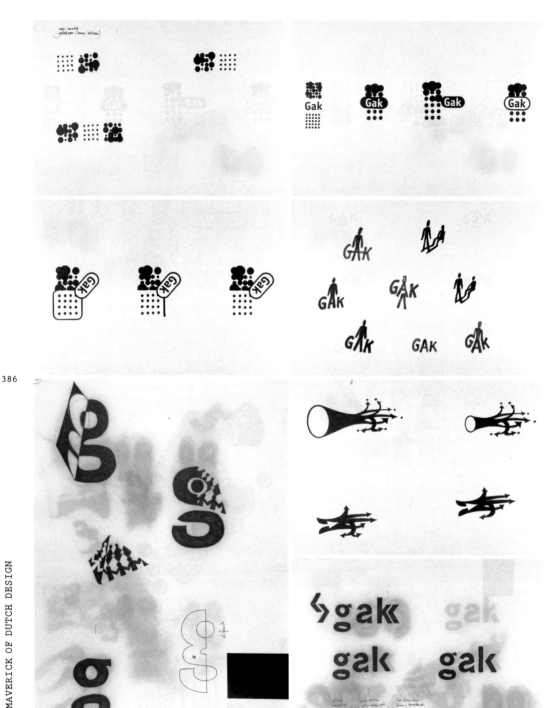

Sketches for GAK (Common Administration Office), 1995

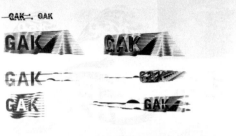

Sketches for GAK (Common Administration Office), 1995

Sketches for GAK (Common Administration Office), 1995
Two sheets (left page, top right and below) show the
first sketches by Andrea Fuchs and Tim Baumgarten
that would develop into the final design

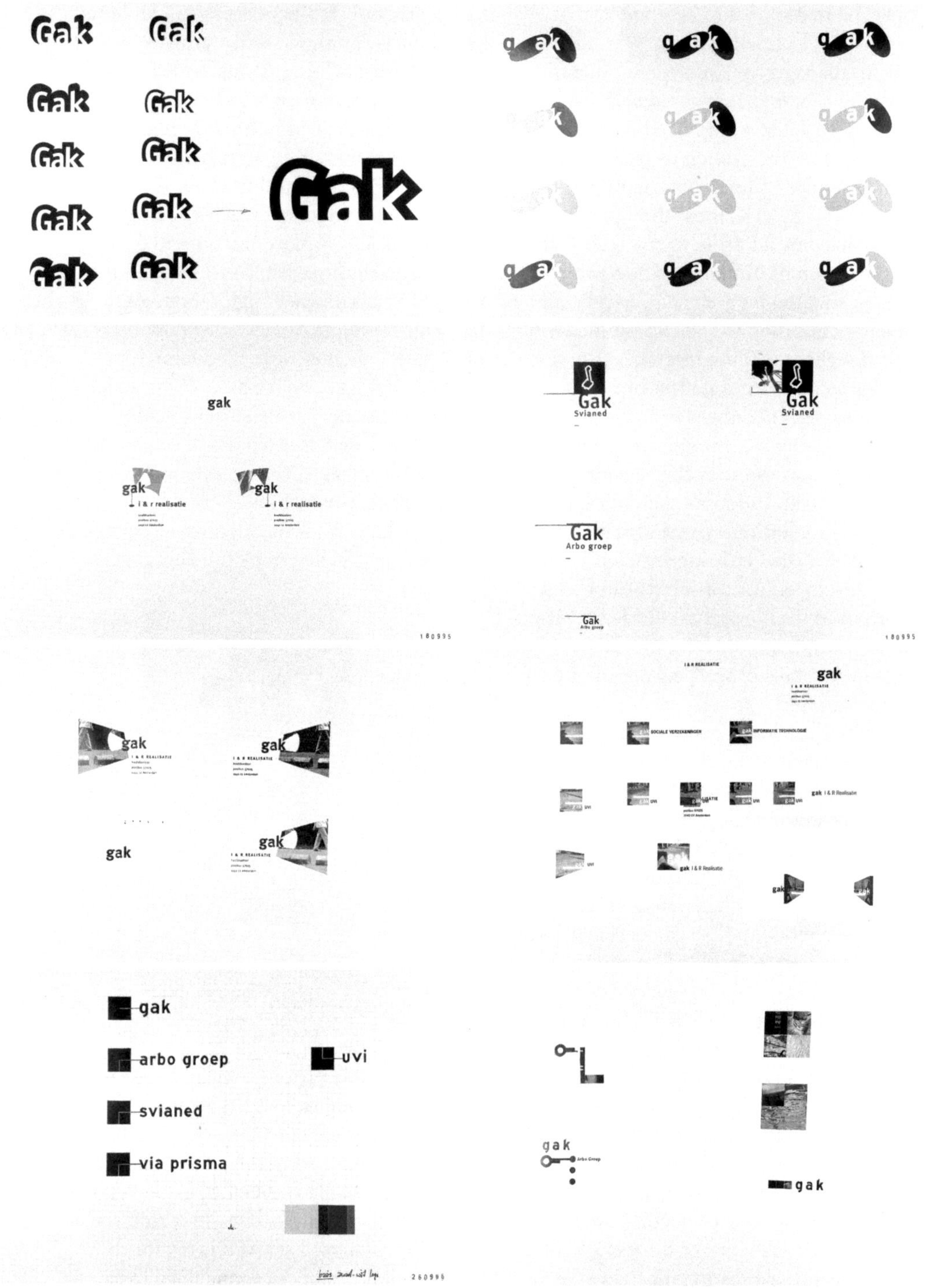
Gak
gak
i & r realisatie
Gak
Svianed
Gak
Arbo groep
180995
I & R REALISATIE
SOCIALE VERZEKERINGEN
INFORMATIE TECHNOLOGIE
uvi
gak I & R Realisatie
gak
arbo groep
uvi
svianed
via prisma
260995

police, he had shown to be good at that.' Meanwhile, Lonneke Jansma was hired as account manager — a new phenomenon at Studio Dumbar, instigated by Kitty, who judged Joost was in need of assistance — registering the numerous projects and organizing the communication between the designers and GAK. Joost thought she was a very welcome addition to the team: 'The steady stream of implementation projects became way too big for me to handle all by myself, in addition to the communication with the client and the internal creative development.'[224] As a matter of courtesy, Joost also designed the stationery of Dorresteijn's own communication agency, and right from the start the two jobs were entwined. In Joost's sketches for Dorresteijn's stationery, one also finds first sketches for the GAK identity, with some ideas developed for the letterhead being repurposed for illustrating GAK activities; visual metaphors for communication become symbols of working together and mutual support.

Renate Boere, an intern at the time, recalls that 'the sketching seemed endless. Every week we, about four interns and three employees, gathered together and Gert judged the result. He looked at the sketches and told each of us how to continue. Our sketches were also discussed with the clients, and we were even allowed to join these meetings!'[225] The abundance of initial ideas, exploring every aspect that could possibly be associated with both the concrete and abstract characteristics of the large social security organization, illustrates the studio's distinctive strategy of 'letting a hundred flowers blossom' before deciding on a definitive direction. In many of the sketches visual metaphors for 'connecting' and 'protecting' are found in photos or drawings of hinges, all kinds of connecting hardware, shock breakers,

ball bearings, carabiners, fasteners, siphons, light houses, meshes, castles, crowds, spirals, joints, helping hands, and so on. A similarly broad expanse of typographic approaches is probed in literally hundreds of small sketches, from sternly modernist to wildly expressive and from hand-drawn to computer-rendered. Meanwhile, all these ideas also explore the potential of each formal approach for variation — the GAK is to become a conglomerate of half a dozen more or less independently operating branches, with an overarching holding and local divisions, each of which needed a distinct identity that visually defined it as part of a whole. In one sketch playing with connections to symbolic themes such as water and joints that were being developed for the identity, a schematic human figure is drawn by Jan Bunk, with

Sketches for GAK (Common Administration Office), 1995 (design: Andrea Fuchs and Tim Baumgarten)

associations on various body parts: 'tear from eye (group oversight) = drop | belly button = honeycomb | joint = ball bearing / hinge.' In an added note he concludes that all of this is 'really far-fetched!'

That may be so, but the search for metaphors not only served ideas for the logos but also laid the foundation for

224   Ibid.
225   Renate Boere, 'Who believes in Aliens?' posted 31 January 2021 on The Secret Bar. Online www.the-secret-bar.nl

GAK (Common Administration Office) board meeting room
(design: Renate Boere)

what would become a thesaurus of visual metaphors and symbolical and atmospheric illustrations in the final design. Each GAK branch would have its own library of photographic images to be used in accordance with the style manual to enliven its stationery, brochures, wayfinding, and so on.

In all its complexity, the new corporate identity needed to be designed and executed in record time; the start of the newly privatized GAK, with its various public and private branches was set for January 1, 1996. Sketching for the job started in May 1995 and by the end of September, the definitive form and structure of the house style were taking shape, designed by Andrea Fuchs and Tim Baumgarten, two German designers in the studio. What followed were months of detailing and implementation, documented in daunting stacks of schemes, schedules, lists and inventories of dozens of sizes and sorts of applications, from letterheads and visiting cards to memos and envelopes to signage and crockery for each of the group's subsidiaries.

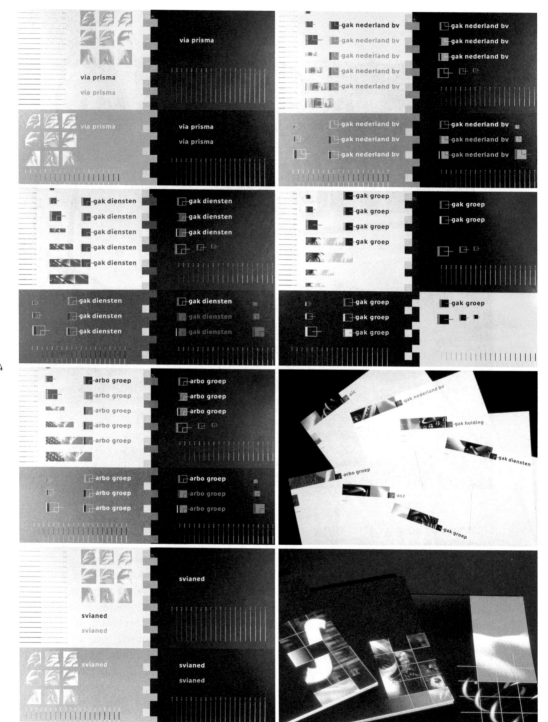

The GAK (Common Administration Office)
identity programme, 1996

In a report by Nijkamp & Nijboer, a corporate identity managing firm, the size and complexity of the commission are outlined: 'The starting point for this inventory is the objective of convincingly presenting the new corporate identity to both internal and external target groups by January 1, 1996. ... This means that a great deal needs to be done in a very short time. The objective is to actually have a basic set of corporate identity carriers with a new corporate identity by January 1.' The report continues by listing the challenges: 'The number of corporate identity carriers is so enormous and the intertwining of paper and automation in particular so dense, that only with very large efforts can much be realized within a short time. ... It was already clear in advance that the breadth and depth of the work field was so great that hardly anyone within the GAK could fully oversee it.'[226] What follows is an inventory of over a hundred pages detailing contexts and briefs for the identity and its implementation in stationery, buildings, corporate apparel, and other representational items.

Tom Dorresteijn played a large part as commissioner, apparently running the account in closer collaboration with the

GAK (Common Administration Office)
logo font by Just van Rossum

studio's designers than with his bosses at GAK. Joost: 'Tom Dorresteijn, as head of Communications at GAK, had played a game of high stakes, because he had

developed a distinct style with us, which he never showed to his directors until it was completely finished. Only then did he go upstairs with a portfolio, saying to us: "Today they'll either cut off my head, or we are going to make a fantastic house

WE ENDED UP WITH TWO TYPES OF PHOTOGRAPHY, 'HUMAN IMAGE' AND 'METAPHORS'.

Joost Roozekrans

style!" It does characterize him: very resolute in what he thinks and he says it outright. Looking back, I found him to be one of the most critical clients I have worked for. When we would discuss the sketches that were presented to him, you could clearly follow his analysis because he thought out loud. And then he would state a distinct opinion. One of those opinions was that photography should be included. That something 'soft' needed to go with it. That's how we ended up with two types of photography, "human image" and "metaphors".'

In the years following the introduction, the identity was further developed, with a bespoke GAK font family designed by Just van Rossum. Joost remarks that 'Just's inspiration was the American high-way letter, the "Interstate", a font with relatively large x-height and short sticks and tails. That was good for legibility in small font sizes, so perfect for forms. At one point Just came to the studio weekly with a new package — it was a very extensive font set.'[227] In addition, uniforms were designed by Liesbeth in 't Hout, Agnes van de Pol was engaged for the design of forms — a huge job in itself — and spatial designs were commissioned from WAACS, a Rotterdam-based design

226   Nijkamp & Nijboer, Inventarisatierapport huisstijl GAK, 15 September 1995.
227   Joost Roozekrans: Zoom conversation, 21 June 2023.

& consultancy firm.[228] In October 1999 the finalized house style was documented in a design manual, written and compiled by Joost, who sees the GAK job as 'the most complex and elaborate corporate identity system I have ever worked on. A

> ### THE GAK JOB WAS A KIND OF 'HOUSE STYLE GENERATOR', A SYSTEM FOR PRODUCING COUNTLESS SUB-STYLES
>
> Joost Roozekrans

kind of "house style generator", a system for producing countless sub-styles. With a bespoke image bank, its own serif and sans fonts plus a mono-spaced font for forms. Thousands of forms were re-written and systematically redesigned.'[229]

What remains of the house style, on which an entire team worked full-time for about five years, are a dozen digitally printed proofs of the design manual. A planned larger offset print run never materialized, because practically at the same time the manual was presented, the government decided to, again, review the structure of the welfare state. The Ministry of Social Affairs had concluded that it had lost its grip on employment services, and decided to take back control. The 'tripartite' managing of social security was cancelled: 'The privatization of WW and WAO[230] is off the table; the implementation of employee insurance will become a government task. The role of the social partners in social security has thus been all but eliminated.'[231]

This meant that the GAK was dismantled, with its public tasks taken over by a new governmental organization, the UWV.[232] For all its breath and depth, the GAK commission was not only very

profitable for the studio while it lasted — it was also one of the shortest-lived house styles in the Studio's history. Millions had been invested in designing and implementing a corporate identity that became obsolete within a few years after its introduction because of changing winds in the Capital. Joost recalls that at first he was flabbergasted and frustrated: 'How could they possibly…? And then you pull yourself together and realize again that design is an applied art serving clients and their political agendas. A lesson in perspective.'[233]

THE DANISH POST HORN

In the same period the GAK commission started, Studio Dumbar received a request connected to their long-standing work for the Dutch PTT. The Danish Post ask the Studio to collaborate with Copenhagen-based design firm Kontrapunkt on a new identity. An important intermediary was, again, PTT's Ootje Oxenaar, who's expertise was 'loaned' to Danish Post as a consultant for four months in 1993, to 'assist in the design project … offering support in the decision phase'.[234] A remarkable decision in the design was to keep the traditional emblem for the Danish 'Royal Mail', a heraldic

Danish Post logo, 1994

crowned post horn with two arrows. In the Netherlands Studio Dumbar had in most cases succeeded to replace traditional heraldry with more contemporary symbolism, but the Danes were apparently less open to redesigning national symbols. The design, therefore, focused on colour

228 The Studio Dumbar team, with Michel as creative director and Joost as team leader, further consisted of Andrea Fuchs, Tim Baumgarten, Job van Dort, Rene Toneman, Michael Lugmayer, Jan Bunk and Marcel Sloots.
229 Joost Roozekrans, email, 19 June 2023.
230 WW (Werkloosheid Wet) is the Dutch Unemployment

Act, WAO (Wet Arbeids Ongeschiktheidsverzekering) covers disability insurance.
231 Jochen van Barschot, 'Sociale partners raken buiten spel' (Social partners get sidelined), in *NRC Handelsblad*, 20 November 1999.

232   Het Uitvoeringsinstituut Werknemersverzekeringen
       (Employee Insurance Administration Institute), officially
       started on 1 January 2002.
233   Joost Roozekrans, email, 19 June 2023.
234   Helge Israelsen, director general of P&T, Denmark, in a
       letter to W. Dik, Chairman of the PTT, 15 January 1993.

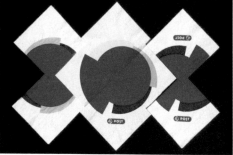

Various applications of the
Danish Post logo

and typography, offsetting the main deep red with yellow, green, and blue circle fragments. It is the most successful of several design commissions and pitches for foreign postal services that were triggered by the international acclaim for Studio Dumbar's PTT design. But back in the Netherlands, critic Ron Kaal saw it as evidence of Studio Dumbar's adherence to 'the school that believes thinking becomes nobler when done with a different organ than the brain'. He points to the varying argumentations for the PTT and Danish Post designs, observing that 'in one instance one argues for the necessity to discard the post-horn motive for postal services (in the Netherlands) because it has become old-fashioned and dysfunctional in our times of satellite communication. In another instance one stresses the necessity to keep the post-horn motive for the (Danish) postal services in order to keep the link with the past'. And he concludes: 'Such lack of logic is the price to pay for thinking with the heart.'[235] Although he obviously meant this in the most disparaging way thinkable, he is actually quite right; Gert's mantra of 'not listening to your client' does not mean that he refuses to hear them. In both cases the Studio answered the brief

235   Ron Kaal, 'Vingerafdrukken van Studio Dumbar; de filosofie van het teveel', in *NRC Handelsblad*, 28 March 1996, Agenda, p. 3.

236   Gert Dumbar, letter to Helge Israelsen, Director General of Danish P&T, 14 June 1995.

237   Knud B. Pedersen, letter to Gert Dumbar, 28 June 1995.

with a reasoned response to the client's heart-felt departure points.

A rather funny clash of cultures that underlines the differences in argumentation outlined above arose at the presentation of the design manual to the Danish Post's management board. In June 1995 the board had returned the manual's proof with four small sentences loosely grouped around the new logo on the first page firmly crossed out. In four languages, it reads 'This happens only once in a century', translating the ancient Latin phrase *Post saeculum evenire*. In a letter, Gert asks the general director to reconsider because the enigmatic sentence adds 'a certain lightness of touch, a certain playfulness' that does not, in his view, 'discredit' seriousness — 'indeed there may very well be mutual enhancement. ... The new house style for the Danish Postal Services is meant to serve for a long period of time. A

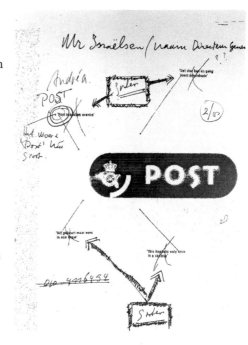

Title page of Danish Post design manual with Gert Dumbar's comments on the board's crossing out four sentences in the design: '[make] the word "Post" big here.' And twice: 'bigger'

Danish Post design manual, 1995

humanistic approach, as described above, seems to be a sound condition. ...' He associates the 'riddle' with the pea in Hans Andersen's famous fairytale 'The Princess and the Pea' and concludes that the piquing sentences on the manual's first page 'could

help to keep the colleagues on their toes and the house style lively'.[236]

All this is vintage Gert Dumbar — the reference to lightness and playfulness and the stressing of 'stylistic durability'. The board wouldn't budge, though. Deputy CEO Knud B. Pedersen replied with his own reference to folklore: '. ... we would be seriously afraid that the recipients (professional users as well as employees in Post Denmark) might imagine themselves back in the fairy tale of "The Emperor's New Clothes".'[237] Exit *Post saeculum ...*

Trompe-l'oeil design on cars of the Centraal Bureau Wegenbelasting' (Central Bureau of Road Tax), 1997. Gert: 'These cars would patrol the streets, also at night, to check whether drivers had paid their taxes and mandatory insurances. The design actually started off as a little joke – also a kind of anamorphosis, that could actually be quite dangerous: it looks like the road just continues through the vehicle. But the client liked it, so it was realized'

Poster for Hommage à Toulouse-Lautrec, International Poster Exhibition in France, 2001 (design: Gert Dumbar, photo: Lex van Pieterson)

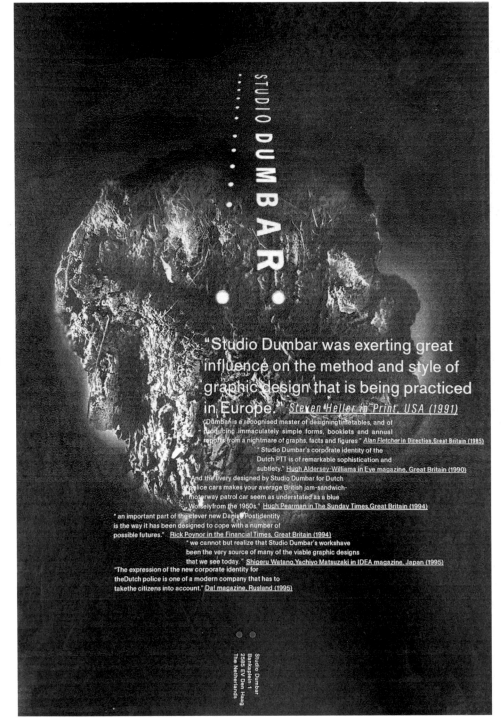

STUDIO DUMBAR

"Studio Dumbar was exerting great influence on the method and style of graphic design that is being practiced in Europe." *Steven Heller in Print, USA (1991)*

"Dumbar is a recognised master of designing timetables, and of producing immaculately simple forms, booklets and annual reports from a nightmare of graphs, facts and figures." *Alan Fletcher in Direction, Great Britain (1985)*

" Studio Dumbar's corporate identity of the Dutch PTT is of remarkable sophistication and subtlety." *Hugh Aldersey-Williams in Eye magazine, Great Britain (1990)*

And the livery designed by Studio Dumbar for Dutch police cars makes your average British jam-sandwich-motorway patrol car seem as understated as a blue Wolseley from the 1950s." *Hugh Pearman in The Sunday Times, Great Britain (1994)*

" an important part of the clever new Danish Postidentity is the way it has been designed to cope with a number of possible futures." *Rick Poynor in the Financial Times, Great Britain (1994)*

" we cannot but realize that Studio Dumbar's work have been the very source of many of the viable graphic designs that we see today. " *Shigeru Watano, Yachiyo Matsuzaki in IDEA magazine, Japan (1995)*

"The expression of the new corporate identity for the Dutch police is one of a modern company that has to take the citizens into account." *Da! magazine, Rusland (1995)*

Studio Dumbar
Bankaplein 1
2585 EV Den Haag
The Netherlands

Studio Dumbar promotional leaflet, 1996

THE HAGUE ROTTERDAM FRANKFURT SHANGHAI

Throughout the 1990s the studio grew steadily. A remarkable trend shows when one looks at a timeline of major commissions in Studio Dumbar's history between its start in 1977 and Gert's retirement in 2003. The data visualization is revealing: the first years are marked by steadfast clients who provided a constant work flow, like NS, PTT, Rijksmuseum, Aegon and the Ministry of Agriculture. The second decade shows a growing amount of sometimes massive one-off jobs, done in a relatively short time. Of course, in both periods there are shorter and longer relations with clients, and more or less ad-hoc commissions and ongoing commitments always ran parallel. But almost all long-term associations with clients originate before the studio's move to Bankaplein in 1991. This could well be explained by the growth of the studio and its concurrent organizational evolution: more and larger teams can simultaneously handle more large-scale, short-term commissions. On the other hand, it may also indicate a changing culture — a shorter life span of designs, and clients who more easily switch designers when they feel their image is not up to date anymore. Gert has consistently advocated 'stylistic durability', by which he means designs that can survive short-lived trends and period styles, and this initially led to lasting connections with clients. But it changed in the 1990s — many Studio Dumbar corporate identities still survived for decades (the Police, Groningen, and NOB identities, for instance), but they were developed in a relatively short time, as one-off jobs. Yet another factor could be the faster-changing staffing of clients' design and communications departments. Gert has always cherished long-standing relationships with commissioners at the top of the client's hierarchy, the directors and CEOs, and he laments the downgrading of client representatives to 'marketing managers whose only concern is that the end product should not irritate anyone — like the famous slogan for a Dutch stain remover: "It foams but will not scratch".' Kitty too noticed that the trade changed, which — in her and Michel's view — called for action: 'The communication with commissioners shifted from the boardroom to the middle management — mostly young graduates with a Communications BA. Our frustration was that advertising agencies often ventured onto our terrain, with less of a portfolio, but with stories that appealed to the marketeers, who prioritized communications advice over design proposals. Michel and I felt the lack of that component, but Gert, who hates marketeers, didn't want to hear it.'

GERT LAMENTS THE DOWNGRADING OF CLIENT REPRESENTATIVES TO 'MARKETING MANAGERS WHOSE ONLY CONCERN IS THAT THE END PRODUCT SHOULD NOT IRRITATE ANYONE'

The change in atmosphere is acutely felt by Vincent, who had left the studio in 1988 to start his own design bureau (Barlock, with Hélène Bergmans and Marc van Bokhoven, also former Studio Dumbar designers). He returned by Gert's invitation to lead a team in 1997, to stay for another decade. 'When I came back, it was an entirely different studio. They had moved to the big place at Bankaplein and there were real teams on several floors. Gert mostly focused on cultural commissions — they created profile for the studio, a French way of thinking.' Vincent continued working for the Ministry of Agriculture — he was known in the Studio as 'mister Agriculture'

— until he started his own Buro Van Baar in 2008, taking the client with him.

The privatized National Forestry Administration (Staatsbosbeheer) is the only one of the former Ministry of Agriculture departments that still uses its original logo. All government organizations have meanwhile adopted a uniform 'Rijkshuisstijl' (State corporate identity), designed by Studio Dumbar in 2008. It meant the end for several identities developed by the Studio for the Dutch government.

Among these was the house style for the Dutch Ministry of General Affairs, the Prime Minister's office. For this design, of 2002, Studio Dumbar combined a stylized version of the Dutch national coat of arms with a thesaurus of colour-coded rectangular shapes for the ministry's various sub-departments. The font used is Eureka, designed by former Studio Dumbar intern Peter Bil'ak. A few years after the introduction of this identity, in 2005, a commission concluded that 'making visible the coherence [of the various government ministries and services] starts with using one vignette for all utterings of the national government'.[238] A project was initiated to clean up the clutter, symbolized in a 'wall of shame' on which a mottled assortment of heterogeneous logos for countless government institutes is collected.

After a pitch with five bureaus, Studio Dumbar's design was chosen. Critics denounced it as a lazy copy of the Studio's identity for the Ministry of General Affairs — indeed it reuses a slightly modified version of the crest of arms designed for the Prime Minister's office. Tom Dorresteijn, Studio Dumbar's former client at GAK, who had partnered with Michel in 2003, after Gert left, answers in Dumbarrian fashion: 'We

238   Report Commission Wolfensperger, quoted in Ed Annink, Hestia Bavelaar (eds.), *De stijl van het Rijk — The visual identity of the Dutch Government.* The Hague, 2010, p. 145.

239   Ibid.

240   See: Mark Schalken, 'Kritisch verlangen: Hugues Boekraad meerstemmig', in Rens Holslag, Jaap van Triest (eds), *Visuele retorica*, Breda, Avans hogeschool, 2006, p. 31.

never made a secret of that — it was a good version [of the crest].'[239] The point of departure was to keep things as simple as possible for a design that should be used and varied by around 150 different governmental organizations. The uniform State Logo was further detailed after comments by among others the Dutch Hoge Raad van Adel (High Council of Nobility — the Dutch authority on heraldic matters) and complemented by an extended 'Rijksoverheid' font family designed by Peter Verheul. Joris Demmink, chair of the house style committee, summarized the client's thoughts: 'timeless, distinguished and business-like'.

SHOWCASING THE WORK

Moving and enlarging the Studio, combined with its by now international status of leading design firm, strengthened the desire to collect the work of the previous years. A first attempt at publishing a concise but authoritative selection of the Studio's œuvre was made in 1990,

coinciding with the move to Bankaplein. The book, titled *Connections and Contradictions in Design*, with prospected texts by Hugues Boekraad and Kathy McCoy, among others, was proposed to Edward Booth-Clibborn, the publisher for whom Studio Dumbar had also made the successful *European Illustration annuals*. Although this book was never realized, its design was thoroughly prepared in literally hundreds of sketches by several designers, notably Robert Nakata.

Nakata's 'meticulousness' that Vincent described is seen in minute sketches and calculations for proportions, typographies, and illustrations, including hand-drawn blocks of text to test sizes and line spacing. Also here, a wide range of visual associations with Studio Dumbar's work is sketched and a variety of page layouts are tested. Boekraad later stated that his text 'was never published because in the end Dumbar needed a different book'.[240] Gert recalls 'the book project faced endless delays and discussions, also with authors, and at some point Kitty pulled the plug

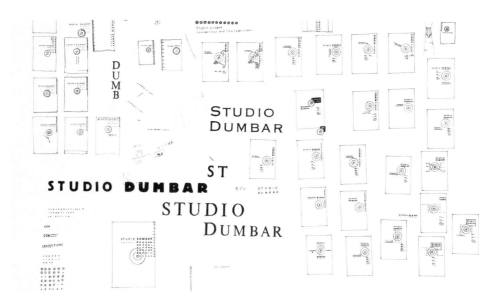

Sketches for *Contradictions* book on Studio Dumbar, 1991 (design: Robert Nakata)

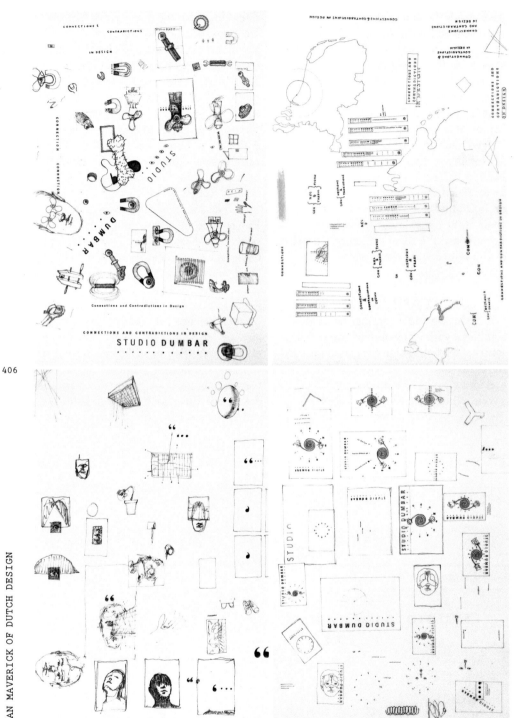

Sketches for *Contradictions* book on Studio Dumbar,
1991 (design: Robert Nakata)

GERT DUMBAR | GENTLEMAN MAVERICK OF DUTCH DESIGN

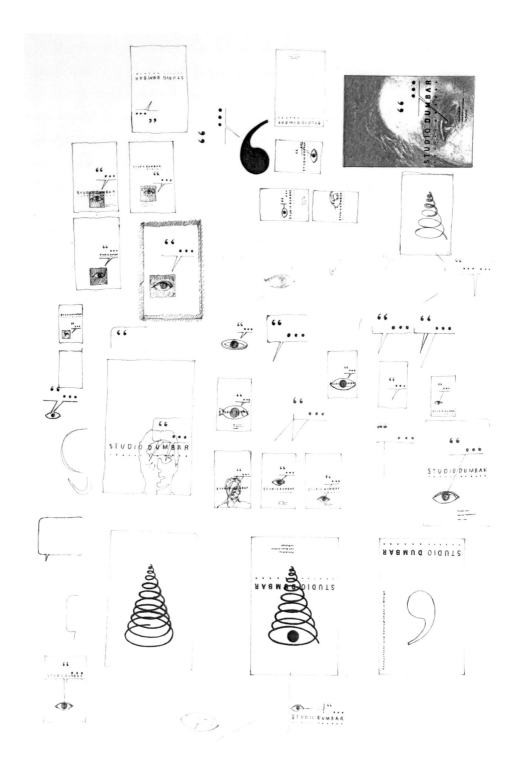

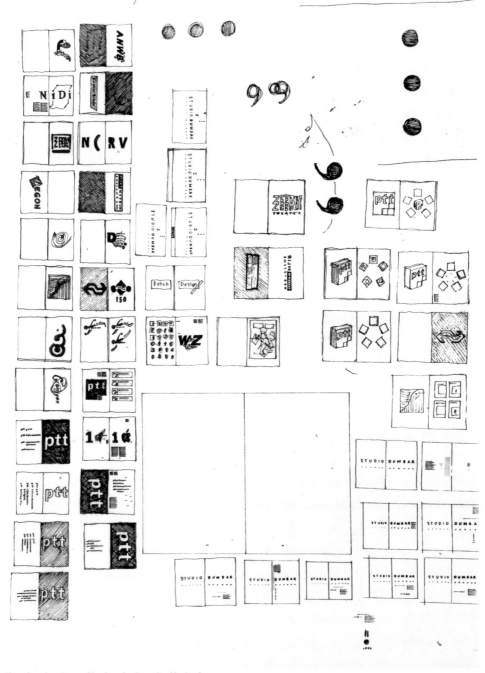

Sketches for *Contradictions* book on Studio Dumbar,
1991 (design: Robert Nakata)

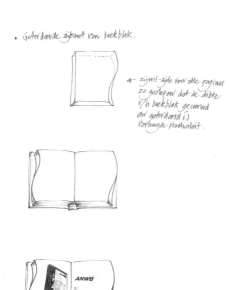

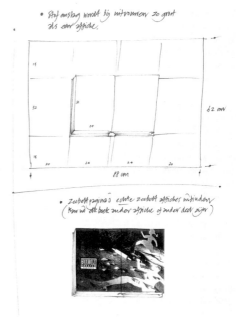

Sketches for *Behind the Seen* book on Studio Dumbar,
1994 (design: Joost Roozekrans)

on it'. A few years later, a second attempt was made, this time resulting in *Behind the Seen*, published in 1996 by German publisher Hermann Schmidt Verlag. Also for this book, hundreds of sketches are made, by Allen Hori and others. The final design, by Albert Leeflang, settles for a rather straightforward lay-out, showcasing a selection of work on glossy paper. The introductions include texts by Rick Poynor and Studio Dumbar's dearest competitor Wim Crouwel who, after stating that 'the first emotions called up by this work were feelings of irritation', remarks that he is by now 'convinced that Gert Dumbar has made an essential contribution to the history of graphic design.'[241] Rick Poynor details a similar appraisal when he states: 'Equally at home working for an avant-garde theatre group or the Dutch police force, Studio Dumbar has shown time and again that it is possible to extend the graphic conventions of the corporate mainstream. Any account of design innovation in the 1980s would put the studio at the forefront, yet it would not be out of place in a group that included such commercial heavyweights as Wolff Olins, Chermayeff & Geismar, and Pentagram.'[242]

The book was supported by an overview exhibition that travelled from the Netherlands via Germany to Japan, China, Australia, and the United States. In the Netherlands it opened at the Kunsthal, Rotterdam, in April 1996. As usual, Gert's critics in two major Dutch newspapers offered their comments. For his part, *de Volkskrant*'s Hub. Hubben was rather lenient with his review of a 'cozy house style like an toppled grab bag'.[243] Ron Kaal made the earlier quoted mistake that Dumbar seemed to believe that 'thinking becomes nobler when done with another organ than the brain'. He describes the Studio as 'more like a three-ring circus, in which all kinds of things

241   Wim Crouwel, 'The relativity itself', in *Behind the Seen*, 1996, p. 37.
242   Rick Poynor, 'Studio Dumbar: function and pleasure', in *Behind the Seen*, 1996, p. 11.
243   Hub. Hubben, 'Gezellige huisstijl als omgevallen grabbelton', in *de Volkskrant*, 9 April 1996.

HET BOEK

STUDIO DUMBAR

Behind the Seen

Het Studio Dumbar boek met honderden full colour afbeeldingen en drie artikelen over de relativerende kwaliteit van dit altijd spraakmakende ontwerpbureau Gebonden met stofomslag, 216 pagina s, f 178,- in de (design)boekhandel of rechtstreeks bij Uitgeverij BIS. Telefoon (020) 6205171/Fax (020)6279251

Promotional leaflet for *Behind the Seen* book
(design: Albert Leeflang)

'Behind the Seen' exhibition,
Shanghai, 1999

happen at once, than the strict discipline that graphic design traditionally is'.[244] Gert, of course, insists that both could — indeed should — be fruitfully merged. The Bremer *Nordsee-Zeitung* agreed, when the exhibition travelled on to DesignLabor in Bremerhaven, Germany. The reporter sees it as the gist of Studio Dumbar's success: 'He combines things that appear to be irreconcilable, and does so in a very open, group-dynamic process.'[245] Later, the exhibition was shown in Frankfurt, before travelling on to Japan during the month of May 1998, where it was divided over two venues, the Ginza Graphic Gallery

in Tokyo and the DDD Gallery in Kyoto. In the following year it was staged in Shanghai, China, curated by Xu Wang who started 'an international alliance' between Wang's studio in China, with Emery Vincent in Australia and Studio Dumbar in The Hague. The collaboration was not very fruitful, apart from exchanging some designers. Alwin Chan, for instance, switched from Emery Vincent to Studio Dumbar, and stayed in the Netherlands. But the link did lay the foundation of what a few years later would become Studio Dumbar China.

244   Ron Kaal, 'Vingerafdrukken van Studio Dumbar; de
       filosofie van het teveel', in *NRC Handelsblad*, 28 March
       1996, Agenda, p. 3.
245   'Streifen-streifenwagen für Holländische Polizei', in
       Nordsee-Zeitung, Bremen, 17 May 1997.

ROTTERDAM

Within a few years after the move in 1991, also the three-story office at Bankaplein started to feel too small for the growing amount of work in the studio. To find more space, Gert, Michel and Kitty now looked to neighbouring Rotterdam to finally start a new Studio Dumbar branch. Kitty recalls that it seemed like a good move, also to satisfy Henri Ritzen's ambition to head his own team. And since Hard Werken folded, Rotterdam did not have a signature design firm anymore, like Amsterdam or The Hague had with Total Design and Studio Dumbar, respectively. Gert: 'Michel has always been excessively a Rotterdammer. He had a house built there. ... I said, we need a bigger office, because we were bursting out at Bankaplein, so Michel started looking in Rotterdam, and I thought "fine, I want them out of The Hague". That was already on my mind. Then we found an insanely beautiful building on the Lloydhaven, which was still a casco. We threw a dinner party there once, while the construction workers were still busy — they joined us for a beer. So Michel had his way, because we already had a kind of agreement that he would take over. And eventually, they were out of The Hague.' In 2003 the Studio did move to Rotterdam entirely.

END OF THE MEASLES

The success of Studio Dumbar, both at home and abroad, not only called for spatial expansion, but also made Gert reconsider some of the studio's idiosyncratic style elements, which were copied ad nauseam by a new generation of graphic designers, worldwide. The free and abundant application of typographical paraphernalia like dots, dashes, and bent lines — called 'the measles' by critics —

and the studio's generous use of staged photography had been adopted so widely that it became a mundane verb: 'to dumbar'. Suggestive of a by now mainstream approach to design, it had lost its appeal to its initiator. The same year as the move to Rotterdam, Gert officially banned the use of both staged photography and 'the measles' in the studio. Gert: 'I had previously prohibited the use of Helvetica, and that was enforced. But when I banned 'the measles' there were of course designers who secretly continued doing it. I kind of liked that. The same for staged photography. And after all, the tear-and-paste work Lex and I did together was inimitable. We put so much time and fun and passion into it — that's where we could let our creative juices flow boundlessly.'

FRANKFURT

Like a few years before in London, international clients triggered thoughts of expanding abroad. Around 2000, large commissions by, among others, Dresdner Bank and its parent, the insurance company Allianz were the main reason for opening a branch in Frankfurt, which was registered in June 2001. Studio Dumbar's Tanja Backe, a native German, was tasked with leading the office. The move was also facilitated by new technologies. Kitty remembers how the introduction of the fax machine in the late 1980s was already a 'big event, because before that we needed to always travel for presentations, which cost huge amounts of time and patience because of endless traffic jams'.[246] Thus German clients such as Bayer and Zanders Paper could already be served at Kanaalweg. In the late 1990s, new internet-based means of communication like the PDF format (first released in 1993) allowed

246   Kitty de Jong, email, 12 May 2023.
247   Klaus Kemp, 'Ex Hollandia Lux: Design von Amts wegen', in *Form* #145, 1994, pp. 50-53.
248   Kitty de Jong, email, 12 May 2023.

249   See: Ansgar Seelen, 'Logo, No Logo', Online PDF, 2004. www.ci-portal.de/wp-content/uploads/LogoNoLogoEssayAS.pdf (accessed 24 January 2024).
250   Kitty de Jong, email, 12 May 2023.

designs to be wired in relatively modest data sizes through the fledgling internet, which smoothed communication between the Frankfurt branch and The Hague headquarters. Another facilitator was the German design luminary Klaus Klemp, an influential advisor on design matters

Allianz logo. Studio Dumbar sketch (left), final design by Claus Koch Design (right), 1998

in Germany at the time, who staged the 'Behind the Seen' exhibition in Frankfurt in 1997. In 1994, Klemp had written an extensive essay on 'the role of government in design' in the Netherlands.[247] 'What has been taking place for some time now in the form of a structural transformation in public institutions in the Netherlands is a revision of the state's self-image.' Klemp observes that the Dutch government is way ahead of their German neighbours in applying market approaches and design principles to government institutions, whether privatized or not. He mentions Studio Dumbar as a prime example of this 'structural transformation', and thoroughly analyses the Police and PTT designs. Klemp ends his article with an advice: 'For German administrative reformers, a visit or two to their smaller neighbour may be advisable.' Small wonder then that Klemp recommends Allianz to go to Studio Dumbar for their new corporate identity.

Again, we see a great variety of sketches, mainly focusing on finding an alternative for the old heraldic eagle, the Reichsadler which, as Kitty remembers, 'was associated a bit too much with Nazi-era German delusions of superiority'.[248] Many sketches explore associations on 'binding together' or 'connecting threads'

that at some point resemble 'hope ribbons' or 'lucky clover'. Related to these explorations are variants of the double-l in the name and accentuations to stress the 'togetherness' suggested by the brand's name. In the end, though, the company was not content and switched to the young German design firm of Claus Koch. They kept the 'eagle', although abstracted almost beyond recognition. Possibly inspired by Studio Dumbar's earlier proposals, the bird and its three chicks — which it kept safe under its wings in the old vignette — are now rendered as three lines (body and two wings). Remarkably, the central line (the body and beak of the eagle) is the same 'l' as the two l's in the brand name, while the 'wings' are derived from the 'i' in a typeface derived from Günter Salden's Attachée typeface.[249] This design grants the logo typographic clarity and consistency, while still echoing the aesthetics of its well-known predecessor. At the same time the new design agreeably downplays the connection to the Reichsadler in the original logo from 1923.

In the meantime, although the unsuccessful Allianz job was well-paid, and the Studio also worked for Allianz daughter Dresdner Bank, founding a branch in Germany proved more complicated and less rewarding than expected. Bureaucratic hurdles consumed a lot of energy and resources, while Tanja Backe went on maternity leave soon after she was appointed head of the office. In addition, as Kitty remarks, German design studios and potential clients now viewed Studio Dumbar as local competitor instead of a foreign source of inspiration.[250] The Frankfurt branch was closed in April 2004.

Breda garbage trucks, 1997

BREDA'S
GARBAGE TRUCK

1997

To mark the introduction of separated garbage collection in the southern Dutch city of Breda, new trucks were adorned with giant close-ups of insects – ants and bees – and short poetic messages singing the praise of garbage collectors and enticing inhabitants to help keep the city clean: 'The ant shows us the way / ants are tiny diligent insects / always busy keeping their nest very clean …' and 'Bees… they work, they work for you. / Be(e) informed, call the bee …'

Gert: 'We used beautiful close-up photos taken by a biologist and I suggested to engage Breda's city poet to write short poetic associations on insects that clean up everything in nature. It looked fabulous, also at night due to the reflective inks used for the type and images'

Studio Dumbar promotional leaflet, 1996

COMPLICATED TIMES

Around the turn of the century, several internal incidents shook up the partnership of the three directors of the Studio, which, seen from the outside, was still thriving and growing — now with branches in The Hague, Rotterdam and Frankfurt. Significant unease was caused by the dissatisfying stint at the Studio of Gert's son Derk, and by Kitty's departure. When Michel and Kitty became partners, in 1989, Gert had stipulated that his son, who studied graphic design, would eventually become part of the Studio, which they had accepted. Derk did an apprenticeship and was employed subsequently, mainly focusing on 'new media', as internet-based media were called at the time. But he didn't feel comfortable, as 'the boss's son', and left in 2001 to start his own design practice. Meanwhile, Gert and Kitty did not extend a contract with a close friend of Michel, who was brought in as organizational talent but didn't function well in Gert's and Kitty's eyes.

Such incidents, concerning people with intimate ties to the Studio's leadership, caused cracks in the collegial collaboration. Kitty, who at the same time had to cope with a divorce and an ailing mother, felt increasingly isolated within the Studio and decided to leave when Gert, after several warnings, had made clear that in his view she didn't perform adequately anymore. He stipulates: 'I received a call from the bank that our finances were insecure — we risked bankruptcy! So I felt forced to ask her to leave.' [251] Kitty's departure was in part triggered by an advice she and Michel had asked from Tom Dorresteijn, their former client with GAK, about his vision for the Studio. Tom analysed the agency's strengths and weaknesses, and concluded that, in due course, Gert would need to retire. In his report, Kitty was criticized for having more on her plate than she could handle, and he advised her to get assistance. Because of Tom's allusion to Gert's retirement, Michel and Kitty kept the report away from Gert for a while, but in the end shared it with him. Obviously, Gert was not amused. In turn, he invited his old friend Jan Willem van der Eb to review the Studio. This led to further — occasionally heated — discussions in which Michel and Kitty argued that Van der Eb was not an expert on business reorganization and too closely associated with Gert. But eventually, during a staff meeting in March 2001, Michel and Kitty agreed to consulting Van der Eb, assisted by Jelle van der Toorn Vrijthoff. Remarkably, Van der Toorn was at the time still a partner in Total Design — a prime competitor — but he had, according

> *IF YOU WANT TO HAVE A SUCCESSFUL STUDIO, YOU NEED A FEW MODELS: KITTY AS THE PUNCTILIOUS WOMAN TAKING CARE OF THE MANAGEMENT AND LOOKING AFTER THE REVENUE, MICHEL WHO MAKES IT HAPPEN, AND THEN A WEIRD GENTLEMAN WHO'S ALSO WALKING AROUND THERE. AND THE FACT THAT THOSE THREE GET ALONG SO WELL, THAT'S VERY IMPORTANT!*
> Gert Dumbar

to Gert, already distanced himself from TD's daily business and had warranted discretion. More important to Gert was that Van der Toorn was decisive in 'turning losses into an over 15 per cent profit for Total Design'.[252] In the same meeting Gert stated that the times of 'endless sketching' were over — a clear indication that the Studio was in dire straits.

All this led to a rift between Kitty and the two other partners. It escalated into negotiations with lawyers, which in Kitty's recollection ended 'shortly after 9/11 in a hotel suite to find out if we could settle without going to court. Even now, twenty years later, I still smile when I remember that event. What started out for me as an assassination of character was solved to my satisfaction and with mutual consent, thanks to my outstanding attorney who, by the way, showed no mercy for [Studio Dumbar's] consultant during that session.'[253] She organized a farewell party at a bar for 'Dumbarians' the next month, not inviting Gert. 'Not difficult to understand everyone's surprise when Gert walked in. Since that day we are the best of friends again.'[254]

In hindsight, Gert stresses the 'model' collaboration between the three partners during more than twenty years: 'If you want to have a successful studio, you need a few models: Kitty as the punctilious woman taking care of the management and looking after the revenue, Michel who makes it happen, and then a weird gentleman who's also walking around there. And the fact that those three get along so well, that's very important! That's the model, and then you put all kinds of very good designers around it.'[255]

Randstad promotional material, 2000

252   Gert quoted in staff meeting minutes, 6 March 2001.
253   Kitty de Jong, 'Frappez toujours', posted 31 January 2021 on The Secret Bar. Online: www.the-secret-bar.nl
254   Ibid.
255   Gert Dumbar: conversation, 5 June 2023.

The same period was marked by what became known as the 'dot-com crash' — the collapse of speculative investments in the booming internet industry of the late 1990s. It caused a minor recession, which did have its effects on budgets for graphic design and communication. Just before that, in 1999, Studio Dumbar acquired a

MICHEL WAS A GREAT FORCE WITHIN THE STUDIO. ORGANIZER, FIRE EXTINGUISHER. AND HE WAS GOOD WITH CLIENTS

Gert Dumbar

major new client: Randstad employment agency, which remarkably switched to Studio Dumbar after being a steady client of Total Design since 1968. The switch coincided with Ben Bos' departure from TD. His Randstad logo was kept in the new identity — it had become an iconic sign, and Bos had already changed Total Design's house letter Helvetica to Frutiger. Michel: 'That account has kept us afloat in those complicated times. Randstad was going through a change, and it took a while before they dared to engage us, so we had done a couple of test commissions since 1996. But once they were in, they stayed for a long time.' It was touch-and-go, though, with economic perspectives darkening after the 'dot-com crash' of 2000. Vincent recalls comments by Randstad employees, saying that if Studio Dumbar had pitched one month later, the job would not have been available: 'Then they would have weathered the storm. But in the end, it was a multi-million job. And ultimately the advantage was that after the recession they could come out fresh and new again. In the meantime, they had bought huge companies in America which were hard

to "align", so they forced that with the corporate identity. For that we set up an international image bank, to make sure that Randstad's image and visual language was the same worldwide.' One of the collateral commissions was the corporate identity for CAPAC, a Randstad daughter focusing on logistics and production workers.

Michel was the clear lead in the Randstad account, and increasingly also in running the Studio, as Gert acknowledges: 'Michel was a great force within the Studio. Organizer, fire extinguisher. And he was good with clients.' It strengthened his idea that Michel should eventually take over. 'I had established something and Michel could continue that in his own manner. He said, "Gert, it will be a very different studio." I said, "of course, I accept that." I discussed it at length with Michel but also said that he did need to get someone else in there, which he did.'

'That was when Tom Dorresteijn came in,' recalls Michel. 'We had met him earlier as a client. He was more a strategist, a communications guy who could value the importance of good design quality.'

SHANGHAI

Times may have been 'complicated', as Michel stated, but that didn't distract from further expansion plans. Already in the 1990s Gert and Leonie had initiated and cultivated contacts with Chinese designers. Leonie had met Xu Wang on a research trip with her business partner Annelies Haase, and Gert's fascination for China stayed, as Joost remembers: 'After I had returned to the Studio by Gert's invitation, in 1999, he one day showed me a newspaper clipping, which was about China and all the adventures to be had there. Not much later he went to an AGI Design Congress and came back saying

'Behind the Seen' exhibition,
Kunsthal Rotterdam, 1998

"we are going to start an alliance with Garry Emery, a renowned designer in Melbourne, Australia, and with Xu Wang", who was in Guangzhou, China. So Gert laid the first stone. Then Michel went to China several times, where, in addition to Wang, he also met Zhengfang Zou, an economist and marketeer from Shanghai, with whom he started Studio Dumbar China, in 2004.' A few years before, in 1999, Studio Dumbar's 'Behind the Seen' exhibition was staged in Shanghai, curated by Xu Wang. Joost: 'That was also the first exhibition of a Western design studio in China. It was mainly a poster exhibition, and it opened with great pomp — Michel was hailed by a choir of 300 children after the opening! Then in 2001, Gert and I organized another version in Beijing, at Tsinghua University. That was at the instigation of our first Chinese intern Jian Zhao — he is now head of the graphic design department there.'

Michel was eager to enter the Chinese and larger Asian market for corporate design; the Studio branch in China was at first called 'Dumbar Branding'. After he had sold his share in Studio Dumbar to Tom Dorresteijn in 2011 Michel gradually developed the Chinese branch into his own design firm, MdB Associates, later De Boer Wang

Studio. With local partners he started an educational institution, DeTao Masters, with which he was connected till his untimely death in 2021. Studio Dumbar China was founded in 2004, with Studio designers Bela Marady and Marc Holtman assisting Michel in Shanghai. Joost followed a few years later, after Michel had persuaded him: 'I initially said no, but Michel said, "try it for a few months, and then you decide whether to stay." That seemed like a good deal. And within three months I knew: wow, great city. I stayed for ten years, got married and started a family there.'

GERT RETIRES

Meanwhile, Gert — now in his early sixties — increasingly distanced himself from the daily business of his Studio. 'I had kind of seen it. I was repeating myself, in dealing with people, with success. I found that killing. At some point I pretty much knew it all. I wanted to do something different. Ideally, I wanted to restore pre-war French motorcycles. And move more in the direction of art, drawing. And I had a jewel of a house in France with a huge plot of land, so I wanted to pay more attention to that too, to nature. To study that and let it take its course — no interventions, no pesticides. All that combined was my motivation, around 2000. I wanted to do something different, that was it really.'[256]

The Studio he had founded in 1977 had become an influential agency, but at the same time, it needed a makeover to cope with the changing climate, both in business and culture. That at least was Michel's view. 'It was a big studio in those days, thirty people just in the Netherlands alone with two studios, one in Rotterdam and one in The Hague, later merged —

256   Gert Dumbar: conversation, 22 June 2023.
257   Ibid.

that was also an efficiency move. You had to switch gears — it all had to happen anyway, something had to change in those days.' In the aftermath of the two reviews of Studio Dumbar's current functioning and future perspective, Gert sold his share to Michel, which necessitated the sale of the office on Bankaplein and move the studio to Rotterdam. Michel invited Tom Dorresteijn as new partner: 'I bought all the shares from Gert at the time. But 100 per cent Studio Dumbar was not a healthy situation. Then we had 9/11 on top of that, a studio just opened in Frankfurt, bad timing, well that's part of it, but it turned out well.'

The Studio kept Gert's name, which by then was a precious asset — a world-renowned brand — also after Michel sold his shares to Tom in 2011. With creative director Liza Enebeis, a former intern at Studio Dumbar and designer at Dumbar-offshoot Barlock, the firm had indeed become 'a very different studio', as Michel had predicted. Still, although it is now part of a global network of design

Gert Dumbar's drawing of Leonie ten Duis reading on a summer afternoon in the garden of their house in Pezuls, France

agencies, DEPT, it proudly flaunts its roots in the studio that Gert founded. Gert rather stoically declares: 'We had created something good, that was functioning

well … a world name. And I'm very good at letting things go. I knew I could let go of the studio and not get excited about it anymore. I just wanted to move on to something else. Eventually, that came about, also because of Leonie, who said, "you should go to the art academy". But that came later…' [257]

IT WAS NOT AN EASY TIME, WE HAD DIFFICULT DISCUSSIONS ABOUT A NUMBER OF ASPECTS. NEVERTHELESS, GERT AND I PARTED VERY WELL

Michel de Boer

Looking back, Michel summarizes: 'It was not an easy time, we had difficult discussions about a number of aspects. Nevertheless, Gert and I parted very well. That, of course is not self-evident, or actually it's often the opposite. So it must be said that that is very special. We parted very well and we remained good friends, that's very important. But the studio had changed, with Gert and also Kitty gone, so it didn't feel like the right place for me anymore. We had deeply believed in what was our strength: developing ideas — we were an ideas factory. And that aspect changed. The world changed.'

Pulchri Studio, 2002-2003
(design: Dennis Koot)

Najaarstentoonstelling

14 september t/m 6 oktober 2002

Bovenzalen, Voorhout- en Tuingalerie
Geopend dinsdag t/m zondag 11.00 - 17.00 uur
Dinsdag 17 september is Pulchri Studio gesloten
Lange Voorhout 15 | 2514 EA Den Haag | T (070) 346.17.35

Pulchri Studio, 2002-2003
(design: Dennis Koot)

PULCHRI STUDIO

2002-2003

Posters for seasonal art exhibitions
at Pulchri Studio, an artists' association and
gallery in The Hague's centre, founded in 1847
Dennis, musing on the gallery's rich
history and dynamic present: 'I wanted to create
both tension and synergy between digital and
organic formal languages — natural elements from
Spring and Autumn in computer blobs and hard RGB
colours, cheap photoshop effects over ultra-
realistic airbrush-like photo fragments. I made
the 'neon-tube' poster as an extra, a general
promotional poster that the gallery could always
use. Pulchri liked it, but had no budget for it.
But Gert wanted the poster printed and so he
financed it — A0 in 4 Pantone fluorescent colours,
which cost a fortune in 2003!'

Tala Abdalhadi, *Cat Toys – 3733 725378463*,
2022. Performer (in photo): Marie Lucy Vital.
Programme 'Soundscape'/'Madame Jambon',
collaboration Royal Academy of Art with Royal
Conservatoire The Hague, 2022, Korzo Theatre
Photo: Alex Schröder

DUMBAR NOW!

Almost immediately after he was sacked as professor[258] and course leader at the RCA in London in 1987, Gert took up a new teaching assignment at St. Joost Academy in Breda. Once again, it was clad in controversy: for half a year, Gert provided his educational service for free as a gesture of protest against the Ministry of Education's pressure on art and design schools to consolidate and merge into large educational institutes. In Gert's words that would result in 'learning factories, a bio-industry in which bureaucracy will grow inexorably'. In an interview for student magazine *Drift* Gert set off his ideas on art and design education against those of the government: 'Art education is a fragile shoot on a giant tree. It is the exception to the rule. It is not science, not to be learned from books. It is the last patch that cannot be mapped because unpredictable creative processes take place there. You have to leave a creative breeding ground alone, just as you leave rare birds alone. ...

Now that they're forced to blend into large conglomerates, they'll become mere craft-schools ... with an artistic sugar coating and hundreds of computers.'[259] He describes himself as 'a ghost-teacher, just like a ghost-flight — I'm not in the computer, but I do arrive.'

Fostering talent and fighting bureaucracy have been pivotal concerns for Gert throughout his career and they are central to his teaching practice as well. As educator of the next generations of graphic designers, Gert took his open and explorative working method, honed in the studio, to the class room. In October 1994 he accepted a two-year guest professorship at the Hochschule der Bildenden Künste Saar in Saarbrücken, Germany, on the French border. His official teaching assignment was 'visual communication and corporate identity' in the department of design, scheduled in three consecutive days per three weeks. Of course, 'corporate identity' was considered in a broadest

---

258   Concerning Gert's frequent ironic reference to himself as 'professor doctor engineer Dumbar', only the last title is fake; he was a professor at several design schools in the Netherlands and abroad and was awarded an honorary doctorate from Humberside Polytechnic, UK, in 1995.

259   Jan Vlasveld, 'Het kwetsbare kunstonderwijs vermorzeld door de Haagse bureaucratie', *Drift*, no.5, October 1988, pp. 12–13.

Top left: Lai Keng Lam, *Ties*, 2022. From l to r: Yannis Kyriakides, Kim Ho,
Lai Keng Lam. Top right: Kristin Norderval, Anja Hertenberger,
Myra-Ida van der Veen (in photo), *Weaving Home*, 2022. Mid: Juliette Hengst,
Liza Kuzyakova, *Horse 1 + 2*, 2022. In photo: Jose Maria Sta. Iglesia,
Juliette Hengst. Bottom left: *Horse 1 + 2* rehearsal, 2022.
In photo: Britt van den Boogaard, Brecht Hoffmann, Liza Kuzyakova,
Yannis Kyriakides, Juan Montero Palma, Juliette Hengst, Juan Marie.
Bottom right: 'Soundscape' rehearsal, 2024. In photo (t to b, l to r)
Hao-Teng Liu, Maja Mikulska, Beverly Lau, Basia Jagiello, Yicheng Geng,
Alessia Campanella, Suzie Veldhuijzen

© Alex Schröder

Above: Juan Montero Palma, Katherine Teng, Shelene Low Shi Ning, *Colour Language Course*, 2022. Performer (in photo): Magdalena Michalko. Programme 'Soundscape', collaboration Royal Academy of Art with Royal Conservatoire The Hague, 2022, Korzo Theatre. Photos: Alex Schröder possible sense. Gert: 'For an assignment I had said: make a house style for a strange, imaginary company. There was a lad who came up with a kind of employment agency with a logo quoting the motto above the gate of Auschwitz: Arbeit macht frei. I of course said "You can't do that, don't you know what that stands for!" To which he replied, "Of course I know what it means. There is no one in the whole world who is so well informed about the crimes of the Nazis as the German youth." That deeply moved me. He also knew, of course, that you could never use that in real life — it was a provocation. Those kids completely loosened up in my classes.'

What is remarkable in the first place is that students dared to present something as provocative as that at all. With Gert, they dared, and profited from the ensuing discussions, which mostly took place outside the school's premises. 'Next to the academy in Saarbrücken was a Kneipe, café Fürst Ludwig, where they had original prints by Frans Masereel on the walls. I did most of my teaching there. That was so much more fun than a dreary classroom. And they served wine. I had my students present their projects there too. The dean once reprimanded me because I allowed my students to address me as "Gert" and not as "Herr Professor", and lectured in a bar. It testifies to the stiff formal culture that was still prevailing in German education at the time. But he left it to me to do something about it. So I just carried on.'

Besides all kinds of wild experiments, Gert did point to the trade's history and the importance of understanding it. In a course together with design history professor Eva Mendgen on 'typography and reading culture' they stipulated: 'Without knowledge of the history of typography, one cannot build a personal

reservoir of experience on a professional level, let alone find a personal style.'[260] The practical assignment of the course urged students to 'place themselves in the position of the designers of yore, to merge with them ... and still arrive at a personal expression.' And he actively advocated his stance on 'stylistic durability' at the academy — and beyond. In April 1996 his 'Hilfswissenschaftler' (teaching assistant) Undine Löhfelm wrote to the editors of the *Brockhaus Lexikon*, on behalf of Gert, that he missed the entry 'stilistische Dauerhaftigkeit' in the encyclopaedia and hoped to galvanize 'an analysis and thorough discussion' of the phrase.

KABK

THE DIDACTICAL ASPECT IS THAT I INVITE THEM TO USE ALL WORKSHOPS. AND TO EXPLORE HUMOUR!
Gert Dumbar

In addition to several guest professorships, Gert has been a steady teacher at his old school, the Royal Academy of Art (KABK) in The Hague

Yicheng Geng (also in photo),
Hypnopompia, 2023.
Programme 'Soundscape' 2023,
collaboration Royal Academy of Art
with Royal Conservatoire The Hague.
Photo: Alex Schröder

since 2006. Currently he teaches at 'I/M/D', the Bachelor Interactive

260 Brochure for the course 'Typographie "à la maniere de...".
261 IMD website, accessed 24 November 2023: www.kabk.nl/en/programmes/bachelor/interactive-media-design
262 See pp. 248–249.
263 Gert Dumbar: conversation, 5 June 2023.

Media Design, under guidance of Janine Huizenga — a course 'for students who want to impact society by designing meaningful interactivity between people, machines, systems, processes, societies and cultures — where "human" is always the most important factor.'[261]

Multidisciplinarity is a key aspect of Gert's teaching — it was already one of the main reasons he was awarded the Werkmanprijs in 1984, as someone who 'stimulates and expands and integrates with other disciplines [and] who has given the broad and traditional discipline a striking expansion.'[262] In his courses at the KABK, with Brecht Hoffmann, the first assignment is always to start with research, followed by using the woodworking, textile, and metal

Stefanos Constantinides, Dominic Hughes (also in photo). *Melodies of the Abyss*, 2023. Programme 'Soundscape', collaboration Royal Academy of Art with Royal Conservatoire The Hague, 2022, Korzo Theatre Photo: Alex Schröder

workshops at the academy for constructing things: musical instruments, stage sets, costumes — anything beyond paper and screens. 'The didactical aspect is that I invite them to use all workshops. And to explore humour! They are second-year students who are completely free in doing what they want — but they need to do research, read … they need to reflect on an idea and then find the right materials to go with that idea, and ways to craft these materials. And they need to finish on time.'[263]

A special class, called 'Soundscape', involves close collaborations between KABK students of art and design and

Alper Çekinmez (also in photo). *Piece of work*, 2023. Programme 'Soundscape' 2023, collaboration Royal Academy of Art with Royal Conservatoire The Hague, 2023, Korzo Theatre. Photo: Alex Schröder

students at the Royal Conservatoire The Hague, leading to presentations with idiosyncratic instruments in a theatrical setting. 'Soundscape' is an initiative of Gert Dumbar and Martijn Padding, the team is supplemented by among others Erika Bordon, Yannis Kyriakides and Brecht Hoffmann. In true multidisciplinarity it connects all senses — understanding sound, art, design and their relations arises from hearing, listening, seeing and making, but perhaps most of all: from wondering, says Gert. 'Those composers, second-year

429

Dominika Badyla, Mick Peters, *Do not applaud*, 2023. In photo l to r: Max Mekkes, Stefanos Constantinides, Gert Dumbar, Basia Jagiello, Jakub Cerulík, Nadia Sotirova Abadjieva, Niko Schroeder. Programme 'Soundscape', collaboration Royal Academy of Art with Royal Conservatoire The Hague, 2022, Korzo Theatre. Photo: Alex Schröder

students and higher, have never made a musical instrument with their own hands. With us, they go to the wood workshop,

Pam Breedveld & Fernande Bloemen. *Spinning Top*. 2023. From l to r: Pam Breedveld, Dominic Hughes, Inez Nuijten, Adèle Houssin. Programme 'Soundscape' 2023, collaboration Royal Academy of Art with Royal Conservatoire The Hague, 2022, Korzo Theatre. Photos: Alex Schröder

they learn to solder and weld, they go to the textile workshop and together with art and design students they learn to make musical instruments. In this collaboration, music and matter come together.' In a veritable Gesamtkunstwerk, students are challenged to not only design and make musical instruments and compositions, but also costumes, theatre settings, choreographies and scenarios — and to perform the result before a live audience.

Such projects and the ensuing performances revive the atmosphere of Dada happenings and sometimes remind one of Futurist Luigi Russolo's *Intonarumori* — literally 'noise tuners'— strange acoustic instruments intended to vastly broaden the range of what could be considered 'musical sound'. While it may thus seem that Gert teaches old-school avant-gardism, he stresses the aim of providing space for his students to freely experiment and invent and build their own tools to explore the boundaries of their trades, or better, transgress them in collaborations that familiarize them with all departments of the academy.

Gert's signature course is on 'Humour as a strategy for design'. Its main aim is to teach students 'to use humour and absurdity in a project. This can be of vital importance to your later development.'[264] While stipulating not to 'listen to your tutors too much' — an echo of his advice 'not to listen

to your client'— the various instalments of the course introduce students to a critical review of design's avant-gardes, challenging them to both understand and mock such icons of design and art history as Bauhaus, Futurism, and Dada, traditions such as the still life and crafts such as furniture making. At the same time, the course underscores the well-established effectiveness of humour and absurdity in formulating a critical commentary on social and cultural phenomena such as fast food, the fashion industry or capitalism in general. All while stressing 'teaching goal nr.2.34.2.5: Learn to whistle your way through your work'.[265] 'You have to trigger the kids! In many teaching assignments, the solution is embedded in the question. In our assignments, the question provokes utter confusion. It teaches students to cope with the unexpected — it's a course in serendipity!'[266]

GERT DUMBAR HAS SHOWN ME THAT LIFE ISN'T HELD TOGETHER BY LOGIC, AND WE'D BETTER LAUGH ABOUT IT, SERIOUSLY

Jeroen Meijer (IMD graduate, 2022)

Thus, Gert connects Pierre Bayle's observation that 'reason just serves to confound everything'[267] to a more contemporary French philosophical

264   IMD Course syllabus, May 2019.
265   IMD Course syllabus, May 2020.
266   Gert Dumbar: conversation, 5 June 2023.
267   See pp. 201, 207.

Inez Nuijten, Adèle Houssin, Niko Schroeder, *Submerge*,
2023. Photos with Adèle Houssin, Inez Nuijten. Programme
'Soundscape' 2023, collaboration Royal Academy of Art
with Royal Conservatoire The Hague, 2023, Korzo Theatre
Photos: Alex Schröder

Indra Joachimsthal, Haevn Aalbersberg,
Mateusz Godlewski, Akiko Mik, *Shells of Light*,
2023. Programme 'Soundscape' 2023, collaboration
Royal Academy of Art with Royal Conservatoire
The Hague. Photos: Alex Schröder

tradition, that mocks the Enlightenment's pretensions of objective truth and scientific neutrality: 'I'm teaching on the basis of Alfred Jarry's philosophy of 'Pataphysics. It mimics being scientific, but totally isn't. That's already containing a boundless amount of humour. And it forces you to stop doing what you're doing — very refreshing. 'Pataphysics is a wonderful tool against conformism, a splendid weapon against the bourgeoisie and capitalism. It orders the unordered.'[268] In a syllabus, Gert points out that the study of 'Pataphysics — according to Jarry 'the science of imaginary solutions'— can also be an effective antidote to 'the looming slumber of intellectual laziness in the curriculum.'[269]

> *I'M TEACHING ON THE BASIS OF ALFRED JARRY'S PHILOSOPHY OF 'PATAPHYSICS. IT MIMICS BEING SCIENTIFIC, BUT TOTALLY ISN'T. THAT'S ALREADY CONTAINING A BOUNDLESS AMOUNT OF HUMOUR*
>
> Gert Dumbar

Beyond philosophy, the French connection manifests itself in Gert's insistence on joie de vivre, which he embeds in his teaching practice as much as he had done in making sure his 'Dumbarians' not only worked hard but also had fun in the Studio. One of his students at KABK tells that Gert would give him € 10 and the assignment to go out and come back with a bottle of red wine and glasses.[270] Ada Lopes Cardozo, then head of KABK's graphic design department and in her words '(officially) Gert's boss', recalls that 'being part of an institute I had to tell Gert things like: "Don't drink wine in the classroom with students." And he would cheerfully reply: "Of course, I understand, you are right." The next day I saw him drinking wine with students in the courtyard of the Academy … elusive.'[271]

'Elusive' may be the single best word available to characterize Gert. He escapes being pinned down to principles or methods — although he clearly has them, as we hope to have demonstrated in this book — by continuously and mischievously undermining them. His stance as a teacher is the same as his creative direction of the Studio: 'In order to bolster the power of imagination, I try to infuse my projects with humour and absurdism. Time and again I try to make my students become specialists in change. And with fun and magic, students sometimes manage to become magicians, inventing ploys to escape definitions.'

A thought arises: maybe Gert had no problem in 'letting things go' as he stated concerning his departure from the Studio, simply because he continued doing what he always did. He appears to agree when he says: 'Of course it's a continuation of what I've been doing all along, in the Studio, in Zeebelt. I'm just carrying on. In a creative profession, you can keep going. There is no retirement. All you need is a clear mind and a healthy body. And a good marriage helps, too. And I have a good marriage. With that you can go on forever. There will be a lot written in the coming years about people who have simply carried on with their active lives and who can also be innovative. That is very important, to have so much experience and be able to pass it on in an open way … A principal here at the KABK once said, "Gert, you are the oldest teacher here, and you do the youngest things!"'[272]

433

268 Gert Dumbar: conversation, 5 June 2023.
269 IMD Course syllabus, May 2020.
270 Max Bong, posted 31 January 2021 on The Secret Bar. Online: www.the-secret-bar.nl

271 Ada Lopes Cardozo, 'The conductor', posted 31 January 2021 on The Secret Bar. Online: www.the-secret-bar.nl
272 Gert Dumbar: conversation 22 June 2023.

ASSIGNMENTS FOR ART ACADEMIES

For his courses on 'Soundscape' and 'Humour as a strategy for design', Gert and his colleague Brecht Hoffmann issued a syllabus brochure each year, outlining the assignment, its backgrounds and aims. The main introductory texts in these brochures are reproduced here and on the following pages.

SOUNDSCAPE is an initiative of Gert Dumbar and Martijn Padding, the team is supplemented by among others Erika Bordon, Yannis Kyriakides and Brecht Hoffmann.

MADAME JAMBON

The 'Madame Jambon' project offers a collaborative platform for KC and KABK students to redefine Oskar Schlemmer's *Triadic* ballet through portable musical instruments, fashion, compositions, performances, and film. Open to second-year students and above, the project encourages interdisciplinary exploration and creative innovation. Participants design portable instruments and captivating costumes inspired by Schlemmer's ballet, with the possibility of merging them seamlessly for live performances at the Korzo Theatre during the Spring Festival. Guided by professors, students utilize KABK workshops to craft instruments and engage with the Fashion department for costume realization. Following the live performance, students transition to filmmaking, capturing their performance's essence on location and editing it into a cohesive film.

Through this multimedia approach, students explore the intersection of music, fashion, and visual storytelling, showcasing their collaborative vision and artistic expression. 'Madame Jambon' fosters creativity, imagination, and interdisciplinary collaboration, enriching students' artistic journey.

MADAME POIRE

The collaborative project 'Madame Poire - The Orchestra of the 21st Century' unites students from the Royal Conservatoire (KC) and the Royal Academy of Art (KABK) to create a grand manifestation of sound and image, set to debut at the Korzo Theatre in April 2023. Building on past successes, the project aims to foster collaboration between KC and KABK while exploring the fusion of sound, image, and music with tangible materials. Divided into five parts, students begin by designing and constructing unique musical instruments, followed by composing original pieces and rehearsing for performance. The project embraces open-ended exploration, with the instruments and final plan expected by mid-December. Filming and recording of the performance will document the project's journey. Guidance is provided by a team of specialists, and participants earn academic credit upon successful completion. 'Madame Poire' encourages creative experimentation, blending traditional and digital art forms to craft an innovative orchestral experience for the modern era.

MADAME CITRON: AN ORCHESTRA AND MORE

'Madame Citron: An Orchestra and More' is a collaborative project between the Royal Conservatoire (KC) and the Royal Academy of Art (KABK), aiming to

responsible for compiling the submissions. Students engage in interdisciplinary research, creating seaworthy objects from recycled materials embedded with messages on plastic pollution, drawing from principles of 'Pataphysics and interdisciplinary collaboration. The project, spanning a semester, culminates in mid-July with the launch of these sea objects. Notably, renowned artist Theo Jansen

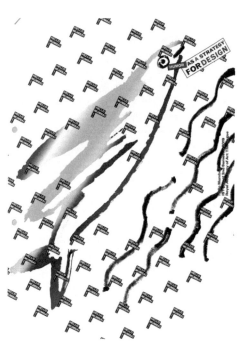

merge music and sound with image and matter. Running from September to April, it culminates in a performance at The Hague's Korzo Theatre. Goals include fostering cooperation between KC and KABK students, linking intangible elements like sound with tangible materials, and gaining performance experience. Participants craft unique musical instruments using KABK workshops, using them in compositions and performances. A video manual showcasing instrument usage is required. The project comprises two parts: pre-intermission short performances and post-intermission orchestral or solo pieces. Specialist guidance is provided, with credit points available upon completion. While humour and analogue methods are encouraged, they're not obligatory. The project emphasizes portfolio-worthy performance recordings, offering students a platform for innovative expression and interdisciplinary collaboration in the arts.

contributes, showcasing his wind-powered beach animals. Throughout the project, lectures are held to enrich participants' understanding of the issue, and upon completion, the marine objects are recycled, promoting sustainability. Ultimately, the project highlights the crucial role of artistic innovation in addressing environmental challenges, promoting creativity, sustainability, and community engagement.

'Hello Mumbai' was a collaboration between the departments Interactive Media Design (I/M/D) and Interior Architecture & Furniture Design (IAFD), with Ernie Mellegers (lecturer/tutor IAFD) of the Royal Academy of Art, The Hague. The final presentation was at Zuiderstrand (South Beach), The Hague.

HUMOUR AS A STRATEGY
FOR DESIGN
Gert Dumbar and Brecht Hoffmann set up within the Royal Academy's Interactive Media Design department (headed by Janine Huizenga).

HELLO MUMBAI

The Royal Academy of Art in The Hague, Holland, launches 'Mumbai: Hello Mumbai!' to combat global oceanic plastic pollution. This project urges art schools worldwide, especially those near the sea, to address this pressing issue. Emphasizing the sea's historical significance and current environmental peril, the initiative aims to instigate collective action. Participants undertake a global design marathon, crafting YouTube videos to raise awareness and propose solutions, with the Royal Academy

LA BANANE
D'ONCLE ALFRED

The project 'La Banane d'oncle Alfred: A fruit bowl as a laugh machine' integrates humour, self-analysis of laughter, electronics, and sound to foster creativity among students at KABK. Emphasizing interdisciplinary approaches reminiscent of the Modernist movement, it encourages students to blend various disciplines like image, sound, fine art, graphics, fashion, and music into their projects. Divided into four main subjects, students create a video of their laughter, design a laughing fruit bowl, develop an interactive laughing wallpaper, and craft postcards featuring their work. Guided by teachers from the Sonology department, students analyze laughter elements for their videos. They then delve into still life art history to design and construct

role of humour in design. Students conduct research, select a target corporation, design a large-scale logo representing its misdeeds, and construct it using recycled materials. The final presentation features the logo installation, with students dressed in corporate attire for a lively costume party. Success is measured by the project's ability to provoke laughter and amusement, particularly from parents, to their children's work.

HYPES AND MORE

The 'Hypes and More' project explores the historical roots and contemporary manifestations of hypes, focusing on their impact on societal norms and individual expression. It traces hypes back to historical rebellions against social norms and highlights their prevalence in modern social media and cultural establishments. The project aims to critique the uniformity fostered by hypes while encouraging participants to embrace absurdity and creativity. Through interdisciplinary collaboration, participants develop anti-hypes that challenge the status quo and celebrate individuality. They

unique fruit bowls with moving, laughing pieces. Additionally, they should create a funny coffee table to accompany the fruit bowl and design an interactive laughing wallpaper. The project concludes with a final presentation in the IMD department hallway.

MULTINATIONALS HA HA

The project 'Multinationals' at The Royal Academy of Art in The Hague, Netherlands, challenges students to creatively address environmental issues and corporate responsibility. Through satire and critical analysis, students critique multinational corporations' denial of ecological concerns perpetuated by political and economic interests. Inspired by 'Pataphysics, the project aims to disrupt traditional educational approaches by infusing humour and absurdity to stimulate critical thinking. It emphasizes collaborative teamwork, research skills, independent thinking, and the

create short videos to showcase their anti-hype concepts, emphasizing humour and alternative creative approaches. The project goals include fostering interdisciplinary collaboration, developing storyboard skills, and utilizing KABK workshops for hands-on learning experiences. By challenging conventional design norms and embracing individual expression, participants engage in intelligent design while exploring the transient nature of cultural trends.

CHANEL NO. 5

'Chanel No. 5 (Fall in love with beauty but do not stumble)' is a critical examination of contemporary fashion and cosmetic industries, highlighting their exploitative practices and societal impacts. It critiques the fashion industry's reduction of individuals to consumer dolls manipulated by capitalism, resulting in uniformity, ecological harm, and exploitation. The cosmetics industry perpetuates excessive

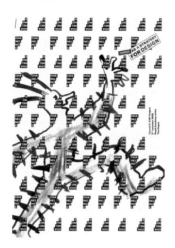

makeup use and harmful products while neglecting recycling efforts. Men's fashion features exaggerated attire and tattoo trends that often lead to regrettable choices. The project involves creating a caustic advertisement film that features performers dressed in exaggerated fashion inspired by societal critiques. It also involves designing packaging for an imaginary cosmetic product to be promoted in the film, all infused with humour and satire. Inspired by 'Pataphysics, it aims to provoke critical reflection on industry norms and advocate for alternative perspectives. Through creative expression, 'Chanel No. 5' encourages a critical reflection on the societal implications of the fashion and cosmetics mass industries, and to creatively communicate their findings with a short video where humour is key.

BAUHAUS LAUGH HOUSE

The 'Bauhaus Laugh House' project at the Royal Academy of Art in The Hague explores the critical examination of the Bauhaus. Despite its utopian ideals, the movement had a darker side, as evidenced by the controversial actions of key figures, such as Le Corbusier's fascist sympathies, J.J.P. Oud's collaboration with German occupiers, Mart Stam's misguided idealism in Stalin's Russia, and Franz Ehrlich's dark architectural commissions for the Nazis.

Students are tasked with critiquing these aspects in a scathing yet humorous and absurd manner, using Bauhaus products as metaphors. The

project aims to foster creative thinking and critical reflection while integrating humour into the design process. Through research, workshops, and creative projects, students delve into Bauhaus history, create interactive objects and wallpapers, and design postcards meant to be sent to the Bauhaus Museum in Dessau, Germany.

The project underscores the complexities of Modernism and challenges conventional narratives in art and design. It encourages students to question established norms and think outside the box, pushing boundaries in their creative expression. By addressing historical fringes and engaging with the Bauhaus legacy, students gain a deeper understanding of the movement's impact on society.

The project concludes with a final presentation where students have the opportunity to showcase their work. It is possible that the project may be published, highlighting the students' contributions to the discourse on Modernism. Ultimately, the project serves as a reminder of the importance of integrating critical thinking and humour into artistic practice, echoing Leonardo Da Vinci's timeless words: 'Where spirit does not work with the hand, there is no art.'

BAUHAUS LAUGH HOUSE 2

Scientifically, laughter is proven to be a potent, side-effect-free medicine, enhancing physical and mental well-being. Infusing humour into design elevates its appeal, captivates viewers' attention, and transcends language barriers, making complex concepts more accessible. Inspired by the doctrine of 'Pataphysics, a secret department within KABK embraces humour and absurdity to invigorate the curriculum and combat intellectual stagnation.

The project aims to critically explore the history of Bauhaus while integrating humour into design. Leveraging KABK's diverse workshops, students engage in hands-on experimentation, encouraged to think outside the box and challenge conventional teaching methods.

437

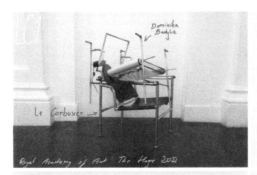

'De Buis'
W. Tümpel

Corina V
Interactive Media Design
Royal Academy of the Arts, The Hague
1st semester 2022

Peter Keler

Dev Bajaj
Department Interactive Media Design
Royal Academy of Art, The Hague
1st Semester 2022

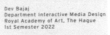

Takehiko Mizutani

Ella Suzanne Oudhof
Department Interactive Media Design,
Royal Academy of Art, The Hague
1st Semester 2022

438

'Bauhaus Laugh House' postcards
Project Royal Academy of Art, The Hague
Top l: Dominika Badyla; top r: Corina Vettore Gimenez;
mid l: Dev Bajaj; mid r: Ella Suzanne Oudhof;
bottom mid: Julian Pohl

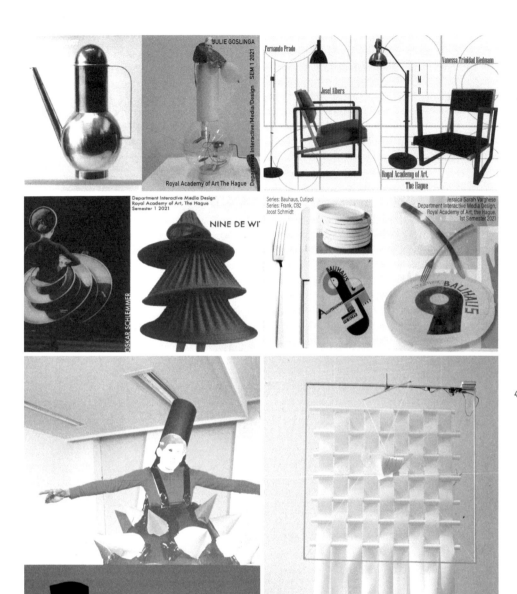

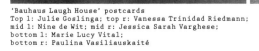

'Bauhaus Laugh House' postcards
Top l: Julie Goslinga; top r: Vanessa Trinidad Riedmann;
mid l: Nine de Wit; mid r: Jessica Sarah Varghese;
bottom l: Marie Lucy Vital;
bottom r: Paulina Vasiliauskaité

Students embark on various tasks, from creating short films about laughter to studying Bauhaus history and designing interactive laughing objects. They reimagine Bauhaus concepts with a humorous twist, infusing creativity and critical reflection into their work. The culmination includes producing interactive laughing wallpapers and designing postcards to send to the Bauhausmuseum in Dessau, Germany.

By embracing humour as a design strategy, KABK fosters a culture of innovation and creativity among its students. Through critical inquiry and imaginative expression, students challenge historical paradigms and push the boundaries of conventional design practices. The project serves as a catalyst for meaningful discourse, inviting reflection on the role of humour in design and its potential to transform society. Ultimately, it underscores the importance of humour in fostering engagement, creativity, and critical thinking in design education.

JOLLY TRAFFIC SIGNS

The 'Jolly Traffic Signs' project at KABK focuses on injecting humour into the urban landscape through reimagined pedestrian traffic signs. It seeks to foster interdisciplinary collaboration and creativity by utilizing various design disciplines and workshops. Participants are tasked with creating a 2-minute laughing video, designing two interactive traffic signs,

and strategically placing them in pedestrian areas. Inspired by Remi Gaillard, the project aims to engage pedestrians in unconventional ways while enhancing traffic flow. Two short films documenting the signs' design process and their real-world interactions are also required. By encouraging creativity and collaboration, the project aims to

bring joy and connection to urban environments, challenging traditional design approaches and emphasizing the importance of humour in design education.

THE ARROGANT SAUSAGE

The project 'The Arrogant Sausage' delves into the critical examination of the international food industry, particularly focusing on the unethical practices of food multinationals. It addresses the paradox of food abundance coexisting with widespread malnutrition, caused by the manipulation of food choices by profit-driven corporations.

The introduction highlights the significant advancements in agriculture and food supply chains, drastically reducing famine rates globally. However,

it also sheds light on the proliferation of unhealthy food choices driven by capitalist interests, leading to detrimental health effects for consumers.

The goal of the project emphasizes the importance of investigative research, teamwork, interdisciplinary collaboration, and the strategic use of humour and absurdity in design. Students are tasked with investigating the unethical conduct of food corporations, crafting demands for change, and presenting their critiques in a visually striking manner.

The project unfolds through various stages, including selecting a food multinational and presenting an intelligent and clear analysis of their shady dealings, turning that data into a list of demands, presenting a scale model of the plan, and constructing giant sausages made of discarded wood as symbolic representations of corporate malpractice. Each sausage serves as a platform for presenting findings and demands, with the logo of the targeted corporation prominently displayed on top of it.

The conclusion underscores the power of humour and absurdity as communication tools, highlighting the symbolism of the sausage in different cultures. The project concludes with a presentation to professors, providing students with an opportunity to showcase their critical perspectives and demand accountability from food corporations.

In essence, 'The Arrogant Sausage' project encourages students to challenge the status quo, confront corporate greed, and advocate for a more ethical and sustainable food industry. It represents a creative and thought-provoking endeavor aimed at sparking meaningful dialogue and driving positive change in society's approach to food production and consumption.

THE CRYING SAUSAGE

'The Crying Sausage' project delves into a critical examination of the global food industry, highlighting its flaws and absurdities while acknowledging its role in reducing global hunger. It critiques multinational corporations' practices, such as McDonald's use of harmful additives and Unilever's contribution to environmental damage. Participants will investigate industry misconduct and translate their findings into a short, humorous film no longer than 3 minutes. Through interdisciplinary collaboration, they will integrate fields like filming, graphics, and music to deliver engaging content with humour and absurdity. Utilizing KABK's workshops, students will create costumes and stage sets while incorporating typography and original film music. Inspired by the Doctrine of 'Pataphysics, the project emphasizes creativity and absurdity in education, aiming to communicate important ideas effectively. Overall, the project seeks to use humour to provoke contemplation without advocating for specific actions like vegetarianism, embracing the universality of bodily functions in its approach.

character, showcasing their storytelling abilities. Overall, the project fosters a culture of playful creativity and collaboration, enriching the design education experience at KABK.

LAUGH AND OBJECT

The Austrian philosopher Otto Neurath (1882-1945) is, together with artist/designer Gerd Arntz, the inventor of the pictogram, a visual language that transcends the language barrier. To paraphrase Neurath's motto: Words divide, humour unites. But

441

BANANA RACE

The 'Banana Race' project at the Royal Academy of Art in The Hague promotes interdisciplinary creativity and humour in design education. Students are encouraged to explore various disciplines such as sound, image, and graphic design while utilizing workshops like wood and metal to develop innovative concepts. Humour and absurdity are key components, challenging students to break from convention and push design boundaries. The project comprises creating a banana vehicle capable of autonomous driving and participating in a banana race. Additionally, students transform their hands and feet into characters inspired by the works of artist Mario Mariotti and produce a multimedia fairy tale featuring the banana as the main first, the following: there is not enough laughter at the KABK! It has been scientifically proven that laughter is a free medicine without side effects. A bout of laughter raises the heart rate and deepens breathing, causing more oxygen to flow to the brain. According to William Fry, professor of psychiatry at Stanford University (USA), one minute of laughter equals ten minutes on a rowing machine. Humour works with an unexpected element, a kind of strobe light of contradictions. This project concerns humor, laughter, and turning this into a spatial element; a piece of 'furniture' that is designed to move in response to its maker's laughter. And the end result being a short film.

LA BANANE D'ONCLE ALFRED 2

The project 'La Banane d'oncle Alfred part 2' is a continuation of its predecessor and focuses on comic book heroes. Comic heroes originated from comic books and are globally recognized figures. There are various types of genres of comics ranging from incredibly sad, to absolutely hilarious.

Similar to the first project, the goal of part 2 aligns with encouraging students to integrate humour seamlessly into their creations, allowing their imagination to run untethered.

In this project, students are required to choose an existing comic book hero and incorporate it into their laughing fruit project. They must create a life-sized version of the hero using three-dimensional materials, ensuring it stands beside the laughing fruit bowl from the previous project and expresses hearty laughter itself. The character should have an emotional expression, using movement or light to achieve this. Additionally, students must create a laughing wallpaper featuring their comic book hero and design two postcards documenting the charactes and the final presentation.

The conclusion emphasizes the importance of embracing Alfred Jarry's

ideas regarding 'Pataphysics, which can be valuable throughout students' academic and professional careers. Overall, the project encourages students to explore the intersection of humour, creativity, and cultural icons, fostering imaginative and engaging creations.

ANTS

The 'Ants' project delves into the evolution of building construction waste, highlighting the shift from a culture of reuse to one dominated by disposability and its environmental impact. Inspired by the collaborative nature of ants, participants aim to emulate their efficiency and adaptability in addressing waste management challenges. Lasting the entire second semester, the project involves constructing a house using scraps sourced from the academy's rear courtyard and throughout Den Haag and should embody the spirit of a chosen artwork and incorporate a militant citation advocating for shelter and hospitality. Teams also collaborate across departments to design and build a corresponding boat, remaining consistent with the house's theme and capable of sailing from the newly constructed apron across the canal. The project emphasizes information collection, teamwork, and exploration of diverse design ideas, fostering autonomy and creative expression. By engaging with societal issues and advocating for environmental stewardship, participants embody the industrious spirit of ants while addressing contemporary challenges in waste management and design.

Top left: Suzie Veldhuijzen, *Suziephones*, 2024. In photo l to r: Andrew MacLeod,
Jonathan Veldhuijzen, Alessia Campanella, Kaat Vanhaverbeke
Top right: Maja Mikulska, Mads Rosairus (both also in photo), *Beautiful Sludge*, 2024
Bottom left: Lai Keng Lam (also in photo), *24zzz*, 2024
Bottom right: Gert Dumbar welcoming the audience; in the background: Alper Çekinmez,
Thomas Wenas, Kim Ho. 'Madame Citron' project, 2024
All photos: Programme 'Soundscape', collaboration Royal Academy of Art with Royal
Conservatoire The Hague, 'Spring Festival', 2024, Korzo Theatre.
Photos top r, bottom l: Alex Schröder; top l, bottom r: Renate Boere

Amnesty International Year Book 1979-1980 cover,
focusing on political prisoners (design: Gert Dumbar)

DESIGN FOR THE COMMON GOOD

When in 1972 two prominent protagonists of Dutch graphic design, Wim Crouwel and Jan van Toorn, debated the ethical, cultural, and political do's and don'ts of the trade,[273] Gert seemed to be a sceptical but silent bystander — he had on several occasions declared that he didn't see much in the discourse on design's social responsibility. He is quoted in a rather disparaging column in *NRC Handelsblad* of 21 July 1977 by art critic Philip Peters, as saying that a designer 'fortunately' does not have a clear task in our society. 'One is given the occasional opportunity to take a socially critical stance. But in general, that doesn't amount to much.'[274] That does not, however, mean he thinks there is no place in design for a social or cultural-political ethos. Gert was well aware of design's ethical discourses — he read Victor Papanek's seminal *Design for the Real World* and was influenced by Andreas Fuglesang's insistence on using 'appropriate technology and conceptualization', especially in communicating with illiterate people. Fuglesang's ideas resonate in Gert's designs for pictograms.

While Gert is not an outspoken utopian thinker — although he is an unswerving advocate of 'the Good Life'— he did address 'the real world' on a number of occasions that triggered his concerns as a citizen as well as his interest and expertise as a designer, either by invitation or by his own initiative.

---

273   See p. 91.
274   Philip Peters, '6 Haagse ontwerpers', in *NRC Handelsblad*,
        21 July 1977, p. 6. In a vitriolic review, Peters scoffs a small
        exhibition of six graphic designers from The Hague at
        the Gemeentemuseum, among them Gert Dumbar,

Ootje Oxenaar and Heinz Edelmann. Clearly, he expects designers to be more aware of their social responsibility and is astonished by the 'gullible bad-boy's talk, uttered by some of them' in the exhibition's accompanying brochure.

পুরাতাপনী : ২৫৩৯২৪

গণস্বাস্থ্য ও পুনর্বাসন কেন্দ্র
(সাবেক বাংলাদেশ হাসপাতাল)
১৩২, নিউ ইস্কাটন রোড,
ঢাকা-২, বাংলাদেশ

Phone : 253924

Gonoshasthaya-o-Punarbashon Kendra
(People's Health & Rehabilitation Centre)
FORMERLY BANGLADESH HOSPITAL
132, New Eskaton Road,
DACCA-2, BANGLADESH

XXXXXXXXX October 25, 1972

Mr Gert Dunnbar,
c/o Tel Desian Associated
Emmapark 14
The Hague
Holland

Dear Mr. Dunnbar,

It was a great pleasure to meet you in Holland last month.
As we discussed then, I would like you to design a graphic picture which we could
give to the village women in our project area in Bangladesh to remind them about
taking their Pill. Although this is perhaps the most important, we would also
be interested in the following:1)Posters to educate people in Family Planning
2) reminding people to take their medicine at the right time and in the right
quantity (i.e. 1 spoonful/tablet XX in the morning at midday and at night:before
the meal/after the meal. 3) reminding XXXXXXXX parents to take their children
to be vaccinated. 4) posters about preventable diseases (cholera, smallpox,
typhoid, polio, diptheria, tetanus, tuberculosis) 5) warning against unhygienic
habits - for example, getting worms through walking in the fields without sandals.
6) posters about growing nutritious food, like spinach and groundnuts.

I am looking forward very much to hearing from you,

Yours sincerely

Zafrullah Chowdhury

গণমুখী স্বাস্থ্য ব্যবস্থা বাস্তবায়নের পরীক্ষামূলক কেন্দ্র—সাভার

First organised Field Hospital for Muktibahini and Refugees in the Eastern border of Bangladesh.

Letter from Zafrullah Chowdhury (Dacca,
Bangladesh) inviting Gert to design posters
for his family planning project

Team of designers working on the Bangladesh project.
At the head of the table: Titus Yokarini, then chairman
of the Dutch graphic designers association GVN.
Gert Dumbar sits on the right

BANGLADESH

One of the first was his response to a request by his old high school friend, Jan Willem van der Eb, an economist who worked with NOVIB.[275] Bangladesh, then one of the poorest countries in the world and still reeling from the aftermath of a devastating civil war with Pakistan, needed professional advice on a project to promote family planning. The project was initiated by Zafrullah Cowdhury, a doctor who had been treating the wounded during the war and who later became the country's first Health Secretary.

In 1972, in the same year as the legendary debate between Crouwel and Van Toorn, Gert assembled a small workgroup of designers, mostly from Tel Design, collaborating with the Dutch graphic designers' union GVN. 'In the villages for which this campaign was meant, visual communication did not exist — no advertisements, no billboards, nothing. And the villagers were illiterate. So we made visual stories around the contraceptives that were used and were distributed there.'[276] The group collected

Poster from Bangladesh warning for
contamination risks between mothers
and children (source unknown)

images that represented wellbeing — a zinc roof instead of a straw one, only two children instead of eight or nine mouths to feed — and combined these with images of the contraceptives: the pill and IUDs. Students from the medical department

275 NOVIB (since 2006 Oxfam Novib) is a Dutch NGO focused on fighting poverty and promoting equal rights. It was founded by Nobel-laureated economist Jan Tinbergen and others in 1956 as 'the Netherlands' Organisation for International Support' in response to the devastating

276

flooding of the southern Dutch province of Zeeland in 1953. Although an NGO, it was and is responsible for managing a sizable part of Dutch government spending on 'development aid'.

Gert Dumbar: conversation, 12 January 2023.

Photos provided by the Bangladesh project
organization as context for the family planning
project. The top right photo shows the building
site for Chowdhury's People's Health and
Rehabilitation Centre in Dacca

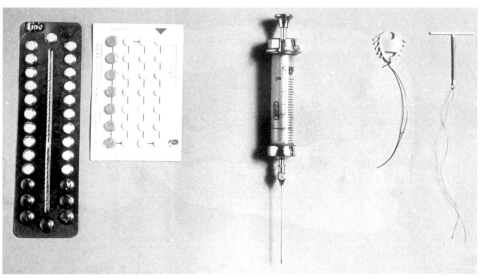

The pill and other birth control methods, photographed for the Bangladesh family planning project

of Dacca University would go the villages with the posters and tell the stories connected to them: If you use these means, you'll be able to have just two children and you'll have money for a zinc roof and for your children's education. 'So these posters were designed to serve as illustrations and reminders of the stories told by the medical students,' says Gert. 'Incidentally, this is how Chowdhury started a phenomenon that later became known as the "barefoot doctors": to have the doctors come to the villages instead of the villagers having to travel to the city. The posters often were the only images in such villages, so they were quite conspicuous. We just had to prevent them being used for other purposes — Jan Willem had heard that scribes went around the villages to write things down for people who couldn't read or write. But there was no paper, so they used whatever was available — potentially also our posters. That is why I designed a pattern, printed on the back side to prevent the posters from disappearing from view because they were used as writing paper.'[277]

Although not a stranger to self-promotion, Gert never boasted of such voluntary work. 'I found it fascinating to put graphic design to use in a different way, to in a sense design for the real world — I've read Papanek and met him a couple of times. But I didn't feel comfortable with advertising such projects. They worked — the Bangladesh project was highly successful, as a study by Dacca University concluded — and that was enough.'[278] Referring to the contemporary debate on the social responsibility of graphic design, Gert asserts: 'Jan van Toorn talked about engagement, but never worked for what we then called the "Third World" — we did it, but didn't talk about it, no one knows about that. You may say in hindsight that it was trendy engagement, but for Bangladesh we did in my view develop something really new in visual communication for the illiterate.'[279]

449

277   Ibid.
278   Ibid.
279   Gert Dumbar: conversation, 29 April 2021.

Photos, sketches, and final poster (right page) for
the Bangladesh family planning project

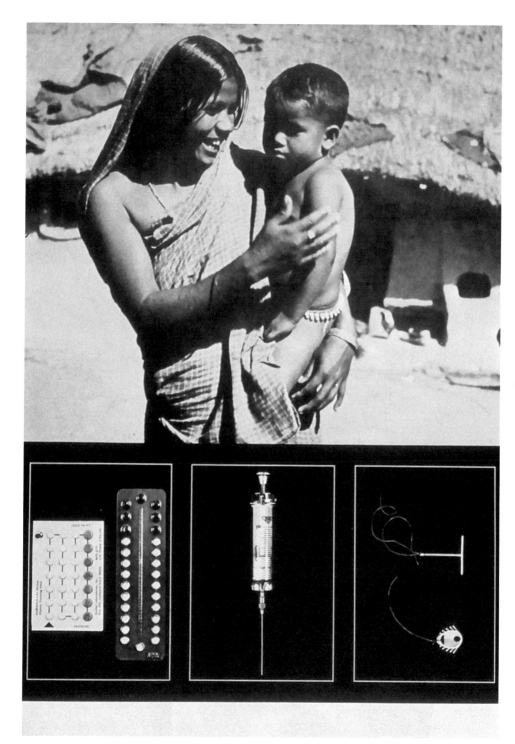

Doctors and students from Dacca medical university
showing and explaining the family planning posters
to villagers

'ARM : RIJK = NO BALANCE'

Opened by minister of Culture Marga Klompé and Prince Claus, this exhibition consisted of some eighty panels with photos and diagrams of developmental projects in 'Third-World' countries such as Tanzania, with accompanying texts and information on economic and social challenges. In addition to showing concrete examples of aid, such as an incubator specifically designed

'Arm : rijk = geen verhouding', 1973

for Vietnam, it also introduced a 'World Trade game', which demonstrated the gaps and dependencies between rich and poor countries. The exhibition, commissioned by the International Institute of Social Studies on the occasion of its twentieth anniversary, was held from 5-18 February 1973 in Noordeinde Palace in The Hague and travelled on to various other places in the Netherlands.

Gert's papier-mâché figure of a caricature-like capitalist with oversized cigar sits on (or if you will, crushes) a flat silhouette of someone who is obviously larger, but clearly powerless. The 'capitalist's' hands are folded as if in pious prayer, but

his relaxed posture, comfortably sitting in his arm chair, suggests nonchalant ignorance of the pale shadowy figure's suffering beneath him.

'ARTICLE 11'

To celebrate the bicentennial of the Déclaration Universelle des Droits de l'Homme et du Citoyen (Universal Declaration of Human and Civil Rights), during the French revolution of 1789, the French organization Artis 89 invited 66 international designers to make a poster. From the Netherlands Anthon Beeke, Jan van Toorn, Hard Werken and Studio Dumbar responded. Gert chose to highlight article 11 of the Declaration: 'The free communication of thoughts and opinions is one of the most precious rights of man.' In his papier-mâché set, with a painted backdrop above a sandy

'Article 11' poster, 1989

'Gitanes' poster, 1991

his introduction to the publication of the fifty posters, curator Alain Weil remarks that Gert was among the very few who 'chose to make use of the Gypsy woman to denounce tobacconism.' The others were Anthon Beeke (with an image that suggests an X-ray of soiled lungs and the sardonic slogan 'Happiness is the longing for repetition'), Gerard Paris-Clavel (ironically stating that Tout va bien over a stained stencil of the dancer), Alain Le Quernec (with a deadpan 'Advertising kills') and Makoto Saito (who depicts the famous dancer-in-smoke icon as a fart from a hairy butt). In a set photographed by Lex van Pieterson Gert stages cut-out versions of the silhouette as two ladies who are thrashing the dirt from a charred pair of lungs. Carpet beaters replace their original fans. The only text is the brand name 'Gitanes', rendered in a spiky outline — as if the letters had served as ash trays. The image itself is eloquent enough to make any other text redundant.

455

desert landscape, a figure hovers like an astronaut in space, connected to a pen by a red lifeline. The instrument of communication is held by an arm sprouting from two legs that seem to literally grow from the number of the article. Scissors threaten to cut the umbilical cord between one's thoughts and expressing them. The entire design, photographed by Lex van Pieterson, evokes a feeling of imminent danger, of the perennial fragility of this 'most precious' right to publicly state one's point of view.

GITANES

In 1991, the French cigarette brand Gitanes wanted to celebrate its iconic packaging design — the silhouette of a gypsy dancer veiled by blue and white whiffs of smoke. The brand issued a call for entries for an Hommage à Max Ponty, the designer of the original package. In

Gert Dumbar, sketch for Rio conference poster, 1992

UN CONFERENCE RIO 1992

In June 1992, the second United Nations Conference on Environment

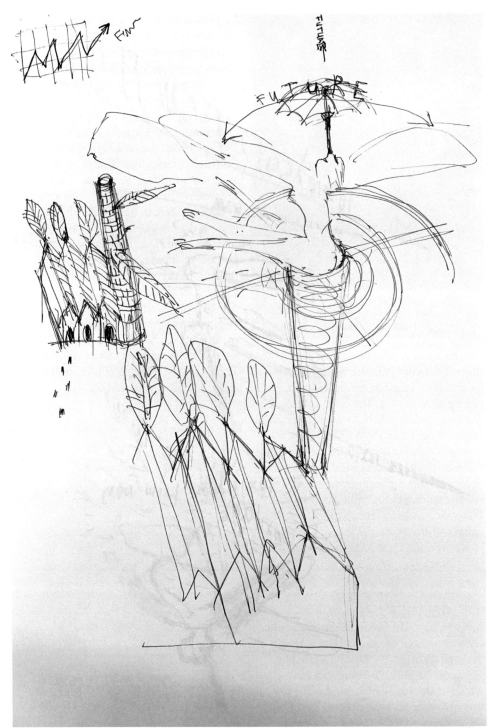

Gert Dumbar, sketch for Rio conference
poster, 1992

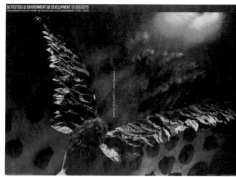

Rio conference poster, 1992

and Development was held in Rio de Janeiro, Brazil. Its grand ambition was to 'define the future paths of the relationship between humanity and the world ... preserving and respecting nature.' One of the cultural projects accompanying the conference was '30 Posters on Environment and Development', curated by Brazilian graphic designer Felipe Taborda. The briefing stipulated that the posters 'should not denounce anything done against the environment ... but should rather be a vision of an integrated solution of progress and nature ...' Gert answered by sketching an angel-like figure flying towards a rosy future. In the final poster, the wings consist of large green leaves, illustrating the slogan 'Man needs wings to green the world'.

GRAPHIC MESSAGE FOR ECOLOGY

In Japan, the most active organization for presenting and promoting Japanese and international graphic design is Ginza Graphic Gallery (GGG), connected to the Dai Nippon printing company. The GGG hosted Studio Dumbar's 'Behind the Seen' exhibition in 1998, and invited Gert in the following year as one of twenty foreign designers, next to twenty-nine Japanese, to convey a 'graphic message for ecology'. Not hampered by Rio '92's briefing, Gert used the podium to denounce industrial air pollution. His charcoal drawing looks like a caricature self-portrait with angry eyes and irritated nose above a brick chimney. Again, the image needs no words to communicate the message.

RUSLAND DUITSLAND DEN HAAG: SOME THOUGHTS ON A DUTCH DESIGN INSTITUTE

In the fall of 1990, a group of distinguished gentlemen gathered to advocate the foundation of a Dutch national Design Institute in The Hague. Among them Gert (as president and, with Studio Dumbar, sponsor), Ootje Oxenaar, Jan Willem van der Eb and Jelle van der Toorn Vrijthoff. That the latter two were

457

'Graphic message for Ecology' poster, 1999

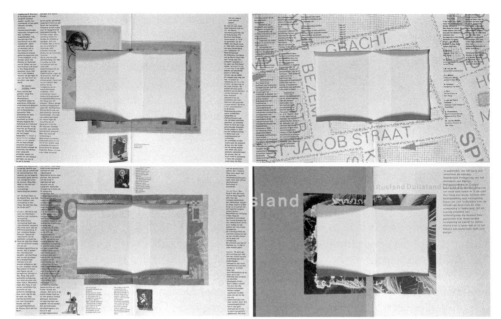

Rusland, Duitsland, Den Haag: Some thoughts on a Dutch Design Institute in The Hague,
double-page spreads, 1990 (book design: Frans van Mourik)

Amsterdam residents seemed to be no problem. Still, the initiative was triggered by an at times fierce competition between three cities, Amsterdam, Rotterdam, and The Hague to house the Design Institute after the Ministry of Culture had stated such an institute should be established. Studio Dumbar designed a remarkable publication — a book with a large die-cut hole at its core, symbolizing the missing centre. Around it, the text argued The Hague's inevitability as the Institute's residence while the illustrations referred to the city's rich design heritage. Mentioning illustrious Hague predecessors in advancing graphic design such as J.F. van Royen, Vilmos Huszár, Piet Zwart, Paul Schuitema, and (government) institutions already present in the Residence, such as the PTT and the SDU (State Printing and Publishing house), the activists elaborated a long list of cultural, historical, political, and economic arguments for The Hague,

bolstered by the city's commitment to finding and financing a representative domicile.

The book's title refers to the graphic revolution that spread from Russia via Germany to the Netherlands in the 1920s

Rusland, Duitsland, Den Haag,
book cover, 1990

and 1930s, anchoring The Hague as one of the international centres of graphic design innovation.

In their support for a Design Institute, the Dutch government had

---

280   Gert and Derk Dumbar: 'A Safe Place', Utrecht Manifest, 2007.

stressed the importance of industrial design, but the gentlemen of the Hague committee were sceptical. Ootje Oxenaar:

Rusland, Duitsland, Den Haag,
book wrapping, 1990

'When the spoon makers and handkerchief designers would have to share an institute with graphic designers you'll get a faceless mammoth organisation.' Hein van Haaren: 'The ministry of Culture should leave industrial design to the economists.' Gert Dumbar: 'It's time for a "Piet Zwart Institute" for graphic design in The Hague.'

The group's focus on graphic design may have worked against them — in the end the Design Institute was established in Amsterdam in the former Fodor Museum as a place for all design disciplines. British design generalist and journalist John Thackara was appointed as its first director.

A SAFE PLACE: PICTOGRAMS FOR DISASTER AREAS
— with Derk Dumbar

In 2007, Gert and his son Derk proposed prototypes for a series of pictograms to be used in disaster areas worldwide. When large-scale disasters —natural or man-made— happen, large groups of people gather in makeshift places, harboured by international organizations such as the Red Cross or the United Nations. 'In such refugee camps,' Gert and Derk argue, 'there is a lack of everything. One of the reasons why so many things go wrong in these environments is faulty communication resulting from language barriers, illiteracy, and cultural differences. ... Under such circumstances, how can one help people find answers to their most basic questions? ... A standardized set of pictograms can help by unequivocally indicating where these answers are to be found.'[280]

The design builds on Gert's experience with Bangladesh and with the pictograms Studio Dumbar designed for several clients, notably the 'foot & mouth' pictograms for the Ministry of Agriculture.

The actual pictograms were designed and developed by Derk, who also organized

Signs warning for agricultural contamination risks, signalling a prohibition of animal transportation (top) and indicating contaminated farms (bottom), 1986 (design: Studio Dumbar for Ministry of Agriculture)

Disaster pictograms exhibited at Stroom, The Hague, 2008
(idea and design: Derk Dumbar)

the extensive research for the project in workshops in Iowa, Shanghai, Paris, and The Hague. The pictograms were then further developed into a prototype set,

Disaster pictograms exhibited at Stroom, The Hague, 2008

presented at the Utrecht Manifest biennial for Social Design in 2007. Gert and Derk admit their prototype 'is based on Western visual culture and rhetoric, simply because that is our cultural background. At the moment, we are consulting international specialists of disaster relief and aid work, in order to find out which themes and terms we need to develop into new and universally applicable symbols.'

Although several international organizations showed keen interest, the further development of the project became bogged down in bureaucracy, as Gert recalls: '"Very interesting" said one civil servant after another and delegated it to an assistant, who also said "interesting" and so on, ad infinitum.'[281]

281   Gert Dumbar: conversation, 12 December 2023.

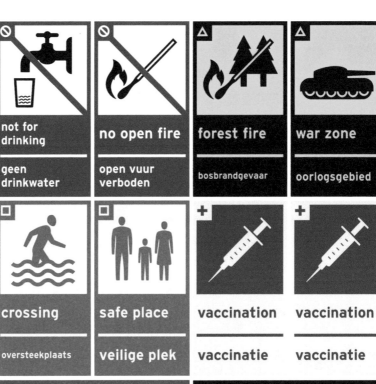

Disaster pictograms, 2008
(design: Derk Dumbar, Rieme Gleijm)

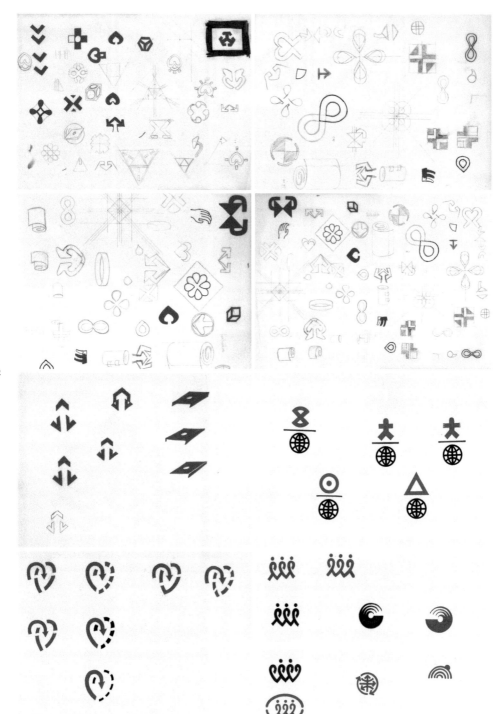

Unrealized sketches for a competition for the identity of Doctors Without Borders

DOCTORS WITHOUT BORDERS

1990s (year unknown)

Gert Dumbar: 'We tried to keep it very simple, so it could be applied as stencil on all kinds of materials. We didn't want to be paid for it — instead, I became a patron'

'1:4' POSTER

1996

A consortium of European NGOs and broadcasters started a campaign to fight ageism, based on the prediction that 'in the 21st century, 1 in 4 Europeans will be over 60'. The EU-supported programme invited creatives to 'volunteer their services in the fight against ageism' and conceive 'opinion-forming TV commercials' to be broadcast throughout Europe. Gert Dumbar was on the jury that judged the proposals. The poster outlines the problems to face: higher life expectancy leads to a longer active life for today's young adults who often discriminate against older people. 'Put yourself in their shoes', the poster suggests, because 'one day they will be yours'

INTERNATIONALE AFFICHE GALERIJ (INTERNATIONAL POSTER GALLERY)

2004

In 1994, Gert Dumbar and friends, among whom DEV's (Aesthetic Design Department PTT) director Hein van Haaren and collector Martijn Le Coultre, started a foundation advocating a public 'poster gallery' in one of two underground tramway stations that were being planned to ease public transport in The Hague's inner city. This 1200 meter 'Hague Tram Tunnel', officially known as 'the Souterrain', was designed by Rem Koolhaas' bureau OMA and opened in 2004. The

Foundation succeeded in realizing a ninety-metre-long sloping walkway with climatized display cases in order to provide museum conditions for exhibiting posters from collections all over the world. The programming of the altering exhibitions is done by The Hague's municipal archive in collaboration with collectors worldwide

'1:4', 1996 (poster design: Bob van Dijk)

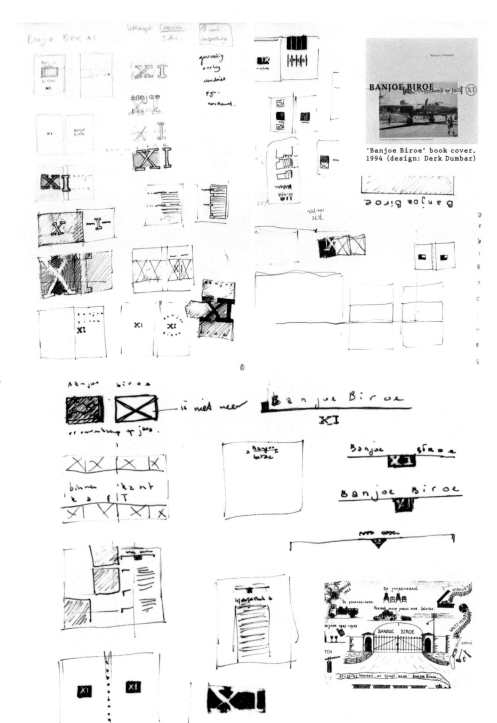

'Banjoe Biroe' book cover,
1994 (design: Derk Dumbar)

Sketches for a book on women's prison camp
Banjoe Biroe, 1994 (design: Derk Dumbar)

BANJOE BIROE

1994

Gert Dumbar, his mother An and sister Petra were
detained there from 1942-1945 during the Japanese
occupation of Java, Dutch East-Indies in the Second
World War. The book collected stories from various
authors and was issued as a free publication by
ANDO printers, The Hague

Monument for 161 soldiers from The Hague who died
between 1945 and 1962 in the former Dutch East-Indies
and New Guinea; Scheveningen, 2002
(design: Gert Dumbar)

OORLOGMONUMENT

2002

The names of the soldiers are carved
vertically into the eight-metre-long stone wall,
arranged in such a way that a horizontal line of text
appears in gold accentuated letters, written by poet
Anton Korteweg: 'Op welke grond werden ze gelegd /
in vreemde aarde' ('On which ground they were laid / in
foreign soil')

468

Dance Party poster 'Dog', for Royal College of Art
(design: Gert Dumbar)

SQUARING
THE CIRCLE

Max Bruinsma & Leonie ten Duis

CONCLUDING REMARKS

In November 1995, a panel of both seasoned and young graphic designers pondered 'The Dumbar Phenomenon' during a public debate at the Rietveld Academie in Amsterdam. Participating in this forum was one of the most distinguished clients of the Studio, Ootje Oxenaar from the Dutch PTT. Also present was Gert's esteemed colleague and adversary, as famous himself, Wim Crouwel. And there were two younger designers, both in a way influenced by Dumbar, but at the same time also critical about his work: Chris Vermaas, an excellent typographer and teacher and Paul Postma of the upcoming bureau of Koeweiden Postma Designers. Postma recalls how as a student he heard the wildest stories about Dumbar and his collaborators at the Studio: 'Because of all this, the man grew to almost mythic proportions.' And Chris Vermaas, who travelled around the globe, working and teaching in Barcelona, New York and Mexico, noticed that in all of those places students were collecting the work of Studio Dumbar, emulating and often copying it.

During the debate, Crouwel was clear and consistent: 'Dumbar's opinions and his formal language are contrary to mine,' he stated. 'Studio Dumbar is an exponent of the purely emotional movement that criticized modernist rationalism in the 'seventies and eighties'. In Crouwel's view a lot of this was plain mockery, practical jokes at the expense of a stunned public. Some of it 'aspired to a sort of superior light-heartedness', but he wondered if it ever 'communicated outside a small circle of elite clients and admirers'.[282]

However one looks at it, one has to disagree with Crouwel here. Consider only the gargantuan pile of news stories, trade magazine reports, design critiques, interviews, and references to Studio Dumbar in general and specialist media world-wide during the Studio's 25 years

Quotes from: Max Bruinsma, 'The Dumbar Phenomenon', in *IDEA* magazine, #255, 1996.

with Gert, and you're bound to conclude that the circle is far from small — it spans the globe. And in a sense, Gert 'squared' it. The 'elite side' of the Studio's output — wildly experimental things for Zeebelt and like-minded clients — was closely enmeshed with what one could call the Studio's 'corporate' side. Far from separating 'experimental' from 'realistic' work, Gert profoundly connected the two in the Studio's practice. Not necessarily with regard to the formal outcome, but on a deeper level — that of a design mentality and methodology. Zeebelt experiments may have directly influenced larger and much more public jobs such as the Holland Festival, but the eagerness to explore non-obvious directions and experiment with a great range of possible solutions can be seen also in strictly regulated corporate identities, such as Dutch Railways, PTT (Mail, Telephony and Telegraphy), the Ministry of Agriculture, GAK and many others. Studio Dumbar's annual reports for corporate clients and their design manuals for large house styles are a case in point. The manuals, for instance, intimately link a thoroughly systematic approach

AN ESSENTIAL FOUNDATION OF GERT'S MENTALITY AND METHOD IS HIS EMPHASIS ON SKETCHING. WITH A PENCIL, HE STIPULATES

— necessary for warranting the consistent application of the identity by the client's designers and DTP-ers — to a playful interpretation of the system. Of course, the manuals are authoritative. They say: 'This is how it should be done.' But they also say: 'Come play along with us'. The graphic and editorial design of these manuals themselves lead by example; beautifully — sometimes exuberantly — packaged, they try to seduce rather than dictate.

This strategy of seduction mirrors Gert's personality. Averse to hierarchies and authoritarian directives, he fostered play and space for adventure. He may have switched from the fine arts to design early on in his professional education, because he needed 'an outside perspective, a client, with a clear and concrete problem', and would 'rather play in an orchestra than as a soloist', but he never gave up his longing for artistic autonomy and freedom. His stance vis-à-vis clients and modernism reflects this freedom of spirit. Gert is not 'serving' clients, nor is he following or advocating a design ideology — he is in respectful but critical conversation with both. With that — and alongside a mostly younger generation of 'postmodern' rebels — Gert has been a strong and early voice of protest against modernism's 'International Style' dictates that pervaded design and architecture from the 1950s to well into the 1970s. At the same time, and sometimes rather paradoxically, he harks back to modernism's roots in the playfully irreverent and rebellious styles and creative methods of the early-twentieth century avant-gardes. More 'Van Doesburg' than 'Mondrian', Gert values clear structure — as long as it leaves room for 'diagonals': play and humour. With that, Gert has been a central and effective advocate of granting creative autonomy and room for experimentation to designers. Rather than providing clients with a 'crystal goblet', he claims visibility and authorship for designers.

An essential foundation of Gert's mentality and method is his emphasis on sketching. With a pencil, he stipulates. 'Sketching needs to be done artlessly with

283   Gert Dumbar: conversation, 17 March 2023.
284   Ibid.

a pencil or marker. That doesn't work on a computer — it's not spontaneous, the line is not nice, the colours are ugly and it's not clumsy enough. It needs to be klutzy. First sketches are extremely important!'[283]

One can see this, again, as a testament to Gert's rootedness in the fine arts where sketching is the foundation of all work: 'The freedom, the personal, experimental approach, the risk-taking that is possible in the arts is for me also essential for design.'[284]

> ## THE FREEDOM, THE PERSONAL, EXPERIMENTAL APPROACH, THE RISK-TAKING THAT IS POSSIBLE IN THE ARTS IS FOR ME ALSO ESSENTIAL FOR DESIGN
> Gert Dumbar

Such a mentality of open experimentation and iterative sketching stimulates the imagination and challenges designers — as well as clients and recipients — to look beyond the obvious. In this view, design is less about 'problem solving' than about finding imaginative, even sometimes puzzling, answers to a client's brief. At the same time, Gert would not have been so successful if beneath the cheerful surface of much of the Studio's output there hadn't been a thoroughly rational, systematic, and controlled machinery; the design professionalism that governed large corporate and institutional commissions. It is often unheeded — a 'music box' needs a well-constructed engine to produce a coherent sound.

Gert has shown an amazing talent in attracting young like-minded creatives. Part of that talent is the balance he and Michel sought between what one could characterize as 'expressionists' and 'functionalists' — a productive mix of creative mavericks and solid professionals, every so often combined in one person. Add to that mix young interns who are given ample space to continue and deepen their unbiased explorations of the craft, and you get what Studio Dumbar has become famous for: 'modernism with a smile' as Gert himself prefers to term it.

'Serendipity is one of my silent design principles,' Gert states. Openness to unexpected, unforeseen paths and events in the creative process, and the alertness to respond to them when they open up promising new directions, are foundational features of the Studio's methodology. As Louis Pasteur is reputed to have said, 'Serendipity only favours the prepared mind', and Gert's has been thoroughly primed by his upbringing and his studies at The Hague's Royal Academy and London's Royal College of Art, where he has consistently confronted high-modernism with its counter-movements — most notably Dada and Pop art.

On that foundation, Gert and Studio Dumbar have always operated at the nexus of corporate design and artistic experimentation. This is rare in the history of graphic design; while many famous agencies and studios have made outstanding artistic work parallel to their solid 'commercial' output, very few have succeeded in merging the two fields as successfully as Gert and Michel did in Studio Dumbar. Some would have preferred to keep the two separate — to refrain from injecting serious design commissions for powerful institutions with artistic ambiguity and playfulness. As Chris Vermaas stated during the debate on 'the Dumbar phenomenon' in 1995, Studio Dumbar and Ootje Oxenaar, with their designs for government, the police and the Dutch bank notes, were the main culprits of 'Micky Mousing' the official face of the Netherlands. Their work, according to Vermaas, resulted in 'a government that looks far too friendly, because Studio Dumbar's work is always joyful, also in situations where joyfulness isn't appropriate'. And he continued: 'It can be wrong to disguise the hard and serious essence of things under a merry toy surface. It deprives them of their reality, of their "thingness".'

Ootje Oxenaar replied that, rather than eroding the 'thingness' of reality, Studio Dumbar has stripped power and its means of communication of its grimness: 'I think it is so nice that this cheerfulness is of such high quality, that it can be a perfect cultural face of a country. Such designs would be impossible under a totalitarian regime — dictators don't like merriness and humour.'

the Studio's work, as Wim Crouwel termed it, found its way outside the protected niche of the graphic design avant-garde, is perhaps Gert's greatest achievement. His younger colleague and fellow rebel Gerard Hadders is in no doubt: 'I actually think Gert is the most important graphic designer in the Netherlands of the last thirty, forty years. The breadth of his work! And he has elevated corporate design to a form of art.'[285]

OPENNESS TO UNEXPECTED AND UNFORESEEN PATHS IN THE CREATIVE PROCESS, AS WELL AS THE ALERTNESS TO RESPOND TO THEM WHEN THEY OPEN UP PROMISING NEW DIRECTIONS, ARE FOUNDATIONAL FEATURES OF STUDIO DUMBAR'S METHODOLOGY

As mentioned before, Studio Dumbar consolidated and popularized new directions in graphic design, which it spearheaded in their work for cultural clients, and made them practical for institutional clients. That the 'elite side' of

285   Gerard Hadders: conversation, 17 November 2023.

The popular Studio dog, Beer
(photo: Lex van Pieterson)

INDEX

475

477

BIBLIOGRAPHY

· Annink, E. & Bruinsma, M. (2008) *Lovely Language: Words Divide, Images Unite*, Rotterdam: Veenman Publishers.
· Annink, E. & Bruinsma, M. (2010) *Gerd Arntz: Graphic Designer*, Rotterdam: Uitgeverij 010.
· Annink, E. & Bavelaar, H. (eds.) (2010) *De stijl van het Rijk: de visuele identiteit van de Rijksoverheid*, The Hague: Stichting Design Den Haag.
· Bakker, W. (2006) 'Design in de supermarkt', *jongHolland*, 2, pp. 14-23.
  —, (2011) *Droom van helderheid: huisstijlen, ontwerpbureaus en modernisme in Nederland, 1960-1975*, Rotterdam: Uitgeverij 010.
· Beeren, W. (1979) *Actie, werkelijkheid en fictie in de kunst van de jaren' 60 in Nederland*, Rotterdam: Museum Boymans-van Beuningen.
· Bojko, S. (1975) 'Tel Design', *Projekt Visual Art & Design*, 106(3:75).
· Bayle, P. (1697) *Dictionnaire historique et critique*, Rotterdam: Reiniers Leers.
· Boom, W. (ed.) (1980) *Het kader van grafisch ontwerpers*, Eindhoven: Lecturis.
· Bruinsma, M. (1984) 'Points of View on Design Education'. *Rietveld Project #23*, Baden/Amsterdam: Alliance graphique internationale/Rietveld Academie.
  —, (1991) 'Anthon Beeke: De geest moet wapperen', *art_i*, 3(10/11), Amsterdam: Maatschappij Arti et Amicitiae.
  —, (1993) 'Gert Dumbar: Er zijn geen wetten,' *Items*, 1.
  —, (1996) 'The Civilized Anarchy of Studio Dumbar', *Graphis*, 52(301).
  —, (1996) 'The Dumbar Phenomenon', *IDEA Magazine*, 255.
  —, (1996) 'Prettig gebrek aan plechtstatigheid: Het handelsmerk van Studio Dumbar', *Items*, 2.
  —, (1997) 'The Aesthetics of Transience', *Eye*, 25.
  —, (1998) 'Official Anarchy: Dutch Graphic Design', *The Low Countries, Arts and Society in Flanders and the Netherlands. Yearbook, 1997-1998*, Rekkem: Ons Erfdeel.
  —, (2017) 'Creative Civil Servants: A Century of Dutch Design Education', www.maxbruinsma.nl/DesignEducation.htm.
· Bruinsma, M. & Kuitenbrouwer, C. (1989) 'Het zondagse spiegelbeeld', *Items*, 30.
· Conradi, P. (2001) *Iris Murdoch: A Life*, London: GB Gardeners Books.
· Crouwel, W.H. (1988) *Over functionalisme en stijl*, Nuth: Drukkerij Rosbeek.
· Debord, Guy (1967) *La Société du Spectacle [The Society of the Spectacle]*, Paris: Editions Buchet-Chastel.
· Duis, L. ten & Haase, A. (1999) *The World Must Change: Graphic Design and Idealism/De wereld moe(s)t anders: Grafisch ontwerpen en idealisme*, Amsterdam: De Balie/Sandberg Publication, 18.
· Fallon, A. (2019) *Roots #51*, Eindhoven and Amersfoort: [Z]OO Producties and Wilco Art Books.
· Gane, M. (1990) 'Ironies of Postmodernism: Fate of Baudrillard's Fatalism', *Economy and Society*, 19(3).
· Haase, H. (1954) *Zelfportret als legkaart*, Amsterdam: De Bezige Bij.
· Hefting, P. (1983) *Het ptt bedrijf: denkbeelden methoden onderzoekingen*, The Hague: Staatsbedrijf der PTT.

· Hefting, P. (1986) 'Grafisch vormgevers en beeldende kunst: Studio Dumbar', *Kunstschrift*, 2.
  —, (1992) *Tel Design 1962-1992*, Amsterdam: Uitgeverij BIS.
· Hogenstijn, C.M. (2005) *Het algemeen Welzijn van het Volk. Deventer in de Patriottentijd*, Nijmegen: Katholieke Universiteit Nijmegen.
· Holslag, R. & Triest, J. van (eds.) (2006) *Visuele retorica*, Breda: Avans Hogeschool.
· Horton, I. & Furnée, B. (2018) *Hard Werken: One for All, Graphic Art & Design 1979-1994*, Amsterdam: Valiz.
· Hubben, H. (2000) *Het tomeloze talent in grafisch Nederland*, Amsterdam: Buitenkant Uitgeverij.
· Hutcheon, L. (1989) *The Politics of Postmodernism*, New York: Routledge.
  —, (1998) *Irony, Nostalgia and the Postmodern*, Toronto: University of Toronto Press.
· Huygen, F. (ed.) (2015) *The Debate: The Legendary Contest of Two Giants of Graphic Design*, New York: Monacelli Press.
  —, (2015) *Wim Crouwel: Modernist*, Eindhoven: Lecturis.
  —, (2021) *Total Design 1982-1996: een ontwerpbureau in transitie*, Amsterdam: Stichting Designgeschiedenis Nederland, www.designhistory.nl/wp-content/uploads/2021/01/TD-Totaal.pdf.
· Huygen, F. & Boekraad, H.C. (1997) *Wim Crouwel: Mode en Module*, Rotterdam: Uitgeverij 010.
· Huygen, F. & Dercksen, M. (2020) 'TD en Studio Dumbar werken samen voor de ANWB', designhistory.nl/2020/td-en-studio-dumbar-werken-samen-voor-de-anwb/.
· Kinross, R. (2000) *Anthony Froshaug: Documents of a Life*, London: Hyphen Press.
· Lippard, L. (1966) *Pop Art*, London: Thames and Hudson.
· Lyotard, J.F. (1992) *Answering the Question: What is the Postmodern?*, Sydney: Power Publications.
· Maan, D.F. (1982) *De Maniakken*, Eindhoven and The Hague: Lecturis and Meermanno.
· Martin, B. (1981) *A Sociology of Contemporary Cultural Change*, New York: St Martins Press.
· Middendorp, J. (2002) *Ha, daar gaat er een van mij!: Kroniek van het grafisch ontwerpen in Den Haag 1945-2000*, Rotterdam: Uitgeverij 010.
· Niermeyer, M (ed.) (1982) *Informele Kunst 1945-1960*, Enschede: Rijksmuseum Twente.
· Pijbes, W. (ed.) (1996) *Behind the Seen*, Mainz: Verlag Hermann Schmidt.
· Poynor, R. (2003) *No More Rules: Graphic Design and Postmodernism*, New Haven: Yale University Press.
· Poynor, R. (2008) *Jan van Toorn: Critical Practice*, Rotterdam: Uitgeverij 010.
· Rock, M. (2010) 'Ameridam: The Dutchification of America', www.2x4.org/ideas/2010/ameridam-the-dutchification-of-america/.
· Roozekrans, J. (ed.) (2021) *The Secret Bar*. Self-published.
· Roskam, A. (ed.) (1997) *Politievormgeving*, Den Haag: Ministerie van Binnenlandse Zaken.
· Sagitarius (1869) *Parlementaire Portretten: De aftredende helft van de tweede kamer der Staten generaal*, Amsterdam: Loman en Verster.
· Seago, A. (1995) *Burning the Box of Beautiful Things*, Oxford: Oxford University Press.
· Seelen, A. (2004) 'Logo, No Logo', www.ci-portal.de/wp-content/uploads/LogoNoLogoEssayAS.pdf.
· Sloterdijk, P. (2013) *You Must Change Your Life*, London: Polity.
· Triggs, T., Shaughnessy, A. & Gerber, A. (eds.) (2014) *Graphics RCA: Fifty Years and Beyond*, London: The Royal College of Art.
· Truijen, E. (1993) *Brieven van een designer, een autobiografie*, Delft: Faculteit van het Industrieel Ontwerpen.
· Voorneman, R. (1995) *Banjoe Biroe, een vrouwenkamp op Java*, Kampen: Boekcommissie.
· Wang, X. (1998) *Studio Dumbar: Graphic Designer's Design Life*, Beijing: China Youth Press Publishers.
· Wilk, C. (ed.) (2006) *Modernism 1914-1939: Designing a New World*, London: V&A Publications.
· Witte, A. & Cleven, E. (eds.) (2006) *Design is geen vrijblijvende zaak*, Rotterdam: NAi Publishers.
· Woods, G., Thompson, P. & Williams, J. (eds.) (1972) *Art Without Boundaries 1950-70*, London: Thames and Hudson.
· Zwagerman, J. (2011) *Alles is gekleurd: Omzwervingen in de kunst*, Amsterdam: Arbeiderspers.

SHORT BIOGRAPHIES

Gert Dumbar, whose career presently spans more than fifty years, has consistently worked to improve graphic design and visual communication, in the Netherlands, as well as abroad.

Dumbar was born in Indonesia in 1940, where he lived for several years before emigrating 'home' to the Netherlands with his family. He studied painting and graphic design at the Royal Academy of Art in The Hague and concluded his studies in the post-graduate graphic design programme at the Royal College of Art in London. Dumbar has held several academic appointments, including a professorship at the Royal College of Art in London, the University of Bandung (ITB) in Indonesia, Cranbrook Academy of Art in Detroit, USA, and DesignLabor in Bremerhaven, Germany. His most recent appointment, in 2003, is at the Royal Academy of Art in The Hague.

He has served on many juries, together with, among others, I.M. Pei, Alessandro Mendini, and A.R. Penck. He has received numerous degrees from, among other institutions, Humberside Polytechnic and the English Southampton Institute.

Memberships include the Alliance Graphic International (AGI), the British Designers and Art Directors Association (D&AD) and the Dutch Association of Graphic designers (BNO).

Dumbar is married and has two children, a daughter and a son, and a grandson.

AUTHOR/EDITOR

Max Bruinsma (1956) is an independent design critic, editor, curator, editorial designer, and teacher. He was editor-in-chief of Eye, the international review of graphic design in London; Items, the Dutch review of design; and Iridescent, the ICOGRADA peer-reviewed online journal of design research. He studied art, architecture and design history in Groningen and Amsterdam, the Netherlands. Since 1984, his critical writings have featured regularly in art and design journals worldwide (including *Eye*, *Idea*, *ID*, *Blueprint*, the *AIGA Journal*, *Étapes*, *Form*). Bruinsma published and edited several books on graphic and new media design, and taught at numerous design schools in the Netherlands and abroad. Until 2021 he was core tutor Transmedia Storytelling at Camera Arts, Lucerne University of Art and Design, Switzerland. One of his latest publications is Design for the Good Society, the final publication of the Utrecht Manifest Biennial for Social Design, 2015. In 2005 he received the Pierre Bayle Prize for design criticism. A generous selection of his writing can be accessed at

maxbruinsma.nl.

AUTHOR

Leonie ten Duis (1942) studied graphic design at the Royal Academy of Art in The Hague. There she met Gert Dumbar, whom she would later marry. She worked as a designer at TelDesign for a few years and then studied Art History at Leiden University. For fifteen years she collaborated with art historian Annelies Haase on various projects in the field of art and design, including curating exhibitions, organizing international conferences on graphic design, and publishing books and essays. Together with Haase, Ten Duis wrote *The World must Change/ De wereld moe(s)t anders* (Amsterdam, 1999), an innovative and seminal book on graphic design and idealism.

VISUAL EDITOR/BOOK DESIGN

Renate Boere (1970) is a designer, researcher, editor, writer, and organizer of lectures and symposia. She teaches at the Willem de Kooning Academy and shares her expertise at various national and international universities.

Boere works mainly in the social and cultural sector, often in collaboration with artists, other creatives, and writers. Establishing Studio Renate Boere in 1995, she has continuously initiated projects that investigate graphic design practice and connect the meaning of design with social issues. Over the past few years, Studio Renate Boere has won several international Design Awards in the book design category. Her designs tell the context of the book in an intellectual, visual, and interactive way.

In 2002, Boere started as a programme co-ordinator at Zefir7-BNO-The Hague. Zefir7 consists of a group of designers who organize monthly lectures on design. Together with design critic Ed van Hinte, Boere started a co-working space for creatives from different disciplines to collaborate on shared research projects while developing individual practices.

renateboere.nl

PUBLISHER

Valiz is an independent international publisher that addresses contemporary developments in art, design, urban affairs, and visual culture. Our books offer critical reflection and interdisciplinary inspiration in a broad-based and imaginative way, often establishing a connection between cultural disciplines and socio-economic questions. Valiz is based in Amsterdam, and connects with authors, artists, designers, institutes, bookshops, distributors and readers worldwide.

valiz.nl

ACKNOWLEDGEMENTS

479

In reviewing and analysing the work done at Tel Design and Studio Dumbar between 1967 and 2003, we have focused on Gert's role as creative director and founder of his Studio, and selected designs that in our view best represent Gert's mentality and working method. While we have aimed to demonstrate the breadth and depth of commissions the Studio took on in the quarter century of Gert's leadership, our ambition was not to give an exhaustive overview of all work done under Gert's creative direction.

Considering the vast number of designers who worked for Studio Dumbar during this period, either as interns, freelancers, or staff designers, we could not speak with all. Although we have credited designers whenever possible, we could not acknowledge each individual's creative input.

Thus, the texts on Gert's time at Tel Design and Studio Dumbar are by their nature subjective accounts that by no means pretend to be definitive.

What we do hope to have achieved is a description of Gert's life and work in the context of the times — the 1970s, 1980s and 1990s — and his impact on graphic design and visual culture in the Netherlands and abroad.

We wish to warmly thank all those who have been of invaluable help to us in collecting and reviewing the material and have given us a view from the inside: Gert Dumbar, Vincent van Baar, Robert Nakata, Henri Ritzen, Joost Roozekrans, Gerard Hadders, Abe van der Werff and Hilary Buruma. Leonie thanks Jan Noordhoek for his inspiring advice. For sharing their insights and knowledge, we also express our heartfelt gratitude to Kitty de Jong, Michel de Boer, Ko Sliggers, Ootje Oxenaar and Wim Crouwel, in fond memory. Special thanks also to Brecht Hoffmann, David Grantsaan and Simon Pillaud for helping us with sorting, documenting and digitizing the vast archive, and to the excellent team at the Haags Gemeentearchief for their generous assistance. Many thanks as well to Renate Boere and her brilliant team of book designers.

Max Bruinsma & Leonie ten Duis

Colophon

Authors: Max Bruinsma, Leonie ten Duis
Editor: Max Bruinsma
Visual editor: Renate Boere, with
Gert Dumbar, Max Bruinsma,
Leonie ten Duis
Image research: Brecht Hoffmann
Reproduction photography and
digitizations: Simon Pillaud/Valiz,
Brecht Hoffmann, Michel de Boer and
many others, with thanks to Haags
Gemeentearchief, Wendy Louw and
colleagues
Copy-editing: Leo Reijnen
Proofreading and index: Elke Stevens

Graphic design: Studio Renate Boere
Typefaces: Adobe Calson Pro,
Prestige Elite Std
Paper inside: Munken Print White 15 100gr
Paper cover: Fedrigoni Arena Natural
Rough 200gr
Lithography: Gaëlle van den Dool
Printing and binding: Wilco Art Books,
Amersfoort, Netherlands
Publisher: Valiz, Amsterdam,
Astrid Vorstermans

© All rights reserved, Gert Dumbar/Valiz,
The Hague/Amsterdam, 2024
And authors, architects, artists,
photographers
Valiz, Amsterdam www.valiz.nl

For works of visual artists affiliated with a
CISAC-organization the copyrights have
been settled with Pictoright in Amsterdam.
© Pictoright, 2024

The authors and the publisher have
made every effort to secure permission
to reproduce the listed material, texts,
illustrations and photographs. We apologize
for any inadvert errors or omissions. Parties
who nevertheless believe they can claim
specific legal rights are invited to contact
the publisher.
info@valiz.nl

International distribution
NL/LU: Centraal Boekhuis, www.cb.nl
Belgium: EPO, www.epo.be
Europe (excl UK/IE, NL, BE) and Asia:
Idea Books, www.ideabooks.nl
GB/IE: Central Books,
www.centralbooks.com
USA, Canada, Latin America: D.A.P.,
www.artbook.com
Australia: Perimeter,
www.perimeterdistribution.com
Individual orders: www.valiz.nl;
info@valiz.nl

This publication was made possible
through the generous support of

creative industries
fund NL

het
cultuurfonds

JHF Jaap
Harten
Fonds

ISBN 978 94 93246 33 1
Printed and bound in the EU, 2024

V